Feel So Fine

Joe Turner, publicity photograph

Feel So Fine

Big Joe Turner — The Boss of the Blues

A Bio-discography

Derek Coller

Hardinge Simpole

Hardinge Simpole
An imprint of Zeticula Ltd
Unit 13
196 Rose Street
Edinburgh
EH2 4AT
Scotland
http://www.hardingesimpole.co.uk

First published in 2023

Back Cover illustration: Big Joe Turner and Paul Williams'
appearance at the New Year's Dance in Bluefield Auditorium,
shown in the advertisement, took place in 1958.

ISBN 978-1-84382-232-5 hardback
ISBN 978-1-84382-233-2 paperback

Dedication

To the multitude of musicians who have given me so much pleasure, and to the many, many friends, who educated, encouraged, and helped me, as well as sharing my enjoyment, listening to so many great players and singers, both live and on record, during the past eighty years.

And to my family who have provided such splendid support upon which my jazz and blues enthusiasm could thrive.

A photo from the set of "Shake, Rattle and Rock!"

A still from the movie "Shake, Rattle and Rock!"

Contents

Illustrations

Foreword

"Have No Fear – Big Joe Is Here"

I first heard Big Joe Turner in the late 1960s when Atlantic's six volume series 'The History Of Rhythm & Blues' attracted the interest of soul music fans – as did anything that had the Atlantic stamp on it. The series featured Atlantic records from 1947 through to 1964 with the first volume featuring sides by the likes of Frank 'Floorshow' Culley, Tiny Grimes, Edna McGriff, The Orioles, and Big Joe Turner - his 'Chains of Love' from 1951. The second volume included the original 'unexpurgated' version of 'Shake Rattle & Roll' and the third volume a rocking cover of 'Corrinne Corinna' – they sparked an interest in the real roots of rock prior to the impact of rock & roll.

Fast forward to 1971 when I discovered Charlie Gillett's ground breaking 'Sound Of The City,' learning about artists such as Louis Jordan, Wynonie 'Mr. Blues' Harris, Roy Brown, Eddie 'Cleanhead' Vinson, Tiny Bradshaw and of course Big Joe Turner who I learned had been a singing bartender in Kansas City in the 1920s and had made his first commercial recordings in 1938 with pianist Pete Johnson.

Gillett described Big Joe as "a relatively obscure name, moving restlessly from one record company to another without achieving any national hits.... Only when he signed for Atlantic in 1950 did he become known to black record buyers".

These included 'Chains of Love' in 1951, 'Sweet Sixteen' in 1952, 'Honey Hush' in 1953, 'TV Mama' 1954 (recorded with the Chicago blues legend Elmore James) and "the novelty blues", 'Shake Rattle And Roll' - and how Big Joe (then in his early 40s) became an unlikely rock and roll star.

Big Joe in fact had 78s issued in the UK going back to 1939 - on Parlophone, Brunswick, MGM and London Records.

There were a few Big Joe albums available in the UK including an album on Fontana in 1965 (Joe had toured the UK in 1965 with the Humphrey Lyttleton Band along with Buck Clayton - he was voted as Best Male Singer by the *Melody Maker*.) His other UK albums including those for Atlantic in 1967, Stateside in 1968 and Philips from 1970 were considered 'jazz' albums.

It wasn't until UK reissue companies such as Ace, Charly and Flyright began releasing great albums of jump blues and boppin' R&B in the late 1970s and early 1980s that I got to hear the artists I had read about in Gillett's tome including many of the records Joe had waxed for indie labels in the 1940s and 1950s – and there were plenty of them!

It is important to realise just how significant his recordings were.

His late 1930s sides waxed with the great boogie pianists and jazz combos and his early 1940s jump and boogie recordings are regarded as being from the dawn of R&B.

On visits to London in the 1980s I bought everything I could by Big Joe (usually second-hand) from shops like Dobell's and Mole Jazz and also from mail order outlets including Sailor's Delight and Red Lick.

These included albums released on Ace, Charly, Official, Mr. R&B's Jukebox Lil label, Savoy Jazz, Pathe Marconi, a great Atlantic double, MCA, Kent, United, Arhoolie, Riverboat, albums featuring Joe's AFRS Jubilee broadcasts, unissued recordings and alternate takes, Atlantic jazz albums, Bluesway, the French Black & Blue label plus his albums on Norman Granz's Pablo label.

In 1983 I reviewed (for the UK magazine 'Pickin' The Blues') 'Blues Train' an album Joe had cut for Muse recorded with Roomful Of Blues (an inspired choice) and produced by Doc Pomus.

I received a letter of thanks from 'The desk of Doc Pomus' and corresponded with Doc which led in turn to me writing letters to Big Joe directly. Joe's wife Pat told me Joe didn't write too good but he enjoyed getting the letters and Christmas cards.

When CDs hit the market my shelves bulged with more great releases from Rhino, Specialty, President, Rev-O-La, MCA and many other labels.

Writer and critic Ralph Waldo Ellison is quoted by Charlie Gillett as saying Turner's music was "infused with the spirit of good natured optimism....which was characteristic of the south western states during the twenties".

Joe's ability to improvise lyrics and use his stock phrases throughout his recording career was endearing and the often paid compliment that Joe "could sing the Los Angeles telephone directory and make it sound good" is apt.

Bandleader, singer, songwriter and R&B expert Billy Vera who supported Big Joe on a number of occasions told me: "Joe Turner was the loudest singer I ever played with - even in his later years when he was so large he needed to sit during his performance. But even then, he was still the Boss Of The Blues."

Tony Burke
(Blues & Rhythm Magazine)

Introduction

Big Joe Turner was the greatest of the blues shouters. For more than five decades, from Kansas City saloons to Carnegie Hall, through the swing era, rhythm and blues, rock and roll, and soul music, Joe Turner sang, never wavering. Small bands, big bands, trios, pianists, rock groups, choirs, all styles of accompaniment rocked to his rhythm. Joe Turner was like a force of nature, making everyone feel fine.

As musicians, writers and critics have said or written over the years:

"Turner's huge voice rolls like thunder...." (Don DeMichael)

"The acoustic miracle that is Turner's voice...." (Gary Giddins)

"A superb blues-shouter of impeccable intonation and infectious beat..." (Barry Ulanov)

"... the epitome of the jazz-influenced blues singer." (Stanley Dance and Yannick Bruynoghe)

"Majesty". (Whitney Balliett)

"He has a tear in his voice." (Ray Charles)

"I think he's a wonderful blues singer." (Jack Teagarden)

"... the heaviest of all jazz-blues singers; rolling along with the impact of a Sherman tank." (Max Jones)

During a lifetime of singing throughout the United States, with trips to Europe, Australia and Mexico, Big Joe Turner was the subject of myriad interviews and articles, followed by numerous appreciations thereafter. Yet despite this outpouring of thousands upon thousands of words, no full length biography of him has to date been published. This volume is an attempt to remedy that omission by providing a long overdue bio-discography of Big Joe Turner, a starting point from which the singer and his music can be further studied and appreciated.

This writer did not embark on this project as a musician, as an expert in Kansas City jazz, as a blues authority or as a citizen of the U.S.A., but as an admirer and a jazz enthusiast. Joe Turner was a favourite from early in my life of appreciation of this amazing music.

Time, of course, plays tricks on our memories. One year merges into another, chronology wanders, names and places are forgotten or misplaced. With incomplete information it is easy to make erroneous connections. This story is true but are the details?

So it was with Joe Turner and his contemporaries. Interviewed about their early careers, sometimes ten, twenty, thirty or more years after the event, it is not surprising that there are conflicts, contradictions, and uncertainties, between various accounts. Even Turner's interviews give differing details. Did he meet Pete Johnson at the Sunset or the Backbiters' Club? Did he gain entry to a club when underage by drawing a moustache on his lip, by putting on a false moustache or actually growing one? It is hoped the reader will appreciate that the chapters detailing the 1920s and 1930s are the writer's best efforts to unravel this confusion, to select the "most likely" chronology.

Joe Turner's sessions with Pete Johnson, those on Vocalion/Parlophone, such as *Roll 'Em, Pete* and *Goin' Away Blues* were essential listening to jazz fans in the 1940s, as were the Decca/Brunswick recordings, with *Wee Baby Blues*, *Piney Brown Blues* and *Lucille* being marvellous examples. Initially I collected the records, then began gathering whatever discographical and biographical details came to hand. That is the background to my attempt to do justice to one of the great voices in jazz and blues. **This is my tribute to Big Joe Turner.**

Joe Turner, July 16, 1946. Promotional photograph by E.F. Joseph, Oakland, CA. courtesy Peter Vacher Collection

Acknowledgements

Lynn Abbott (Tulane University)
Steve Adamson
Mary Katherine Aldin
Dave Alvin
Ray Astbury
James Austin
Trevor Bannister
Dave and Ann Bennett
Tony Biggs
Bill Brown (Australian Jazz Museum)
Yannick Bruynoghe
Tony Burke (*Blues & Rhythm*)
Mark Cantor
Maureen Chapman
(Concorde Club Archives)
Martin Colvill
Stanley Dance
Liz & David Driver
Nesuhi Ertegun
(Atlantic Recording Corporation)
Sharyn Felder
Robert (Rob) Ford
Paul Garon
Pete Goulding
Dave Green
Charles (Chuck) Haddix
Nigel Haslewood
Tad Hershorn (Institute of Jazz
Studies, Rutgers University)
Franz Hoffman
Trevor Huyton
Wolfram Knauer (Jazzinstitut
Darmstadt)
Daniel Kochakian
Len Kunstadt (*Record Research*/Spivey
Records)

Graham Langley
Doug MacLeod
Barney McClure
Mack McCormick
Bob McGrath
Hans J. Maurer
Kurt Mohr
David Nathan
(National Jazz Archive, UK)
Steve Newland
Paul Oliver
Bernie Pearl
Dave Penny
Rod Piazza
Bob Porter
Howard Rye
Brad San Martin (Digital Archivist,
Apollo Theatre)
Lori Schexnayder Tulane University)
Nancy Sefton (GS Management)
Tony Shoppee
Nevil Skrimshire
Chris Smith
Hal Smith
Elizabeth Surles (Institute of Jazz
Studies, Rutgers University)
Geraldine Turner
Peter Vacher
Steve Voce
Gary Von Tersch
Melissa Weber, (Tulane University)
Phil Wight
Kevin Williams, (Tulane University)
Val Wilmer
Dimitri Wischnegradsky (Jacques
Demetre)

Tulane University, New Orleans, is home to the William Ransom Hogan Jazz Archive.

The cooperative spirit and generosity of jazz and blues researchers is of the highest order. All those acknowledged here delved into their files and collections to try to answer my queries or to meet my requests, and I am greatly indebted to them.

Very special thanks are due to the following:

Ray Astbury researched Afro-American newspapers for whatever references to Big Joe Turner he could find, whether news items, news reports or advertisements. Or, if we were fortunate, even a rare review of an engagement. One dare not try to compute the hours Ray must have spent delving through more than forty years of so many publications, from *The Pittsburgh Courier* to *The Fresno Bee*, from the *Chicago Tribune* to the *Huntsville Mirror*.

Tony Biggs was always ready and willing to answer my queries about Joe's records. His own tribute to the singer, the highly recommended and self-published *Shout It Out*, is brimful with colour photographs of Joe Turner's record labels.

Tony Burke, editor of the authoritative magazine, *Blues & Rhythm*, published since 1984, was an enthusiastic supporter of my efforts, with numerous suggestions and offers of help.

Chuck Haddix, co-author of *Kansas City Jazz*, was ever-willing to respond to my questions about Joe Turner and the city of his birth, and to provide newspaper cuttings where relevant.

Chris Smith, so knowledgeable about the meanings and sources of blues lyrics, and whose regular column in *Blues & Rhythm*, "Words, Words, Words," is required reading, was always helpful and informative in discussing Joe Turner and his use of traditional lyrics.

Bob McGrath for his diligent and enthusiastic work on the illustrations.

Any errors within these pages are, of course, this writer's responsibility.

1

"... a fantastic period of corruption and jazz growth"

In 1821 French fur trappers established a settlement (originally Cansez) at the juncture of the Missouri and Kansas rivers. This became the frontier town of Kansas City, eventually growing into one of the major conurbations of the U.S.A. It is in the State of Missouri, while a smaller Kansas City is across the river in Kansas.

Situated in "the heart of America," Kansas City is within Jackson County, through which passed three major trails westward - the Santa Fe, California and Oregon. Combined with its prime position as a Missouri River port, the town became an important staging post on the pioneer trail. After the Civil War (1861-1865) the city boomed, becoming a centre for beef and grain. In 1853 its population was 2,500. By 1900 it was nearly 164,000 and by 1940 it was 400,000. Over ten per cent of the population was African-American, rising from 17,567 in 1900 to 41,574 by 1940.

In the latter part of the 19th century, cattle drives would arrive in the city, their cowboys bone-weary and saddle-sore after the long, tiring weeks on the trail, wanting rest and recreation, drinking, gambling, whoring; and Kansas City tried to meet their needs, an endeavour which continued unabated into the 20th century.

K.C. had a reputation as a wide-open town and one imagines, as in a Western movie, a place all lights and rowdiness, gambling and noise, saloon girls and shootings, with the good citizens waiting for John Wayne or Randolph Scott to ride into town to clean it up.

It took a little over a hundred years for Kansas City to be called the "Crime Capital of the United States". The events leading to this labelling took place during the administration of T. J. Pendergast.

In Kansas City, to amend the meaning of Oscar Hammerstein, II's lyric, "They'd gone about as far as they could go"

***

Thomas Joseph Pendergast (1872-1945) moved to Kansas City in 1893 to work for his brother Jim, a saloon owner who had already established himself as a force in the city's politics. Tom became an alderman in 1910 and when Jim died in 1911, replaced him as chairman of the Jackson County Democratic Party. In a close-fought election in November 1925, he won political control of the city. "A few days later he appointed Henry F. McElroy as city manager. Together, they opened the gates for a fantastic period of corruption – and jazz growth ....."[1]

Pendergast's power over Kansas City and its environs, which lasted until 1939, was gained by "fraud, manipulation and violence at the ballot station, as well as by attention to the problems of the poor, the immigrant, the black."

Tom Pendergast

This benevolent bribery included distributing food, clothes and coal to the poor, as well as organising Thanksgiving and Christmas parties for needy children. (It was reported that in 1935 12,000 children went to Convention Hall for a "Christmas give-away".) As Superintendent of Streets in 1900 Pendergast had found 250 jobs for fellow Democrats. In 1931, to mitigate the effects of the Depression, he inaugurated a $5 million building programme, which gave Kansas City what Driggs and Haddix describe as "the magnificent art deco court house, city hall and municipal auditorium." They also claim that Kansas City is unwilling to allow Pendergast any historic credit for transforming Kansas City from a dusty cow town to the Paris of the Plains.[2]

It so happened that Pendergast's Ready Mixed Concrete Company provided the materials for the building work. In addition, Pendergast was a major shareholder, nearly 50%, in The Sanitary Service Company, which had the contract for collection of the city's rubbish. Among his other holdings was the T.J. Pendergast Wholesale Liquor Co., which became the Pendergast Distributing Co. when prohibition was enacted.

Thus Pendergast's policies were financially beneficial to him and his cronies, as well as aiding the city's criminal underworld. However, it must be said, on the credit side, that these same policies also shielded Kansas City from the worst effects of the Depression.

The 18th Amendment, the National Prohibition Act (or the Volstead Act), was enacted in October 1919 and came into effect in January 1920. It was poorly drafted, with many exemptions allowed, and provision for enforcement greatly underfunded. It all conspired to provide another profit-making opportunity for the criminal gangs. The bootlegger had arrived.

In 1926 TJ Pendergast made a deal with the notorious gangster, Johnny Lazia. This gave Lazia influence within the police department, making it easier for him to run his rackets, while Pendergast gained access to Lazia's voting block and, no doubt, a share of his ill-gotten gains. It was after this arrangement that K.C. truly became a wide-open town. There was no respect for the laws on alcohol, prostitution or gambling, with illegal saloons, bootlegging and brothels ignored by the authorities, as were casinos, horse-racing, the numbers racket, slot-machines and so many other methods of parting punters from their money.

City manager, Henry McElroy, when queried about the number of one-arm bandits in K.C., cynically answered: "Nobody but a sucker would put a nickel, dime or quarter into a slot machine. If the slot machine didn't get the sucker money something else would."[3]

Nathan Pearson, in *Goin' To Kansas City*, writes that "Prohibition enforcement ceased altogether. There were no felony convictions for Prohibition violations in Kansas City during the entire period of that law – this in a city famed for its bars, nightclubs and speakeasies."

Dave Dexter, who was born in Kansas City and worked there as a reporter said: "Pendergast, in many ways, did much to swell Kansas City's income. He smiled on gambling, he endorsed the pleasure districts as long as their inhabitants paid his collectors a regular 'operating' fee. He encouraged the opening of niteries and rubbed out any laws which might necessitate a spot's closing before sunrise."[4]

As might be expected, there is no consensus on the number of watering holes to be found in Kansas City during the 1920s and '30s. *The Kansas City Future* reported that the city had more nightclubs per capita than any other, three hundred or more clubs, saloons, hotels, joints and dives, giving rise to its reputation as a "hot, wide open town". In 1938 the *St. Louis Post Dispatch* reported that Kansas City had more than 500 bars in an area of 15 blocks.

This proliferation of bars, saloons, cabarets and dance halls meant work for musicians. Most establishments employed instrumentalists, whether a solo pianist, a small band or a full orchestra. These employment opportunities attracted musicians from other states and cities, contributing to the growth of Local 627 of the American Federation of Musicians. More will be heard of this in a later chapter.

Dave Dexter provided some interesting murder statistics for the Pendergast era. In 1927 the homicide rate in Kansas City was higher than it was in Chicago, 16 for each 100,000 population, compared with 13.[3] In 1928 there were 89 murders in K.C., with only three murderers being sentenced to hang. That same year in England, which had a population eighty times larger, there were there seventeen murders, with just two unsolved.[5]

Boss Tom Pendergast

He pinpoints the ambivalence about the Pendergast era by quoting an editorial from a 1930 *Kansas City Star*: "For the last four years, with all its faults and failures, Kansas City probably has had the most efficient city government in its history."[6]

On June 17, 1933 Frank 'Jelly' Nash was being escorted to Leavenworth Penitentiary, arriving at Kansas City's station, before being driven to the prison. As Nash and his escort reached the station car park they were met by bursts of machine-gun fire. Nash, three policemen and a federal agent were slain. It has been described as a bungled attempt to rescue Nash, but perhaps it was an execution to silence him. Whatever the reason, Kansas City acquired the title, Crime Capital of the United States.

Johnny Lazia, who was believed to have arranged the ambush, was shot to death shortly afterwards. Infamous bank robber 'Pretty Boy' Floyd, who had been happy to make Kansas City his base in 1930, was also suspected of involvement in the 'Union Station Massacre', but always denied it.[7]

The change in Kansas City's and Pendergast's fortunes began when the Volstead Act was repealed on December 5, 1933. Later, in 1938, a crackdown on other illegal activities began when an erstwhile colleague of Pendergast's, Lloyd Stark, became Governor of Missouri. With his eye on a bid to become President, Stark began a clean-up in Kansas City. This gradual erosion of Pendergast's empire continued until his political demise in 1939. As a result, employment opportunities for musicians in Kansas City diminished until they were no more favourable than in any other city.

Over the years Pendergast had become addicted to gambling on the horses, his losses growing ever larger, until he took money from the State insurance fund to cover them. In 1939 he pleaded guilty to two counts of income tax evasion, was fined and sent to prison for fifteen months, of which he served twelve. With his health deteriorating after his release, he was incapacitated when he died on January 26, 1945.

In their 2013 biography of Pendergast, Larsen and Hulston ended on a note of ambiguity when they wrote: "Pendergast may bear comparison to various big-city bosses, but his open alliance with hardened criminals, his cynical subversion of the democratic process, his monarchistic style of living, his increasingly insatiable gambling habit, his grasping for a business empire, and his promotion of Kansas City as a wide-open town with every kind of vice imaginable, combined with his profound compassion for the poor and very real role as a city builder, made him bigger than life, difficult to characterize."[8]

His political enemies called T. J. Pendergast "a ruthless leader of a corrupt political machine that had made Kansas City a hotbed of vice and crime."[9]

This corrupt political machine had, by creating the conditions in which musicians could find plentiful employment, also made the city a hotbed of jazz and blues, one in which musicians and singers could learn and thrive and compete, to become among the best of their generation. One of the singers was called Joe Turner.

2

"I had singing on my mind."

(1911 - 1930)

In the same year that Boss Tom Pendergast began his flagrant rise to power by becoming chairman of the Jackson County Democratic Party, Joseph Vernon Turner was born on May 18, 1911, in the black section of Kansas City.

He was Joseph Turner, Junior. His father, born 1880, was from San Antonio, Texas, and mother, nee Georgia Marshall, born 1892, was from La Belle, Missouri. The 1910 Census shows them living at 540 Cherry Street in Kansas City. There was one sibling, Katherine (Katie), born in 1908.[1] Joe never asked his mother how she and his father met.[2] Georgia was reported to be one of ten daughters, but her son never mentions any of his aunts.

An application for a licence, dated September 3, 1907, for a wedding to take place the following day, shows Joseph aged 29 and Georgia aged 17, details which fail to match with other official documents quoted here. This application, found by Ray Astbury, lists Joseph resident at 508 Cherry Street.

Joe Turner said of his father, "[He was] killed by a train when I was four years old, while on a fishing trip [3]," so it is understandable when he said, "I don't know too much about him"[4]. He told Whitney Balliett, "My father was a cook at the Baltimore Hotel and the Muehlenbach Hotel, and he was a fisherman, too. He caught crayfish in the lakes and ponds and streams....."[5]

Joe's recollection would mean that his father died in 1915, though there have been reports (in John Chilton's *Whos' Who of Jazz*, for example) that the train accident did not happen until Joe was 15. However, his father's death certificate, also traced by Ray Astbury, reveals that Joe Senior died at the age of 36 in July 1918. The certificate does not have the exact date of death, it being given the same date as the certificate (July 6, 1918), while his date of birth and the names of his parents are listed as "unknown". It does confirm that Joe's father was a labourer and that the cause of death was "Railway traumatism accidental (multiple injuries)"

One memory of his father was going to see the circus shows which came to town.

> "My father used to take me. We never missed one. We used to go see the parade in the morning. My sister and I would have balloons and cotton candy. Afterwards, we'd drink all the lemonade we could for a nickel."[6]

After she was widowed, his mother worked in a laundry, pressing shirts. Later she managed a block of apartments and remarried. While Georgia was working, the children were raised by their maternal grandmother, who they knew as Mrs Harrington. At school Joe seems to have been no bother - when he attended -

but a poor pupil, failing to learn to read and write. He said his education was "elementary at an early age,"[7] but "I used to sing in school. That's about the only thing I got good in school was singin'."[8] He spoke of going to Lincoln School, though Charles Haddix has pointed out that Lincoln was a High School, not a grade school.

> "We'd duck school a lot – I didn't get past the sixth grade anyway – and go down to the river and fish and swim."[9] "I always wanted to do what the big boys did. They used to swim in the Missouri River and even though I couldn't swim very good, I'd jump in, too .... I decided to take up fishing. I never did turn out to be a good fisherman, but I've caught an awful lot of crawdads."[10]

In later years he used his lack of education as inspiration for one of his songs, as he did with other aspects of his life. *Can't Read, Can't Write Blues* was recorded for United Records and he reiterated this phrase in other ad-lib blues. In 1974, on the Pablo label, he sang *For Growin' Up*, a "composition" sounding very spur-of-the moment, in which he sings of being born in a ghetto and being a runner (a numbers runner, presumably), with his mother always looking for him. He also mention his grandparents, with a photograph, like many other black families at that time, of world heavyweight champion "Jack Johnson on the wall".

But it was music which increasingly occupied his thoughts. ".... ever since I was a kid I had singing on my mind. I started singing around the house."[11] This interest grew at school and continued "as a teenager, with the kid's quartet in the park."[12] "I sang a lot on the streets, me and a bunch of the boys."[13]

He told Val Wilmer about having a lot of fun with the quartet, singing in the park, adding,

> "I never did play any instrument, though I did try to play drums but it didn't work out too good. Of course, then, I had no idea of going into the business professionally.[14]

With Peter Guralnick he was a little more specific, saying, "I wanted to play drums, but I had two left feet."[15]

He recalled one group of musicians that would play at his house.[16] He tells how they played a gas pipe with one end covered, had an old banjo and how they tried for the jug band sound, blowing across the mouth of a crock gallon jug, making the bass sound "to keep the beat – boom, boom, boom!"[17] There was a large Jew's harp with a bell on it, a tin tub and a washboard to also carry the rhythm, plus a blind violinist.

> "Then there was a guy who played a tin pot with a handle on it with string and a tin can connected to it. They played all the old songs, like *Swanee River, I'm In Love With You, Honey, The Yanks Are Comin' [Over There]*, and *St. Louis Blues*."[18]

Georgia, Joe, Katie. 1930s

Blind singers were a common sight in the streets of America in the early twentieth century, with men such as Blind Lemon Jefferson, Blind Willie Johnson and Blind Blake just three who later became famous in the annals of blues history.

Although Joe Turner never learnt to read music, his general musical education continued when he began, perhaps in 1921 or 1922, to guide blind musicians around the streets of Kansas City, as he has described in various accounts:

He told Leslie Gourse how he learned by following two street singers, a harmonica player and a guitarist. Then he earned fifty cents a day by leading a blind man around with his guitar, singing with him, suggesting he was twelve when that happened.[19] ("Those blind blues singers would make quite a bit of change during the day.")[20]

"I started as a little boy. I used to carry a blind man around when I was about ten. He was a guitar player and I used to make songs to go with it. I guess I've been making them up ever since then."[21]

"I did that off and on for two or three years, but I can't remember those singers' names."[22]

"I used to sing around on the streets. Lead a blind man all over town. He played the guitar and I used to lead him, sing and help him make his living that away. I didn't know who he was, I just ran into him on the street. I used to help him back and forth across the street whenever I'd see him. I hung around, picked up the habit of singin' along with him. My mother didn't know where I was at. I told her I was helping a blind man around, making some money."[23]

On another occasion he said,

"My mother used to have a switch ready when I'd show up home from singing, but I'd grab her and hug and kiss her and show her all the money I'd made, thirty or 40 cents. The blind man finally came to my house and asked my mother if I could continue to work for him. She told him that if he would promise to make me wear a little straw hat to keep the sun off me, I could have the job of leading him around, but only after school".[24]

"Or I'd go down from the house a block or two in the morning and find one of the blind blues singers standing on a corner. I'd stay with him all day and we'd cover the town. He stopped on corners and sang and I passed a tin cup. We went into restaurants, too, and when I was old enough I sang along. I made up words – blues words – to go along with his guitar music...."[25]

It is surprising, contrary as it is to the gospel beginnings of so many blues and soul singers, that church music did not have a greater influence on Joe Turner. His view for this is also unusual:

"My mother used to take me to church all the time, but I didn't really think it was the proper thing to do – to sing in the church."[26] Though there was one apparently ill-judged musical experiment when,"with this girl, and while all the people were busy, we slipped on over to the piano and started wailin'."

The experiment was not appreciated by the congregation and Turner said he never sang in the church again.[27]

The Turners were not a musical family. Turner said, "I never heard my mother sing a note and she didn't play no music, and my father didn't either."[28]

But there were records in the house, so BJT heard the classic blues singers, the Smith ladies, Bessie, Clara, and Mamie, and Ethel Waters. Waters, he said, was "the only singer I ever adored."[29] He also mentions "Leroy Carr, Lonnie Johnson and a lot of people that I don't even know now."[30] To James Austin he said, "I used to love Ethel Waters" and of Leroy Carr, "He was good".

Turner told Stanley Dance that Ethel Waters' *Shoo Shoo Boogie Boo was* one of the first records to give him a kick[31], a memory recalled in his *Crescendo* memoir,

> "The first record I really got enthused about was Ethel Waters singing a number called *Shoo Shoo Boogie Boo*. We had an old-time Victrola there and whenever my mother wanted to get me out of bed, she'd put that on. I'd wake up when I heard that music and I'd get right up without any trouble".[32] (This title by Miss Waters was recorded on June 27, 1929.)

Another singer who received his admiration was the little known Clarence Rand - "a beautiful man, a crooner before Bing Crosby's time."[33]

Sitting for hours, as he told Leslie Gourse, he listened to records of different styles - folk, blues and pop songs,[34] I always could remember pretty good and I'd sit there and and get 'em down, and then I could do it like they did."[35]

Around 1923 came a serious blow.

> "When I was twelve years old …. There was a fire and I had to jump out of a second-storey window of the apartment we lived in and I broke everything. [It seems that "broke everything," actually meant that both ankles were fractured.] Doctor said I'd never walk again. I was in the hospital two months and after that I crawled around on the floor for a year, until I got sick of it and grabbed onto chair backs and pulled myself up and started to walk again.[36]

More than fifty years later he philosophised, "The doctor said it would give me trouble later on, and it has."[37]

It is most likely that this serious accident was the point at which Turner stopped attending school and, when recovered, gradually found ways of supplementing the family's income. One assumes that for a time one of these ways continued to be leading blind musicians around the town, part of his further induction into the field of entertainment.

After his recovery, when he was about thirteen, he began to learn songs from an uncle by marriage, Charlie Fisher. (In one interview he said it was Katie's brother-in-law,) Quoted in another interview, he said, "I wanted to learn how to sing and I was fascinated by that."[38]

To Whitney Ballett he said,

Charlie Fisher played piano in a night club and he also played on a piano in the hall downstairs in our house. He taught me the new tunes and I listened to two other uncles, who played guitar and banjo and violin."[39]

And to Val Wilmer,

"He (Fisher) used to play a whole lot of piano. Every time he got a new tune, he used to come home and start banging on the piano, and we were all excited. As soon as we learnt the words, we'd sing and have a ball. Mostly I used to go sing songs like *Ja Da* – hit songs, you know."[40]
"I kept right up with all the music. In fact, I was around a bunch of musicians all the time,"[41] perhaps referring to the jug and washboard band. "I was only interested in music then – I ate and slept that stuff. I'd be sitting on the side of the bed till late at night, thinking up some blues. And every time some new blues records came into town, the man would call me up and I'd be right down at the store."[42]

"The man" was the music man "at the store downtown - I had to pass right by there - he'd always beckon: 'Come on in, I've got the new batch in here.' He liked music, too, so he'd play all the new records for me. I didn't have too much dough, so I offered to pay him a little at a time, if he let me take some home. He said: 'Tell you what you do. When you learn a record, you let me know, and I'll come to the club and hear you sing.'
".... And he used to bring his family to hear me. In fact, later on he got him a night club of his own, and he made me a singer in his joint."[43]

Unfortunately, neither the name of this perceptive jazz lover nor of his club are given.

Perhaps this is relevant to another story:

"A bunch of Italians, they give me a nightclub. I had an outdoor garden. I used to have a band. They give me the band in the back. From then on I ain't lookin' back."[44]

Again, no names are mentioned.

"Until then I sold papers, had a horse and wagon and sold junk." It was while he was a peddler that he had further opportunity to practice his blues songs; as he said, "improvising the words"[45]

Or, he told Balliett,

"I did all kinds of jobs. I shined shoes and sold papers and worked with a man had a double team and a wagon and hauled paper boxes and like that. I'd lead horses around the stockyard and make a couple of bucks, and I had me a job in a hotel making breakfasts for the waiters."[46]

This last comment ties in with his description as a dishwasher in the 1930 census and with his telling Leslie Gourse that he did not get his first singing job until he was twenty-one.[47] After the labouring jobs he would have found employment for a year or two as a bar-tender, his singing an unpaid added attraction.

The 1930 census shows that Georgia had married Lonnie P. Murry, a hotel dishwasher, and they were living at 830 East 8th Street, Kansas City. (In the census for 1940 the surname is spelt Murray.) Katie has left home, presumably married, but Joe is living with his mother and step-father. He too is shown as a dishwasher.[48]

Missing here are Turner's teenage escapades in his search for any cabaret or club where blues and jazz were to be heard. These will be found in the next chapter, as we go from the Roaring Twenties into the Kansas City jazz of the thirties.

3

"Let me sing with your band."

(1930-1934)

By the mid-1920s Kansas City's reputation for open-all-hours gambling, drinking and music making was well established. The big bands of Bennie Moten, Walter Page, George E. Lee, Thamon Hayes and others, later to include Count Basie and Andy Kirk, were thriving, as were territory bands, such as those led by Troy Floyd, Clarence Love, Alphonse Trent, Tommy Douglas and Paul Banks. Nationally known bands were in town for one-nighters or theatre shows. Week long theatre bookings at the Newman or the Mainstream were not unusual. On October 31, 1936 the Paseo Ballroom was the venue for a battle of the bands, Duke Ellington versus Count Basie. The jam sessions featuring local and visiting musicians became legendary, none more so than the one which took place at the Cherry Blossom on December 18, 1933, when local tenor players Lester Young, Herschel Evans and Ben Webster battled the 'King,' Coleman Hawkins, who was in town with the Fletcher Henderson orchestra.

Count Basie recalled other bands who were active when he arrived in K.C.: the [Original] Blue Devils and Chauncey Downs, while the territory bands included Jesse Stone, Jap Allen and Clarence Love.[1]

Joe Turner commented on out-of-town bands like Earl Hines and Duke Ellington,

"They'd come two or three times a year and play one-nighters and whenever in town, otherwise or nearby, all the greats came in for a jam session till all hours in a.m."[2]

"Oh, it was really jumping. There was music all the time and we had some pretty wild cats out there. Of, course there was Count Basie's band and Andy Kirk's, and Jimmy Lunceford was often there. And Julia Lee .... she and her brother, George, they used to have a good band. And all the musicians used to play at the Sunset one time or another, people like Mary Lou Williams, and Ben Webster. That town was really on fire, bouncing. I ain't never found no town like that since."[3]

Another recollection was,

"There was always lots of good music goin' on with Hot Lips Page, Lester Young, Pete Johnson and Count Basie hangin' around. When those guys would get the place jumpin' – well, I just had to join in and be a part of that music, some way. I couldn't play an instrument – so, I just started singin'. All the folks seemed to like it real fine and before long, I was doin' more singin' than bar-tending."[4]

Or, as Joe put it in his song, *Piney Brown Blues*,

Well, I've been to Kansas City, girls, and everything is really all right
Well, I've been to Kansas City, girls, and everything is really all right
Where the boys jump and swing until the broad daylight

And as he said on another occasion, "I wasn't making much money but look at the fun I was having!"[5] He told Robert Palmer[6], "We might get $25 a night, if it was a real good night. Or, more often, $10. A lot of times you would just work for tips". With the same attitude, commenting on low pay, Count Basie said: "Actually, things weren't as bad as they seemed, because prices were low and tips from gangsters high." [7]

Basie, in his autobiography, reported,

"There were good musicians everywhere you turned. Sometimes you just stayed in at one place and sometimes you might hit maybe two or three more, but you could never get round to all the jumping places in that town in one night. There were just too many."[8]

Pianist and bandleader Jay McShann arrived in K.C. in the mid-thirties and was immediately converted,

"...there was always somewhere to go and something to see and listen to. During that time, see, they didn't close the joints. Joints stayed open – they didn't have no lock and keys to them because they stayed open 24 hours (laughing). .... I hated to go to sleep because I was afraid I'd miss something."[9]

Saxophonist John Williams declared that, "Any musician that migrated to Kansas City and was broke, there was two places you automatically had a job, it was $2 a night and all you could drink." "If you were a musician in Kansas City you had it made. You were a big shot. All the illegal things, they did them like they were legal. They didn't bother to prosecute. The law was in every night for a shakedown .... the bars were open 24 hours a day. 3 o'clock in the morning and they're in there partying."[10]

It was in this 'scholarly' atmosphere that Joe Turner's education in jazz and blues continued, eventually leading to graduation with honours.

Turner has said that he did not become a professional singer until he was twenty-one, though it is possible the addition of singing to his bartending duties contributed to his income. Throughout his teens, as listed in the last chapter, he would have searched for day jobs wherever he could find them. Accordingly, his vocalising would have been a spare time occupation, though his latter-day work as a bartender, then a singing-bartender, were steady steps towards becoming a blues-shouting professional.

As an adult Turner was six-feet-two inches tall, weighing about 250-lbs. An imposing figure, he must also have been born with a powerful constitution, else he could never have survived the thousands upon thousands of miles he travelled in the course of his career. In 1930s Kansas City he would have needed all the energy and enthusiasm of youth to do labouring jobs during the day and then shout the blues until the early hours.

The Hole in the Wall

So the question is, did his career commence, semi-professionally at least, at The Kingfish or at the Hole in the Wall? In a 1945 interview for *Metronome*, Turner said that he began to sing the blues at a spot called The Kingfish, whereas in 1958 he is quoted saying,

"I started singing the blues in Kansas City at a place called The Hole in the Wall on Independence [and Harrison]. I was taken there by my sister, I was about 13 or 14 and I had been singing on the streets with a bunch of kids. Then I started singing in taverns".[11]

Joe Turner's sister said his mother spoilt him, making her, Katie, take him every where she went. Joe said he "liked to bug her, because he was devilish".[12] But Katie seems to have done her share of spoiling, later escorting him to rent parties and saloons. Even if he was fourteen or fifteen years old, his sister still would have been very young. Joe said, "I used to go around buffet flats with my sister, who was a dancer. She used to take me out to cabarets once in a while. The cats used to ask me to sing the blues and finally the boss of a place called The Kingfish, a little beer parlor and bootlegging joint asked me to work for him."[13] Turner says he was about fifteen and that he had followers from the South Side who came to hear him. "I ran into Pete Johnson at this Kingfish place. Pete had a job there playing piano; this was in 1926."[14] Joe repeated this to jazz writer Max Jones, "Me and Pete, we started together at the Sunset – though I met him before that at a place named the Kingfish."[15]

In 1945 Turner endeavoured to describe to Inez Cavanaugh what nights in the various clubs could be like,

"All the working people came in early and got high and had a ball and then things would kinda quiet down and finally there wouldn't be nobody in there except the bartender, waiter and the boss and we'd start playing the blues about three o'clock in the morning. People used to say they could hear me hollering five blocks away. It would be in the still of the morning and the boss-man would set up pitchers of corn likker and we'd rock. Just about the time we'd be starting to have a good time, here would come the high hats and we'd set the joint on fire then and really have a ball 'til ten or eleven o'clock in the day. Sleep? Who wants to sleep with all that blues jumpin' around?"[16]

Pete Johnson,
early 1920s

Pete Johnson (1904-1967) was a pivotal influence on Joe Turner's music. He had switched from drums to piano in 1926, becoming a brilliant jazz and boogie pianist. Along with Albert Ammons and Meade Lux Lewis, he was a member of the famous Boogie-Woogie Trio of the 1940s. He lived in relative obscurity after he settled in Buffalo in 1950. Seriously ill in 1958, he did not really recover, though in that year he made an appearance at the Newport Jazz Festival, as well as undertaking a European tour with Jazz at the Philharmonic. Both were in the company of Joe Turner.

It is uncertain to which club the next quotation refers - The Hole in the Wall or The Kingfish or a speakeasy unknown.

> "Way back in Kansas City, when I was about twelve, I used to hang around a nightclub where there was a good band. At the afternoon rehearsals I would sing with them. But the boss would never let me in at night. He wanted me to start work cleaning up the joint but I said, 'I don't want to clean up, I want to sing'. He said I was much too young, but finally, Pete Johnson, who was playing piano in the band said, 'Give him a chance'; and I was in."[17]

It is likely that Turner's progression in the various saloons and speakeasies began as a cleaner, next as a waiter, and then as an assistant bartender. He said,

"I became interested in music while working as a waiter for Piney Brown .... sat in on sessions singing with Duke Ellington, Count Basie, Father Hines and others – then a teenager."[18]

Ellington has been quoted as saying:

"When we were playing the Booker T. Washington theatre in Kansas City, we went to hear Joe Turner sing the blues every night, all night. Pete Johnson was playing piano for him and it was a real kick."[19]

The Backbiters Club

The next step was to the Backbiters Club. Turner said of the owner of this saloon in Little Italy,

"There was a cat had a joint. His name was George Stone. He was a little, short fellow. He wore high-button shoes, a derby and he used to wear a 20-dollar gold piece all the time, hanging across his chest. Oh, he was something – a real, swingin', high-class cat."[20]

Singer George Melly, perhaps mishearing Turner during a 1965 conversation, wrote, "His first real job was George Dorne's nightclub".[21]

Mr. Stone is believed to have shown great skill in sneaking Turner in and out of his establishment without catching the eye of the juvenile authorities.

It was here, in a speakeasy which he called "low and degraded," that Pete Johnson said he first met Joe Turner[22], perhaps meaning where they first worked together. "He used to come to the place where I was playing and he was always accompanied by a host of admirers. These fellows with him wanted to hear him sing, so I let him and that is how he got started with me." Johnson also said, "Before he became a full-time singer, he was an assistant bartender at a nightspot called The Black and Tan. He would just take off his apron and get up and sing. And people would be crazy about him."[23]

In a number of interviews Turner has told the story of how he got into the club, each with a slight variation in the details. What follows are edited versions of these stories.

He began by hanging around outside the Backbiters Club on Independence Avenue and Troost, listening to Pete Johnson on the piano. He and his pals also liked to watch the dancers in action.

"They used to put paint on the windows, so the children couldn't see through. But I'd go round there in the daytime, get me a razor blade, and shave me off some eyeholes, so I could see what's going on later at night. My mother used to think I was in bed, but I'd be down there every night, hanging around that joint."[24]

For a time his brother-in-law was the club's doorman/bouncer, watching for concealed weapons, but when he left to take another job, Turner saw his opportunity to gain entry. As he told Val Wilmer,

> "I went in there with a moustache, made with some eyebrow pencil, had my daddy's pants and shirt on. The man throwed me out every time he'd catch me. Then he got tired of throwing me out. Then Pete and me started working together."[25]

In some versions he puts on a false moustache or actually grows one, is wearing his daddy's hat, or the clothes belong to his brother-in-law. In one he describes this happening at the Sunset.

> "I was already tall and I'd slip the hat down over my eyes and go in with a crowd. The musicians would tell me, 'Go home, little boy' but I'd bug them and say I could sing, and finally one night they let me. There was no mike in those days, but I got up there and sang blues songs, and they were surprised I could keep time so good and that I had such a strong voice. I sang a couple of songs and the man who owned the joint liked them and the people liked them. The man asked me how old I was and I told him twenty, and he looked at me and said, 'Your mama know where you are?' and I told him my sister did. And I started working there at weekends, He paid me two or three dollars." [26]

Another variation on this theme was:

> "So I told Peter Johnson, 'Let me sing with your band, Daddy'. He said, 'You can't sing in this nightclub, you're too young'. I said, 'Well, if you don't tell nobody, won't anybody know I'm here. All these people, they're busy doing what they're doing'. So he said, 'Okay, what can you sing?' I called him off some tunes and we took off."[27]

And another......

> I got by the door, slipped past the people and made my way over to the piano. Pete Johnson was playing and I stood around by the piano and asked, 'Let me sing with your band?' Well, he just laughed at me and said, 'Can you sing?' I said, 'Yeah, I can sing a little bit' and he said, 'We ain't got time for no little bit singing.' So I said, 'You play what you wanna play and whatever you play I'll sing'.

> PJ: Right now we're playing the blues. You ever heard the blues?

> JT: Yeah, I hear 'em every day.

> PJ: What key do you wanna hear?

> JT: I don't know about no key, let me feel around and see what's happening,' and that was it." [28]

"The Backbiters' Club had an upstairs and a downstairs. I sang with Pete Johnson and he had Murl Johnson on drums and a saxophone player."[29]

Count Basie was probably referring to the Backbiters Club when he said,

"The first time I met Joe he was working down on Independence Avenue. He was the bartender down there in a basement joint where they used to serve whiskey by the dipper. Big Joe was the singing bartender. He would sing his numbers right behind the bar while he was mixing drinks. He'd be hollering the blues and dipping that good taste, and also taking special care of all the cats he knew. He was in charge of the whole business down there."[30]

Joe's next move was to the Black and Tan Club, sometimes called the Black and Tan Cotton Club, at Charlotte Street and Independence.

The Black and Tan Club

"We moved to the Black and Tan Club, which had been a furniture store and had a balcony and all. An Italian named Frankie owned the place and he wanted to make me the manager. I said I didn't want that but I would get the entertainers and the waiters if he'd let me learn to tend bar. The bartender was Kingfish and he was older. Part of my job was to get the bootleg whiskey and part was to take off my apron and sing with the band when things were quiet. Kansas City was wide open, and sometimes the last show would be at five in the morning."[31]

"First thing they started me off by bringing in the whiskey. I'd go back to the stash, get the whiskey and bring it in the nightclub in big pitchers ... I'd wash glasses and help around the bar and I learned how to mix a few drinks .... In bootleg days they didn't have too many mixed drinks. They had red whiskey and they had white whiskey and that red whiskey was what they called needle whisky and corn liquor was white, kinda yellow lookin'".[32]

To add to the confusion of reported dates and names of clubs and various "Sunsets," there had to be a club called The Kingfish and a bartender given the nickname of "Kingfish". The latter was Jesse Fisher, described as "a famous mixologist on 12th Street".[33]

At this time many club owners were preparing themselves for the probability that Franklin D. Roosevelt would become the next President of the United States. They knew that FDR's victory would mean the repeal of the Volstead Act. By refurbishing their existing clubs and opening new ones they hoped to be ready for the changed circumstances after Prohibition.

Hawaiian Gardens

In 1932 the Black and Tan was closed, refurbished and reopened as the Hawaiian Gardens, with Joe and Pete retained. The *Kansas City Call* for July 15, 1932 carried the announcement that:

New Nightclub, Hawaiian Gardens, Opens Tomorrow
Sadie McKinney headliner, with 7-piece Hawaiian Gardens
Serenaders, including Pete Johnson, piano, Abie Price, drums.
Plus singing bartender Joe Turner.

The Gardens catered to both races but was segregated. Turner described his work on Charlotte Street as, "All round bartender, vocalist"[34] Abie Price was the leader of the group.

In September 1932, as part of a crackdown on illegal drinking and gambling, Federal agents closed 11 clubs, including the Hawaiian Gardens. Pete Johnson and his musicians were arrested during the raid. When Federal agents subpoenaed Johnson, he refused to testify, on the advice of the owners of the Gardens. No doubt they were very persuasive. The not-so-fortunate Turner and Kingfish landed in jail[35], probably briefly, as Turner has spoken of the speed with which arrangements for bail were normally made - "Boss man would have his bondsman down at the police station before we got down there .... we'd just walk in, sign our names and walk right out."[36]

Reporting Turner's arrest, the *Kansas City Call* for October 7, 1932 names him as an assistant bartender, living at 803 East 8th Street.

The Cherry Blossom

"After Prohibition ended we moved to the Cherry Blossom at 18th and Vine. It had been a theatre and it had great big dance floor. George E. Lee had a band there and his sister Julia Lee played the piano and sang. She was a beautiful brown-skinned woman with personality plus."[37]

The Cherry Blossom, 1822 Vine Street, opened on April 8, 1933 in what used to be the Eblon Theatre. [38] As the name implies, it was Japanese-themed, with twelve waitresses in Japanese costumes. Joe Turner and Kingfish were behind the bar and Pete Johnson was solo pianist. The *Kansas City Call* for April 14, 1933 reported that 1,176 attended on opening night. The club was open 24 hours.

Quoting Joe Turner:

"We were at the Cherry Blossom two or three years and then I left town with Pete Johnson's band and travelled to Chicago and St. Louis and Omaha and back to K.C. again. We moved around, back and forth and in and out, but we never went too far from home."[39]

It would seem that the statement "two or three years" was not meant to be taken too literally, because "At the end of January 1934, the Cherry Blossom suddenly went dark and the owners disappeared with the club's payroll."[40]

Joe Turner:

I guess I was around nineteen when I started going all over with Pete's band, playing dances and breakfast parties. It was a six-piece band. I used to get a chance to sing with Bennie Moten when they'd come to town. I'd run up there and tell 'em that I'd like to sing two songs if they wanted me. And then I used to sing with Ben Webster, Jo Jones and all the cats out of Basie's band. We had jam sessions every Friday night."[41]

"My mother was running an apartment building at Eighth and Charlotte then and I'd show apartments for her, but I always kept one back for me and my gang. I went into the Sunset Club. Piney Brown ran it and I was a bartender and still sang. When the place was empty, the band would play real loud and I'd go outside and sing through one of those big paper horns, up and down the street, and the people would come. I thought I was somebody when I got enough money together to buy a paper horn and a baton so that I could direct the band when I wasn't singing."[42]

Turner has mentioned other saloons in which he worked, prior to his famous sojourn at The Sunset. He was a singing bartender at a club run by George Breshere, on Independence Avenue[43]. and no doubt the same at The Smokehouse and The Peacock Inn.[44] At Curly and Stout's Place Turner was employed as a "singing show manager,"[45] while Murl Johnson has spoken of his friend Pete Johnson playing "on Independence Avenue for a fellow named Curly".[46]

Subway Club

This was another place with a reputation for its many all-star jam sessions. "The Subway was a tiny club in the basement of 1416 [sic; actually 1516] East 18th Street where, past a doorman and down a narrow stairway, were the swingingest jam sessions in town."[47]

Ross Russell in his Kansas City jazz history writes that The Subway was operated in connection with a bar and restaurant on the street floor; occupying the basement of the premises. It was popular with visiting swing bands, black and white, Benny Goodman, the Dorsey Brothers, Fletcher Henderson, etc.[48]

Joe Turner has said he worked at The Subway but details of his employment are not known. He may only have been referring to joining the jam sessions there.

Now we are approaching the end of 1934 and the opening of a major new club, with Joe Turner no longer a singing-bartender but a singer who sometimes served behind the bar.

4

"That town was really on fire."

(1934-1936)

Felix Payne, 'Piney' Brown and Ellis Burton were three non-musicians frequently mentioned by jazzmen when recalling the 1930s. Pianist Sammy Price said they were "like godfathers actually for most musicians. They understood problems, financial problems ...." [1] However, Joe Turner's connection was with Felix Payne and, especially, 'Piney' Brown, rather than with Ellis Burton, who ran the Yellow Front saloon.

Payne (1884-1962) was Afro-American, a business man and a close ally of Tom Pendergast. Among his holdings was the *Kansas City American*, which he published in opposition to the main black newspaper, the *Kanas City Call*. He owned a number of saloons, including The Subway and The Sunset Cafe. Both were managed by Walter 'Piney' Brown, who was also black. The following quotations indicate the respect in which Brown was held. A few days after he died, in November 1940, Turner recorded his famous *Piney Brown Blues* as a tribute. This included the verse:

Yes, I dreamed last night I was standing on 18th and Vine
Yes, I dreamed last night I was standing on 18th and Vine
I shook hands with Piney Brown and I could hardly keep from cryin'.

A later version, titled *Old Piney Brown's Gone*, has the lines:

Down on 18th and Vine, where old Piney Brown got his start
Down on 18th and Vine, where old Piney Brown got his start
He was a goodtimer, was a playboy from his heart

The last time I saw old Piney, he was standing on 18th and Vine
The last time I saw old Piney, he was standing on 18th and Vine
I'll tell the world, sure was a friend of mine.

Eddie Barefield, saxophonist, said, "Piney was like a patron saint to all musicians. He used to take care of them. In fact, he was like a father to me." [2]

Count Basie, pianist and leader,

"Piney Brown was the man-about-town in Kansas City in those days, and by the way, he was the nicest guy you'd ever want to meet in the world. When you were with him, you never had to worry about anything, because he always took care of the bill." [3]

Buck Clayton, trumpeter,

"Piney Brown was a big time sportsman in Kansas City that everybody loved. He was also the father and the professor of all the pimps in Kansas City and there used to be quite a few of those in town."[4] Which singer Myra Taylor[5] confirmed, "He was a pimp, you know," in addition to being a heavy gambler.

Some confusion has been caused by there being two Brown brothers, one nicknamed 'Little Piney' and the other 'Big Piney'. The former was Walter, who ran the Sunset Clubs. He was almost certainly born in 1900. The latter was Thomas Jefferson Brown, who was 34 when he died in August 1932. He was a well-regarded businessman and baseball club owner.[6] Walter 'Piney' Brown is reported to have been the manager of The Subway, though later than 1930. Chuck Haddix has a poster for the club, circa 1930, which shows Ed Brown as the manager.[7]

The Sunset Club

"After The Kingfish we moved out South and worked at a place called the Sunset – this was a little dictier ... one small room in the back of a grocery store. Fella served whiskey out of his hip pocket for twenty-five cents a pint ... forty cents for a set -up (lemon and ice).[8]

Turner's description of this Sunset club hardly fits that of the Eastside Musicians Sunset Club or perhaps the Sunset Crystal Palace but, when he talks of only three entertainers (himself, Pete Johnson, piano, Murl Johnson, drums), of a loudspeaker running from the joint out into the street, of the boss calling "Roll 'Em, Pete" and telling him during a lull to "Call 'em in, Joe," it seems it could be one of these to which he is referring.

All the references to the Sunset convey the impression that Turner and Johnson worked there for many years. Ben Webster has spoken of seeing the duo at the Sunset in 1932 or 1933, while Joe Turner certainly alludes to earlier years. Yet the available evidence suggests they were there from late 1934 to late 1935, then working periodically in the years between 1936 and 1938. Johnson was the one more frequently employed.

One possible piece of evidence that there was an early Sunset Club can be found in a story in the December 23, 1938 issue of the *Kansas City Times* which reports that "*Roll 'Em* was born 5 years ago at the 12th Street's Sunset Club." It depends how accurate is the reporter's "five years".

The *Kansas City Call* of November 9, 1934 carried an advertisement announcing the opening at 12th and Woodland of the Eastside Musicians Sunset Club. "Rearranged, newly decorated and said to be the most beautiful Night Club in Kansas City," the entertainers named included "Little Skippy, a shake dancer," Miss Josephine Byrd and, doubling from the Harlem Nite Club each nite, George E. Lee and his sister, Julia. Also on the bill were "Mr. Joe Turner, blues singer, moaning the blues throughout the night. Music by Pete and his Little Peters, with guests Hot Lips Page on trumpet and Eddie Durham on trombone". The manager was Piney Brown.

Announces Its New Opening at 12th and Woodland

Rearranged, newly decorated and said to be the most beautiful Night Club ever to run in Kansas City. Positively the greatest array of entertainers ever presented. From St. Louis Nite Club comes little Skippy, known as the fastest and cleverest little "shake" dancer in these parts. Miss Josephine Byrd, formerly of the Green Pastures, singing and dancing all the late numbers. Mr. Joe Turner, blues singer, moaning the blues throughout the night. Music by Pete and his Little Peters, assisted by Eddie Durham and Lips Page. Doubling from the Harlem Nite Club each night, will be George E. Lee and his sister, Julia. Bennie Moten with his entire band, Maceo Birch and

Known on the street as the Sunset Club, rather than by its formal title, there is no mention of the numbers racket and the dice games in the basement.[9]

Damning with faint praise, bassist Gene Ramey said, "The Sunset was not a bucket of blood but you might see some fighting in it and you'd have to break out of there."[10]

Murl Johnson was not related to Pete Johnson, but they were life-long friends. His memory of this time was, "When Pete first went to work at the Sunset there was only a piano and drums. The drummer then was a fellow named George. When George left I started to work with him and they also hired Joe Turner to sing the blues. Then the Sunset got to be a very popular place and when the big bands got to town they would always flop [flock?] to the Sunset Club. White and colored musicians, it was always something going on all night. When all the musicians would get off their jobs they would come by the Sunset Club and jam."[11] Piano and drums became a trio when saxophonist Walter Knight was added and eventually Pete Johnson was leading a septet. Ben Webster also recalled working in the group.

It is difficult to know how to place Turner's recollection that he "started at the Sunset about 1931. I was nineteen or twenty years old" and "The Sunset capacitated about five hundred and just about the size of Birdland. I was bartender at the Sunset Club, Also their talent scout, including myself. About four bartenders and ten or twelve waitresses on weekends."[12]

It was at the Sunset that Joe Turner and Pete Johnson's partnership was cemented, playing together night after night, putting together their compositions, encouraged by the musical history which was taking place around them. This was where they won their city wide fame, which would soon make them jazz stars, thanks to local journalist, Dave Dexter, and to the visiting John Hammond.

That local fame can be judged by the recollections of fellow musicians as they counted the impact which singer and pianist made upon them. Drummer Jesse Price:

"I have known Joe Turner since 1931 when …. he worked with Pete Johnson at the Sunset Club at 12th Street and Vine. Of course, that was the greatest place for the musicians and Joe Turner was the boss man around then. Jimmy Rushing was at the Reno Club, downtown, and Basie only had three reeds, two trumpets, one trombone, drums, bass, guitar, with Basie at the piano, but Joe Turner was holding his own at the Sunset."[13]

Drummer Jo Jones:

"I remember we used to play behind Joe there [the Sunset]. There was a place close by (across the street in fact), called the Lone Star. Joe Turner would start to sing the blues at the Sunset and then he'd go across the street and sing the blues at the Lone Star and we were still playing all this time. Joe would socialize there for a while and stop in the front and have breakfast and then he'd come back into the Sunset, go up to the microphone and sing some more blues, and we'd have been playing all the time. Often we'd play for an hour and a half straight like that."[14]

Pianist Mary Lou Williams:

"A wild Twelfth Street spot we fell in regularly was the Sunset, owned by Piney Brown, who loved jazz and was very liberal with musicians. Pete Johnson worked there with bass and drums, sometimes with Baby Lovett, a New Orleans drummer who became one of Kansas City's best. Now the Sunset had a bartender named Joe Turner and while Joe was serving drinks, he would suddenly pick up a cue for blues and sing it right where he stood, with Pete playing piano for him. I don't think I'll ever forget the thrill of listening to Big Joe Turner shouting and sending everybody, night after night, while mixing drinks."[15]

Pete Johnson said that Turner did not tend bar at the Sunset; he just sang. The advertisement for the grand opening would seem to confirm this, though comments by Mary Lou Williams and Turner himself suggest otherwise.

Saxophonist John Williams may not have been referring to the Sunset when he said,

"Joe Turner .... was the bartender who waited on the waitresses, not the public, and he'd be chasin' and pourin' and he'd get high about three o'clock in the morning and start singing the blues. He wasn't getting paid for that, he just sang the blues."[16]

Reporter Dave Dexter wrote, "Along the rocking Twelfth Street East of downtown Kaycee was the Sunset Club, a modest nitery.... Pete Johnson, Sam (Baby) Lovett, drums. Behind the bar, a massive man, Joe Turner. [17]

Tenor man Ben Webster:

"I think about the Sunset .... that could be 1932 or 33 and the band would be Pete and Merle (sic) Johnson on drums, Mouse Randolph on trumpet and me. I lived down the block from the Sunset then. They had a mike on the bandstand and one of the speakers was out in the street. If the joint was empty, Piney Brown would say, 'Better call 'em, Joe'. Then we'd blue the blues for 45 minutes and Joe would sing 'em. The place filled up and then Piney would say: 'Cut it back, Joe,' so he could serve some drinks. And those days Joe would depend on tips. One day somebody asked him for *Trees*, you know that ballad, and Joe wanted the tip. Well, I heard Joe Turner sing *Trees*. And believe me, the Trees Blues .... the funniest s--- I ever heard in my life. I swear Mouse cried."[18]

Turner's ability to satisfy a customer with his version of a 1930s ballad with lyrics starting "I know that I will never see, a poem lovely as a tree" confirms that his repertoire was far wider than expected. His singing of *It Don't Mean A Thing (If It Ain't Got That Swing)* at this time was commented upon, while a little later he was featuring such standards as *I Can't Give You Anything But Love* and *On The Sunny Side of the Street*. One of his favourites from the Kansas City days, a staple in his repertoire and in his discography, was an old ballad, *When The Morning Glories Wake Up In The Morning*. Sometimes it was recorded just as *Morning Glory* or *Morning Glories*, with Joe receiving composer credit for *Morning Glory* (on the Pablo "Life Ain't Easy" album) and for his versions made as *Early Morning Blues* and *Cocka-Doodle Doo*.

Tips did have their effect on the group's repertoire! Turner told Peter Guralnick

"We was doing boogie woogie, we was singing all pop songs, *Swanee River*, anything a sucker wanted to hear we done it. We didn't miss. If the people come and request, say, *I'm The Sheik of Araby* – BOOM, got you covered. Give me the money and we've got it going for you.[19]

Pianist Earl Hines:

"You can't beat the originals ... Joe Turner was the first person I ever heard sing the blues, other than the ones I heard when I was a kid. ... Joe

Turner was the first I heard sing that 'B-y-e, B-y-e' and I thought it was the most exciting thing I had ever heard .... And Joe Turner, he would keep going with them, until he got hotter and they got hotter until that final chorus when everything was rockin'." [20]

One of the first public address systems in town was installed behind the bar for Joe Turner's use, although he didn't really need it because he had a voice with the quality and dynamics of a trumpet, enough to fill a club larger than the Sunset. The system was connected to a loudspeaker over the door of the club and facing the important intersection of Twelfth Street with Paseo and Highland. When Big Joe, backed by the two-piece rhythm section, burst into song, the entire neighbourhood knew it ... On some occasions, Turner would dispense with the amplifying system and, stepping into the street, begin "calling his children home."

Trumpeter Oliver Todd:

"The Sunset was home to Joe Turner and Pete Johnson .... Turner would shout the blues in the Sunset and then continue singing out into 12th Street, 'calling the children home,' as Turner said. Joe would sing right out the door and even the people on the streetcar going by would be hopping."[21]

Pianist Count Basie:

"Later on, he was working ... at Piney Brown's Sunset on Twelfth Street with Pete Johnson playing piano with Murl Johnson, and sometimes Baby Lovett, on drums. They were something. When I heard him that first time, I said to myself, 'Jesus I never heard anything like this guy'. He was the blues singer in that town. Anybody who came to Kansas City talking about singing some blues had to go listen to him."[22]

Trumpeter Buck Clayton:

"I used to love to hang out in the Sunset Club and listen to Joe Turner and Pete Johnson. Joe was young and had just switched over to being a singer as he formerly had been a bartender. They used to knock me out every night.[23]

Pianist Jay McShann was especially enthusiastic, particularly about the special talent that Joe Turner had.

".... when he sang the blues, he would make those words up as he goes. Especially if he was inspired, he would say something different every time. But how he could do that I don't know. It was something that was natural for him."[24]

"The thing that really amazed me was that Joe would keep singing for thirty or forty minutes straight through." ... "Pete would *Roll 'Em* for on

Count Basie, 1930s

piano for maybe ten minutes, then Joe would come back [and] sing ten or fifteen minutes. They'd play one tune and it'd last forty-five, fifty minutes, and that was a set. A one-tune set … I'd never seen anything like that."[25] "Man, I heard Pete and Joe and Joe could holler those blues for 45 minutes on one tune."[26]

Dave Dexter confirmed that "When they 'felt it,' Pete and Joe would start a boogie which might run anything from 10 to 75 consecutive choruses, Joe singing a few, Pete taking a few, the tenor coming in and so on."[27] One musician less enthusiastic was leader Andy Kirk:

".... We moved to 1212 Woodland. That's when I heard a lot of Joe Turner, the famous blues shouter. He was working at Piney Brown's, right around the corner on 12th Street. Turner and boogie-woogie pianist Pete Johnson kept rolling out blues till four or five in the morning. I didn't have to go to the club. It came to me through the windows. Sometimes I'd get so disgusted: all that blues shouting and boogie woogie kept me awake."[28]

Pete Johnson remained at the Sunset until December 1936, but Joe Turner left in September 1935. On Saturday, September 21, he was due to open at the Night Hawk Tavern, as reported by The *Kansas City Call* (September 20, 1935). The same newspaper, November 15, 1935, advised that Turner was now manager of the Lone Star Indoor Gardens, with Miss Billy Keith of Chicago as featured singer and dancer.

The Chicago Defender of October 12, 1935, announced "Ray Nance and his Rhythm Barons - the Sunday Afternoon Varieties, starting October 20 at Club DeLisa. Guests to include Adelaide Hall, Art Tatum, Earl Hines .... and Joe Turner." Was it Big Joe?

Joe Turner, late 1930s

5

"We're just waiting for John Hammond"

(1936-1938)

John Hammond, 1930s

John Hammond was the next major influence on Joe Turner's career. Hammond (1910-1987) was in the fortunate position of being born into a wealthy family ("My mother was a Vanderbilt, my father was a banker"), so he was able to indulge his love of jazz by promoting the careers of such musicians as Count Basie, Benny Goodman, and Billie Holiday. He produced the famous "Spirituals to Swing" concerts in 1938 and 1939. Over a forty-five year period, 1932 to 1977, he was a prolific record producer, making influential jazz records and albums for Brunswick, Vanguard and Columbia, among others.

***

Pete Johnson has said that the experimental radio station W9XBY had a wire from the Sunset Club and that John Hammond had heard his and Joe Turner's broadcasts. Hammond's autobiography makes no mention of this. In it he tells only how, at 1 a.m. one morning in 1936, probably in March, he went to his car, which was parked outside the Congress Hotel in Chicago. Spinning the dial for some music on his car radio, he was stunned to hear for the first time the Count Basie nine-piece band. Listening to its nightly broadcasts persuaded him he must go to Kansas City, which he did in July 1936.

Count Basie, left, with John Hammond, late 1930s

Although his autobiography fails to date his visit to Kansas City, he has been quoted as saying it was in late March or early April, 1936[1], though it was in fact in July[2]. Pete Johnson says that Hammond came to K.C. with Willard Alexander, an M.C.A. (Music Corporation of America) booking agency executive, but Hammond's book does not mention Alexander. Nor does it name Dave Dexter, although it is certain that he was Hammond's guide. Dexter was

Down Beat's correspondent in the city and Hammond was a fellow writer for that news magazine. Also in town at the same time, with the Louis Armstrong orchestra, was Louis' agent Joe Glaser, who proved to be more interested in Andy Kirk than in Count Basie.

Pete Johnson. at Cafe Society. 1939

Neither does *John Hammond on Record* say that he saw Joe Turner and Pete Johnson while he was in town. However, elsewhere he is quoted as saying:

"I'll never forget the first night. I went to the [Reno Club]. Basie had a show .... eight p.m. to four a.m. So I was there at eight o'clock and stayed until four that night. Then Basie said to me, 'Come on, John. I'm gonna take you to the Sunset.' I had never heard Pete or Joe at that time. Joe Turner was singing at the bar and Pete was in the back room playing .... A room apart and it was unbelievable. Joe's invention was endless."[3]

Confirming this, Count Basie wrote:

"So we took him by the Sunset to hear Pete Johnson and Big Joe Turner, which of course he had already heard about, and those two cats damn near killed him because they were swinging so much. He just sat there shaking his head and slapping his hands."[4]

Joe Turner said that when he sang risque blues songs Hammond "pretended he was going to duck under the table, he was so embarrassed."[5] Turner has also been quoted as saying that Hammond wanted him to join Basie for the trip to New York, but the singer declined,

"I was working with Pete Johnson ... and I never sang with a twelve-piece band with arrangements. I was a little awkward singing with those arrangements. So I told him I'd rather not go. I'd .rather wait until he came back here sometime and bring me and Pete Johnson to New York."[6]

A possible personnel for The Little Peters, Johnson's band, around this time, as given by Murl Johnson, was Bob Hall, Clarence Davis, trumpets, Walter Knight, alto, Curtyse Foster, tenor, Pete Johnson, piano, Clint Weaver, bass, Murl Johnson, drums.[7]
Curtyse Foster claimed that Hammond never heard the full band.

"Every time he came in to hear the band, he didn't get ... the full unit. Invariably some of the musicians would be off getting drunk. Hammond made three or four trips down to the Sunset and never did hear the full band."[8]

Even had he heard the complete unit, it is doubtful whether Hammond could have found work for it in New York City.
Perhaps the musicians followed the example of their leader? Visiting musician, John Williams, said, "Pete (Johnson) and a drummer played at Piney Brown's place on 12th in Kansas City. But they were always high."[9]
Johnson and Turner may have toured with this or a similar personnel. As mentioned earlier, Turner told Whitney Balliett that he "left town with Pete Johnson's band and traveled to Chicago and St. Louis and Omaha and back to Kansas City again."[10] Though Joe did suggest to Val Wilmer that the touring began around 1930: "I guess I was around nineteen when I started going all over with Pete's band, playing dances and breakfast parties. It was a six-piece band."[11]

The outcome of Hammond's visit was that an enlarged Count Basie orchestra was signed by Willard Alexander to join Benny Goodman's on the M.C.A. roster. This was the beginning of the Count's rise towards the top of the big band hierarchy. For Turner and Johnson however, any benefit was slower to materialise. Pete Johnson has said that in 1936 he and Turner did have engagements in New York at the Apollo Theatre and at the Famous Door. But, in fact, these did not happen until 1938.

For now, Kansas City remained home for Joe Turner and Pete Johnson. They continued at the Sunset until there was a parting of the ways caused by the pianist's habit of pleasing his lady admirers at the saloon by buying them drinks, using money taken from his and Joe's kitty.[12] Turner reacted by moving across the street to the Lone Star.[13]

The rift lasted some months but was healed by 1938, to their mutual advantage, when they travelled together to New York at John Hammond's invitation.

A few years on, Joe had further cause for complaint. He told Doc Pomus how Pete Johnson had cheated him of royalties for songs which he, Turner, alone had composed. After these songs were discussed, prior to a record session, Johnson would go the publisher or the record company, advising them of the songs and claiming co-authorship of Turner's compositions. When Joe got wise, he stopped talking about his songs prior to a recording session.

The Lone Star

It may have been 1934 that drummer Gus Johnson, Jr., (born 1913) was referring to in this early mention of The Lone Star, "Joe Turner wasn't singing when I got to Kansas City. He was the janitor, cleaning up the place at the Lone Star. Later on, he tended bar and after he had learned all the blues, they started letting him sit in and sing. Pete Johnson was playing piano there and I was sitting in with him the night I met Jo Jones."[14] (Gus Johnson was told that Jones had just joined Count Basie's orchestra.)

The Lone Star was sited at 1708, East 12th Street. Bassist Gene Ramey said, "The Lone Star, where Pete Johnson was playing, was directly across from the Sunset. It was a nightclub, a little like Jimmy Ryan's in New York, a little less crowded than the Sunset.[15] "..while trumpeter Orville Minor stated, "Right across the street was the Lone Star, where Joe Turner was..."[16]

When he wasn't playing the Sunset, "Turner was generally across the street at the Lone Star, a club run by Frank Duncan, the famous Kansas City Monarchs catcher. (Duncan was once married to Julia Lee.)"[17]

A 1936 or 1937 advertisement for The Lone Star from the *Kansas City Call*, reproduced in *Goin' To Kansas City, is* headlined, "Joe Turner, King of the Blues, starring with Safronia's New Mammoth Floor Show".

Despite all the music making, Joe Turner still had time for romantic adventures. He may have met Carrie, surname unknown, by now, as both were living in K.C. in 1936. In the 1940 census they were entered as man and wife.

Pete Johnson recalled one evening in particular, "Joe and I were working but he at one spot (Lone Star) and I across the street (Sunset) ... It seems Joe's girl friend married another fellow and poor old Joe really got the blues. And that night when I was through my work and in the place that Joe was working, Joe got up on the stand and really sang the blues from his heart that he made up as he went along."[18]

Perhaps this inspired Turner's 1944 recording for Decca, *It's The Same Old Story*, later repeated in *Johnson and Turner Blues*, recorded for National in 1947.

> Please Mr. Johnson, don't play the blues so sad
> … … … I lost the best girl I ever had.

The *Kansas City Call* for December 4th, 1936 reported that Joe was with Edith Griffin at Wolf's Buffet. while the December 18th issue carried a surprising news item. The "entertainer" description and the age make it likely, though not certain, that this is our Joe Turner:

Entertainer Is Arrested
Mrs. Addie Harison Shot By Joe Turner
(cutting appears opposite)

The report states that Joe Turner, entertainer, 25, was arrested after shooting Mrs. Addie Harrison. Turner shot her at his home at 1320 Euclid Avenue. He had known her for two years and shot her in an attempt to "frighten her away" because she wouldn't "leave him alone". Mrs. Harrison declined to press charges.

As a name, Joe Turner is far from uncommon. Big Joe has often been confused with a contemporary of his, the stride pianist Joe Turner (1907-1990). At least two budget CD releases of Big Joe Turner material have photographs of the piano-playing Joe Turner on the front of the insert. In more recent years there has been a bass-guitarist named Big Joe Turner, leading his "Blues Caravan".

The Reno Club

The Reno Club, at 602 East 12th Street (or 12th and Cherry) was where the Count Basie orchestra gained its local reputation. It was small in size, a whites-only club. "It was run by gangsters. But there was no trouble," said singer Myra Taylor.[19] Sol Stibel was the manager.

Trumpeter Richard Smith recalled, "The Reno Club's early Monday morning "Spook" breakfasts would often be sparked by the heralded appearance of Big Joe Turner …. surrounded by a cheering section from his Sunset Crystal Palace gig…"[20] Count Basie organised these breakfasts, which began on October 28, 1935, following an advert. in the *Kansas City Journal-Post* of October 26, 1935. They were held on a Monday, beginning at 4 a.m.[21]

Entertainer Is Arrested

Mrs. Addie Harrison Shot By Joe Turner

Mrs. Addie Harrison, 25, 1807 East Thirteenth street, suffered a bullet wound on the left side of the body, when she was shot Monday evening, December 14, at 1320 Euclid avenue.

Police arrested Joe Turner, 25, an entertainer, whose address is at 1320 Euclid avenue, early Tuesday morning, and booked him for investigation in connection with assault with intent to kill.

Turner admitted shooting Mrs. Harrison on Monday evening at his apartment, in an attempt to "frighten her away," he told police officers.

He said he had known her for over two years and had begged her recently to "let him alone," he told police officers.

Miss Harrison was taken to General hospital No. 2 from which she was released on December 15.

Turner was released by the police

Writer George Hoefer, claimed that Turner had worked at the Reno Club, singing between sets by the Count Basie group.[22] This may be a reference to Turner's guest appearances at these breakfast gigs.

The Elks

In the 1950s Jerry Wexler was a key figure at Atlantic Records. In 1936, when he became a student at Kansas State College of Agriculture and Applied Science in Manhattan, Kansas, he made many trips into Kansas City to catch the music scene. "At The Elks I heard Joe Turner, that magnificent shouter, then a singing bartender, whom twenty-five years later I wound up producing."[23]

Pianist Jay McShann noted, "Joe would work with everybody, a different group every night in town,"[24]

Wolf's

Jay McShann had arrived in K.C. towards the end of 1936. In August 1937 he began working, alongside drummer Harold Gadson, at a saloon called Wolf's on 18th and Vine. McShann said, "So I went to a club called Wolf's Buffet. This was just a piano and drums over there, that's all they had. (The owner) would bring in guys like Joe Turner to come in and sing the blues on the weekend."[25] "Those were some great sessions."[26]

By April 1937 Turner was part of 'Your Hit Parade' at the Lone Star cafe[27] and he was there in August, the *KC Call* for August 13, 1937 reporting on "musicians gathering for 'jam session' at the spook breakfast on Friday morning". Then Miss Edith Griffin's name appears again, listed with Turner at Piney's Tavern.[28]

(A rumour concerning Johnson and Turner, Benny Goodman and Teddy Wilson appeared in *The Pittsburgh Courier* of March 26, 1938. It reported that Pete Johnson and Joe Turner "will be imported to take up the slack when Teddy Wilson's present notice allows him to step out and form his own outfit". Wilson did not leave Goodman until March, 1939, and this odd rumour proved to be just that. It did suggest, however, that the singer and pianist were being noticed outside the boundaries of Kansas City.)

When, in May 1938, John Hammond asked Turner and Johnson to come to New York to work at the Famous Door on 52nd Street, he did not know that the singer and pianist had parted, but his invitation caused them to revive their partnership.

On May 24, 1938, at 3:30 p.m., Joe Turner and Pete Johnson boarded a train to take them from Kansas City and into New York to sample the big time. No doubt it was Hammond who persuaded Willard Alexander to finally sign the duo to M.C.A., a fact reported in *Down Beat* for June 1938, though it referred to two bands being signed, those of Joe Turner and Pete Johnson! The *Kansas City Call*'s version was, "John Hammond, field agent for the Music Corporation of America, made the arrangements for their contract with MCA and their engagement at the Famous Door," which began on Friday, May 27.[29] The Famous Door, though only a small club, seating about ninety customers, featured top jazz musicians and bands. During the summer of 1938 it even hosted the Count Basie orchestra. The Count opened there on July 11 for a six week booking which turned into fourteen, closing on November 12.[30]

During their stay on "Swing Street" Turner and Johnson appeared on Benny Goodman's Camel Caravan ("Camel cigarettes are slower burning; they give a milder, cooler, more fragrant smoke"). The broadcast of May 31st was heard by a teenage Bob Inman, who perhaps having missed or misheard an announcement, noted that the duo played *The Blues*.[31]

There was also a discouraging engagement at the famed Apollo Theatre, where they were scheduled to play for a week, commencing Friday, June 17. Louis Armstrong and his Orchestra topped the bill. It is not clear if the Famous Door job was combined with that at the Apollo or if the 52nd Street engagement had ended.

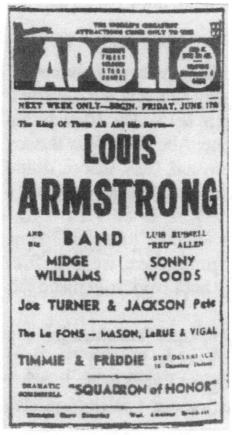

New York Amsterdam News, June 18, 1938

Not only was Pete Johnson called "Jackson Pete" in a newspaper ad. for the Apollo, but the duo failed to impress the audience. Marge Johnson said that the fault lay with the person who planned the programme. Instead of letting Joe and Pete do a blues number, they were told to do a ballad, *I'm Glad For Your Sake, I'm Sorry For Mine*. The audience began stamping their feet and beating their hands together. She continued, "Joe and Pete couldn't imagine what was happening and the curtains were closed. To quote Pete, it was a good thing they closed them or they'd been throwing rocks at us'. Louis Armstrong was on the same programme and as they passed him he said, 'That's show business'".[32]

The Apollo story does pose one or two questions. Were they allowed only one number per show? Would not that song have been dropped after the audience reaction? Did they see the week out? It has been suggested that they played only the one night. Perhaps they were appearing on the Wednesday amateur night, but the Apollo advertisement would seem to discount that. It must be remembered that Marge Johnson's account is second-hand; she did not meet her husband until 1949.

JOE TURNER and PETE JOHNSON

—IN PERSON

Making Their First Appearance in Kansas City, Kansas, since a Successful Triumph in New York, at The

WAYSIDE INN

1932 NORTH FIFTH STREET

A BLUE MONDAY SPECIAL

SEPTEMBER 12

Added Attraction: Edith and Earnie

HENRY PAYNE, PROP.   BILL JENNINGS, MGR.

Unknown newspaper, September 9, 1938

Turner told Whitney Balliett, "After our show with Goodman, we auditioned at several places, but New York wasn't ready for us yet, so we went back to K.C."[33] Pete Johnson says one of the places they tried was Kelly's Stables.

Of their return to K.C. Joe said, "Everybody laughed when we got home. 'Hey, you couldn't make it in New York City, man.' We'd say, 'Yeh, yeh, we're just waitin' for John Hammond to call us back,' and they'd shake their heads and laugh again."[34]

Back in their home town, Turner and Johnson worked at The Lone Star, as reported by the *K.C. Call* for July 1, 1938, but they did fit in other gigs. There is, for example, an unsourced advertisement for the Wayside Inn which states that on Monday, September 12, 1938, Joe and Pete were making their first appearance in Kansas City, Kansas, since "a successful triumph in New York".

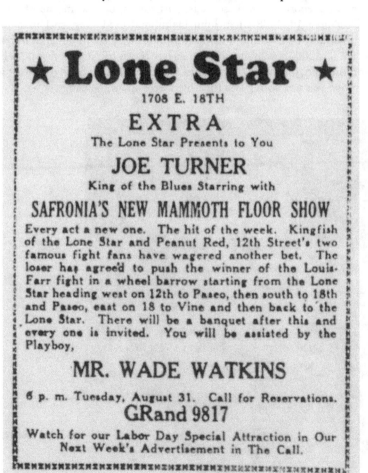

Kansas City Call, September 9, 1938

Between August and December 1938 it is probable that Joe Turner continued at The Lone Star, as did Pete Johnson, until at some point he returned to work at the East Side Musicians Sunset Club. During 1938 the partnership made at least one guest appearance on the Vine Street Varieties radio show, broadcast by WHB from the Lincoln Theatre on Saturday afternoons from 3 pm to 4 pm. The band on the show was led by drummer Jesse Price.[35]

The *Kansas City Times* (December 23, 1938) reported that both Joe Turner and Pete Johnson were at the Lone Star when the call to appear at Carnegie Hall was received. Alto player Walter Knight and drummer Murl Johnson were also in the group. This report confirms that Pete Johnson received a long-distance call on Monday, the 19th, received travelling money from New York on Tuesday, and after a celebration that night, he and Joe caught the train at 11:45.

Another report varies these facts, particularly on the means of travel. It was December 19, 1938 when John Hammond used Western Union to wire Joe Turner and Pete Johnson, confirming their Carnegie Hall appearance and their fee of $200. It was suggested that bus travel to New York would be the most economic. They were to appear in the "Spirituals To Swing" concert which Hammond was promoting and their lives were about to change.

Joe Turner

6

"The boogie got moving"

(1938)

In 1938 John Hammond found his backer for a Carnegie Hall concert to be called From Spirituals to Swing. This would present, as he put it, "Negro music from its raw beginnings to the latest jazz".[1] Or, as stated in the programme, "The Music Nobody Knows". The backer was *The New Masses*, the literary magazine of the American Communist Party, though Hammond believed that editor Eric Bernay arranged the sponsorship because it was a worthwhile venture, rather than to push a political agenda.

The concert, which took place on December 23, 1938, was dedicated to the memory of the great blues singer, Bessie Smith, who had died in September 1937. It was a sell-out, with chairs on the stage to accommodate as many people as possible. On the programme was gospel (Mitchell's Christian Singers and Sister Rosetta Tharpe), blues (Sonny Terry, Big Bill Broonzy, Ruby Smith, Helen Humes, Jimmy Rushing and Joe Turner), boogie-woogie piano (Albert Ammons, Meade Lux Lewis, Pete Johnson), New Orleans jazz (Sidney Bechet) and swing (Count Basie orchestra and groups).

Turner spoke a few years later of the backstage nerves they had experienced.

"We had never worked in anything more than small nightspots .... The afternoon of the concert the four of us [Turner and the three pianists, Johnson, Albert Ammons and Meade Lux Lewis] were in Carnegie Hall, sizin' up the situation and tryin' not to let on to the others just how scared each of us was. That hall and stage looked just so big to us – and it kept lookin' a little bit bigger by the minute ... Everything turned out all right though. As soon as the boys hit the first beat and the boogie got to moving – why you could feel that audience pickin' up on that beat. They had never heard anything like that before. Everything started jumping and then it didn't seem to make no difference whether we were in the Kingfish back in Kansas City or in Carnegie Hall. I started singing – and I wasn't scared."[2]

John Hammond's memory of Turner's appearance on stage was,

"Joe shoved the microphone out of his way, as though flicking lint from a lapel, picked up the beat and started shouting the blues in an open-throated tone that carried to the far reaches of the hall. Joe Turner was amongst us and feeling well."[3]

CARNEGIE HALL GOES "SCOT."

Joe Turner's 12th Street "Music" Puts 'Em in the Aisles.

(By the Associated Press.)

NEW YORK, Dec. 23.—Joe Turner, Kansas City Negro cabaret singer, was one of the swingdom Cinderellas to bring down the house tonight in staid old Carnegie hall, stronghold of classical music, in an all-Negro concert covering "Spirituals to Swing." The dress circle and the galleries applauded with the same gusto rendered to Toscanini and other Bach-Beethoven-Brahms boys.

Turner, wearing the same green-tinged suit and yellow shoes he uses in the small Lone Star cabaret in Kansas City, put 'em in the aisles with some real old low-down "scat" singing. (Sorry, it can't be described —you have to hear it. It's hot, with a lot of boops.)

He did his own "Joe Turner Blues," a Kansas City and Negro favorite called "Roll 'Em," and a bit of good-natured whimsy entitled "You Low-Down Dog," his rich, deep voice rocking Carnegie's far-flung walls without the aid of a microphone.

It was Joe's second trip to New York—he came here last spring for Benny Goodman's Carnegie concert —and he wasn't a bit nervous.

"I just got up there and gave it to 'em," he said, "—and I hope they liked it." They did.

His Lone Star co-star, Pianist Pete Johnson, another "boogie-woogie" luminary, said working Carnegie hall was easier than the cabaret.

"There aren't a lot of people drinking and yelling at each other," he explained, "so you don't have to play so loud."

Meade (Lux) Lewis, a mahogany-skinned car-polisher from Chicago who also applies a deft touch to a piano, played selections that bore the far-from-classical titles of "Honky Tonk Train Blues" and the "Yancey Special," among others.

Kansas City Times, December 24, 1938

Joe Turner, with backing by Pete Johnson, sang *Low Down Dog* and *It's All Right Baby*. They were part of his standard repertoire for the rest of his career. Hammond had the concert recorded on acetate discs and in 1959 much of the music was issued on Vanguard LPs. More recently it has appeared as part of a three-CD set, which also includes the 1939 From Spirituals To Swing concert.

Newspaper reports the day after the concert included an uncredited one by Association Press stating

> "Turner, wearing the same green-tinged suit and yellow shoes he uses in the small Lone Star cabaret in Kansas City, put 'em in the aisles with some real old low-down 'scat' singing".

His songs are given as *Joe Turner Blues*, *Roll 'Em* and *Low Down Dog* - "his rich, deep voice rocking Carnegie's far flung walls without the aid of a microphone."[4] Another also used "scat" in an unfamiliar way, "There was Joe Turner, dusky young scat singer from the Lone Star Cabaret in Kansas City[5] ..." and reviewer, John Chapman, wrote that Joe could "shrivel a microphone just by breathing in".[6]

The concert was an undoubted success, generating huge publicity for the performers, while the rich and upper-class of New York City were primed for the opening of "The wrong place for the Right people," Cafe Society.

7

"The wrong place for the right people."

(1939-1940)

Cafe Society was the brainchild of a man whose background was in the selling of shoes, Barney Josephson (1902-1988). It was to be an integrated nightclub, with no mob influence and no colour bar for entertainers, staff or customers, and Josephson found the ideal talent-spotter for his new club in John Hammond. Cafe Society opened in the basement at 2 Sheridan Square on December 28, 1938, with Billie Holiday, the Boogie Woogie Boys, and trumpeter Frankie Newton and his band. Jack Gilford was comedian and master of ceremonies.

Some sources quote January 4, 1939 for the opening of the club, while researcher Ken Vail gives December 30th.[1] In his autobiography however, Josephson refers more than once to December 28th. He had forgotten to obtain a cabaret licence but put the show on anyway.[2]

Writing in 1945, George M. Avakian, Master Sergeant U.S. Army, reminisced about being taken by Steve Smith of the Hot Record Society, principally to hear Meade Lux Lewis, "The club opened during the Christmas holidays of 1938 .... we went on 'our' opening night; namely, the second night."[3] Avakian does not mention Joe Turner, just Billie Holiday and the Frankie Newton orchestra, neither is Joe shown on the initial advertisements for the club. This probably confirms that Turner and Johnson did not appear on the bill until January 4th, despite both Josephson and Billie Holiday's recollections, though Holiday did write in her autobiography, "I'll never forget that opening night. There must have been six hundred people in the joint, celebrities, artists, rich society people. And a big hitch ... nobody could go on until we had the cabaret licence." Then the licence arrived and at 11:30 the show began. Turner, she said, killed them.[4]

Joe told of his friendship with Miss Holiday,

"I used to bug her all the time 'cause I used to go in her dressing room and use her brown powder and put it on my face. She used to throw me out. I used to walk with her during the intermissions. She would walk up and down the street to get some fresh air, so me and her got to be good friends."[5]

On December 30th, two days after the club opened, Turner and Johnson made their first recordings, *Goin' Away Blues* and *Roll 'Em, Pete* for the Vocalion label. These exciting, classic titles immediately became a part of jazz history. Upon the record's release, Dave Dexter wrote that the two titles "are just about the finest blues exhibitions to be made into permanent form, Joe's famous 'Well yes, yes' shouts are there – and so are Pete's rockin' rhythms and improvisations. The Lone Star atmosphere is there. It's inescapable." Some eighty years later, pianist Jim Turner referred to

"The seemingly endless inventiveness of Big Joe Turner with his booming blues vocals and his lyrics and Pete Johnson with his flawless boogie-woogie - these were true geniuses whose excellence, in my opinion, has yet to be surpassed."[6]

During her stay at Cafe Society Billie Holiday introduced the song for which she is rightly celebrated, the anti-lynching *Strange Fruit*. This was recorded for Milt Gabler's Commodore label on April 20, 1939, with backing by the Frankie Newton band. Made at the same date was *Fine and Mellow*, credited to Miss Holiday, though Gabler has said that he and Billie worked on the lyrics at the club the night before the session. The traditional nature of these verses might also explain why Joe Turner told Larry Cohn that he composed the song. Doc Pomus, for one, believed this claim, which at least merits consideration.[7]

Barney Josephson, in his autobiography, writes:

"The women were all crazy over Big Joe. He was largely unschooled, unlettered, don't think he ever spent a day in school. He was tall and slim and never stopped moving while he sang. He had an endless repertoire of blues, not just the slow, sad blues of the Deep South, but 'pepped it up some' he would announce," before going into *Cherry Red*.[8]

Producer George Avakian recalled that

"The blues shouting of Joe Turner, teamed with Pete Johnson, was one of the highlights of Cafe Society history. (Joe's) favorite drink at the bar was a rugged thing known as a peppermint stick (mainly a large quantity of rye) ... Turner, incidentally, used to shout *The Sheik of Araby* in fine style."[9]

Joe also told James Austin that he sang a lot of pop songs at Cafe Society, including *The Sheik* and *Red Sails In The Sunset*.[10] One writer has even incorrectly quoted Avakian as saying that Turner was singing *Shake, Rattle and Roll*, the 1954 song, at Cafe Society.

Turner is not mentioned in the club's advertising on a regular basis, but that cannot be taken to mean he was not appearing. Helen Humes, who was the featured singer at Cafe Society between 1941 and 1943, commented that during her stay Joe Turner worked there "on occasion".[11]

New York's *Daily News* (February 1, 1939) claimed, "You'll be hearing a lot more of Joe Turner, colored scat singer at Cafe Society," while the *New York Times* (April 23, 1939) advised that "Joe Turner provides the hectic ballads with loose-jointed abandon". An advert. in the same paper (March 5, 1939) asked:

HAVE YOU HEARD?
"I ain't had no butter since my
cow been gone"
as sung by
BIG JOE TURNER from KANSAS CITY
The new blues shouter who is making
musical history

New York Times, March 5, 1939

Turner was back in the Vocalion studios on June 30, 1939, to record three titles with Pete Johnson and his Boogie Woogie Boys (Hot Lips Page, trumpet, Buster Smith, alto, Johnson, piano, Lawrence Lucie, guitar, Abe Bolar, bass, Eddie Dougherty, drums (*Cherry Red, Baby Look At You, Lovin' Mama Blues*) and one title (*Cafe Society Rag*) with the three pianists, Johnson, Ammons and Lewis. In addition, four titles from Cafe Society broadcasts have surfaced on the Document label, one with backing by Frankie Newton's band (*Sunny Side of the Street*) and three with Pete Johnson (*Low Down Dog, Honeydripper, Early Morning Blues (When the Morning Glories....).*

Pete Johnson and Joe Turner, unknown location, 1939. Photograph courtesy Peter Vacher Collection

Joe Turner, the Boogie Woogie Trio and Billy Holliday [sic] were advertised to play at the Apollo Theatre for one week, commencing August 11th. Also on the bill were Willie Bryant, Tip, Tap and Toe, and Teddy Hill's Orchestra. It was not unknown for performers at Cafe Society to sometimes double up, if Josephson agreed. Writer George Hoefer says Turner's initial Cafe Society run was for an uninterrupted nine months and this may well be correct. He mentions a theatre tour with the Boogie Woogie Boys, which ties in with a Chicago appearance nine months after Cafe Society opened. [12]

On or about September 15th, 1939 Harry James and his Orchestra opened a four week booking (there is a review in the *Chicago Tribune* of September 17th) at the "Panther Room of the College Inn" of the Hotel Sherman in Chicago. Also featured in the show were the Boogie Woogie Trio (Ammons, Lewis and Johnson) and Joe Turner. (In February 1939 James had recorded a trumpet-and-rhythm session, with Albert Ammons on two titles and Pete Johnson on two.) Drew Page, who played in the James' reed section, recalled the gig with the Trio and Big Joe, as well as the fact that there was "a jitterbug team of eight kids"![13] There were broadcasts on both NBC Red and Blue networks, via WMAQ, as well as on local radio, some nightly, except Mondays.

Issues of the *Kansas City Call* for October and November confirmed the Hotel Sherman engagement and that Joe and the Boogie-Woogie Boys ended their stay on Saturday, November 4th, before returning to New York and Cafe Society. The *Indianapolis Recorder* (November 18th, 1939) reported that the final night of the singer and pianists' stay "had the entire Panther Room patronage rocking …."

From left, Meade Lux Lewis, Joe Turner, Albert Ammons, Pete Johson, Cafe Society, c. 1939

Replacing the Frankie Newton group, pianist Joe Sullivan brought a mixed band into Cafe Society on November 24th, with Turner, the Boogie Woogie trio and Hazel Scott the main entertainment. This Cafe Society cast was due to play a midnight benefit concert at the Apollo theatre on December 15th. The club also announced a Swing Festival to run from December 18th-25th to celebrate its first anniversary, with featured performers Joe Turner, Ida Cox, the Boogie Woogie Trio, Hazel Scott, James P. Johnson and the Joe Sullivan unit. In addition Cafe Society was to present its first anniversary Swing Festival at Carnegie Hall on December 31th, 1939, with Sonny Terry and Big Bill Broonzy replacing Johnson and Jack Teagarden's Orchestra instead of Joe Sullivan's.

Daily Princeton, December 14, 1939

A December 1939 advertisement advises that Cafe Society is the "Rendezvous of Celebs, Debs and Plebs", has the "Most Exciting Music Ever to Hit New York", and it's the place "Where Swing is King". The Famous Boogie Woogie Boys are the headliners, alongside Joe Sullivan's New Band, Hazel Scott and Big Joe Turner.

A tempting news item from Columbia Records – or, more likely, John Hammond – advised there were plans to record a W.C. Handy "Blues Album," with Billie Holiday, Joe Turner, Jimmy Rushing and a Count Basie small group. Like many good ideas, this was another which failed to blossom.

During Joe Sullivan's stay of just over six months there were a number of personnel changes in his unit before arriving at the line-up used for a Vocalion recording session. Two of the four titles made by Joe Sullivan and his Cafe Society Orchestra on February 9th, 1940, had vocals by Joe Turner *(Low Down Dirty Shame/I Can't Give You Anything But Love)*. The musicians were Eddie Anderson, trumpet, Ed Hall, clarinet, Danny Polo, clarinet, tenor, Sullivan, piano, Henry Turner, bass, and Johnny Wells, drums, with two men from the Count Basie orchestra added for the recording, Benny Morton, trombone, and Freddie Green, guitar. The previous month, January 15th, Turner had sung on two titles by The Varsity Seven *(How Long, How Long Blues/Shake It and Break It)* for Varsity Records.

Joe Turner, early 1940s

The United States Population Census for 1940 has Joe Turner (Jr.), with his "wife," Carrie Turner, living at the Woodside Hotel on Seventh Avenue, New York. That same year we learn that Georgia was living in Grand Rapids, Michigan, with her second husband, Lonnie Murray (sic), a road digger, aged 44. Joe's sister, Kate, had by this time married and become Mrs. Bryant, with two sons, Jerry and Charlie. In later years Big Joe was to advise Jerry, saying, ".... I have a nephew whom I encouraged, who is a singing pianist. Also musical instructor in Canada".[14]

Turner and Johnson continued at Cafe Society through February to April, together with the Joe Sullivan group, Hazel Scott and the Golden Gate Quartet. How long this continued is unclear, though in August the singer and pianist made two appearances on the NBC Blue Network radio show, the Chamber Music Society of Lower Basin Street. On the 11th Turner and Johnson performed *Roll 'Em Pete* and *Goin' Away Blues*, while on the 18th they repeated these titles, but Turner, with Albert Ammons on piano, also sang *Turner's Blues*. These titles later appeared on LPs. Dave Dexter talked about Kansas City jazz on the second broadcast.

An intriguing announcement in May was that the "Boogie Woogie Three and Joe Turner will appear in concert with the Boston Symphony Orchestra at Boston Symphony Hall - June 17."[15]

On Tuesday, October 8th, 1940 Barney Josephson opened his second nightclub, Cafe Society Uptown, located at 58th Street, between Park and Lexington Avenues.[16] Turner may have been there, with Johnson, Ammons and Lewis. The Sheridan Square site became Cafe Society Downtown.

A week later, on the 15th, Benny Carter took a small band into the studios to record two titles for the Okeh label, featuring Turner vocals on both, *Joe Turner Blues* and *Beale Street Blues*. For this date Carter concentrated on clarinet.

Turner did have periods when he was "resting" and this was one of them, as a later report in *Down Beat* indicated. Single appearances in October may have been at jam sessions held at the West End Theatre on 125th Street, probably with the Boogie Woogie Trio.

The Boogie Woogie Boys, 1939. Photograph courtesy Peter Vacher Collection.

SERIAL NUMBER | 1. NAME (Print) | | ORDER NUMBER

183

Joseph *Vernon* *Turner*
(First) (Middle) (Last)

271

2. ADDRESS (Print)

2424 - 7 Ave Apt9
(Number and street or R. F. D. number)

NYC *NY* *NY*
(Town) (County) (State)

3. TELEPHONE

(Exchange) (Number)

4. AGE IN YEARS

29

DATE OF BIRTH

May 18 1911
(Mo.) (Day) (Yr.)

5. PLACE OF BIRTH

Kansas City
(Town or county)

Mo
(State or country)

6. COUNTRY OF CITIZENSHIP

U.S.

7. NAME OF PERSON WHO WILL ALWAYS KNOW YOUR ADDRESS

Mrs. Qumel *Turner*
(Mr., Mrs., Miss) (First) (Middle) (Last)

8. RELATIONSHIP OF THAT PERSON

Wife

9. ADDRESS OF THAT PERSON

2424 - 7 Ave Apt9
(Number and street or R. F. D. number)

NYC *NY* *NY*
(Town) (County) (State)

10. EMPLOYER'S NAME

Barney Jolson

11. PLACE OF EMPLOYMENT OR BUSINESS

2 Sherman Square *NYC* *NY* *NK*
(Number and street or R. F. D. number) (Town) (County) (State)

I AFFIRM THAT I HAVE VERIFIED ABOVE ANSWERS AND THAT THEY ARE TRUE.

Joseph Vernon Turner
(Registrant's signature)

REGISTRATION CARD
D. S. S. Form 1

(over)

16—17105

Front and back of Joe Turner's Draft Registration Card, 1940

REGISTRAR'S REPORT

DESCRIPTION OF REGISTRANT

RACE		HEIGHT (Approx.)	WEIGHT (Approx.)	COMPLEXION	
		6' 1½"	200½		
White		EYES	HAIR	Sallow	
				Light	
Negro	✓	Blue	Blonde	Ruddy	
		Gray	Red	Dark	
Oriental		Hazel	Brown	Freckled	
		Brown ✓	Black ✓	Light brown	✓
Indian		Black	Gray	Dark brown	
			Bald	Black	
Filipino					

Other obvious physical characteristics that will aid in identification...............

No ne

I certify that my answers are true; that the person registered has read or has had read to him his own answers; that I have witnessed his signature or mark and that all of his answers of which I have knowledge are true, except as follows:

E H Singer

(Signature of registrar)

Registrar for ..... 36 .... 21 ...... N Y C ...... N Y
             (Precinct)   (Ward) (City or county) (State)

Date of registration ..... October 16, 1940

(STAMP OF LOCAL BOARD)

(The stamp of the Local Board having jurisdiction of the registrant shall be placed in the above space.)

Dave Dexter arranged for a group of musicians associated with Kansas City, including Hot Lips Page, Pete Johnson and Joe Turner, to record six titles for Decca, to be released in a Kansas City Jazz album of three 78rpm records. This successful session was held on November 11th, 1940, with Turner recording just the one title, *Piney Brown Blues*, backed by Page, Johnson and the rhythm section. Dexter says that when this title, backed by Johnson's *627 Stomp*, was released as a single it sold over 400,000 copies.[18]

In his book, *The Swing Era*, Gunther Schuller wrote:

> "One of the most remarkable and moving performances in all of jazz is *Piney Brown Blues* by Joe Turner and His Fly Cats .... *Piney Brown* is here singled out as a uniquely memorable performance of extraordinary expressive power .... [This] is a poignant lament, a heartfelt jeremiad, a profound musical snapshot and document of a time and a place central to the history of jazz."

Schuller continues,

> "Turner in his narrative blues had a remarkable ability to inject emotion and drama into his singing - what a great operatic baritone he could have been! - and nowhere is his singing more moving or expressive than on *Piney Brown*."[19]

The Vocalion and Decca recordings have confirmed that the partnership of Joe Turner and Pete Johnson has to be celebrated as one of the most exciting in all of jazz and blues history.

Subsequently Turner signed a contract with Decca Records which was to keep him busy in the studios throughout 1941, and on November 26th, he made four sides for Decca, accompanied by pioneer stride pianist, Willie 'The Lion' Smith. This was followed, on January 21st, 1941, by a lovely session under the leadership of Art Tatum. Turner sings on two titles, *Wee Baby Blues* and *Last Goodbye Blues*. His accompaniment by Tatum on piano, Joe Thomas, trumpet, and Ed Hall, clarinet, is nigh on perfect.

1941

Under the headline "Joe Turner Back Shouting The Blues", *Down Beat* for March 15th, 1941, reported, "New York – Joe Turner, blues shouter from Kansas City, is back working again at downtown Cafe Society after many months of being unemployed, except for record dates. Turner took Rosetta Tharpe's spot."

Starting in early February (a *New York Times* advertisement confirms he was there on February 12th), this latest Cafe Society engagement lasted until April. Turner had been working with Meade Lux Lewis, Willie Bryant, Mae Diggs and the Henry 'Red' Allen Orchestra.

From left to right, Joe Turner, Pete Johnson, Albert Ammons, Meade Lux
Lewis, Apollo Theatre, August 1939

Early in April Turner and Meade Lux Lewis left Cafe Society Downtown
to join a tour organised by emcee, singer, comedian and leader, Willie Bryant.
Also on the tour were The Peters Sisters vocal group, with Bryant fronting the
Snookum Russell Orchestra. *Down Beat* (May 1st, 1941) gave the schedule
as starting at the Howard Theatre in Washington, for one week, then three-
day dates in Norfolk, Richmond, Newport News, Portsmouth and Lynchburg.
"Group will be on road until at least the middle of May."

Sometime in 1941, perhaps on April 19th, Ahmet and Nesuhi Ertegun
organised their first jazz concert in Washington, at the Jewish Community
Center. Ahmet recalled, "We had booked a terrific line-up, led by Sidney Bechet
featuring Sidney DeParis and Vic Dickenson, and Joe Turner singing with
pianist Pete Johnson. That was my first in-person encounter with Joe."[17] There
were many more such encounters to follow during the 1950s.

It is likely that the tour concluded in New York, when "Harlem Favorite" Willie Bryant was due to headline at the Apollo Theatre for one week beginning Friday, May 9th. With him were, among others, Joe Turner and Meade Lux Lewis, singer Billy Daniels, dancers Tip, Tap and Toe, and the Earl Bostic Band. They were appearing "in a new musical comedy hit, 'Swinging In Society'".

Joe had been due to join an all-star "From Bach to Boogie Woogie" concert at Carnegie Hall on April 23rd, 1941, but his appearance has not been confirmed. This was another Cafe Society presentation, with a jam-packed programme, including Lena Horne, Hazel Scott, the bands of Teddy Wilson, Ed Hall and Red Allen, Count Basie and his Orchestra and others. If Joe had appeared, he no doubt would have been lucky if allocated two songs.

Perhaps he escorted Miss Blanche Brown to the concert. An item in the *Pittsburg Courier* for April 26th, 1940, reported, "Blanche Brown of St. Paul, Minn., is a Washington visitor and the seeming 'after-show' of Joe Turner who sings the blues ..." (It is an odd coincidence that the singer should escort Blanche Brown and that two of his wives had the maiden name of Brown.)

Thursday afternoon, May 15th, there was an open-air entertainment, with Noble Sissle as emcee, to enlist support for the New York Fund. Joe Turner and other Cafe Society members took part. Neither the event location nor the function of the New York Fund were given.

Recordings at Decca were the highlights of July. There was another classic session with Art Tatum and a rhythm section, on June 13th, when four top-of-the-range titles were made, *Lucille*, *Rock Me Mama*, *Corrine Corrina*, and *Lonesome Graveyard Blues*. It would have been surprising if the next appearance in the Decca studios, on July 17th, with pianist Sammy Price, Leonard Ware, guitar, and Billy Taylor, bass, had reached the same standard. It does not, but it still added four rewarding numbers to the Turner discography.

***

Jump For Joy

July 10th, 1941, was the opening night at the Mayan Theatre in Los Angeles for "A Sun-Tanned Revue-sical" featuring Duke Ellington and his Orchestra. Dorothy Dandridge, who a decade later was to play the lead in the movie "Carmen Jones", was the female star, the sixty-strong company also including the Duke's singers, Ivie Anderson and Herb Jeffries. When Dandridge left the show, her replacement was Judy Carol.

Pat Willard, who was Ellington's PR for twenty years, wrote detailed notes for the Smithsonian album LP 037, a compilation attempting to recreate the show. Willard explains that towards the end of July, at one of the regular after-show meetings, Ellington convinced everyone that the blues had been neglected by "Jump For Joy" and that the only appropriate reparation was to bring in Joe Turner from New York at once.[20]

Joe received the telegram at Cafe Society and is quoted as saying:

"I had been there five years working in the same nightclub [the club had been open less than three years] .... and I didn't know if I wanted to go to California. But Barney Josephson say, 'Go out there and do the show and come on back when you get ready,' and Duke's telegram say to take the train right away and that's fine because I was scared to fly."[21]

Ellington said:

"I sent for Joe Turner and signed him up. I got so much pleasure listening to him break it up that I completely forgot I had him under contract."[22]

Pat Willard recalled there was no special material for the singer, who sang his own blues until at last the Duke wrote *Rocks In My Bed* for him.[23] Joe claimed he helped write the song, but received no composer credit. It was Ivie Anderson who recorded the title with Ellington, while Turner made it for Decca on September 8, with accompaniment by pianist Freddie Slack. In addition, the policeman's sketch, "Shhhh! He's On The Beat," was expanded to include Joe Turner.

Turner joined the revue early in August, perhaps by the 4th, and it was a nerve-racking experience for him.

"I used to get so scared with singers like Herb Jeffries around but Duke would try to bring me on. He'd sit in the pit and play the intro four or five times. I'd look down at him and my knees were knocking so much I thought I had St. Vitus dance. Then Ben Webster would play for me and off I'd go. I liked singing with the smaller group as Duke's full band played too much music for me. Duke used to say, 'Come on, Joe, you can make it, you're a pro'."[24]

George Simon wrote a review for the October 1941 issue of *Metronome*, having seen the September 15th performance:

"It took an after-premiere addition to stop 'Jump For Joy'. He was a blues singer who busted into a second-act skit as a cop and commenced to pour out some of the most moving blues-chanting heard on many a stage. They had to call Joe back for more and even then the comparatively small audience wasn't satisfied. He was the only show-stopper in this sometimes fast, sometimes not so fast, moving revue. Duke Ellington's band was supposed to be the featured attraction, but it spends its time down in the pit ... and no matter how hard you try, you can't make a feature of a pit band."

(Others in the cast included Marie Bryant, Willie Lewis and Pot, Pan and Skillet.)

Another review quoted by Willard said, "*Rocks In My Bed* (is) the best American Calypso heard hereabouts. Joe Turner can toss out verses until the milk wagon drives up."[25]

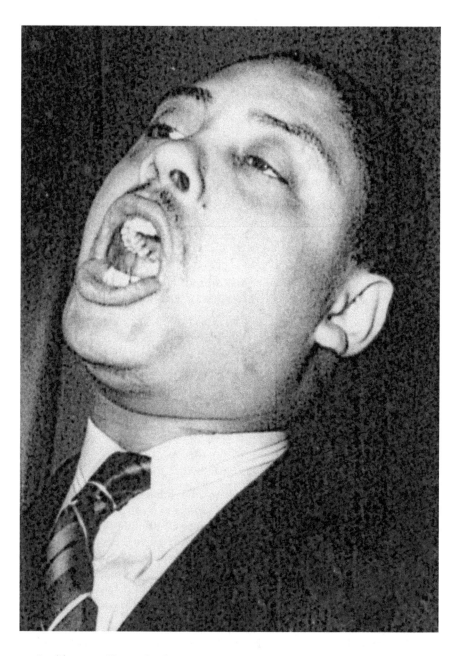

Joe Turner at Decca Studios, 1940

Turner's recording of *Rocks In My Bed* (Decca 4093) is markedly different to Ivie Anderson's with the Ellington Orchestra (Victor 27639). It has additional verses, in typical Turner style, which he no doubt used when singing the number in the revue.

Special moments in jazz remain in the memory and one such from 'Jump for Joy' stayed with the Duke's tenor man Ben Webster. During an engagement at Ronnie Scott's Club in Soho, London, his bassist was Dave Green, who recalled

"I used to drop him off at the White Horse Hotel in Regent's Park after the gig. He knew I loved Jimmy Blanton so he would tell me little things about him. One night, as we were leaving the club to walk to my car he suddenly announced in a loud voice to whoever might be listening, 'Big Joe Turner, Fred Guy and Jimmy Blanton playing the blues ... best Goddam music I ever heard in my life'."[26]

Ben Webster, left, and Dave Green, at Ronnie Scott's Club, c. May 1965, courtesy of Dave Green.

"Jump For Joy" closed September 27th, 1941, after eleven weeks and 101 performances – or more if one consults Wikipedia.

One of Ellington's biographers, Terry Teachout, suggests the audiences enjoyed the show, with the critics inclined to be less tolerant. Among the reasons for the show failing to achieve its goal of transferring to Broadway, he lists the orchestra being in the pit, too many cooks involved in its preparation, using sketches that were not that funny and, in usual Duke Ellington style, leaving everything until the last minute.

It is possible that the show's anti-racist message meant that there was an inclination to overlook its imperfections as an entertainment. Even more important was the failure to generate enough income. The show had to struggle to pay such a large cast, a financial struggle which would have been even greater if it had tried to tour from West to East coast prior to a Broadway opening.

The main sketch writer was Sid Kuller, who claimed to be the inspiration for the revue. Other contributors included illustrious names like Langston Hughes and Mickey Rooney – though that did not stop their sketches being dropped later on. The choreography for the show was by Nick Castle.

Mercer Ellington said that "Jump For Joy" was his father's opportunity "to have his say about racial discrimination".[27]

Duke said

> "There was the first and greatest problem of trying to give an American audience entertainment without compromising the dignity of the Negro people. Needless to say, this is the problem every Negro artist faces. He runs afoul of offensive stereotypes instilled in the American mind by whole centuries of ridicule and derogation. The American audience has been taught to expect a Negro on the stage to clown and 'Uncle Tom,' that is, to enact the role of a servile, yet lovable, inferior."[28]

He also said, "The theme had to do with burying Uncle Tom in the theatre. We buried Uncle Tom in the opening scene."[29]

Parts of the revue were filmed at the Mayan Theatre in the middle of August. Mark Cantor reports that the version in colour, which is held by the Smithsonian Institute, was shot by Harry Carney, baritone saxist in Ellington's orchestra. Turner is seen on stage for a few seconds. The quality of the film is poor, lack of sound is disappointing, but it is still a valuable document. A similar pot-pourri, in black and white, was filmed by Andy and Mary MacKay.[30]

A few weeks after closing at the Mayan, Duke Ellington and his Orchestra opened a one-week engagement on Wednesday, November 19th at the Orpheum Theatre in Los Angeles. Several members from "Jump for Joy" were also on the bill, including Joe Turner, Marie Bryant and Pot, Pan and Skillet.[31]

"Joe Turner in Blues Contest on Coast" reported the *Kansas City Plaindealer* for November 21st, 1941. It continued, "By popular demand the Alabama theatre cafe brings to its Sunday matinee …. a blues singing contest which will feature Joe Turner and other blues singers. The contest is open to anyone who can sing the blues." Among those also appearing were the Whities Lindy Hoppers, who had appeared in the 1936 Marx Brothers' "A Day at The Races" and the 1941 Olsen and Johnson's "Hellzapoppin'".

Joe remained in Los Angeles after "Jump For Joy" closed, making it his base for a number of years. It has been reported that for a time he shared accommodation with Pete Johnson, though by 1944 he was living at his sister's.

It is possible that the partners visited their home town about this time. The *Kansas City Times* (November 24th, 1941) gives no details, but comments that Pete Johnson and Joe Turner's return visits "have been merely to see 'the folks at home'. The boys really are in the money."

Joe Turner at Mayan Theatre, Los Angeles, from film of Jump For Joy, 1941

8

"Joe Turner has gone Hollywood"

(1941-1942)

On many occasions since it opened in 1934 The Swanee Inn (133 N. La Brea) was home to numerous jazz stars including, in the 1940s, Big Joe Turner, Meade Lux Lewis, Art Tatum, the Nat 'King' Cole trio, and Joe Sullivan. Cornettist Bobby Hackett said of it on a radio broadcast, "It was kind of a beat-up place, but it was very cosy". A *Metronome* writer referred to it as "this cosy but frantic bistro on La Brea".[1]

It was to the Swanee Inn that Turner went when "Jump For Joy" closed, joining pianist Meade Lux Lewis. He was there early as October, the *Pittsburg Courier* for the first of November reporting that he was "shouting the blues with Meade Lux Lewis ... at the Swanee Inn". As *Down Beat* (November 1st, 1941) put it, he was to co-feature with Lewis, who had been there since August 19th, 1941: "Lewis, who has done turn away business, is expected to stay for four more weeks at least."

Rather more dramatically, the *Dayton Daily News* for November 9th, 1941 contained a report which read

"The Swanee Inn features one of the great boogie-woogie masters of modern times – Meade 'Lux' Lewis – and 'Big Joe' Turner, who is the best blues singer we have ever heard. 'Big Joe' sings blues the way a baritone steam whistle would if the baritone steam whistle was six feet tall and weighed 220 pounds and had brass gongs for lungs. When he sings *Rocks In My Bed* or *Careless Love*, your ears are hammered and the flesh of your brain is jounced".

Lewis departed towards the end of the year, perhaps after the Christmas holiday. *Down Beat* for January 15th, 1942, reported, "Meade Lux Lewis closed his long run at the Swanee Inn, leaving Eddie Beal .... to assist Joe Turner". However, it was not long before Lewis returned, when Beal left to become Lena Horne's accompanist.

Turner was in Decca's Los Angeles studios on January 29th, 1942, to record *Blues In The Night*, the hit song which gave its title to the film. One other side was made, *Cry Baby Blues*. The accompaniment was by a trio, with the little-known Fred Skinner on piano.

The Pittsburgh Courier for March 14th, 1942, advises that the big items from the coast include "*Joe Turner Blues*-in' it away at the Caprice" (sic). Seven days later the paper again refers to the Caprice and that Turner is "laying 'em in the aisles"

Bass player Red Callender recalled being in Lee Young's band at the 90-seater Capri nightclub in Los Angeles, accompanying Billie Holiday and Joe Turner. The personnel was Paul Campbell, trumpet, Bumps Meyers, tenor, Arthur Twyne (or Twine), piano, Louis Gonzales, guitar, Callender, bass, Young, drums. When Twyne died, his replacement was Jimmy Rowles. For a time Lee's brother, Lester Young, joined as "guest artist" on tenor while working out his AFM union ticket. Campbell was later replaced by 'Red' Mack.[2]

A *Down Beat* news item in the April 15th, 1942 issue, by-lined Oakland, CA., states that John A. Bur-ton (sic) has taken over the management of Joe Turner. "Blues shouter Turner will tour the country after his close at the Club Capri in Hollywood". No details have been found for the proposed tour.

The Capri, at Pico and La Cienega, was owned by Billy Berg, later to open the very well-known nightspot, Billy Berg's. That was in the future, but in 1942 he moved into larger, plusher premises, The Trouville, with 250 seats, in Hollywood, on Beverly and Fairfax. Callender said, "Again we had The Spirits of Rhythm, Joe Turner, Billie Holiday, Slim and Slam, and the Lee and Lester Young band on the bill."[3] whereas Jimmy Rowles mentions The Spirits of Rhythm, Joe Turner, Marie Bryant and Leo Watson; no Billie Holiday, no Slim and Slam. The probability is that Turner and Bryant transferred from the Capri to the Trouville, with Billie replacing Joe a few weeks later. [4]

The Duke Ellington Orchestra was due to begin an eight-week engagement at the Trianon Ballroom in Southgate, CA, on April 2nd. That same evening the Lee and Lester Young band was scheduled to open at the Trouville nightclub. When Duke's drummer, Sonny Greer, was taken ill, Lee could not refuse the opportunity to play with the Ellington orchestra, despite the importance of his own opening.[5] This story does provide a date for the opening of the Trouville.

Callender's recollection, as it applies to Turner and Holiday, has to be treated with caution. Certainly Joe Turner played the Capri in early 1942, as shown by the news item in *Down Beat* for April 15th, 1942, and he, Slim and Slam and the Spirits of Rhythm were at the Trouville when Billie Holiday arrived, towards the end of May, 1942, rather than mid-May reported by John Chilton. The *Boston Herald* (May 26th, 1942) gives, "Billie Holiday is currently singing at the Trouville Club in Los Angeles. She's part of a floor show that includes Slim and Slam, Joe Turner, the Four Spirits of Rhythm and Lester Young's band". Ken Vail lists a broadcast from the club on June 1st which includes Holiday but not Turner. Lady Day stayed for a reported two months, until replaced by Marie Bryant.[6] However, when the *California Eagle* (July 2nd, 1942) advised, "Now that Joe Turner has his slightly-used Packard, he sings out the blues with more gusto", was it referring to his appearance at The Trouville and, if so, did it mean that Billie's stay there was just for five weeks or so? It seems possible.

On Tuesday, July 28th the Negro Cavalry Regiment celebrated 75 years of army service at Cape Lockett, California. Bette Davis recited the "The Star Spangled Banner" and the large cast of black performers included Ethel Waters, Hattie McDaniels, the Berry Brothers, Lena Horne and Joe Turner.

Next is an intriguing sentence in *The Pittsburgh Courier* (October 3rd, 1942): ". . . Joe Turner has gone Hollywood, but grand, and is playing nothing but blondes . . ."

1943

The first news for 1943 is of a January "Jubilee" radio show which featured Billie Holiday, Art Tatum, the Red Allen band and Joe Turner. Unfortunately, Joe's contribution was not included on the resulting AFRS transcription.

Then, from *The Pittsburgh Courier* (February 27th, 1943) came a story of, apparently, drunken skylarks, or worse

> "According to waiters and porters on the Southern Pacific's crack Daylight Limited, Joe Turner and Wynonie Harris, alleged entertainers, really cut 'hawg' upon 'hawg' during their recent rail trip from Oakland to the Angel City. Loud and wrong – all the way – much to the train crew's embarrassment. If Harris and Turner will call by the Courier offices here, we'll have their paid-up membership cards to the 'we ain't ready club' waiting."

It could have been on tour such as this that Lowell Fulson, singer and guitarist, said, without giving a year, "When they packaged me in L.A. there was T-Bone (Walker), Bull Moose Jackson, Wynonie Harris, Big Joe Turner and Jay McShann."[7]

Details of Turner's bookings for most of this year are sparse, though they included another guest spot on the "Jubilee" radio show and probably more stays at the Swanee Inn. A Hal Holly "Los Angeles Band Brief" in *Down Beat* (July 1st, 1943), indicated that Joe had re-joined Meade Lux Lewis at the Swanee Inn. For a short time the Lorenzo Flennoy Trio, with Gene Phillips, guitar, Eddie Williams, bass, were on the same bill.

From September on a little more is known. Tuesday, September 14th, saw the opening, at The Plantation Club at 108th and Central Avenue, "for an extended engagement," of the Baby Simmons' New Revue, featuring Erskine Hawkins ("The Twentieth Century Gabriel") and his Band, Carita Harbert, Dusty Fletcher, Joe Turner, Sleepy Williams, The Two Zephyrs "and the prettiest line of girls on the coast."[8]

At the end of September Joe spent a week in a revue at the Lincoln Theatre (2300 Central Avenue) in L.A., closing on Friday, September 24th. Others on the bill, in addition to the "King of the Blues", were the Lyson Brothers (Juvenile Stars), Bobby Wallace (The Human Instrument), comedian Pigmeat and singer Bardu Ali and his band.[9]

In her biography of singer Joe Williams, *Every Day*, Leslie Gourse writes that on one occasion Joe Turner was unable to make a gig with Pete Johnson and Albert Ammons. The younger Williams (born 1918) deputised for him for six weeks, the first $150-a-week gig that he'd ever had. This was probably an engagement at Frenchy's club in Milwaukee.(Two titles by Williams, with Johnson and Ammons, recorded October 15th, 1943, have been issued on Document DOCD-1003.)

In October an advertisement proclaimed "New York Comes To Phila", referring to a show at the Club New Yorker in Philadelphia. The accompaniment was by trumpeter "Chas. Gaines' Orch.". It is likely that the show ran from October 26th to November 1st. The ad. also stated that Turner was "featured in 'Stormy Weather,'" though this was an error if the reference was to the 1943 movie.[10]

In the last days of November, he sang *Low Down Dog* on a "Jubilee" radio show, presumably accompanied by Pete Johnson and Albert Ammons, who were also present, along with emcee Ernie Whitman, Fats Waller, The Delta Rhythm Boys, and Harlan Leonard and his Orchestra.[11] Titles from the broadcast were distributed to military radio stations on an AFRS (Armed Forces Radio Service) transcription. (Jubilee was a programme which initially featured black artists and was intended for black servicemen.)

Turner's return to action is confirmed by a news item in *Capitol News* for December 1943 stating, "Joe Turner is back in circulation again, working nightly at Hollywood's Swanee Inn with Meade Lux Lewis." Joe Sullivan is believed to have returned to the venue about this time, *Down Beat* for May 1st, 1944, reporting he had just completed a 16-week run there.

Fats Waller, who had been on the "Jubilee" radio show with Joe only a matter of weeks previously, died on December 15th, 1943, aged 39. The *Los Angeles Tribune* for December 27 included a tribute to Fats by Big Joe (see overleaf).

1944

Joe Turner was still at the Swanee Inn on January 24th, 1944 when he and Lewis made "soundies" (three-minute films to be shown in special juke boxes) of *Roll 'Em* and *Low Down Dog*. Lewis is in top form, but Joe is not seen; an actor (Dudley Dickerson) mimes to his singing. The plots are amateurish, the music first-class. Turner was paid $100 for the rights to record these two compositions, affirming that the two songs were his "exclusive property".[12]

It was the February 14th, 1944 edition of the *Los Angeles Tribune* which contained just one line, stating, "Joe Turner got a rejection slip from the army". No other information is given, but one assumes that Joe's weight was a factor in his failing to pass a medical.

The singer remained at the Swanee Inn into April, with Joe Sullivan at the piano.[13] A *Metronome* report said of Sullivan and Turner, "they alternate throughout the evening," but Santa Monica's *The Samojac* (February 23rd, 1944) states that "Shoutin' Joe" "is accompanied by Joe Sullivan, famed Chicago pianist". It also lists the Lorenzo Flannoy (sic) Trio as the intermission group. *The Capitol News*, August issue, reports Sullivan returning to the Swanee Inn and that "Big Joe works off and on at the spot and comes and goes whenever he pleases."

YEAH, MAN!
Happy as a Baby Boy...

With a Brand New Christmas Toy!

In loving memory of one of the greatest musicians 'in the world — the one and only Fats Waller —

I wish you

A Very Merry Xmas and A Happy New Year

"Live while you're young
"Love one another"
"Roll 'em, boy . . .
"Let us jump for joy!"

The philosophy of your friend,

JOE TURNER

Thomas 'Fats' Waller died December 15, 1943 on board the Santa Fe's Super Chief en route from Los Angeles to New York City.
The *Los Angeles Tribune*, December 27, 1943, included this tribute to the great pianist, composer, singer and entertainer by Big Joe Turner."

Turner himself said, "I used to play out to the different nightclubs in Hollywood. Worked in the Swanee Inn out there for years. I got pretty well acquainted with a lot of people."[14]

On May 1st, 1944, Joe began a lengthy tour with "Little Beau and his Orchestra," opening in Detroit at Sunnie Wilson's Ballroom, site of the famed Graystone Ballroom.[15] One news report said, "Chavis Sherriff, 'Little Beau' as the cats refer to him, brings his 15-piece orchestra....."[16] Sherriff was the arranger and also played tenor saxophone. Other musicians named are Buddy Burdette, tenor, James Phelps, baritone, and Count L. Carrington, piano, Sheila Guyse, vocals.

After two days (May 6th and 7th) at the Sunset Terrace Dance Palace in Indianapolis, the tour continued through Kansas City and Chicago, as well as most of the Southern states, and a foray into Canada. *The Chicago Defender* for June 17th, 1944, under the line "Joe Turner to Southwest," referred to highly successful engagements through Florida, Alabama, Mississippi and Louisiana, before touring Texas, his first into the Lone Star state. The issue of August 5th, 1944 called it a six months tour of the East, South, West and Southwest. These press releases, complete with hyperbole, no doubt emanated from Joe's personal manager, John A. "Precisely" Burton.

The known dates for the tour with Joe Turner, are:

May 1944

1	Sunnie Wilson's Ballroom, Detroit, MI
?	Municipal Auditorium, Kansas City, IL
6	Sunset Terrace, Indianapolis, IN
7	Sunset Terrace, Indianapolis, IN
20	Wichita, KS
23	Port Stanley, Ontario, Canada
24	Port Stanley, Ontario, Canada
26	Buffalo, NY
27	Wilmington, DE
30	Banner Warehouse, Burlington, NC

June 1944

2	Charleston, NC
3	Savannah, GA
5	Tampa, FL
6	Two Spot Club, Jacksonville, FL
8	Pensacola, FL
9	Dragon Ballroom, Mobile, AL
10	Hattiesburg, MS
19	Beaumont, TX
24	Baton Rouge, LA

The Daily Times-News (Burlington, NC), May 23, 1944

July 1944

- 7   last date in Texas
- 8   Colorado Springs, CO
- 15   Rose Room, Wichita, KS
- 21   Lincoln Ballroom, Columbus, OH
- 27   Elberta Beach, Sandusky, OH
- 28   Saginaw, MI

The date of the Saginaw booking has been shown also as July 29th. Whichever date is correct, it is believed to be the one on which Joe's participation in this tour ended; though matters are not straightforward. The Little Beau orchestra was due to play in Milwaukee on August 4th, and there is no mention of Turner.

However, a later news item tells of Turner leaving his band to fly to New York from Milwaukee to record for Decca on August 8th, "but will rejoin it in Beloit, Wisconsin, after a few days rest." This news release appeared in three newspapers in Chicago, Philadelphia and Pittsburgh, while there is a Band Routes column which has "Joe Turner and his Orchestra" playing in New York City, N.Y., on August 9th and 10th.

Where the mystery deepens is that Turner started an engagement in Chicago on August 5th, reaching there from New York. Assuming the Chicago booking to be correct, one wonders about the source of the "flying to New York to record for Decca" story. *The Chicago Defender* heading was "Joe Turner To Record New Hit"! It is difficult to believe that the record company would find it necessary to go to such lengths to record Big Joe. In any case, there is no documented recording session by Turner that week in August and there are no relevant gaps in Decca's New York matrix listing.

On the balance of probabilities it would seem that Turner's part in the Little Beau tour ended in Saginaw at the end of July. He then travelled to New York, perhaps to appear briefly at a "Broadway hot spot", before arriving in Chicago in time for his August 5th opening. Whether the Decca recording session was cancelled or postponed, was a publicist's fantasy or an error of some kind, is unknown.

The *Chicago Defender* news item states, Cabin In The Sky - Monday, August 5th, Joe Turner "world's greatest blues singer will join Pete Johnson and Albert Ammons, 6352 Cottage Grove Avenue. Turner will come directly from New York where he recently set a new all-time record at a Broadway night spot."

Down Beat confirmed the Cabin in the Sky engagement, adding that it was two years since the singer and pianists had played together. It also indicated that their next port-of-call was the Forest Park Hotel in St. Louis, starting September 11th but, as we shall see, that date was put back to November.

A sign of the times was that the Four Cracker Jacks were to be part of the 'Sepia Sensations' twice-nightly variety show at the Club Zombie in Detroit, commencing Labor Day (September 4th), only to cancel when one of the quartet received his draft papers. Joe Turner was booked as their replacement. Starring in the show were the "boogie-woogie piano-swing team" of singer Helen Humes and pianist Connie Berry, comedy duo, Apus and Estrellita, and "the ladies of the chorus adding their spice and beauty," or, as they were later called, "ten lovely sun-kissed beauties". Music by the Harold Wallace Orchestra.[17]

The *Detroit Tribune* for September 16th, 1944, noted, "Joe Turner, recording star of the blues, is one of the reasons why the Club Zombie has been packed all week long". In the same issue, a reviewer wrote, "Joe Turner is a real sensation with both the male and female patrons. He (send?) some torrid blues from his big frame".

"Sepia Sensations" continued for three weeks, to be followed the week commencing September 25th by "Fall Varieties", headlined by singer Bobbie Caston, with a contortionist, a comedy duo and a song and dance trio. Big Joe Turner was retained. This revue was again advertised in the *Detroit Times* for October 3rd, 1944, confirming Joe was present until at least October 6th.

While in the city Turner took part in a jazz concert organised by local deejay Bill Randle, at the Detroit Institute of Arts on, Saturday, September 30th. Also appearing were pianist Pete Viera, plus the Ted Buckner Jam Band. A long-serving alto player in the Jimmy Lunceford Orchestra and the brother of the famous organist, Milt Buckner, Ted Buckner composed *The Art Institute Jump* to premiere at the concert. For his part, Randle was to become a nationally known radio presenter.[18]

Joe's final session for Decca was held in Chicago on October 30th, 1944. Four fine titles were recorded, with accompaniment by Pete Johnson, piano, Ernest Ashley, guitar, and Dallas Bartley, bass. (Other dates and locations have been given for this session; refer to discography.)

Reviewing *Rebecca* and *It's The Same Old Story*, Dave Dexter wrote

"Comes now a reunion of two famed jazzmen, Big Joe shouting the blues with Pete playing backgrounds impeccably, as in the old days. The lyrics are stale – Joe has waxed them previously – but he's in good voice and the trio behind him doesn't sag."[19]

For Decca, the musicians' strike had lasted until October 8th, 1943, when the company reached an agreement with the A.F.M. It was not until November 11th, 1944 that Columbia and RCA Victor conceded.

On November 3rd Joe Turner started a two-week engagement, nightly except Sundays, at the Circus Snack Bar of the Forest Park Hotel in St. Louis. [*St. Louis Post-Dispatch*, October 29th, 1944] He was backed by the two pianos of Albert Ammons and Pete Johnson, who had been in the city since September and were already duetting at the hotel.

1945

Fletcher Henderson and his Orchestra opened a week's engagement at the Paradise Theatre in Detroit on January 5th, the bill also including dancer Peg Leg Bates and the dynamic trio, Turner, Ammons and Johnson. Next, the trio were top of the bill for a week at the Metropolitan Theatre in Cleveland, Ohio, where the Joe Webb led the nine-piece house band.

The show at the Apollo theatre in New York, commencing January 19th, 1945, for one week, headlined Boyd Raeburn and his Band and revue, as well as Albert Ammons, Pete Johnson and Joe Turner.

For the next engagement Turner was solo, appearing at the Club Bali in Washington, D.C. The advertisement in the *Washington Evening Star*, January 26, 1945, claimed:

Nationally known Colored Stars
JOE TURNER
Esquire's No. 1 Boogie Woogie

Pianist and Blues Singer
MELROSE COLBERT
Cafe Society Singer
Coleridge David Band

It is not known if the *Evening Star* had advance warning that Turner had won an Esquire Silver Award, for best male vocal, voted on by a panel of critics and published in *Esquire*'s 1945 Jazz Book. (Louis Armstrong received the Gold Award.)

Joe's recording career resumed in 1945, when he began a two year association with National Records. His first session was on February 2nd, in New York, where he was united with Frankie Newton and Pete Johnson, while his second was on May 10th, in Chicago, with a less certain personnel. National was started by Al Green, strictly as a money-making concern. He was a business man who knew nothing about music, so he hired Herb Abramson, who was at university, to be a part-time record producer; or, as *Cash Box* put it, "serving in the role of director of artist and repertoire". Abramson[20] said that, "The first people I signed up were .... Pete Johnson and Joe Turner." This was his initial influence on Turner's career, with more to follow in the years ahead. Three of the National release are reported to have entered the Top Ten in the r&b charts of the time, *S.K. Blues* reaching number 3, *My Gal's A Jockey* number 6, and *Still In The Dark*, number 9.

While he was in New York it was reported by the *Baltimore Afro-American* that Turner was playing a week's engagement at the Apollo with Cecil Scott's Orchestra. Singer Marva Louis, wife of Joe Louis, was the headliner, with dancer Peg Leg Bates and "Deek" Watson's Brown Dots also on the bill. However, an Apollo advertisement for the week of March 2nd-7th lists all those artists except Joe Turner.

On March 8th Luis Russell "and his Celebrated Orchestra" headlined an appearance at the City Auditorium in Galveston, Texas. Also in the cast were Joe Turner, Peg Leg Bates and Milton Buggs and Nora Blount. Three days later, March 11th, Turner, Bates, Buggs and Blount were part of a Saturday dance and stage show "for Negroes" at the Harvest Club in Beaumont, Texas. Buggs and Blount were advertised as "blues singers" while Joe Turner was a "composer".

Joe is reported by John Chilton to have toured with the Luis Russell Orchestra during 1945, with *Blues Who's Who* adding that they worked dances across the U.S.. Tours with the Teddy Wilson and Lionel Hampton bands have also been listed, but without details.[21]

On March 23rd Turner was back at the Paradise Theatre in Detroit for another week. On this occasion the headliner was the Tiny Bradshaw Band, with Billy Ford, trumpet and vocal, Count Hastings, tenor, and Gene Rogers(sic), piano. Other acts included Joe Turner, Moke and Poke, and Melrose Colbert, "ballad stylist". Film buffs may like to know that the featured film was "Dr. Maniac," starring Boris Karloff.

Dallas was the next known stop, where Joe opened on Sunday, April 1st, for a four-week, five nights a week stay, as an extra added attraction at Claudia's "Negro nightclub". Dancers Stomp and Stompie; Frankie Walker, also a dancer, plus singer Benita Loparez were others featured. "Each week, on Wednesday and Thursday nights only, a white spectator section is provided." During his stay in Dallas Joe was a guest, on April 13th, 8:45 - 11:45, at the Dallas Jazz Club, with "the regular jazz combination".

In a 1946 recording for National, Turner sang, "Don't like to brag, don't like to boast, I'm sharp when I hit the coast." and he was back in Los Angeles in May, appearing at the Palomar Ballroom on Friday, May 11th.

Ted Yerxa, a jazz critic for the *Los Angeles Daily News*, had a weekly half-hour radio show which ran from late 1944 to early 1947. It was broadcast over KPAS, Pasadena, was sponsored by the Coastguards and featured jazz musicians. Joe Turner made two known appearances on the show, the first on July 4th, 1945, the second the following year.

In August Turner took the plunge and opened his own club. News items confirmed[23] that "Joe Turner now fronting (and singing) at Joe Turner's Blue Room, Central Avenue." and that "Joe Turner last month opened his own 'Blue Room' in downtown Los Angeles. Specialising in chicken and hot biscuits, Kansas City style, Joe frequently shouts a song to keep things moving inside his emporium."[24]

Down Beat, August 1945, stated, "Joe Turner, who has been featured at many niteries here, was slated to open his own on August 2nd. Spot, located at 9900 Central Avenue, will be known as Joe Turner's Blue Room." The same paper for September 15th, 1945, reported, "Joe Turner and his wife, who operate Joe Turner's Blue Room nitery, have been denied a liquor licence by state control board, which ruled spot too close to residential neighborhood."

Nothing further has been noted about the liquor licence. There may have been a successful appeal or perhaps the Turners struggled on without a licence. *Capitol News* lists Big Joe and the Blue Room each month until and including February 1946 and "Joe Turner's Blue Room" was advertised in the *Los Angeles Tribune* for December 31st, 1945. Presumably the struggle was abandoned early in 1946, though a news item as late as September 1946 contained the unlikely statement, "he owns a spot known as the Blue Room".

Even an interview in *The Negro South* (June 1946) contained the optimistic view:

> "Besides being a singer, Joe is a business man. The first floor of his two-storey apartment building in Los Angeles has been converted into the popular Joe Turner's Blue Room, which specializes in fried chicken and steaks".

The article continued: "Over a year ago, Joe met the right girl in Los Angeles. She's young and attractive and a very good housekeeper".

Joe Turner, Los Angeles, 1945

Joe Turner outside the Blue Room

These references confirm that there was a marriage in 1945, the bride's name being Lou Willie Brown. A feature in *Ebony* of March 1954 says they met in Los Angeles, got engaged in Detroit and married in Chicago. In May 1945 the new Mrs Turner travelled to Los Angeles to join her "hubby".

In October 1946 Turner recorded his *Miss Brown Blues* for National, but this seems to be too early in the marriage for it to be autobiographical! One verse starts gallantly,

But you ain't seen nothin', 'til you see the little girl they call Louella Brown
She's a real fine baby, yes, the kind you have to have around

While the next starts less romantically,

Well, she took all my money, got hold of my best friend, too
And I opened my big mouth, she said, "Big boy, you know what you can do"

Top, Joe Turner,, Dew Drop Inn, New Orleans, bottom, interviewed by The Negro South staff writer.1946,

And many years later, for United, Turner recorded *Fun In Chicago*, with the line, "I met a girl in Chicago, name was Lou Willie Brown". One report has the marriage ending in 1965, though the split may have occurred a year or two earlier.

The first Cavalcade of Jazz at Wrigley Field in L.A. was held before an audience of 15,000 on September 23rd, 1945, with a bill including the Count Basie orchestra, the Peters Sisters, Slim and Bam, and Joe Turner.

Joe made another appearance on a Jubilee broadcast in October 1945, singing *S.K. Blues* and *Love My Baby* with the Johnny Otis big band. Known details are in the discography. Otis (1921-2012, born Ioannis Veliotes, of Greek heritage) was that rarity at the time, a white musician who became famous in the black world of rhythm and blues. Among his numerous activities, musical and otherwise, he sang, played piano, vibes and drums, and later promoted the long-running Johnny Otis Show, in which his small band accompanied numerous singers, including such stalwarts as Joe Turner, Little Esther Phillips, Eddie 'Cleanhead' Vinson, Lowell Fulson and T-Bone Walker.

On November 14th Turner ("King of the Blues") opened for "an indefinite booking" at the Rose Room nightclub in Dallas, together with bassist Dallas Bartley and his orchestra. The "indefinite" was settled by early December, when a news item has him appearing at the Big Track club in Norfolk, Virginia, probably the second week in December. Turner was then due at the Dew Drop Inn in New Orleans: (Joe Turner) "will be back with a new sack of new songs for Christmas, along with a brand new show".[25] The Dew Drop Inn became a regular stop for Turner over the next twenty years. Presumably, back in L.A., Mrs Turner was looking after the Blue Room.

Information about Big Joe's appearances at the Dew Drop Inn during the 1940s is sparse, except that Dave 'Fat Man' Williams said he played piano for Joe at the Inn. This was perhaps in the late 1940s.

Central Avenue in Los Angeles came to be the equivalent of Twelfth Street in Kansas City or 52nd Street in New York. Sadly, Turner's *Blues On Central Avenue*, recorded in 1941, does not add to our knowledge of this thoroughfare. It is a lament about a married woman, although the final line does say "I met you on Central Avenue"!

Trumpeter Art Farmer's opinion was

"I think Central Avenue was important: also to groups that were really not regarded as jazz groups – like Roy Milton, blues singers, things like that – because they had a lot of work. I wouldn't want to give the impression that Central Avenue was just a jazz place, because it really wasn't. You had Roy Milton and Pee Wee Crayton and T-Bone Walker and Ivory Joe Hunter, Big Joe Turner, and they were much more successful than the jazz was, without a doubt [laughter]. This was their happy hunting ground [laughter]. But, you see, groups like that had jazz players playing with them. That was certainly a big part of the street." [26]

Joe Turner, 1945

1946

March 1946 found Joe Turner at Club 45 (845 Prospect Avenue) in The Bronx, New York. This was advertised as an "All Star Show", probably lasting four weeks. Dinah Washington was the headliner, with Joe in fifth position on the bill.

Saxophonist Floyd Turnham told jazz writer Peter Vacher that in 1946 he was with trumpeter Jake Porter's band on a tour with Joe Turner and Wynonie Harris (1915-1969), a blues shouter in the Joe Turner mode.

> "Made a trip to New Orleans and Texas and on down. I used my own car for transportation. I think I got 5 cents a mile for my car so that paid for my phone – I sent my earnings home. I think that's about the best trip I had"[28]

(It is likely that this tour was actually in May 1947.)

Joe Turner was at the Dew Drop Inn in New Orleans early in 1946, probably in May when he was interviewed for the previously mentioned June 1946 issue of *The Negro South*. Joe was back on the West Coast by June 23rd, when he appeared on Ted Yerxa's "Lamplighter's Jazz Session" broadcast over KPAS,

Joe Turner and his Packard, 1940s

News reports would suggest that Joe was back at the Dew Drop Inn, New Orleans from August 15th for three weeks; at Club Paradise, Port Arthur, Texas, from September 6th for one week; and at the Club Peacock, Houston, Texas, from September 13th for three weeks. Such dates are estimated; a week in show business might be five or six days, or even less. Turner was reported to have arrived in Chicago from Houston on Tuesday, October 1st.

From New Orleans, *The Pittsburgh Courier* for August 31st, 1946, reported, "After three sensational weeks in which he played exclusively to 'standing room only' crowds in the Groove Cocktail Lounge of the Dew Drop Inn and broke all existing records at the gay uptown Crescent City spot ... Joe Turner invades Port Arthur, on Friday night ...".

The news item in the same paper for September 14th, 1946 is also rapturous: "Duplicating his triumphs in New Orleans recently, Joe Turner, the 210-lb song stylist who ranges six feet, two inches in height, was a sensation in the swank

Club Paradise of Port Arthur, Texas, last week, where he won encores at every performance.

"This week, Turner, who is billed as 'the world's greatest blues shouter,' will bring his infectious style and savory songs to the Peacock here (Houston) to open an attractive three-week engagement which must be the envy of any solo artist anywhere in the country.

"Turner features an array of crowd appeal numbers, but the tunes which have been 'breaking down houses' everywhere he has traveled since leaving Los Angeles, where he owns a spot known as the Blue Room, are those which have brought him national fame - *Rebecca, My Gal's A Jockey* and *Piney Brown*."

Joe's next stop was the Windy City, where *The Chicago Defender* for October 5, 1946, told readers,

Joe Turner in DeLisa's Show Opening Friday.

Joe Turner, the man who sings the blues and whose recording of *Piney Brown Blues* swept the country, is the new headliner at the Club DeLisa, 5521 State Street. Turner came to the .... (club) Tuesday night from the Peacock Inn in Houston, Texas, where he 'wowed 'em'. Judging from the reception at his premiere, Chicagoans are well pleased with the kind of singing he offers."

The show in which Joe was starring was titled 'Sound Off" – complete with singers, dancers, impersonator, roller-skater, and contortionist, plus the Fletcher Henderson Orchestra. The run was for two weeks.

For many years the Club DeLisa was a major entertainment location in Chicago. In 1946 it was at 5521 South State Street and run by Mike De Lisa. During Joe's engagement he recorded two sessions for National Records on October 11th and 12th, 1946. Several musicians from the Henderson house band were in the accompaniment, which was led by drummer Red Saunders.

It would seem that "a long string of one-nighters" followed, with a possible booking at the Brown Derby in Chattanooga, Tennessee, before Joe ended the year back in New Orleans, with a one week residence, December 23rd to January 1st, at the Dew Drop Inn.

National advertisement for *My Gal's A Jockey/I Got Love For Sale*, recorded in Los Angeles, January 23, 1946, accompaniment by Bill Moore's Lucky Seven Band.

9

"Don't play no be-bop in here."

(1947-1950)

"Look Who's Back – By Popular Request" is how The Embassy Club "(colored)" in South Hattiesburg, Palmers Crossing, advertised the appearance of Joe Turner and Rhythm Orchestra on Sunday, January 12th, 9 p.m. to 1 a.m.[1]

The Pittsburgh Courier (February 8th, 1947) advised that, "One of the newest teams that loom as big box office is the coupling of Snookum Russell's orchestra and blues shouter Joe Turner. They will tour Dixie and the West". Part of the tour would have been another Sunday "One Nite Only" booking on February 23rd, a return visit to the Sunset Terrace in Indianapolis. It was advertised as Big Joe Turner and His Orchestra, with pianist Snookum Russell's name in small type.

In March and April there was a second tour with Wynonie Harris. *The Chicago Defender* for March 29th, 1947, reported that Wynonie Harris and Joe Turner were touring the South with their 'Blues Battle'. The tour started on Sunday, March 9th, at the Dreamland Ballroom in Little Rock. The reporter excitedly announced,

> "Fans throughout the nation are now discussing the 'Battle of the Blues' ....record crowds have flocked to theatres everywhere they have appeared. When Snookum Russell, 'Be-Bop' maestro, whose orchestra is furnishing the music, was asked his opinion as to who should wear the 'King of the Blues' title, he replied with a smile, 'It is really fun playing for these two guys and as to picking the winner, folks, I'm neutral'."

However, an April 5th report states, "The much heralded battle of blues, featuring Joe Turner and Wynonie Harris, came to a sudden end here (Macon, Georgia) as Harris and Turner quit cold after a wrangle over financial affairs."[2] The April 12th, 1947 issue of *The Chicago Defender* advised that Snookum Russell had signed Max Bailey to replace Turner and Harris.

Turner and Harris continued touring together after the dispute with Russell. There were scheduled appearances by them with Russell at Chicago's Savoy Ballroom on Easter Sunday night, April 6th, and at Detroit's Forest Club ballroom the following night, Easter Monday. Their accompaniment, if they appeared, is unknown.

Another advertised date was at The Keyhole in San Antonio, "coming Thursday, May 1st," the floor show included Turner and Harris, vocalist Marion Abernathy and King Porter and his Orchestra. New Orleans was also part of their tour. The following Wednesday, May 7th, "Joe Turner and Wynonia (sic) Harris .... and their recording orchestra" were at the Arlington Casino in Opelousas, while on the 12th, with vocalist Savannah Churchill and Jake Porter's orchestra, they appeared at an afternoon benefit for the Texas City Disaster Victims, at the West Side Auditorium in Port Arthur.

Joe Turner
And
Wynonia Harris
The nation's greatest
blues singers and their
Recording Orchestra
THE
Arlington Casino
Wed. Night
May 7th
Reservations limited
Better call today.

Daily World, May 4, 1947

    Turner was reported to have had a booking during May at the Club Cobra, in Los Angeles, with no mention of Wynonie Harris. That same month he was scheduled to play the Earle Theatre in Pittsburgh.

In July both singers were in New York, where they made three titles, including a two-part *Battle of the Blues*, for Aladdin records. (Their "patcha, patcha" routine on this title was repeated nearly forty years later, when Turner and Jimmy Witherspoon duetted for Pablo Records, except that "all day long" became "all night long".) Turner and Harris continued these musical hostilities off and on for several years.

Jimmy Witherspoon (1923-1987), also a noted blues shouter, had seen Turner in 'Jump for Joy'. He told Chip Deffaa,

> "I was always inspired by him. Joe and I became close. I used to go to his house, right here in Los Angeles, before I was singing professionally ....
> When I first started singing, he said I was going to be a great blues singer.
> He said that at the Club Alabam".[3]

Witherspoon has also been quoted as saying that he heard Joe at Alex Lovejoy's Breakfast Club, though no year was given.[4]

The July 19th, 1947 edition of *The Pittsburgh Courier* carried an Atlanta, GA, news item headlined, "Joe Turner Tours with 'Vout Woman'" and advising that Turner and vocalist Marion Abernathy "joined forces this week for a new 'Battle of the Blues' which will keep them on the road and in the public spotlight for more than three months. Forming a new 'Swing Parade' unit, the pair will tour the South and Mid-west, ending in New York."

On tour with Turner and Abernathy was reedman Jim Wynn and his Orchestra, their dates including: August 23th at the Yacht Club, Dallas ("For White Only"), August 26th at the Rose Room, Wichita, Kansas and September 14th at the Sunset Terrace, Indianapolis. However, Marion Abernathy was well advertised for other engagements for all of August, which places a question mark against this particular "Battle of the Blues" tour.

Turner had a three-night engagement at The Zanzibar in Sacramento, CA, October 10th, 11th, and 12th, with vocalist Helen Wilson and The Peter Rabbit Trio also advertised.

It was in October that Joe Turner and Pete Johnson renewed their partnership. They were at the Tappers Inn, Richmond, before moving on to San Fancisco where, towards the end of that month, they were at Fillmore Street. On October 23rd they opened at Blackshear's Supper Club for a two week engagement, ending November 4th, with Jack McVea "and his Door Openers" also on the bill.[5]

Tenor player Jack McVea reminisced, "I recorded four sides with him, using my group with Pete Johnson on piano (at that time Pete was travelling with Big Joe). My group was appearing at Harold Blackshear's (ex-heavyweight fighter) Club in San Francisco .... Big Joe worked with my group and actually broke up the show."[6]

In San Francisco they recorded, November 6th, 1947, four titles for Aladdin with the McVea band. Also about this time Joe, using the title Big Vernon, with just Pete at the piano, made a two-part *Around The Clock Blues* for the Stag label.

Turner and Johnson were scheduled to return to the Zanzibar in Sacramento on November 17th to appear in a one-nighter "Blue Monday Jamboree".

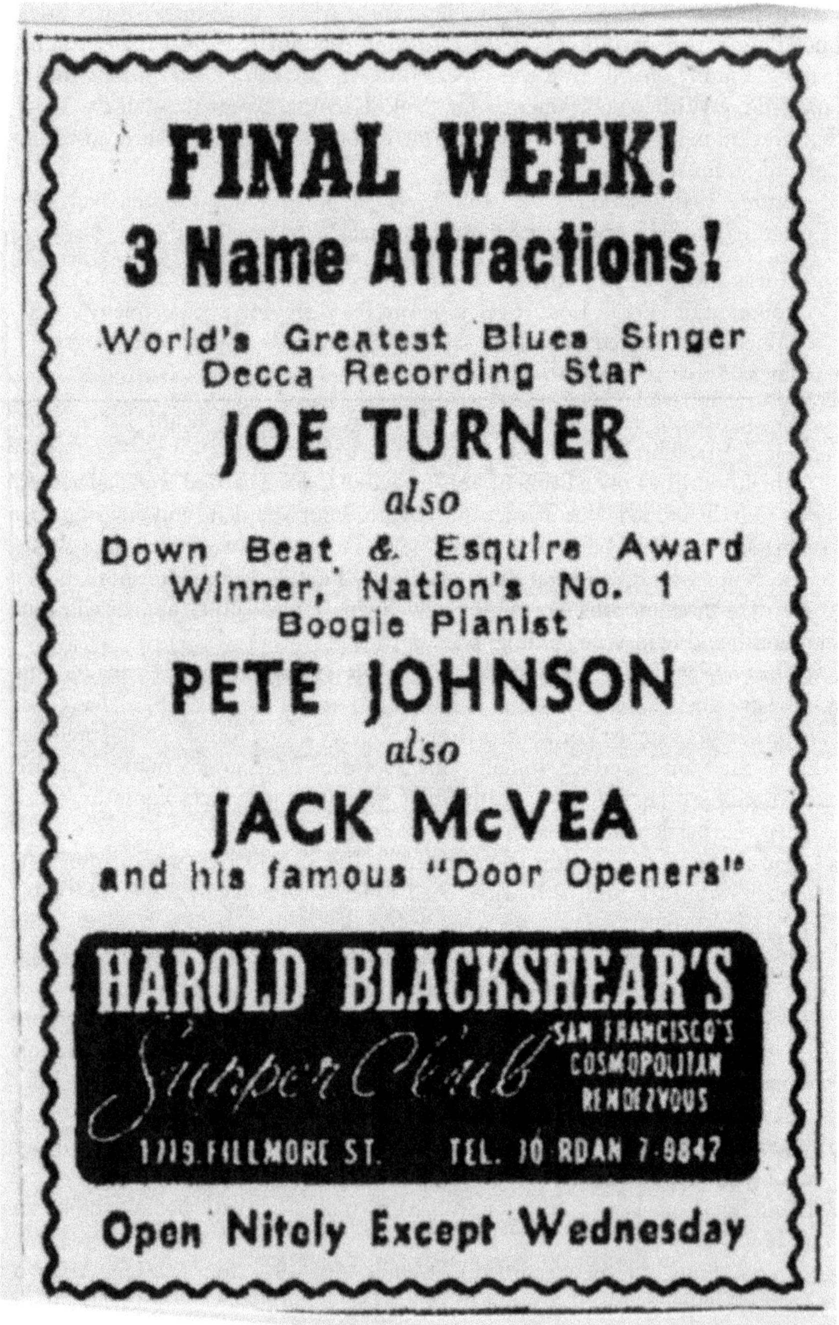

San Francisco Chronicle, October 27, 1947

Then Turner was off to Chicago, where he recorded for National on November 29th and December 9th, 1947, but was back in Los Angeles shortly afterwards. *Down Beat* (December 17th, 1947) reported, "Pete Johnson and Joe Turner now at the Venus Club on Third Street in San Francisco". Next came two "Just Jazz" concerts, the first at the Municipal Auditorium in Long Beach, on Friday, December 26th. The same cast (Benny Goodman Quintet, Kay Starr, Pete Johnson, and Joe Turner plus "a tolerable group of local musicians,") appeared the following day at the Shrine Auditorium on Jefferson Boulevard. The "tolerable group of local musicians" included Ernie Royal, trumpet, Vido Musso, Wardell Gray, tenors, and Don Lamond, drums. For his set Turner was accompanied by Pete Johnson at the piano and a rhythm section. A short review in the *Daily Trojan* , January 5th, 1948, reported that Joe sang "a few old bawdy blues songs," but that he also "had a seasonal song for the kiddies with lyrics about someone tacking (sic) a stocking because Santa Claus was in the vicinity". [It is unlikely that this seasonal song is connected to the *Christmas Date Boogie* which Turner recorded for National in 1948.]

Deejay Gene Norman, often in partnership with Frank Bull, promoted a series of jazz and blues concerts in Los Angeles during the 1940s, using such titles as "Just Jazz," "Dixieland Jubilee" and "Blues Jubilee". Four excellent Turner/Johnson titles recorded at the Shrine concert were issued on RPM and Modern.

It was perhaps at this time that the duo also worked at the Memo Cocktail Lounge.

1948

Joe Turner was scheduled to follow Amos Milburn and then T-Bone Walker into The Dew Drop Inn in New Orleans on or about February 22nd, probably for a two-week stay. This may be the occasion he is reported to have been accompanied by the Dave Bartholomew Band.[7]

In May, into June, he and crooner Dan Grissom appear to have been on tour in Texas with a "Blues v. Sweet" package, including one-night stands at the Library Auditorium in San Antonio on May 1st and Liberty Hall in El Paso on June 19th. For the latter engagement, Joe is "King of the Blues," Grissom is "Idol of Sweet Music" and the music is provided by trumpeter 'King' Jake Porter.

Joe is solo for his next known appearance, on Friday, July 30th, with Jimmy Liggins and his Orchestra, for "One Big Night" at the Palomar Ballroom in Fresno, CA,

Turner's recording activities would suggest that he spent a lot of time between June and December in Los Angeles. In June he made eight titles for the *Down Beat* and Swing Time labels, owned by Jack Lauderdale, while a further ten were made for M-G-M. All these had Pete Johnson at the piano.

Trumpet player on the *Down Beat* sessions was Art Farmer who, in a few years, was to become very well-known in modern jazz circles, working with Gigi Gryce, Benny Golson, Gerry Mulligan and the Clarke-Boland Big Band. In an interview, Farmer recalled

"One time I played a gig with Big Joe Turner and he was singing the blues. Just me, my brother (Addison, a bassist), and a drummer. I'm playing background behind Joe, and right inside the song – he makes up lyrics as he goes along – he says, 'Play me the blues, don't play no be-bop in here!'"[8]

Joe Turner and Pete Johnson, 1948

A one-nighter during the third week of September was at the Congo Club in Kansas City, where Joe sang with The Sweethearts of Rhythm all-female orchestra and *The Los Angeles Times* (October 13th) included a classified advert. for an appearance by the Kay Starr-Joe Turner Revue at the Million Dollar theatre. Jack McVea told Swiss researcher Johnny Simmen that his band worked at the Million Dollar Theatre in 1948, where the artists played one-week residencies. The band personnel was Sammy Yates, trumpet, Jack McVea, tenor, Gene Phillips, guitar, Frank Clark, bass, and Rabon Tarrant, drums. No pianist was mentioned.

Unconfirmed was a report in *The Cash Box* (Los Angeles, September 11th, 1948) that "Folks South and East can be on the lookout for a real treat when Jimmy Witherspoon and Joe Turner hit the road for a long tour".

The fourth Cavalcade of Jazz was held in Chicago at Wrigley Field on September 12th, 1948, when the stars include Dizzy Gillespie, Frankie Laine, Joe Adams, the Sweethearts of Rhythm, Little Miss Cornshucks, Jimmy Witherspoon and Joe Turner.

Turner was back at the Congo Club towards the end of October, taking part in a fund-raising concert with Rob Parrish, the Four Girl Friends and pianist Lorenzo Flennoy's combo.

Referring to two titles recorded October 28th for the Dootone and then Coast labels, Pete Johnson recalled, "There was a man that was talent scout for M-G-M records, his name is Dootsie Williams. We cut the records when I was out in Los Angeles."[9]

Williams said that he was unable to sell or lease the Joe Turner sides he recorded, so had to issue them himself.[10]

On October 26th Joe, with Pete Johnson, was due to open an engagement at the Skybar, in Cleveland, Ohio. How this ties in with the above mentioned Dootone session is not known.

In November, in Hollywood, Turner made an appearance on a "Jubilee" broadcast, accompanied by pianist Lorenzo Flennoy's trio. One title, *Cherry Red*, appeared on an AFRS transcription.

Might it also have been in 1948 that Ornette Coleman, alto saxophone, later a leader of the avant garde movement, "worked with r&b groups, eventually forming his own and backing singers such as Big Joe Turner"?[11] Another unknown date was when Turner appeared as a guest with the King Porter band at the Sportrees Music Bar in Hastings, Michigan; Porter, trumpet, Billy Mitchell, tenor, others unknown.

Big Joe seems to have spent the Christmas/New Year period headlining a review at the Music Bar in Detroit. Other singers and dancers were on the bill and the orchestra was led by veteran pianist T.J. Fowler.

1949

Blues Who's Who's itinerary for Joe Turner in 1949 is "club dates through South," including two in New Orleans, at The Rhythm Club and the Dew Drop Inn. *The Pittsburgh Courier* for April 2nd, 1949 advised, "Repeating old triumphs made over the past few years in Frank Painia's tradition-steeped Dew Drop Inn, New Orleans, is 210-pound song man, Big Joe Turner, billed as 'the world's greatest blues shouter'".

Without quoting a specific year, critic Ralph J. Gleason mentioned a concert which contained Joe Turner, the Stan Kenton All Stars and bassist Vernon Alley's band. This was no doubt the April 11th, 1949 "Just Jazz" concert promoted by Gene Norman at the Shrine Auditorium.

The Pittsburgh Courier reported in its August 6th, 1949 issue, "Big Joe Turner who opens at the Baby Grand Cafe in New York on August 1st for a limited stand, is now being managed by Maceo Birch, former band mentor for Count Basie. This marks Big Joe's first New York appearance in many years...." The *New York Amsterdam News*, seven days later, had an ad. for the Cafe at 319 West 125th Street. Joe Turner, "blues at its best," was starring in "Blues-Time Variety Parade", also featuring "America's youngest tenor sax virtuoso, Morris Lane". The trio was led by Walter Bishop, presumably pianist Walter Bishop, Junior.

In *Lady Day's Diary*, Ken Vail lists a plan by Joe Glaser's Associated Booking Corporation to organise a tour by Billie Holiday and Joe Turner. This was about November 1949, but it failed to materialise. Towards the end of the year Turner was playing "an extended residency" at the Ace of Clubs in Baton Rouge, Louisiana, during which he recorded two titles for the Rouge label. In December he travelled to Houston, no doubt for an engagement. While there he met guitarist Goree Carter, who introduced him to Sol Kahal.

Freedom Records was owned by Soloman 'Sol' M. Kahal, who was "only in the business to put his name on some song copyrights and hope for a hit which would give him a steady income."[12] Recordings were made at the ACA Studios. Freedom survived for about four years; when it folded, Kahal became the manager of a Shipley Doughnut shop in Houston.

Asked about the Joe Turner records on Freedom, Houston-born guitarist Goree Carter told Dick Shurman

> "That's about the onliest one I recorded behind because he was down and he didn't really have no place to go .... he came in one day, him and his wife and this is where he wrote this number, *Adam Bit The Apple*, he saw a picture on the wall, of Adam in the forest, and he wrote that song right at the table .... We started rehearsing with Joe and got him a record for Freedom, and that's when he got his break...."[13]

Christmas morning Turner was in San Antonio, Texas, to entertain at the Woodlake Country Club.

1950

A 400-word report in *The Pittsburgh Courier* (July 15th, 1950), under the heading "Big Joe Turner Wins New 'Raves' in Dixie," gives an indication of Joe's engagements during the first part of the year. It refers to him being "... in the midst of a current Dixie tour that will last six months" and that he is the "toast of Southern music lovers.

> "(He) has already covered key cities and nightspots in Georgia, Tennessee, Texas and Louisiana. In Atlanta he had a crowd-winning two-week stand at the commodious Royal Peacock Club, formerly Top Hat, and he was equally a 'rave' in Nashville, where he sang 'em indigo for a full month. Several weeks were reeled off working in the 'name' niteries of San Antonio, Houston, Galveston and Fort Worth.

"Long a hit in the Crescent City, Joe, who has been brought back to New Orleans about four or five times by popular demand, was back at work in Frank Painia's tradition-steeped Dew Drop Inn, 2836 LaSalle Street, for three solid weeks – and he really packed 'em in."

The writer, Lucius Jones, refers to Joe's personal manager, "the missus, Mrs. Lou Willie Turner", accompanying Joe "for a promising three-week stand in the magnificent Ace of Clubs, new and modern night spot of Baton Rouge, La, only eighty-five miles from Creole City.

"Present plans call for Joe Turner to travel coast to coast with a package show, for which bookings can be made direct through Joe Turner, 6612 Maryland Street, Chicago 37, Ill. On all the present one-nighters in Dixie, Joe Turner has been 'fronting' the swing-minded Otis Ducker combo, which has had a long stand at Dew Drop behind the famous Edward Blachard (sic) Gondoliers."

[When altoist Otis Ducker recorded for Decca in New York in April 1950 his combo was Melvin Lastie, trumpet, Plas Johnson, Alvin Tyler, tenors, Reveal Thomas, piano, ---- Carter, bass, June Gardner, drums.]

In April 1950 Turner recorded four titles, including a remake of *Lucille*, in New Orleans for the Imperial label, owned by Lew Chudd. His accompaniment was a small group led by Dave Bartholomew, trumpeter and arranger, who was to feature again in the Turner history. Fats Domino is the pianist on these titles.

A sleeve note to a long-play reissue of this session states

"During the late 1940s he was a regular attraction at the infamous Dew Drop Inn on La Salle Street. Turner was also booked out-of-town by the Dew Drop's proprietor, Mr. Frank Pania (sic), who paired him with the Inn's house band, Edgar Blanchard's Gondoliers, for dates throughout Louisiana and the Gulf Coast."[14]

Another sleeve note quotes Dave Bartholomew:

"Joe used to be in and out of New Orleans all the time. He was very good friends with the guy who owned the Dew Drop Inn, Mr. Frank Painia. Frank had a hotel and a restaurant and he could feed you and help a guy out. You didn't need a lot of money. These were some of Joe's lesser years, though he was still very popular on the nightclub circuit. Joe loved my band and every time he came to town he had to have us. He tried to get us to go on the road with him, but we were just too busy."[15]

Frank Painia (1911-1972) was African-American. He opened the Dew Drop in 1945 and ran it until 1972.[16]

The Dew Drop Inn title seems to have been a casual one. A photograph shows a sign reading DEW DROP CAFE, BAR & COCKTAIL LOUNGE. Below that is another, HOTEL – FLOOR SHOWS, Fri. Sat & Sun.17. The Inn, apparently, was also famous for its female impersonators and no doubt other entertainment.

At The Dew Drop it was reported that Turner's cocktail of choice was a shot of whiskey, plus a dollop of Louisiana hot sauce. To quote Jeff Hannusch, "One Dew Drop regular recalls Turner's claims to be able to outdrink anyone and everyone … One of Turner's memorable drinking escapades occurred one evening in Bogalusa, Louisiana, after spending the entire day at the bar. Just before showtime he climbed into a parked car, locked the doors and promptly fell asleep. Blanchard's group played Turner's intro three times but to no avail." When he was found it took an assault upon the car to rouse the sleeping singer, but he did finally make it on stage.

An entry in a May 1950 *Billboard* reported that singer Felix Gross and his band "left [Los Angeles] for Kansas City and points east last week" for a scheduled two month tour. The personnel was Frank Leviston, trumpet, Henry Sloan, trombone, Joe Swanson, tenor, T.B. Watson, piano, Al Adams, bass. No drummer is listed. The paper adds: "They'll probably be joined by Joe Turner before completing dates."

Later in the year Turner was at The Oasis in Los Angeles. He was probably accompanied by drummer Lee Young's combo, which worked at The Oasis during 1950. Young's personnel was Parr Jones, trumpet, Maxwell Davis, tenor, Dudley Brooks, piano, and Billy Hadnott, bass. It seems likely that Joe's booking at the Oasis closed as Billie Holiday's started, on Friday, September 15th. Another gig in the Los Angeles area was on September 23rd, when "Big Joe Turner's Orchestra" was advertised to play for a dance at The Airport Club in Abbeville.

In October Joe was working again at the Dew Drop Inn on New Orleans' La Salle Street. In December, or thereabouts, trips to Houston provided the opportunity to record a number of titles for the Freedom label.

Record buyers were well catered for during the year. National records were advertising Turner's coupling of *Nobody In Mind* and *A Low Down Dirty Shame* in January, while in March *Billboard* reported from New Orleans that *Adam Bit The Apple* on Freedom should be watched. In April the paper said that Freedom was riding the r&b charts with *Still In The Dark*. Other releases in the year were:

week of June 10	*Just A Travelin' Man/Life Is A Card Game* - Freedom 1537	
week of June 24	*Feelin' So Sad/Moody Baby* - MGM 10719	
week of August 19	*Story To Tell/Jumpin' Tonight* - Imperial 5090	
week of October 21	*Feelin' Happy/You'll Be Sorry* - Freedom 1540	
week of December 2	*Back Breaking Blues/Empty Pocket Blues* - Aladdin 3070	

10

"Best R&B Artist of 1954"

(1951-1954)

1951 was the year when Joe's "lesser years" started to give way to more prosperous times.

On January 19th, 1951, "Count Basie and his All-Star Sextette" headlined an engagement at the Club Juana in Detroit. Also on the bill were Joe Turner, song stylist Rose Mitchell and one-arm and one-legged dancer, Crip Heard. Basie moved on after January 28th, but Joe became top-of-the-bill from February 2nd, with pianist Todd Rhodes and his Orchestra. When trumpeter Dizzy Gillespie and his Orchestra arrived for a February16th-25th booking, Big Joe remained as part of the show.[2]

Guitarist, singer Lowell Fulson is known to have been on the road during early 1950 and 1951, his accompaniment including Ray Charles on piano. Also in the band may have been Earl Brown, alto, and Eddie Piper, drums. In view of the lengthy tour Turner undertook in 1950, it is likely that his trip with Fulson did not happen until 1951. Whichever year, Charles expressed his admiration for Turner, saying:

> "In Texas I got to play piano behind acts like T-Bone Walker and Big Joe Turner. Sometimes they were on the same bill with Lowell and our band would back 'em up. I especially loved playing behind Big Joe. I had grown up with his records and here I was on a stage with him. That man has so much weeping in his voice. If it was just you and him in a room, he could sing the blues at you till you'd break down and cry. I don't care how cold-blooded you might be, he'd get to you. .... he has a tear in his voice. And I ain't even heard anyone sing the blues so raw and so pure."[1]

Count Basie, who had disbanded his full orchestra a year earlier, continued with a small group for most of 1951. However, he was tempted to lead a big band again for a one-week run at the Apollo Theatre in New York. The band, built around the sextet, opened on Friday, March 30th, 1951, with Joe Turner as the band's singer. The *New York Age* lists singer Irene Williams, with pianist Herman Chittison's Trio, and comedian Pigmeat [Markham] in the show, plus dancer Bill Bailey, Rose Hardway and Norma Miller's Chorus.

Frank Schiffman, the long time manager and co-owner of the Apollo, wrote brief review cards for artists appearing at the theatre. Just one of these cards has been found which relates to Joe Turner. It is headed "Count Basie Band," and the entry is for April 5th, 1951. Apart from Basie, the performers are named without comment, though Schiffman noted, "Large band. Played show well. Basie excellent. Band only fair. Business helped materially by excellent show, including Bill Bailey".

Ahmet Ertegun, head of Atlantic Records, has told the story of signing Joe Turner to his company.

"So Joe Turner came in [to Basie's orchestra], and he wasn't that kind of singer. He was the greatest blues singer, Kansas City style blues singer of them all. He has a voice nobody can match. But, Joe and Basie never got together. The band would finish and Joe would still be singing .... I took him to the bar after the show [the opening night at the Apollo] and he was feeling very depressed .... finally I said, 'Listen, come with us and we'll make some hit records".[3]

And Joe did.

To Tom Fox, Ertegun explained that Basie had refined his arrangements over the years and those for the stage had become more sophisticated. Turner, with limited if any rehearsal, found it very difficult. He missed his cues and the audience jeered. Ertegun tracked him to Braddock's bar on 126th Street, which was where Joe agreed to record for Atlantic, signing a three-year contract.[4]

Ertegun wasted little time getting Turner into the studio. On April 19th four titles were recorded, *The Chill Is On*, *After My Laughter Came Tears*, *Bump Miss Susie* and *Chains of Love*. Harry Van Walls was the leader of the accompanying band.

Ertegun continued, "I wrote *Chains of Love* with Van Walls; well, actually, I wrote it but I gave half to Van Walls because he played the piano introduction."[5] The song was originally to be called *Three O'Clock Blues* and according to Jerry Wexler it was a rewrite of *Mecca Flat Blues*. Again to Tom Fox, Ertegun said, "I wrote, with his help, a song called *Chains of Love* and Jesse Stone wrote a beautiful arrangement. That became a big hit"[6] On the label the composer credit for the song went to "Harry Van Walls and A. Nugetre". (Ertegun used a pseudonym for his songs because he did not want to embarrass his family!) *Chains of Love* was in the rhythm and blues charts for 25 weeks, reaching second spot for four of those weeks. It is believed to have sold a million copies.

Ebony magazine for March 1954 said, sensationally, of *Chains of Love* that it was "a blues number so potent that when he introduced it at a dance in Lake Charles, Louisiana, all the men and women in the club started fighting."

Also in April, National released *Rocks In My Bed/Howlin' Winds*. The following month, the week of May 19th, the first of a series of successful releases for the Atlantic label appeared. Atlantic 939 coupled *Chains of Love* and *After My Laughter Came Tears*, with the first song becoming a staple of Turner's repertoire for the next thirty years.

A May issue of *Billboard* reported that Turner was now signed to SAC (Shaw Artists Corporation) and that he was to tour with a Helen Humes package, also starring "singer" Dusty Fletcher, exotic dancer Rita Thomas, and the Hal Singer Band. Hal 'Cornbread' Singer was a tenor player, while Dusty Fletcher's 1946 hit record was *Open The Door, Richard*.

The report stated that there were "at least a dozen of these disc packages making the standard r&b rounds in the one-nighter hinterlands".

"The Humes-led package kicks off its tour Friday (4th) in Cincinnati and will continue on thru Columbus, Akron, Lexington, Louisville, Knoxville, Nashville, Atlanta and Memphis."

Known dates for the "Swing Parade of 51" are May 10th at the Lyric Theatre in Lexington, Kentucky, and June 2nd and 3rd at the Palace theatre in Dayton, Ohio. There is also a photo showing Humes and Turner at the Palace Theatre in Memphis.

Despite the Apollo set-back, Turner made a number of appearances with Count Basie during the summer. (Basie had re-organised a big band for a May-to-August tour.) They played a concert and a dance, "10 until 2," at the Municipal Auditorium in Charleston on June 16th and a dance at the Chilhowee Park auditorium, with "a reserved section for white spectators," in Knoxville, Tennessee, on June 18th. "Count Basie and his Orchestra, featuring Joe Turner and the All-American Rhythm Section" were advertised to appear at the Regal theatre in Chicago for one week, starting Friday, June 29th, and a concert at the TV-Playhouse in Kansas City, on July 6th.

It appears that Joe went from Kansas City to New Orleans, the *Detroit Tribune* (July 14th, 1951) reporting that he was "now held over at the Dew Drop Inn." But he was back with Basie on August 10th/11th, for Friday and Saturday nights at the Lagoon in Salt Lake City.

In July *Billboard* stated, "Blues shouter Joe Turner will join Joe Morris' 'Cavalcade of Blues' package as an extra attraction to play a series of 31 one-nighters in the Texas-Louisiana area for promoter Howard Lewis". Mobile's *The Gulf Informer*, (July 28th, 1951) reported:

"Texas blues fans will be getting a double dose of their favorite musical product when the Joe Morris Blues Cavalcade teams up with one of America's all-time favorite blues stylists Joe Turner on an 18 city tour of the South-west during the month of August. Joe Morris, the ex-Lionel Hampton trumpet star and arranger, is a perennial favorite in the Texas area and is now returning with what he believes is the greatest edition of the 'Blues Cavalcade'."

In addition to Turner and Morris, the Cavalcade starred singers Laurie Tate and Bill Mitchell. The tour, which was of 18 dates rather than 31, was focused on Texas (Big Spring, San Angelo, Lubbock, Wichita Falls, Mexia, Dallas, Forth Worth, Houston, Corpus Christi, Beaumont, Austin, San Antonio, Galveston, Waco, Sherman), but with three detours, one into New Mexico (Hobbs), then two into Oklahoma (Lawton and Oklahoma City).

On August 24th he was scheduled to open at the Flame Show Bar in Detroit. The *Detroit Times*, August 23rd, 1951, announced that "One of the busiest blues specialists these days is Joe Turner... He's perhaps best known for his version of *Too Many Women Blues* but his latest, *Chains of Love*, is changing hands fast across the country's record counters." Joe was still advertised at the same venue on September 3rd.

The Flame Show Bar booking seems out of step with the dates for the Joe Morris tour. Or with the item in the *Detroit Tribune*, for September 15th, 1951, "the Joe Morris Cavalcade of the Blues, featuring the popular Laurie Tate and co-starring blues singer Joe Turner has extended its second tour of Texas and the Southwest in order to cover an additional 30 cities".

Whatever the accuracy of these reports there can be no doubt that Turner and his fellow artists were continually on the move. A September report in *Billboard* states, "Joe Turner has been set for a series of 22 one-nighters on the West Coast as a result of his hit waxing of *Chains of Love*." One of these dates was at the Eagles Auditorium in Seattle on the evening of September 18th, 1951, with the advertisement announcing that "Joe Turner and Orchestra" would appear.

Another complication with the blues package tours is the possibility that the artists might have had an arrangement whereby they could miss occasional performances in order to take better paying solo gigs. As with any engagement, an artist could fail to appear, perhaps due to illness or transport problems. It was not unknown, for example, for a two week engagement to be halved if business was poor during the first week.

Turner's dates for November included:

November 2nd and 3rd, at the Club Morocco in Little Rock, Arkansas, featuring a "Battle of the Blues" with Christine Kittrell.

November 21st to 24th, with Count Basie and his 16-piece Orchestra, Club Riviera in St. Louis, but not on the 22nd. (Basie's final dates with his small group were in October. He then rehearsed a new orchestra, the April in Paris unit, and he remained a big-band leader until his death in 1984.)

November 22nd, with Dinah Washington, Earl Bostic and Clyde Terrell, the Auditorium, Atlanta, Georgia. (Presumably a scheduled absence from the Club Riviera engagement.)

San Francisco was Turner's location towards the end of 1951. *Down Beat* (November 2nd, 1951) stated, "Joe Turner doing a number of gigs out of the Bay area in Stockton and elsewhere, using Ernie Lewis to front a band, which occasionally featured Teddy Edwards on tenor." The same issue noted that Joe was included in two shows at the Berkeley High School Auditorium.

The Pittsburgh Courier for December 1st, 1951, reported, "Dance – Big Double Attraction"; Joe Turner, along with tenor-player Hal Singer's band, would be at the Keystone Club in Silsbee, Texas, on Saturday, December 8th.

The final three months of the year saw the release of another four records

week of October 13:	OK 6829	*Cherry Red/Joe Turner Blues* (a reissue)
week of November 17:	Atlantic 949	*The Chill Is On/Bump Miss Susie*
week of December 8:	Swing Time 269	*Christmas Date Boogie/ How'd Ya Want Your Rollin' Done*
week of December 15:	Fidelity 3000	*Life Is A Card Game/When The Rooster Crows*

Joe Turner Atlantic 949 Ad Pic *Cash Box* 1 Dec 1951

1952

During this year Joe made a number of trips between New York and New Orleans, fitting in many other cities along the way, including Detroit, MI., where he played the Paradise Theater between January 4th and 10th. He was in the Big Apple on January 20th, 1952, when he recorded five titles for Atlantic, including *Sweet Sixteen* and *Poor Lover Blues*. *Sweet Sixteen* entered *Billboard*'s Rhythm and Blues Records charts at the end of April. It spent four weeks in the top ten in "Best Selling Retail", and seven weeks in "Most Played Juke Box," reaching third place.

The Atlantic session went into overtime, but Turner made it to the WLIB-New York studio in time to appear on the a.m. Nipsey Russell Show, on which he sang *Chains of Love*. *Billboard* reported him sleepily stifling yawns over early morning coffee.

At the end of January he was at the Hippodrome in Richmond, VA, "with Billy Mitchell". Top of the bill were The Clovers, followed by Joe Morris and Laurie Tate. He was scheduled to appear with Joan Shaw and her Blues Express Orchestra at the Coliseum in Evansville, Indiana on February 9th, and again at the Sunset in Indianapolis on the 10th. On February 14th he was in Muskegon, MI, at the C.I.O. Hall.

"Joe Turner, Count Fisher Packin' Em In At George's" was the *Indianapolis Recorder* headline, April 5th, 1952, for Turner's appearance at George's Bar and Orchid Room between March 31st and April 5th. On Easter Sunday, April

13th, 1952, Big Joe Turner versus Gatemouth Brown was the blues duel at the Rosenwald Gym in New Orleans. The duo were then to play New Iberia, Ponchatoula, Algiers, Biloxi, Donaldsville, Port Allen and back to New Orleans at the San Jacinto. Top of the bill at the Earle Theatre in Philadelphia, April 25th to May 1st, was 13-year-old pianist Frankie "Sugar Chile" Robinson, with Turner also present. The reviewer in the *Philadelphia Enquirer* (April 26th, 1952) advised that "Joe Turner warbled a couple of songs that didn't make much sense."

Joe was in New York by Friday, May 9th, to play another week at the Apollo, this time with the "new" Count Basie orchestra. Also on the bill were The Five Keys. Then it was on the road again, and by May 31st he was in Austin, Texas. He was reported in New Orleans, at the Dew Drop Inn, on June 6th, 1952, then, with Ray Charles on the bill, there followed a series of one-nighters in the South, the cities visited including Houston, Dallas, Oklahoma City and, on June 23rd, Little Rock, Arkansas.

An appearance with Hal Singer and his Band at the Trianon Ballroom in San Diego on June 28th was advertised as "What A Nite!" Also with tenor man Hal "Cornbread" Singer's band was a Saturday, July 19th dance and show at the Marigold in Fresno. These dates formed part of Turner's California tour which trade magazine *Billboard* advised had wound up on July 20th, to be followed by a string of one-nighters down to New Orleans, where he would open at the Dew Drop Inn on July 25th for one week, before moving on to the Orchid Room in his home town, starting August 5th. A later report stated that his opening night in Kansas City was Standing Room Only.

On Labor Day 1952, September 1st, in Augusta, Turner was scheduled to start a short tour with the singer and guitarist Lowell Fulson's band, playing thirteen dates through Florida.

He had returned to New York by September 23rd, 1952, for a recording session for Atlantic, from which two titles were issued. Then it was off on the road again, one known date for which was a one-niter concert in Youngstown, Ohio, on September 23, alongside Ruth Brown and Willie Jackson. The latter played alto and baritone, and also sang.

In 1952, though the date is uncertain, Joe was reported at the Baby Grand in New York City Also on the bill was a "terrified" singer-songwriter called Doc Pomus. Pomus, who had been strongly influenced by Joe's early recordings, called at Atlantic's offices the next afternoon and by chance met his idol. As he said, ".... from that day on I wrote for him, trailed him around and finally became old and mature enough to become a close, close friend and we were 'podners' until he passed away"[7].

The *Chicago Defender* for October 25th, 1952, reported, "Joe Turner's just completed weekend at Sportman Club in Newport, Kentucky, was one of the biggest on record for that Bluegrass spot. Joe will play the fabulous Glass Bar (of the Midtown Hotel) in St. Louis for a week beginning October 24th." From Friday, November 7th, he was due to play a week at Uncle Tom's Plantation in Detroit.

1953

As the New Year began and at the behest of his agency, the Shaw Artists Corporation, Joe Turner, again with Ray Charles, headed South once more. One gig involved a dance date on the 4th of January in Houston, Texas.

Towards the end of February he was due to appear at the New 504 Club in Chicago, with drummer Jump Jackson's band and The Five Blazes vocal group, probably for a week's engagement. By May he was in New Orleans and there on the 12th he recorded his fourth session for Atlantic. The accompaniment was by a band directed by trombonist Pluma Davis, the musicians being drawn mainly from the Edgar Blanchard group. Four titles were recorded, but only two were released, *Honey Hush* and *Crawdad Hole*.

Trumpeter Frank Mitchell, a member of Edgar Blanchard's band, recalled, "Joe would perform at the Dew Drop from Thursday to Saturday. During the week Frank [Painia] would book him around the area in towns like Slidell, Gulfport and Biloxi. We sounded real good behind Joe. He called his Atlantic label and told them, 'Look, I got a good band and some new material. Let me go into the studio and cut.'"[8] But Charlie Gillett, in his history of Atlantic Records, reported it differently, "In May 1953 Ahmet suggested that Joe get himself into a studio nearest where he happened to be, which was in New Orleans." (There have been stories that, despite his lengthy discography, it was difficult to organise Turner into a recording studio.)

Mitchell continued:

"I lived around the corner from the J.M. Studio but I never got in it until I went in with Joe in 1953. At that session we did *Honey Hush* and *Crawdad Hole*. After the session me and Edgar came back to the Dew Drop. Frank said to us, 'Y'all ought to be ashamed of yourselves. That was some of the worst shit I've ever heard'. We just looked at each other because we thought we did pretty good. But a month later the record was number one in the country and Frank was walking around with his chest stuck out because it was his band on Joe's record."[9]

Turner told Val Wilmer:

"I made *Honey Hush* down in New Orleans and that kind of kicked off a different beat there. It started going like a house on fire, but before you knew where it was, all those cats like Elvis Presley and Bill Haley and Fats Domino come humping. And it was nothing but the blues with a good jump beat. Yeah, that *Honey Hush* kicked it off and the others took me over the top."[10]

Edgar Blanchard's drummer, Alonzo Stewart, recalled:

"We picked a lot of guys up and made them great. We did the *Honey Hush* session with Big Joe Turner when he was doing nothing but singing around the Dew Drop. Then this record comes out and pow, Joe's a big star."[11]

When Stewart joined Blanchard and the Gondoliers in 1953, the personnel was Frank Mitchell, trumpet, August 'Dimes' Dupont, alto, baritone, Warren Hebrad, tenor, Edward Santino, piano, Blanchard, guitar, and Stewart Davis, bass.

By 1953 Ray Charles was leading his own group. *Down Beat* reported that he and Joe Turner "are doing a swing of Texas concert dates, July 14th through 30th".

An August *Billboard* reported that Ahmet Ertegun and Jerry Wexler were flying down to New Orleans to cut a session with Joe Turner and Ray Charles. They did record Charles, but there is no known date with Turner.

Phil and Leonard Chess were famous for their numerous blues releases on the Chess label, including those by Muddy Waters, Little Walter, Howlin' Wolf, Sonny Boy Williamson and many others. Wexler wrote, "Even though Phil and Leonard Chess are our main competitors, they're also our friends. They've arranged this session for us...."[12]

Left to right, Jerry Wexler, Ahmet Ertegun, Joe Turner - playback time

"This session" featured Joe Turner with a small group of veteran blues players, including Elmore James on guitar. Jerry Wexler and Ahmet Ertegun were in the studio when four titles were made, only two of which were initially released, but these were hits when they came out in December. Recorded in Chicago on October 7th, 1953, they were:

TV Mama
>the one with the big wide screen
>She's got great big eyes and little bitty feet
>And in the waist she's so nice and neat

Oke-She-Moke-She-Pop
>Step into my Roadmaster
>This time we're going to ride in class
>We gonna talk about the future and forget about the past.

Talking with Steve Propes about this session, Turner showed his disinterest in the details of his backing groups: "I didn't pay too much attention to who they got because there was always an argument who ... they wanted and all that ... yakity-yak stuff. I said, 'It's your money, you want to do it, go ahead and do it, fine with me, as long as he keeps time.'"[13]

Big Joe's status with Atlantic at this time was such that when Leonard Chess said that he had "an agreement with Muddy Waters that if Muddy's records stopped selling, he could always work for Leonard at his house," Jerry Wexler could joke that he and Joe had the same kind of deal. "Joe told me, if our company ever gets into trouble, I can always get a job as his chauffeur".[14]

Joe Turner with trumpeter King Kolax band, date c. 1954

Turner was at the Toast of the Town in Chicago for a stay due to end on October 10th. This may have been the time he played the club when trumpeter King Kolax led the house band. The following day, Sunday, he was at one of his regular spots, the Sunset in Indianapolis, in a 'Blues Parade' with pianist/vocalist Floyd Dixon. *Billboard* had him "entertaining nitely at Cadillac Bob's" in Chicago, during October, but with no specific dates. Also in the Fall, he appeared in concert, a Rock and Roll Party, at the Cleveland Arena, featured alongside the Buddy Johnson Orchestra, Fats Domino, Dakota Staton, Red Prysock and eight vocal groups. The producer was Alan Freed, who was making his name on local radio by playing the music of black rock 'n' roll artists. Freed was to become increasingly influential during the 1950s.

Honey Hush, which had been recorded in May 1953, was released the week of August 15th and became number one in the *Billboard*'s Rhythm and Blues Chart for eight weeks, commencing the week of December 5th. It was reported in an October *Billboard* that, "Joe Turner, whose Atlantic waxing of *Honey Hush* hit the national (r&b) charts last week after grabbing attention in New Orleans, is set for a string of one-nighters thru the Texas area with his ork, starting October 10th until November 22nd. After that the vocalist goes into the Louisiana-Mississippi territory where he will work until January."

Under a Houston by-line, the *Indianapolis Recorder* for November 14th, 1953 reported that the Blues Cavalcade, featuring T-Bone Walker, 'Big Wheel' Joe Turner and Lowell 'Everyday' Fulson would be appearing in the city "this week". On the same day, *The Pittsburgh Courier* carried a news item from San Antonio headed, "T-Bone Walker Under Bond Because of 'Tea'": "T-Bone Walker was freed here last week on $2,000 bond after having been jailed on a narcotics charge, accused of having marijuana in his possession. The guitarist was nabbed in a raid by city detectives following his packed Library Auditorium engagement with Joe Turner."

Jerry Wexler again, "In December of 1953, we [Wexler and Ahmet Ertegun] recorded Joe ourselves, returning to Cosmo's studio in New Orleans, where we cut the bulletproof *Midnight Cannonball*. Joe just kept getting stronger, better, bigger in every way."[14] The illustriously named trombonist on the date was Worthia G. "Show Boy" Thomas, who confirmed that he had recorded with Turner.

From 1945 to 1956 the J&M Studio, run by Cosimo (Cosmo) Matassa, was situated on North Rampart Street. It was the only serious studio in New Orleans at the time, with a reputation for the high quality of its recordings. (In 1956 Matassa moved to larger premises.)

For the present, it has to be assumed that all the weeks and months unaccounted for were spent on the road, part of the endless touring. One is disinclined to dispute *Ebony* magazine's claim that Joe had travelled as much as 75,000 miles in one year.

1954

Joe Turner's activities can now be documented in greater detail, partly due to columns in *Down Beat* and *Billboard*, but to a greater extent by Ray Astbury's searches into the archives of Afro-American newspapers.

January 1954

23   Griffin Brothers and their Band, plus "Big" Joe Turner (Hear him sing *Honey Hush*), plus singer Chuck Willis. Columbia Township Auditorium, Columbia, SC.

29   Joe (*Honey Hush*) Turner plus Roy Milton and His Orchestra. Durham Armory, NC.

30   "Big Joe" '*Honey Hush*' Turner, Griffin Brothers Orchestra, T-Bone Walker, Chuck Willis, Municipal Auditorium, Charleston, WV.

February 1954

3   Joe Turner – engagement at the Crown Lounge, Chicago, IL

12   "Fats" Domino and his Orchestra, Joe Turner, famous for "*Honey Hush*," and Edna McGriff, Valley Arena, Holyoke, MA.

16-21   Joe Turner – Ebony Club, Lockland, OH.

THE CASH BOX

★ AWARD O' THE WEEK ★

"SHAKE, RATTLE AND ROLL" (2:57)
[Progressive BMI—Calhoun]

"YOU KNOW I LOVE YOU" (3:08) [Lou Willie Turner]

JOE TURNER
Atlantic 1026

JOE TURNER

● Joe Turner is really loaded with this one. "Shake, Rattle and Roll"

has everything. Great beat, simple tune, Turner vocal, and a sockful of punchy phrases that combine to make up a terrific lyric. Add this to the fact that Turner is currently one of the hottest record salesmen in the business and you have a mighty potent piece of wax. The under lid, "You Know I Love You," is a slow romantic blues, well done, but destined to be lost in view of the upper deck.

Sometime in February he was with Chuck Willis at Lloyd's Manor in Newark, New Jersey.

He was in New York for an Atlantic recording session on February 15th. That was when he recorded the seminal *Shake, Rattle and Roll*, a version of which later cemented Bill Haley's claim to rock 'n' roll fame.

Shake, Rattle and Roll was released the week of April 17th and *Billboard* reported, in its usual optimistic way, "though only out this week, this disc has begun to roll up impressive sales figures". The optimism was justified when the record held the number one spot in the rhythm and blues charts.

An advertisement in *The Chicago Defender* announced, "Joe '*Honey Hush*' Turner starring at Crown Propeller Lounge, opening Tuesday, March 2nd. Sax Mallard and his band." The assumption is that this booking, probably for two weeks, was in addition to the one scheduled to commence on February 3rd.

Then we have Turner's known engagements from the end of March to early June.

March 1954
26   Big Joe Turner, Guitar Slim and his Orchestra,
                 Woodlake, San Antonio, TX.

April 1954
12   Joe Turner, T-Bone Walker, Guitar Slim and his
                 Orchestra, Dreamland, Omaha, NE.
16   Joe Turner, with pianist/singer Smiley Lewis and his
                 orchestra, Veterans Memorial Building (city and state unknown).
18   Joe Turner with Smiley Lewis and his Orchestra,
                 Labor Temple ballroom (city and state unknown).
30   Joe Turner (*Honey Hush*) and Smiley Lewis,
                 Sacramento Memorial Auditorium, CA.

May 1954
11-16   engagement at unknown club, Oakland, CA
19   Joe Turner, also Smiley Lewis and his Orchestra,
                 McElroys Ballroom, Portland, OR
20   Joe Turner with Smiley Lewis and his Band,
                 Evergreen Ballroom, Tacoma, WA.
21   Smiley Lewis and His Famous Orchestra, also in
                 person Joe Turner, Armory, Spokane, WA
22   Joe Turner, "Hear Him Sing "*Honey Hush*" with
                 Smiley Lewis and his Band, Eagles Auditorium,
                 Seattle, CA.

June 1954
5   Smiley Lewis with "Big Joe" Turner and the
                 "*Honey Hush*" Band, Palladium, El Paso, NM.

Joe trying out a new song with Lou Willie (*Ebony*, March 1954)

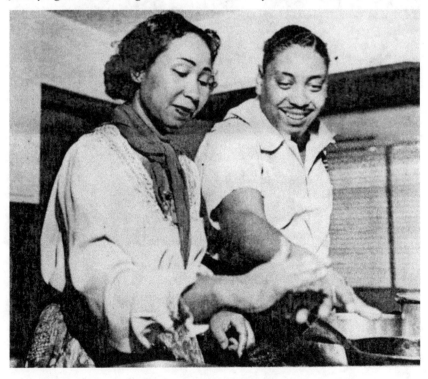

Joe and Lou Willie in the kitchen (*Ebony*, March 1954)

circulation, published a feature article about Turner in its March, 1954 issue. It reports he and his wife, Lou Willie, living in a $22,500 house in the Park Manor district of Chicago, together with dog Rusty. The article also states, "Joe gives wife most of the credit for his success in past nine years. She has been a settling influence on carefree bluesman," and, "For a number of years Mrs. Turner traveled with her husband as business manager on one-nighters. [She] quit because driving was too dangerous."

Amos Milburn and Big Joe (*Ebony,* March 1954)

Joe was at New York's Apollo for the week of June 11th-17th. This was a "Gala Week" at the Apollo, with The Spaniels vocal group the headliners, Arnett Cobb and his band, and "King of Blues" Joe Turner, followed by a week in another revue at the Howard Theatre in Washington, DC., June 18th-24th. Then onto the San Francisco area for a series of "very successful one-nighters," for John Burton and Manny Schwartz, "up the coast as far as Vancouver," before going into the Apache Inn, Dayton, Ohio, July 8th-12th. Four days later, July16th-18th, it's The Tally Ho in Long Branch, New Jersey, then he is off on tour again, including a July date at the Madison Rink in Chicago, with Fats Domino and Muddy Waters. It may also have covered appearances in two of disc-jockey Alan Freed's productions, one of which was on July 25th in the Armory in Akron, Ohio, with a full house of 3,100, of which a third were white teenagers. In addition to Turner they heard, among others, Faye Adams, The Five Keys and the Joe Morris orchestra. The other Freed show was in "the cavernous Cleveland Arena" on August 29th, together with Fats Domino, Clyde McPhatter, the Drifters and others.

The *Cash Box* issue of July 10th, 1954, featured Atlantic Records on the front cover. In the Disc Jockey Poll, Rhythm and Blues, *Honey Hush* was the "Most Programmed Record" and Joe Turner was "The Most Programmed Male Vocalist".

A *Billboard* news item (June 1954) states that "Guitar Slim, T-Bone Walker and Joe Turner have been set for a second tour thru the Texas area from July 30th to August 24th. There are no open dates. The trio's last trek thru Texas, which ran for 30 days, was one of the most successful booked by Howard Lewis this year". Known dates are:

August 1954

?	Turner and Memphis Slim, Magnolia Ballroom, Atlanta, GA
10	Turner with T-Bone Walker, plus Guitar Slim and his Orchestra, Woodlake Country Club, San Antonio, TX

From *Billboard* for August 21st came the following: "Atlantic record stars Ruth Brown and Joe Turner made a number of film shorts last week for TV use. The shorts, emceed by Willie Bryant, feature the singers doing their top record hits." They were shot for Studio Films, who had purchased Snader Telescriptions. These were for a 13-part television series with the encompassing title of "Showtime At The Apollo." Filmed in a New York studio, with reaction shots from a Wednesday amateur night Apollo audience, the new recordings were interspersed with older Snader material. Joe was accompanied by the Paul Williams band, Jimmy Brown, trumpet, Eddie Silver, tenor, Paul Williams, baritone, Freddie Johnson, piano, Steve Cooper, bass, Belton Evans, drums. *Shake, Rattle and Roll* appeared in the episode titled "Stars Over Harlem" and *Oke-She-Moke-She-Pop* in that called "Variety Time". In 1957 the titles appeared in compilation feature films, *Shake, Rattle and Roll* in "Rhythm and Blues Revue" and *Oke-She-Moke-She-Pop* in "Rock and Roll Revue".[15]

Still from Showtime at the Apollo, 1954

These Studio Films were ostensibly all-star, including acts such as the Delta Rhythm Boys, the Count Basie Sextet, the Lionel Hampton and Cab Calloway orchestras, Sarah Vaughan, Herb Jeffries, Nat King Cole, Ruth Brown, Martha Davis, and Faye Adams.

During the week of filming, Joe's *Shake, Rattle and Roll* was number 6 on *Billboard*'s R&B Best Sellers in Stores listing. Ruth Brown's *What A Dream* was at number 3. And in the week of September 25th, Joe's *Well All Right* and *Married Woman* were released by Atlantic. By October the sales of Joe's *Shake, Rattle and Roll* record were vibrant enough for the song to replace *Honey Hush* in the advertising for his engagements.

Other *Billboard* reports were that "Chuck Willis and Joe Turner are set for Eastern one-nighters during late September" and, in October, that they were "also off on a Southern tour that will cover Florida and Alabama come November". Dates included, in late August/early September, along with pianist/singer Memphis Slim and The Spiders, an appearance at the Municipal Auditorium, Kansas City, Illinois and, on October 2nd, Big "Joe" Turner, Chuck Willis and his Orchestra, at the Arcadia, Providence, Rhode Island.

Big Joe was in New York on October 19th, 1954, when he recorded again for Atlantic, though the four titles were either unissued or rejected and then remade the following January.

In October and November the tour with Chuck Willis continued, first with a series of one nighters in the East, followed by Florida and Alabama. On November 6th, Turner and Chuck Willis, each with "his orchestra," were featured in an FAMU Victory Ball at the Tallahassee Skating Rink, in Florida. They also appeared in a special Thanksgiving dance and show at Selden Park in Brunswick, Georgia on November 26th. December 2nd found Turner, with the Choker Campbell Orchestra at the Riverside Ballroom in Phoenix, Arizona.

Walter 'Choker' Campbell (1916-1993) played tenor saxophone. As a leader, he became well-known in the r&b field, working with Joe Turner on many occasions.

Down Beat, December 29th, 1954, issue, reported from San Francisco, "Joe Turner playing several one-niters on the local r&b circuit in November." *Billboard* prefers December for this tour, saying that Turner and the Choker Campbell group played a successful weekend engagement at the Savoy Ballroom (in Chicago) December 3rd-5th, before leaving on a tour of California.

When the West Coast tour ended, Turner was due to play a series of dates in Louisiana, during Christmas and New Year, including Shreveport on Christmas Eve and New Orleans on Christmas Day.

Joe told one unidentified reporter that "he is very grateful to the Juke Box Operators of America' for naming him the 'Best R. & B. Artist of 1954'".

And as the year changed, perhaps that was when rhythm and blues morphed into rock 'n' roll.

11

"I made all those things before Haley"

(1955-1956)

Before continuing the Turner chronology, a few basic details about major influences on his story in the 1950s will set the scene for the rest of the decade. Atlantic Records, *Shake, Rattle and Roll*, Bill Haley and Alan Freed all, directly or indirectly, played their part.

Atlantic was formed in the previous decade, in October 1947, when Ahmet Ertegun (1923-2006), son of a former Turkish ambassador to the United States, and Herb Abramson (1916-1999) became partners. Both were jazz enthusiasts, but Abramson had had some part-time experience of the record business while at university. He had worked for Al Green of National Records in 1945, where he had recorded Joe Turner with Pete Johnson. Abramson was President of the new company, Ertegun the Vice-President.

After the initial struggle to become established, Atlantic soon settled into a comfortable groove, recording black artists and achieving a satisfactory number of hit records in the rhythm-and-blues charts. Among the instrumentalists, vocal groups and singers, inevitably, was Big Joe Turner.

In those days, when the New York recording sessions took place in the office, one desk was piled one atop the other and space found for the artists involved.

In 1953 Herb Abramson went into the U.S. Army for two years, honouring a commitment made when the service paid for his training as a dentist. To fill the position left by Abramson's departure Ertegun recruited another jazz fan, Jerry Wexler (1917-2008), to take care of administration and promotional work. He bought a 13% stock holding and became an integral part of the operation. In his student days Wexler had heard and appreciated Joe Turner in Kansas City.

Abramson left the army in April 1955, after Dental Corps service in Germany, and returned to Atlantic. He was placed in charge of a subsidiary label, Atco but, no longer feeling part of the team, he asked the other three (brothers Ahmet and Nesuhi Ertegun, and Jerry Wexler) to buy him out, which they did.

Nesuhi Ertegun (1917-1989) had been working for Contemporary Records, but he was getting restless. When, at the end of 1954, his brother and Jerry Wexler asked him to join Atlantic, to help build their album catalogue, especially the jazz side, he was happy to do so, as of January 1st, 1955.[1] He was particularly proud of two Atlantic albums with which he was associated, the "Genius of Ray Charles" and Joe Turner's "Boss of the Blues", despite the latter's disappointing sales.

In later years, with Ahmet Ertegun still at its head, the label became part of the Warner Brothers empire and concentrated on rock groups, many of them British, such as the Rolling Stones, Cream, Genesis and Phil Collins.

The financial arrangements with Atlantic are unclear. It appears that the label treated its black artists better than most companies, without upsetting the industry's status quo. Neil Slaven commented, "The hits continued to come ... He (Turner) still didn't get any royalties but that seems to be the story of his life."[2] However, Big Joe was one of the few artists who was actually under contract to Atlantic.

Authors Justine Picardie and Dorothy Wade have written that Turner's contemporaries, most of whom were black, did not have decent recording contracts. "If they were lucky, they were paid meagre royalties; and often the sum of those royalties was exceeded by the bill for 'studio time' which the artists were required to pay."[3]

Bob Porter, a producer himself, points out that there were two types of royalties: publisher/songwriting royalties and artist or contractual royalties. Atlantic used the standard Musicians Union contract which specified 3-5% royalties payable once the costs of the recording sessions had been recouped. Anyone who wrote songs was paid first, only the artists with the biggest hits got the second. Costs of sessions were cross-collateralized with costs of each session going into one large pot. Much later, in the 1980s, accounting practices changed to have each session stand on its own.[4]

Bassist John Levy, who later became a personal manager and agent, explained to Nat Hentoff in *Jazz Times* for September 2001 ('John Levy: A Personal Manager Beyond Category'): "The recording industry used two separate types of contract: one that they offered to white artists and another that was used for black artists. The royalty rates were usually lower, the advance was always lower and the amount of money they put into promotion was always lower in the black contracts. Except for the black superstars – they get a very good budget ... And sadly, I don't believe that separate black arrangements have really changed that much".

Joe Turner was with Atlantic for eleven years, until his final session in May 1962. In the early years he made numerous hits for the label and he benefited from working for an expanding major rhythm and blues company, run by jazz enthusiasts who had admired him long before becoming record executives.

Shake, Rattle and Roll was written, music and words, by Jesse Stone (1901-1999), pianist, arranger, composer and bandleader, using the pseudonym, Charles E. Calhoun. (He used the Calhoun name when his songs went through the performing rights society B.M.I. and not A.S.C.A.P.) His other compositions included *Idaho, Cole Slaw* and *Smack Dab In The Middle*. Stone was a veteran musician, a contemporary of Joe Turner's in Kansas City, working for George E. Lee and Thamon Hayes, as well as leading his own Blues Serenaders, 1926 to 1928 and in the early 1930s. By the late 1940s he was at Atlantic. An important figure in the label's history, he was also credited by Ahmet Ertegun as doing "more to develop the basic rock'n'roll sound than anybody else ... He was a great, reliable, loose arranger, who could update a five year-old arrangement with a couple of chord changes."[5]

Stone's composition "... *re*mained on the *Billboard* Rhythm and Blues Chart for thirty-two weeks, peaking at number one on three different occasions."[6] Paul Watts has it in the Best Sellers Top Ten for 27 weeks and the Juke Box Top ten for 33 weeks.[7]

Haley's producer at Decca was Milt Gabler (1911-2001). Gabler was a died-in-the-wool jazz enthusiast, running the famous Commodore Music Shop and, between 1938 and 1957, the thriving jazz label Commodore. His catalogue consisted largely of white jazz groups, including numerous Eddie Condon bands, but it also boasted Sidney Bechet, Ed Hall, Willie 'The Lion' Smith and other black artists. He recorded Billie Holiday's *Strange Fruit*, when her own company, Columbia, would not. In the 1950s he was also working for Decca Records, producing jazz sessions, but also more popular artists, including Louis Jordan, the alto playing leader of a well-known jump group.

Milt Gabler in his study, New Rochelle, October 1979. Photograph courtesy Daniel L. Mahony

Gabler described his approach to recording cover versions of black material, "If any of the lyrics were double-entendre I would clean them up. I didn't want any censor with the radio station to bar the record from being played on the air. With NBC a lot of race records wouldn't get played on air because of the lyrics. So I had to watch that closely."[8]

Thus, when he selected *Shake, Rattle and Roll* as a possible follow-up number to Haley's *Rock Around The Clock*, Gabler sanitised Stone's original lyrics. Speaking of this, Johnny Otis said, "The black community always had a wholesome approach to sexuality. 'You're wearin' those dresses, the sun comes shinin' through/I can't believe my eyes, all that mess belongs to you.'" In Milt Gabler's version this became, "You wear those dresses, your hair done up so nice/ You look so warm, but your heart is cold as ice."

Haley's recording of *Shake, Rattle and Roll* sold a million or more copies, further helping rock 'n' roll to move into the mainstream pop field. It entered the charts on August 21st, 1954, reached number 7 and was in the Top 40 for 27 weeks. "Turner's version was caught in the tailwind and moved into the pop charts, reaching 22."[9] This was enough to gain Joe a spot singing the song on the Ed Sullivan Show.[10]

As late as January 1955 Turner's version of *Shake, Rattle and Roll* was still at #15 in the *Billboard* r&b Most Played by Disc Jockeys chart. Like so many of his Atlantic titles, the song was to remain in his repertoire for the rest of his life.

Bill Haley (1925-1981) was a country and western singer, who also played guitar and wore a strange kiss curl on his forehead. In the early 1950s he had a number of small hits with titles such as *Crazy, Man, Crazy* for Essex records, but in 1954 he recorded *Rock Around The Clock* with the Comets for Decca Records. It was not an immediate success, but its subsequent use for the soundtrack of the 1955 film, "Blackboard Jungle," made Haley's name and paved the way for rock and roll's world-wide success. White teenagers, now a powerful section of the record buying public, wanted to hear more of the same, even from a forty-plus-year-old singer like Joe Turner.

Shake, Rattle and Roll was recorded by Turner on February 15th, 1954, and released by Atlantic around the time that Bill Haley made *Rock Around The Clock on* April 12th, 1954. Haley returned to the Decca studio, on June 7th, to record his version of *Shake, Rattle and Roll*, with the resulting success already described.

Joe Turner was philosophical about what happened with Bill Haley. "I made all those things before Haley and the others, but suddenly all the cats started jumping up, and I guess I kinda got knocked down in the traffic."[11]

Later, Turner was to tour with Haley in various rock'n'roll packages and they became friends, with Joe being a guest on Haley's fishing boat, the Comet IV. Joe said

> "I used to travel around with him. I never sang *Shake, Rattle and Roll*, let him sing it. I had a lot of other songs I sing anyway, so it didn't make too much difference to me. Everybody used to say, 'Man, what are doin with him?' I'd say, 'Well, it's alright, He's a nice fellow. I don't care, it don't make no difference to me. 'Nough money out there for all of us".[12]

In his biography of Haley, John Swanson makes the case that Haley's version is the better, "while allowing for the obvious fact that Turner is unquestionably the better singer, the Gabler production is far more exciting than Atlantic's release. His view was that "the Bill Haley cover ... sold more copies than Turner's because it was a better record."[13]

It is interesting that in the Elvis Presley version, the lyrics are closer to those sung by Joe Turner and that in the 1950s Presley had a few prized 78s of r&b singers, including Big Joe, transferred to reel-to-reel tape.[14]

Jesse Stone said:

"At that particular time there was no such thing as rock-and-roll, and those records that were made by Atlantic were sold mostly to black people. There was a bar against playing black music on the big [radio] stations, so Joe Turner's first record was a hit as far as blacks were concerned, but a black hit was nothing like a white hit."[15]

The prominence now given to rock 'n' roll was not universally welcomed by the jazz world.. Critic Leonard Feather said it was not only very rarely jazz, it is very rarely music. Billy Taylor, Jr, pianist and teacher, felt compelled to complain, "Even legitimate blues singers like Joe Turner have suffered. He has to have a Bill Haley-type rhythm section behind him to sell, but of all people, Joe doesn't need someone to make him swing."[16]

Alan Freed (1921-1965) had an hour-long classical music programme on the Cleveland station WJW, but in 1952 he persuaded his manager to allocate him a second hour to host what he called "Moondog's Rock and Roll Party". This pioneered the relay of black music to white teenagers. Following the show's success he moved to New York in March 1954 to work for WINS radio. He quickly gained a very large following of young listeners and as a result was able to produce numerous concerts and tours featuring the most popular rhythm 'n' blues artists, as well as appearing in five rock 'n' roll films. In 1956 he hosted Alan Freed's Rock 'n' Roll dance party on CBS.

Freed was fired in 1959, his reputation ruined, when he was involved in the "payola scandal", the practice of a record company paying a disc-jockey to give priority to playing specific records. He died an alcoholic.[17]

1955

Alan Freed's Rock 'n' Roll Ball played two nights, January 14th/15th, at St. Nicholas Arena, New York. featuring Joe Turner, Fats Domino, The Clovers, Clyde McPhatter & the Drifters, and the orchestras of Buddy Johnson, with Ella Johnson, and Red Prysock. Audiences of 7,500 are claimed, and "nearly half the crowd was white".[18]

Commenting on the show, a January *Billboard* reported:

"Alan Freed's 'Rock-n-Roll' Ball ... was a tremendous success financially, grossing over $24,000. But these eye-opening figures tell only part of the story, for the show had to be seen to be believed. A total of about 12,000 people jammed the hall on both nights. Actually, the word 'jammed' can't begin to describe the solid mass that stood for five hours to see the spectacular r&b show put on by Freed and company. ... The enthusiasm of the audience was transferred to the performers, who reacted to the frenzy with tremendous performances. A finale that lasted about half an hour was rocked in the atmosphere of a revival meeting. With Joe Turner at the mike and Fats Domino at the piano, the entire troupe returned to the stage for a closing that was without parallel."[19]

January 1955 (courtesy Blues & Rhythm archives)

Joe Turner and Alan Freed, mid-1950s

Next came an engagement, January 17th-22nd, with Al "tenor sax" King and his Band, at the Celebrity Club, a nightclub in Providence, Rhode Island, and there was a successful recording session for Atlantic on January 28th, when four titles were made, *Morning, Noon and Night, Hide and Seek, Ti-Re-Lee* and *Flip, Flop and Fly.*

Then, immediately following on was another long tour. "The Top Ten Rhythm and Blues Review of '55" (sometimes the 'Review' became a 'Show,' and sometimes 'Rhythm and Blues' was omitted) included Joe Turner, Bill Doggett's trio, Lowell Fulson, Faye Adams, comedian Al Jackson, Paul Williams' Band, dancers The Spence Twins, The Clovers, The Charms, The Moonglows, and the Moonlighters.

Richmond Times Despatch, January 26, 1955

Originally the schedule was for 60 one-nighters, or 42 according to *Billboard*, but the March 9th issue of *Down Beat* refers to 52 days straight, New York to Texas and back, via New Orleans. One advertisement refers to the Paul "Hucklebuck" Williams Big Band, and an advance report says the artists are "all backed by Paul Williams' 20-piece orchestra." There was "an evening (January 29th) in Richmond, Virginia, when 8000-10000 (sic) were turned away," while only a third of the expected audience of 6000 attended the February 6th event at the Arena in Cleveland. The promoter blamed the mayor and police for being ultra cautious about security.

Known dates, some using the title "Top 12 Rhythm and Blues Review" when The Five Keys were added to the show*, include:

January 1955
28	Norfolk, VA
29*	The Mosque, Richmond, VA

February 1955
1	Court Square, Springfield, MD
2	Ritz Ballroom, Stanford, CT
3*	Syria Mosque, Pittsburgh, PA
4	Trianon Ballroom, Chicago, IL
6	Arena, Cleveland, OH
8	Coliseum, Evansville, Indianapolis, IN
9	Ryman Auditorium, Nashville, TN
10	National Guard Armory, Jackson, TN
11	Opera House, St. Louis, MO
12	New Civic Auditorium Music Hall, Omaha, NE
14	Sportatorium, Dallas, TX
15	Reo Palm Island, Longview, TX
16	City Coliseum, Austin, TX
17	Municipal Auditorium, Oklahoma City, OK
22	Municipal Auditorium, San Antonio, TX
25	Madison Rink, Chicago, IL
26	Municipal Auditorium, New Orleans, LA

March 1955
1	Municipal Auditorium, Raleigh, NC
3	Memorial Auditorium, Raleigh, NC
4	RKE Legion Auditorium, Roanoke, VA
5	Township Auditorium, Columbia, SC
8	Municipal Auditorium, Birmingham, AL
9	City Armory, Durham, NC
10	Tobacco Warehouse, Greensboro, NC
11	Municipal Auditorium, Charleston, WV
12*	Syria Mosque, Latrobe, PA
13*	The Mosque, Richmond, VA

?	Austin, TX
16	County Hall, Charleston, SC
18*	Academy of Music, Philadelphia, PA
20	Buffalo, NJ

Some of these engagements were for one performance only, others were for two each evening. On a few occasions the show was combined with a dance. With reference to the March 13th booking in Richmond, the news item in the *Richmond Times Dispatch* (February 27th, 1955) makes reference "to the sell-out on January 29th and the fact that so many were turned away on the night of the performance......"

With the Top 10 (or Top 12) Rhythm and Blues Review (or Show) behind him, Joe was back on the club and one-nighter trail, including:

March 1955

25	Auditorium, Milwaukee, WI, Joe Turner, The Spaniels vocal group and the Paul Williams Orchestra. This was billed as "Big Rhythm and Blues Show!"
27	Sunset Terrace Ballroom, Indianapolis, with the Joe Morris Band.

April 1955

8	Woodlake Country Club, San Antonio, Texas, with Lowell Fulson ("and His Guitar that Plays The Blues") and ("The Sensational New") Choker Campbell and Orch.

May 1955

?-14	The Blackout Club, Chicago, Illinois

The Pittsburgh Courier for April 23rd, 1955 had announced the winners of the paper's annual poll, with Joe Turner voted the top male blues artist.

During late May to June 13th he was on tour in the South with the Joe Morris combo. This included a gig in Hollandale, Florida and, on the 10th, a "June German Ball, 10 'til 4," at Baldwin's Gymntorium in Martinsville, Virginia. An added attraction here was blues singer Bea Booze. White spectators were charged $1.00.

The tour concluded with another "Annual Colored June German Ball," on June 13 in the Planters Warehouse, Rocky Mount, North Carolina, advertised as "the Biggest Negro Dance in the South". Andy Kirk and his Clouds of Joy and the Joe Morris Band, with singers Joe Turner and Ursula Reed were featured. "Dancing is scheduled to begin at nine o'clock Monday evening and will come to a close at five o'clock Tuesday morning."[20]

Turner, with Joe Morris, was the headliner of the variety show at the Memorial Auditorium in Raleigh, North Carolina, on June 20th. Other dates with Morris accompanying included a dance on July 1st at the Guildford Tobacco Warehouse, Greensboro, North Carolina, and two opening nights at the Club Baron in Nashville, Tennessee, July 6th and 7th. The club advertised that "A special section will be reserved for white people".

On Friday, July 15th, Joe appeared at the Newport Jazz Festival, Rhode Island. Turner sang with Roy Eldridge, trumpet, and Coleman Hawkins, tenor. Jack Tracy commented, "Big Joe Turner didn't have much of a chance when he came on, either, because of the mikes..."

During the summer he was on tour again, under the auspices of Shaw Artists.

July 1955

18   Peps, Philadelphia, Pennsylvania

August 1955

4-7   Apache Inn (nightclub), Dayton, Ohio

19   on stage at the Apollo theatre, New York, for one week, Dr. Jive, plus New Rhythm and Blues Show, with Bo Diddley, The Five Keys, The Spaniels, and Dolores Ware.

Shortly after the Apollo date he was set for another exhausting tour, the second "Top Ten Review" of the year. This was preparing "in St. Louis for tour of 16 states, in more than 50 cities, for 66 consecutive days." Tour was set to start late August for East, mid-West, South and South-West.

The September 3rd edition of *The Pittsburgh Courier*, under a St. Louis by-line, reported that the "Top Ten Review" would open in that city, the start of "an unprecedented series of bookings," of almost seventy consecutive days, taking in fifteen states and into sixty cities and towns. "Many performances will be played in baseball parks to accommodate the anticipated crowds".

An item in the *New York Amsterdam News* (August 6th, 1955) aimed to generate publicity for the start of the Top Ten Revue tour. It was headed, "Joe Turner Sees Blues Taking 'Pop' Spotlight". "In a highly controversial statement made on the eve of his departure as a star of a new revue, Joe Turner, known internationally as The Boss of the Blues, stated that all other styles of music, including the Mambo, will have to take a back seat in 1955 and let the Blues take the spotlight in the pop music world." He "immediately became the crater of a storm of controversy as champions of swing, bop, dixieland, mambo and sentimental ballads, vigorously disputed Turner's prophecy."

When the Review opened at the Kiel Opera House in St. Louis it starred The Clovers and organist Bill Doggett, in addition to Joe Turner, The Five Keys, Bo Diddley, T-Bone Walker, Etta James and Paul Williams and his Big Band. For the remainder of the tour, however, Walker was out and Faye Adams, The Charms, Gene and Eunice, and mc/comedian Al Jackson were in.

Some venues had a segregated area for white spectators, but others had separate performances. A news item advised two shows in New Orleans, "6 p.m. for white patrons and 8 p.m. for colored", as did an advert. for the Birmingham gig, except it was "for white, 4:30 pm; for colored, 8:30 pm."

Known dates are:

August 1955

26   Kiel Opera House, St. Louis, MO

31   City Auditorium, Galveston, TX

September 1955

1	Beaumont, TX
2	Municipal Auditorium, San Antonio, TX.
4	Municipal Auditorium, New Orleans, LA.
5	Sportatorium, Dallas, TX
6	Exposition Hall, Corpus Christi, TX
7	Legion Stadium, Longview, TX
8	Robinson Auditorium, Little Rock, AK
9	Municipal Auditorium, Oklahoma City, OK
11	La Grave Field, Fort Worth TX
13	Coliseum, Odessa, TX
14	Coliseum, El Paso, TX
15	Municipal Auditorium, Amarillo, TX
16	Ice Arena, Albuquerque, NM
20	Armory, Jackson, TN
22	Auditorium, Atlanta, GA
23	Speedway, Dayton, OH
24	Coliseum, Evansville, IN
25	Auditorium, Birmingham, AL
27	Soldiers and Sailors Memorial Auditorium, Chattanooga, TN

October 1955

1	Municipal Auditorium, Charleston, WV
6	The Armory, Burlington, NC
8	Township Auditorium, Columbia, OH
9	Field House, Huntingdon, VA
12	Stambough Auditorium, Youngstown, OH
14	Trianon Ballroom, Chicago, IL
15	Skatarena, Indianapolis, IN
17	Madison Theatre, Detroit, MI
18	Circle Theatre, Cleveland, OH
20	Syria Mosque, Pittsburgh, PA *
22	The Mosque, Richmond, VA *
26	Coliseum, Baltimore, PA
27	Fairgrounds, Indianapolis, IN
28	Arcadia Ballroom, Providence, RI
29	Carnegie Hall, New York City, NY
30	Symphony Hall, Boston, PA

*These two shows (four performances) were titled The Top 12 Rhythm and Blues Show, featuring Bill Haley and his Comets, and with Earl Gaines replacing Gene and Eunice.

In the newspaper adverts. Turner is usually shown fourth or fifth on the bill for most of these package tours, but in the news items he is one of several who might be selected as the main subject of the reporter's comments. He had little sympathy for those who worried about their billing. As he told Val Wilmer,

"I just get out there and do my bit when everyone's hollerin' about who's supposed to be the star of the show. Competition – I call it the chopping block!"[21]

Shaw Artists Corporation promotional photo

Towards the end of the year two movies, both including Joe Turner and produced by Studio Films, were premiered. On October 24th "Rock 'n' Roll Revue" was shown in New York, followed by "Rhythm and Blues Revue" in Baltimore in Christmas week. Both were variety shows, using a mixture of new and old material. Other artists appearing in the first Revue included, among others, the Lionel Hampton and Duke Ellington orchestras, Nat King Cole, Dinah Washington, and Ruth Brown. The second film also had Cole, Brown and Hampton, as well as Sarah Vaughan, Amos Milburn, Martha Davis and the Count Basie Quintet. Turner, who sings one number in each film, originally recorded both songs (*Oke-She-Moke-She-Pop* and *Shake, Rattle and Roll*) in August 1954 for the television series, "Showtime at the Apollo,'" as described in the previous chapter.

In Roanoke Rapids, on Halloween, October 30th, it was reported that "A prankster had the whole town hopping when he played a recording of *Shake, Rattle and Roll* on the chimes amplifier of the First Baptist Church. 'He turned the volume on full blast and, boy, did she wake up the whole town.'" The report, in the *(Raleigh) News and Observer,* ended, "The police have the recording of the jive hit as rendered by Joe Turner and his Blues Kings. They're looking for the prankster."[22]

Joe was in New York for an Atlantic recording session on November 3rd. Two titles were made, *The Chicken and the Hawk* and *Boogie Woogie Country Girl*. When a fanzine editor asked Turner how he wrote the *Country Girl* number, Joe said that he walked down the street and sang it to himself, back to the hotel, down the street for a few hot dogs, back to the hotel, then to a bar for some wine, went to a picture show, walked around New York, "all the time singing the song". In a couple of days, "We go on down the studio, make the arrangements, make the music, set it up and it is just perfect."[23]

Talking to Steve Propes about *Boogie Woogie Country Girl,* Turner said he did not know if Doc Pomus wrote it, but describes walking around New York,

"running them songs through my head … I finally learned it, but I wasn't too sure about it. When I got to the studio, after they had the arrangements made up, the music and everything, it fit right in. We started a couple of times, third time we cut it".[24]

That could be how Turner wrote a song or learned new lyrics, but *Boogie Woogie Country Girl* is credited to Doc Pomus and Reginald Ashby. (Pomus said that he gave 15 per cent of the song to his friend Reggie Ashby in exchange for writing the lead sheets for the band.)

Both Jerry Wexler and Herb Abramson have described how they tried to help Turner to learn new lyrics. Unsuccessful were attempts to send him dubs on the road, as invariably these would be lost, but sending them to the Theresa Hotel in New York, where they provided a portable phonograph also failed, as Joe usually forgot to use the converter for DC current used by the hotel. In the end the solution was for someone to stand behind Joe as he recorded, whispering each line into his ear. Abramson recalled, "He couldn't read so good, so I fell back on a technique learned from his wife, manager, songwriter and vocal prompter Luella Turner. I stood behind him as he recorded and fed him the next line (spoken quickly into his ear) during the unhurried instrumental bars that followed each line he sang."

Doc Pomus (1925-1991), born Jerome Felder, was crippled by polio at the age of six. He was inspired to become a blues singer after hearing a Joe Turner record. They became friendly during their association with Atlantic Records, but lost touch after that, reconnecting many years later. Pomus co-wrote several hit songs with Mort Shuman, including *A Teenager In Love, Save The Last Dance For Me* and *Sweets For My Sweet*. For Turner they wrote, among others, *Love Roller Coaster, I Need A Girl, Don't You Cry*, and, by Pomus alone, *Still In Love*.

Joe travelled to Detroit for an engagement, November 4th-9th, at the Flame Show Bar, where he joined "Willie Bryant, Emcee, Mayor of Harlem"! Then, for one week, probably commencing Friday, November 11th, he was in a "Rhythm and Blues Cavalcade" with The Clovers, The Five Keys, the Solitaires. Annisteen Allen, and Eddie Bonnemore and his Big Band at the Howard Theater in Washington, D.C.

November 18th Turner "and his all star band" appeared at the Sportsman's Club in Petersburg, Virginia, and on the 24th, Thanksgiving night, he and the Paul Williams band were at the Armory in Muncie, Indiana. At the end of the month he and "5 Other Terrific Acts," including Pete Biggs' band, were doing three floor shows nightly at the Orchid Room in Kansas City.

With the bands of Fats Domino and Floyd Dixon, he sang at the Fair Park Auditorium in Lubbock, Texas, on December 10th, then it was off to the West Coast for the remainder of the year. On December 14th, 'Big' Joe Turner was at the Palladium in San Diego, followed the next day, with Floyd Dixon and his Orchestra, at the Riverside Ballroom, Phoenix, Arizona. It was reported that he was playing a series of one-nighters in late December/early January for Manny Schwartz in Northern California, including Sweet's in San Francisco on December 27th.

He was still in California on December 31st for an appearance in a Blues Jubilee, at the Shrine Auditorium in Los Angeles. Altoist Jackie Kelso, who was a member of the accompanying Roy Milton's Solid Senders, has been quoted as saying that he did a tour with Joe Turner, "I remember it was called the Weinberg Tour. Little mining towns in Kentucky, Virginia." Joe was also a guest on the Hunter Hancock television show during this time.

Joe's second recording sessions for Atlantic in 1955 resulted in more hits. In November came *The Chicken and the Hawk* and *Boogie Woogie Country Girl*. *The Chicken and the Hawk*, coupled with *Morning, Noon and Night*, was advertised in *Billboard* in the December 1955 issue.

Billboard's 1955 poll of r&b disc jockeys placed Big Joe Turner at number 2 in the 'Favorite Artists' section. He also had three 'Favorite Records' in the top fifteen. These were *Flip, Flop and Fly, Hide and Seek* and, at number 2, *Shake, Rattle and Roll*.

In its May 18, 1955 issue *Down Beat* announced the introduction "of Annual Awards in Rhythm, Blues Field. .... Because of the tremendous impact the rhythm and blues field has made on popular music in the last year, and because r&b finally appears to have taken a permanent and prominent grip on a large segment of the music buying public, *Down Beat* is instituting an annual series of awards to the top stars in the field." Joe Turner was chosen by the editors as the 1955 Top Male Personality of the Year.

1956

Joe's stay on the West Coast seems to have ended on January 2nd with an engagement at the Dream Bowl in Napa, California, accompanied by the Floyd Dixon Band. Subsequently, a news item in the *Kansas City Plaindealer* (January 20, 1956) has him "resting" in his home town:

> "Both Billy Eckstine and blues singer Joe Turner, both stopping at the Watkins Hotel, stated the first week of the New Year that they were idle until next booking ...."

But by January 14th Joe was playing a dance at Rusty's Playhouse in El Paso, Texas, with Smiley Lewis and the Paul Williams Band. Perhaps this was part of the Texas tour he was reported to be making this month with a package which included Ray Charles, Etta James and Charles Brown.[25]

And there was not too long a wait for the next of the year's package tours. "The Greatest Rock 'n' Roll Show of '56" was arranged by Irvin Field Super Attractions and featured Bill Haley's Comets, as well as Joe Turner, LaVern Baker, Bo Diddley, The Platters, Roy Hamilton, The Drifters, The Five Keys, Shirley and Lee, The Turbans and the Red Prysock orchestra.

The known dates for the show are:

January 1956
19	Auditorium, Birmingham, AL
27	Syria Mosque, Pittsburgh, PA, 3750 seater
28	Mosque, Richmond, VA, 4600 approx seater
29	Birmingham , AL
30	Chattanooga, TN
31	Charlotte, NC

February 1956
1	Township Auditorium, Columbia, SC
2	Memorial Auditorium, Raleigh, NC
3	Memorial Coliseum, Winston-Salem, NC
4	Norfolk, VA
5	Washington, DC

Blue Monday, the Fats Domino biography, puts the total Charlotte attendance at ten thousand.

Singers were top of the bill for two days, February 18th/19th, at the State Theater in Hartford, in a show called "Rhythm and Blues Jamboree of 1956". The Ames Brothers, LaVern Baker and Big Joe Turner featured, with dancer Bunny Briggs and Murray Schaff and his jazz quintet.

In addition to a February 24th recording session for Atlantic, in New York, which produced *Lipstick, Powder and Paint*, plus a new version of the famous 1941 number with Art Tatum, *Corrine Corrina*, this was probably the month when Joe appeared at Gleason's Bar of Music in Cleveland, Ohio.

Ahmet Ertegun, Jerry Wexler, Joe Turner. *Cash Box*, April 2, 1956

He was back in the recording studio in New York on March 6th and 7th to make the major artistic achievement of his time with the Atlantic label. The album, "The Boss of the Blues" (LP1234), with backing by an eight-piece jazz group, including Pete Johnson on piano, is rightly considered a classic.

"The Boss of the Blues: Joe Turner Sings Kansas City Jazz" was produced by Nesuhi Ertegun and Jerry Wexler as a vanity project. As Wexler put it, "... we'd wanted to indulge ourselves and change Joe's groove for one album. .... Ernie Wilkins wrote the charts for a Basie-based octet ....and the arrangements were mean and lean, Joe's vocals salty and strong. The result, *The Boss of the Blues* is sub specie aeternitatis."[27] Or, as Spinoza might have put it, "this album will last forever and a day".

Criss-crossing the Eastern states seems endless. "N. York's Great Rock 'n' Roll Show" was at the Paramount Theatre in Brattle(boro), Vermont, on March 14th. then Joe was solo in New York, appearing at the Baby Grand on March 16th. An Easter Dance, at midnight on Sunday, April 1st, at the Armory Drillroom in Danville, Virginia, starred Turner and the Paul Williams Orchestra. The following evening the same artists headlined a show and dance at the Memorial Auditorium in Raleigh, North Carolina.

Then followed a number of "New York's Great Rock 'N' Roll Shows," with Roy Hamilton, Ruth Brown, Joe Turner, LaVern Baker, Bo Diddley, The Platters, The Clovers and others. April 4th they were at the Carlisle Theatre in Carlisle, PA, the 5th at the Tennessee Theatre in Johnson City and the 6th at the Dalton in Pulaski, Virginia, though Turner was also advertised to appear for the Grand Opening of Club 36 in Petersburg, Virginia, that same evening. On the 7th the venue was the Capitol in Pottsville, PA, on the 12th at the Stratford in Poughkeepsie, New York, and on the 17th the Ohio Theatre in Mansfield, Ohio.

In the meantime Shaw Artists Agency were arranging further package tour dates between April and August.

At the end of April "The Biggest Rock 'n' Roll Show of 1956" began touring, with Bill Haley and his Comets, plus LaVern Baker, Bo Diddley, Joe Turner, Clyde McPhatter, Red Prysock and his BIG rock 'n' roll orchestra and six vocal groups. Scheduled was a 45-day tour of 45 cities, ending on June 3rd, but this was extended to June 5th. "Traveling will be done by bus, with the exception of plane jumps from Omaha to Denver and Denver to Dallas."

(A British dixieland band led by trumpeter Freddie Randall was, bizarrely, to join the show on May 19th as part of an exchange arrangement with the Louis Armstrong All-Stars. An advert in the *Charleston Daily Mail* declared, "Freddy Randall and his combo – first rock 'n roll from England"!)

April 1956

20	Sports Arena, Hershey, PA.
21	Warner Theatre, Atlantic City, NJ
22	The Mosque, Richmond, VA.
23	Victoria Theater, Shamokin, PA

24	Catholic Youth Center. Scranton, PA.
25	The Arena, Philadelphia, PA
26	County Center, White Plains, NY.
27	Mosque Theater, Newark, NJ.
28	War Memorial Auditorium, Syracuse, NJ.
29	The Forum, Montreal, Canada
30	Maple Leaf Gardens, Toronto, Canada

May 1956

1	Auditorium Theatre, Rochester, NY
2	Memorial Auditorium, Buffalo, NY
3	Syria Mosque, Pittsburgh, PA
4	Veterans Memorial, Columbus, OH
5	Memorial Auditorium, Canton, OH
6	Olympia Stadium, Detroit, MI
7	University Fieldhouse, Dayton, OH
8	Arena, Cleveland, OH
9	Cincinnati Gardens, Cincinnati, OH.
10	Indiana Theatre, Indianapolis, IN
11	International Amphitheatre, Chicago, IL.
12	Kiel Auditorium, St. Louis, MO
13	Music Hall, Kansas City, MO
14	Civic Auditorium Arena, Omaha, NE
15	Coliseum, Denver, CO
16	Sportatorium, Dallas, TX
17	Municipal Auditorium, San Antonio, TX
18	Civic Auditorium, Houston, TX
19	Loyola University, Baton Rouge, LA.
20	Municipal Auditorium, Birmingham, AL
21	Chattanooga, TN
22	Greensville, SC
23	Memorial Auditorium, Raleigh, NC
24	Ponce de Leon Stadium, Atlanta, GA
25	Baseball Park, Jacksonville, FL
26	Fort Hesterley Armory, Tampa, FL
27	Dinner Key Auditorium, Miami Beach, FL
28	Sports Arena, Savannah, GA
29	Coliseum, Charlotte, NC
30	Memorial Coliseum, Winston-Salem, NC
31	Township Auditorium, Columbia, SC

June 1956

| 1 | The Mosque, Richmond, VA |
| 2 | Memorial Auditorium, Norfolk, VA |

3	National Guard Armory, Washington, D.C.
4	Syria Mosque, Pittsburgh, PA
5	Municipal Auditorium, Charleston, WV

BILL HALEY

and his Comets headline the Rock 'n' Roll Show of 1956, to be presented at 7 and 10 p. m. May 19 at the Loyola field house. Also in the show are *The Platters*, Clyde McPhatter. La-Vern Baker, Big Joe Turner. The Teen-agers. T h e Teen Queens, Bo Diddley and his Combo. The Drifters. The Flamingos, The Colts and Red Prysock and his orchestra.

Times-Picayune
(New Orleans)
May 6, 1956

The April 20th appearance at the Hershey Sports Arena was advertised as the "Big Rhythm and Blues Show" with Bill Haley and Joe Turner, but also singer Roy Hamilton, while for the May 1st show the *Democrat and Chronicle* reported, under the headline "Rock 'n Roll Show Lively, But Fans on Best Behaviour," that "Five thousand persons, mostly on the sunnyside of 25 .... filled the Auditorium".

Birmingham News, May 10, 1956

On May 11th the *Indianapolis News'* report of the previous day's show contained the opinion that, "Joe Turner could as well have been left off the program as he showed little voice and mere mumbling". Contrary to this, a belated review in the *Detroit Tribune* (May 19th, 1956) states, "Turning the place into an uproar and a dance floor was the boss of the blues, Joe Turner. Yes, the place was really rocking and rolling as 230-lb Joe Turner sang with every ounce of his weight. The old as well as the young stood up and began swaying and jumping as Joe sang with his impressive style".

The opening paragraph of another short review, this time in the *San Antonio Express* (May 18th, 1956), advised, "The police were kept busy at Thursday night's rock-and-roll show, but there were no fatalities and the Municipal Auditorium still stands". It explains that the "gendarmerie .... was (there) to discourage the young audience of 6,000 from bopping in the aisles". The third time they attempted to dance was when "Joe Turner, a soloist with all the vocal volume of a quintet, began his songs after the intermission".

The day after the Birmingham performances, the *Birmingham News* published details of the picketing which took place outside the Municipal Auditorium for the afternoon show for white patrons. "The night show for Negroes was not picketed."

> "Placard-carrying pickets staged a pavement demonstration yesterday afternoon .... but some 2500 persons ignored the pickets to attend a rock-and-roll music concert. The pickets, identified as members of North Alabama Citizens Council, carried signs condemning the fast-beat music, latest craze of the nation's teenagers."

It was also reported that the Citizens Council was campaigning against be-bop and rock-and-roll, saying "the music is degrading".

Among the signs displayed were: "Jungle music promotes integration"; "Be-bop promotes Communism"; "Jungle music aids youth delinquency"; "Why Negro music"; and "Churches must speak out against these anti-Christ forces". One of the signs was carried by Jesse Mabry, who had been convicted the previous month for an assault on singer Nat 'King' Cole.

Teenagers in turn picketed the Council members with a home-made sign, "Rock and Roll is here to stay". The *Birmingham News* reported that the audience, mostly boys and girls of high school age, were wildly enthusiastic but orderly.

Look, a photo-magazine, sent a reporter and photographer to cover the "first couple of shows". A feature entitled "The great Rock 'n' Roll controversy" appeared in the June 26th issue. It included a number of photographs taken at the "Sports Arena" in Hershey, mainly of the audience but with one each of the Comets and LaVern Baker.

Jerry Fuentes has posted audience figures for many of these shows.[26] Depending on the size of the venue, audiences of between 3000 and 10,000 were typical. There was an attendance of 22,500 for the two shows in Detroit and 16,000 in Montreal. 14,000 in Charlotte and 13,000 at the Maple Leaf Gardens in Toronto were the highest for single shows. In Norfolk and Charlotte it was claimed that 5,000 teenagers were turned away. A few venues did not sell-out, for which Bill Haley blamed poor promotion. Birmingham and Chattanooga (1,200) attendances were down due to picketing by white extremists, while in Greenville the second show was cancelled after a bomb was discovered in the hall. Similarly, the second performance on May 28th in Savannah was cancelled, owing to the race relations problems.

Audiences were described at a few of the concerts as "unruly and wild" and early in the tour Bill Haley was twice assaulted as he left the stage. Another comment on a crowd was "energetic but well behaved". Some problems may have been due to an over-enthusiastic audience, rather than racially motivated. *Look* magazine claimed that many so-called riots were caused by over-crowding. "Whenever 7,000 adolescents are jammed into an auditorium which seats 5,000, there are likely to be scuffles...."

Examples of the bus journeys undertaken include, on May 10th, driving overnight from Indianapolis to Chicago, arriving there at 6:30 am; on May 14th, 540 miles from Omaha to Denver, arriving 9 am: May 15th, leaving Denver at midnight to drive 850 miles to Dallas, arriving 3 pm. (Presumably the plans to undertake the last two journeys by plane were cancelled. Too expensive? Too ambitious? An over-enthusiastic press release?)

Another example of the sheer grind of these tours: on May 18th, 1956, after two shows at the Civic Auditorium in Houston, Texas, the group left there at 1 a.m. and arrived in Baton Rouge, Louisiana, at 9:30 a.m. After sleep and refreshment, the singers and musicians performed at Loyola University, before boarding their bus at 1 a.m. for the journey to Birmingham, Alabama.

On May 24th it was a mere 330 miles from Atlanta to Jacksonville.

A combination of stubbornness, confidence and bravery must have been needed to survive a tour such as this. If the miles of travelling were not enough, the performers had to face both the threat of the Klu Klux Klan and the bigotry demonstrated in the Southern states.

Working in Florida with tenor player Choker Campbell's combo, Turner played a Mid-Summer Ball on June 11th at the South Street Casino in Orlando, followed by a gig at the Manhattan Casino in St. Petersburg on June 15th.

Another appearance in what became became a long-running association was on July 12th on Station KTTV in Los Angeles, when he was a guest on the Johnny Otis Show. Subsequently, Turner worked frequently during the next thirty years with Otis, who was a multi-instrumentalist, as well as a bandleader/showman.

Still on the West Coast Joe, with Choker Campbell and his orchestra, Turner played a dance at the Sacramento Auditorium on July 28th and at Sweet's Ballroom in Oakland on August 1st, though by August 8th he and Campbell were in Omaha, Nebraska, at the Carnation Ballroom.

Reviews of Joe Turner's appearances are rare outside the jazz field, but one more perceptive than most appeared uncredited in the *Oakland Tribune* for August 5th, 1956. Tuesday was the last day of July.

Joe Turner of K.C.

One of the great blues shouters to come out of Kansas City in its heyday as a jazz capital Joe Turner, was in Oakland last Wednesday night for an appearance at Sweet's Ballroom with Choke Jackson's band. Turner's early fame came while he was singing with pianist Pete Johnson in the Midwest and when he was featured in a Carnegie Hall concert in 1938. After some years out of the limelight he came back to public notice in the early Fifties as one of Atlantic's leading rhythm and blues artists.

"This music they call rock 'n' roll," said Turner as he waited to go on the stand, "is the same as rhythm and blues, which has been here for a long time. But it just came into wide notice the last few years. The kids like it because it has a beat you can't miss and is easy to dance to. And dancing's coming back."

Ellington Number

While we talked the band was playing an Ellington number in a relatively subdued manner. For one reason the instrumentation was different from the average rock 'n' roll group: Jackson uses a trombone and trumpet in addition to the saxes (a baritone and a tenor), and his rhythm section (piano, string bass, drums) is minus the amplified guitar which usually is considered de rigueur for an R & R group.

When Turner went on stand and began singing the band's style changed. It still played in the basic 4/4 time, but the second and fourth beats were stressed unmercifully. (It is the same weak and strong accent from which Dixieland derives its synonym of two-beat style, though in this pattern the contrast between the stresses is not so pronounced.).

The drummer was conforming to the exaggerated rhythmic pattern by hitting rim shots (in which the body of the stick strikes the metal rim of the snare drum at the same instant the tip of the stick strikes the drumhead) with his left hand, beating cymbal and tomtom with his right, operating bass drum pedal and top hat cymbals with his feet, all in this one - TWO - three - FOUR, one-TWO-three-FOUR mode.

Volume Increases

As soon as Turner had finished the first round of verse and choruses the saxes and brass stepped up their volume. They played the simple, hackneyed progressions involving the tonic, subdominant, and dominant chords, which is all this musical style permits and which is one reason so many jazz musicians deprecate it.

Meantime the pianist, who while Turner sang had been playing the typical triplet pattern near the top of the keyboard, now was working in a lower range—and harder. The bassist joined in the overstressed beat and at the same time swung his instrument as though it was a dancing partner.

Elvis Outrated

Two things were lacking which are found in the ordinary rock 'n' roll group; fortunately or unfortunately, depending upon your point of view. As mentioned, there was no guitar; had there been one the guitarist would have had its amplifier on full and its chording would be obvious. And Jackson, the tenor saxophonist, did not, at least while I was there, play the extremely distasteful, honking type of chorus which is another trademark of the best rock 'n' roll.

As for Turner, the numbers I heard were in the traditional blues pattern and he sang them honestly and with a conviction that distinguishes a great performer—a conviction which I doubt Elvis Depresley could attain if he tried a hundred years.

Oakland Tribune, August 5, 1956

Billboard in June reported that Jim Ferguson, booking agent and manager, "has brought Joe Turner under his wing. Turner and his accompanying band are scheduled to leave shortly on another Southern junket." This junket presumably included the August 13th-18th engagement at the Palms Club, in Hallendale, Florida.

On August 19th he was due to appear with pianist Art Tatum's trio, pianist Mary Lou Williams and blues shouter Jimmy Rushing as part of the Berkshire Music Barn's summer festival in Lennox.

For the nine days between August 29th and September 6th, Alan Freed's Second Anniversary Rock and Roll Show was featured at the Paramount Theater, Brooklyn, NY. with Fats Domino, Joe Turner, Frankie Lymon, The Penguins, the Alan Freed Big Rock 'n' Roll Band (including Freddie Mitchell, trumpet, Al Sears, tenor, Jimmy Wright, tenor, Panama Francis, drums) and others. "Five complete stage and screen shows will be presented daily at popular prices."

Daily News (New York), August 27, 1956

Not long after the Alan Freed show closed, Turner was on his way to Los Angeles to be filmed singing two numbers for "Shake, Rattle & Rock!" a full-length (75-minute) movie, starring Touch (later Mike) Connors. It also included two numbers by Fats Domino and his band. The musical numbers were inserted into a typical B-movie story of a school's board of governors learning to appreciate rock and roll. Turner, accompanied by Choker Campbell's band, sang *Lipstick, Powder and Paint* and *Feelin' Happy*, with the latter song also heard over the opening credits. Mark Cantor advised that production began on August 23rd, and would have lasted about two weeks. One assumes that Joe just made it.

September 9th saw Fats Domino, Big Joe Turner, The Turbans, Dakota Staton, Charlie and Ray, Gene and Eunice, appearing at Sparrow Beach in Baltimore, in the "Last Big Rock 'n' Roll Harvest Ball of the Season". Six days later, he and Choker Campbell were at the Trianon Ballroom in Indianapolis, while later that month Joe was in Cleveland, Ohio, as the final star to be booked by The Ebony Club, before it closed.

Turner and Choker Campbell were on the bill for another "Rock 'n' Roll Revue" on September 19th at the Leona Theater in Homstead (Pittsburgh), alongside the familiar names of LaVern Baker and the Moonglows, plus Carl Perkins, the Monarchs, the Turbans and the Sheppard Sisters. Only four performances during the day on this occasion.

In October, before the next blues package got rolling, Turner was featured at The Sunset in Indianapolis, alongside pianist Floyd Dixon's group. It is unfortunate that the city journals, in this case the *Indianapolis Recorder*, never gave band personnels.

The 1956 edition of the "Top Ten Review" was headlined by Little Richard, pianist and singer, along with Bill Doggett, on Hammond organ with his trio, singers Big Joe Turner, Faye Adams, Etta James, and Tommy Brown, vocal groups The Moonglows, The Five Keys, The Five Satins and The Robins, tenor player Big Jim McNeely and his Big Band.

Known dates are:

October 1956

16	Municipal Auditorium, New Orleans, LA
17	City Auditorium, Galveston, TX
19	Sportatorium, Commerce, TX
20	Municipal Auditorium, San Antonio, TX
22	Municipal Auditorium, Oklahoma City, OK
23	Municipal Auditorium, Knoxville, TN
24	Auditorium, Little Rock, AK
26	Kiel Opera House, St. Louis, MO
27	State Fairgrounds, Indianapolis, IN
28	Memorial Hall, Dayton, OH
29	Armory, Louisville, KY
30	Chilhowee Park, Knoxville, TN

November 1956

3	Auditorium, Columbia, SC
4	Auditorium, Huntsville, AL
5	Soldiers & Sailors Memorial Auditorium, Chattanooga, TN
6	Auditorium, Bluefield, WV
7	Memorial Auditorium, Raleigh, NC
8	Coliseum, Winston Salem, NC
9	Municipal Auditorium, Charleston, WV
11	The Mosque, Richmond, VA
12	Fabian Theater, Paterson, NJ
15	Legion Auditorium, Roanake, VA

Turner was in New York for a November 20th recording session for Atlantic. Of five titles cut, four were released, including *Midnight Special Train, Red Sails In The Sunset* and *Feelin' Happy*.

Three days later, the 23rd, he opened for a return week at the Howard Theater in Washington, DC. Also on the bill were the Choker Campbell band, Etta James, and the Five Satins. Following, on December 1st,, was a booking at the Green Lantern, with Choker Campbell's unit, in Anderson, Indiana.

Sometime late in 1956 Turner was in Little Rock, Arkansas. Guitarist and singer Bobby Rush recalled in his autobiography (*I Ain't Studdin' Ya: My American Blues Story*) that he first met Joe when they both appeared at the Morocco Room in Little Rock;

"Just a few years back I'd been at the Big Rec. in Pine Bluff, standing at the foot of the stage, looking up and watching Big Joe – now I was opening for him".

(Big Rec. was the popular name for the Townsend Park Recreational centre)

"Over the decades, I would get to know Big Joe better …. But what is a natural, absolute fact is that I don't think there is any other person like Big Joe Turner in history. His music life ricocheted around like silver ball in a pinball machine. Bounced from jazz to jump blues, boomeranged to R&B, and jumped right into rock 'n' roll. What most folks say is true – that there ain't no rock 'n' roll without him."

En route to New Orleans Joe, with Choker Campbell, starred at Junior Hatchett's New Orleans Room in Carbondale, Illinois, on December 22nd, The following day he was in the Crescent City, singing at the Labor Union Hall.

Corrine Corrina was claimed to be his fourth million seller. It was in *Billboard*'s R&B chart for ten weeks, reaching number 3. It even entered the pop chart, The Top 100, for seven weeks, climbing to number 43. *Lipstick, Powder and Paint* (coupled with *Rock A While*) spent only two weeks, reaching 12 in the R&B chart..

In the *Down Beat* R&B Personality of the Year Readers' poll Joe came second to Fats Domino. In the Male Singer section he came 14th with 52 votes; Bing Crosby was 13th with 69!

12

"'Long as it sounds good"

(1957-1961)

1957

A rock'n' roll package, again headlined by Bill Haley and his Comets, with Joe Turner in the cast, toured Australia in January, 1957. Also featured were LaVern Baker, The Platters, and Freddie Bell and the Bellboys. *Billboard* reported that the party emplaned on January 3rd and would have a three-day stopover in Manila, but the itinerary given in John Swanson's biography of Bill Haley is more detailed. Leaving on January 1st, the singers flew from Philadelphia to Chicago, then took the train to Los Angeles. From L.A. they flew to Australia, with refuelling stops in Hawaii, Canton (sometimes Kanton) and Fiji. Arriving in Sydney on January 6th, their engagements were:

January 1957

8	Newcastle Stadium, Newcastle, New South Wales
9/10	Brisbane Stadium, Brisbane, Queensland
11/12	Tivoli Theatre, Adelaide, South Australia
14/15/16	West Melbourne Stadium, Melbourne, New South Wales
17/18/19	Sydney Stadium, Sydney, New South Wales
21/22/23	West Melbourne Stadium, Melbourne, New South Wales
24/25/26	Sydney Stadium, Sydney, New South Wales

An item in *The Pittsburgh Courier* (August 10th, 1957) quotes Jerry Wexler extolling, with a sadly incorrect prophecy, the "Joe Turner Sings Kansas City Jazz" album - ".... is destined to be Turner's best seller of all time". The *Courier* writer then indulges in purple prose about the Australian tour "last year" (sic).

> ".... he enjoyed unprecedented success on a tour of Australia where streets were renamed in his honor, mayors of various towns greeted him, and he was also made an honorary citizen of the Down Under country".

It is of course possible that some mayors did greet Bill Haley and all the other artists.

On returning to California, Joe played an engagement with Riff Ruffin, vocal and guitar, at the 54 Ballroom in Hollywood, but some dates in the San Francisco area were postponed. They were replaced by bookings in the South. It was also around this time that he had new representation, the Jolly Joyce Theatrical Agency, who also booked Bill Haley.

"Shake, Rattle & Rock!".

The Southern tour included:

February 1957

6   Rusty's Playhouse, El Paso, Texas (with Jimmy McCracklin & his Orchestra)

9   Lubbock, Texas, ('Big Joe Turner and his Band')

22   Regal, South Parkway, Chicago, for one week, "Al Benson's Rock 'n' Roll Rhythm and Blues Review, featuring Big Joe Turner, 'Daddy of the Rock 'n' Roll Beat'" Also appearing were Arthur Prysock, The Spaniels and altoist Tab Smith's band. Attendance for the week was given as 31, 750.

         (In an advert. in the *Chicago Tribune* for February 24, The Spaniels are replaced by Screamin' Jay Hawkins, while *Billboard* listed Hawkins and Brook Benton.)

26   Club Louisiana, Baton Rouge, Louisiana

March 1957

1   Colonial Theatre, Milwaukee, Wisconsin (with Al Smith's Orchestra)

2   Kentucky Center, Louisville, Kentucky, with Dorothy Ann Ferguson & others.

10   Slavonian Lodge, Biloxi, Mississippi

16   EM Club, Newport, Rhode Island

22   Manhattan Casino, St. Petersburg, Florida (with Choker Campbell Orchestra)

Shake, Rattle & Rock!

May engagements included one on the 11th at Frolics Ballroom, in Allentown, Pennsylvania, a recording session for Atlantic in New York on the 13th, one week at the Casino Royal, Washington, D.C., (though this may have been in June) and an appearance on the 30th at Sparrow's Beach, Annapolis, Maryland. From the 31st he and Choker Campbell had a week's engagement at the Howard Theatre (presumably Washington, DC, also), alongside, among others, Bo Diddley and The Moonglows.

The Atlantic session was with Choker Campbell's septet. Five titles were made, including *Trouble In Mind* and *World of Trouble*. The latter title, coupled with *Love Roller Coaster*, was released the week of June 10th.

June 1957

17   Roberts Show Club, 6622 South Parkway, Chicago, for one week, Big Joe Turner and a complete new show.

24   Planters Warehouse No. 2, Rocky Mount, North Carolina, dance with Joe Turner, Illinois Jacquet, and Choker Campbell.

July 1957

1   Palisades Park, New York, Johnny Mathis, plus Joe Turner.

3   Alan Freed's Rock 'n' Roll Summer Festival, Paramount Theatre, New York, with Chuck Berry, LaVern Baker, Clyde McPhatter and, among others, Joe Turner.

At the end of July he and Campbell, with "lovely Vikki Nelson" and "Torrid Zelma Frazier," and The Pearls were in a "Rock'n'Roll Revue" at the Hippodrome in Richmond, West Virginia. The advertisement for the show gives no indication if this was for one night or longer.

There was a variation to the routine on August 1st. On this occasion Joe and Choker Campbell were the stars of a "White Rock-Roll Dance" at the Auditorium in Bluefield, West Virginia. Admission was $2.00, Colored Spectators $1.00.

On August 13th they were at the Progressive Men's Club in Monroe, Louisiana, on the 15th at the Harvest Club in Beaumont, Texas and on the 22nd they played a dance in Wichita Falls, Texas. There was also an August booking in Denver, listed in *Billboard* without details.

"King of the Blues, Big Joe Turner" was advertised at the Key Club in Birmingham, Alabama, presumably with Campbell, on September 9th, but this same date is quoted for Turner, plus Choker Campbell and his Big Orchestra, playing at O.J.'s Half Acre in Huntsville, Alabama. The singer and Choker Campbell were still together for a dance in the Masonic Hall in Milwaukee on September 21.

Another recording session for Atlantic was held on October 2nd in New York. Four titles were made, of which two were issued, *Teen Age Letter* and *Wee Baby Blues*. When this coupling appeared, *Billboard* excitedly reported,

> "If, when you dig Turner's two sides, you think the pianistics are great, you're absolutely right. On *Teenage Letter* you'll be listening to the crazy fingering of hit-writer Mike Stoller and on *Wee Baby Blues* it's none other than the great Ray Charles."

(Stoller thought it was "quite an honour" to play on his track.)

Atlantic released four Joe Turner records during the year:
the week of March 16,   *Red Sails In The Sunset/After A While*, Atlantic 1131
the week of June 10,   *Love Roller Coaster/World of Trouble*, Atlantic 1146
the week of September 9, *I Need A Girl/Trouble In Mind*,   Atlantic 1155
the week of December 2, *Teen Age Letter/Wee Baby Blues*,   Atlantic 1167

Cash Box, December 28, 1957 (courtesy of Phil Wight.)

During October 1957 Joe was part of "The Fantabulous Rock 'N Roll Show of '57" blues package, alongside Mickey and Sylvia, Annie Laurie, Larry Williams' Band, Bo Diddley's trio, Roy Brown, The Moonglows and others, plus the Ray Charles Orchestra. During the tour there were some variations to the show's name and artists tended to come and go, though Turner is advertised consistently.. Known dates are:

October 1957

4	Roanoke, VA
5	Township Auditorium, Columbia, SC
6	Auditorium, Bluefield, WV
10	The Mosque, Pittsburgh, PA
11	Memorial Auditorium, Raleigh, NC
13	The Mosque, Richmond, VA
15	Bell Auditorium, Augusta, GA
16	War Memorial Auditorium, Nashville, TN
17	Coliseum, Winston-Salem, NC
23	New City Auditorium, Columbus, GA
27	City Auditorium, Birmingham, AL
30	North Side Coliseum, Fort Worth, TX

November 1957

1	Sportatorium, Dallas, TX
2	Coliseum, Waco, TX
5	Liberty Hall, El Paso, TX
6	Sports Center, Tucson, AZ
11	Coliseum, Evansville, IN
12	Cincinnati Garden, Hamilton, OH
14	Tomlinson Hall, Indianapolis, IN
16	Hobart Arena, Troy, OH

Come December there was a weekend jazz tour, 'A Dizzy Evening with Sarah'. Sarah Vaughan was the headliner, with Dizzy Gillespie and his Big Band, Art Blakey and his Jazz Messengers, and Joe Turner as the male singer. Three dates in

December 1957

6	Academy of Music, Philadelphia, PA
7	State Theater, Hartford, CT
8	Mechanics Building, Boston, MA

Turner's dates for December included an appearance in a "Big Stage Show!" at the Booker T. in Richmond, Virginia, with the Five Keys, Vikki Nelson, shake dancer and Choker Campbell. The 'Big Stage Show' possibly ran for one week from December 12th. Then Big Joe, with the Paul Williams' Band, played a

Christmas Day dance at the Memorial Auditorium in Raleigh, North Carolina, followed by the Durham Armory on the 27th.

Joe was little featured in the 1957 polls of *Down Beat* or *Playboy*, though he was voted to third place in the *Melody Maker*'s critics' poll. His 'The Boss of the Blues' album for Atlantic was selected sixth in the Top 20 Jazz Records of 1957 in the *Jazz Journal* annual poll.

1958

1958 began with a New Year's Day show and dance by Turner and Williams at the Auditorium in Bluefield, West Virginia. His only Atlantic session for the year was on January 22nd, when five titles were recorded, with two remaining unissued. This was followed by a week's booking at the Apollo Theatre, commencing Friday, January 31st. Turner was the headliner, the bill also including Tiny Topsy, Lee Allen, The Five Satins and Choker Campbell.

Then it was off to the West Coast, as *Billboard* reported, "Ruth Brown, Joe Turner and Paul Williams will tour California for five or six weeks beginning mid-February." Known dates for the tour are:

February 1958
14   Harmony Gardens, Bakersfield, CA
19   Sweets Ballroom, Bakersfield, CA

March 1958
1   The Eagles Ballroom, Seattle, WA
2   Evergreen Ballroom, Tacoma, WA
10   Elks Auditorium, Los Angeles, CA

The tour, which ended on the 10th, also included bookings in San Francisco, Sacramento and Portland. Paul Williams and his Orchestra featured singer Bobby Parker.

Don Albert was a well regarded trumpet player and bandleader. In 1958 he was running the Keynote Club in San Antonio, Texas, when Turner played there the night of March 19th. Next known are four days at the New Cotton Club, April 18th-21st, in Indianapolis and a one-nighter, April 25th, at the Famous Cafeteria, Sheffield, Alabama.

The *New York Amsterdam News* for June 7th has a photo of Joe Turner and Pete Johnson being handed their tickets by Sammy Price as they board their flight to Europe for a two-week tour, starting at the Brussels World Fair. There is no mention that this is actually a tour by Jazz at the Philharmonic.

The JATP tour was part two of one which started in London on May 3rd, with Ella Fitzgerald and Oscar Peterson. When these stars began solo tours, the remaining musicians, Dizzy Gillespie, Roy Eldridge, trumpets, Coleman Hawkins, Stan Getz, Sonny Stitt, tenors, Herb Ellis, guitar, Ray Brown, bass, and Gus Johnson, drums, were joined by Turner and Johnson.

The itinerary included:

May 1958
19	Theatre du Cirque Royal, Brussels, Belgium
20	Konzerthus Stockholm, Sweden
??	Copenhagen, Denmark
??	Oslo, Norway
24	Kurhaus, Scheveningen, The Netherlands and Concertgebouw, Amsterdam, The Netherlands
26	Tieatro Sistina, Rome, Italy
28	Stuttgart, Germany
29	Munich, Germany
30	Berlin, Germany
31	Hamburg, Germany

June 1958
1	Festhalle, Frankfurt, Germany
2	Zurich, Switzerland
3	Alhambra, Paris, France

The May 20th concert was recorded by Sveriges Radio and a half-hour segment can be heard on pastdaily.com. It ends with Turner singing *Wee Wee Baby*, accompanied by the rhythm section and a dash of Sonny Stitt.

Two titles from the Zurich concert, *I Want A Little Girl* and *St. Louis Blues*, with Roy Eldridge, trumpet, Sonny Stitt, alto, Johnson, piano, Herb Ellis, guitar, Max Bennett, bass, and Gus Johnson, drums, have circulated on tape. *Cherry Red* from the final Paris concert, with Stitt on tenor and Eldridge omitted, is on a Sunset Boulevard CD.

Joe Turner, left and Pete Johnson, right, in Milan, Italy, May 1958, with unidentified fan.

Blues collector Dimitri Wischnegradsky (Jacques Demetre) was disappointed by Turner and Johnson's performance at the June 3rd concert at the Alhambra in Paris. They "played only two or three tunes, not very well and they did not impress the public .... they were a little drunk and did not give their best. After [the concert] we (Pete, Joe, Kurt Mohr and me) spent the whole night at my home, listening to records and asking questions.[1]

Pete Johnson and Joe Turner in Paris, May 1958. photograph courtesy of Jacques Demetre

Following the Brussels concert, collector Yannick Bruynoghe invited Turner, Johnson, Coleman Hawkins and Roy Eldridge to his home, but conversation with Turner was inhibited because of the presence of Hawkins and Eldridge.

> "Hawk considered Turner as a 'country square' in a certain way - who didn't even have a tuxedo with him for such a tour." Turner said he did not like the accompaniment of "this guy on tenor - what's his name - Johnny Stitt, isn't it?"[2]

Kurt Mohr gained one or two interesting details about the singer's recordings for National and no doubt felt that his conversation with Turner was more informative than Yannick Bruynoghe did about his. The former recalled, ".... Joe couldn't clearly remember personnels for each sesion and only ventured a few names of which he was sure,"[3] namely the reaction which discographers appreciate. Bruynoghe's comment was, "He was unable to recognize any accompanying musician - apparently not interested."[4]

A concert at the Tieatro Sistina in Rome on May 26th proved to be a fiasco, caused by promoter Norman Granz' error of judgement, or arrogance, as has been suggested. That evening he had dinner with Sophia Loren and her sister, Maria Scicolone but, perhaps understandably, lingered over the meal. Assuming that a tardy Italian audience would delay the JATP performance, he arrived late at the theatre, starting the concert an hour after the scheduled time. The paying customers were furious. There were boos and paper missiles. The concert was cancelled after Stan Getz had played his set and Dizzy Gillespie had struggled through one number. Joe Turner and Pete Johnson did not perform. And ticket money was refunded.[5]

Another Jacques Demetre photograph of Joe Turner in Paris, 1958

The other side of Granz is found in this quotation from his biography,

"I've always funded everything myself. And I think it gave me more latitude in the end to do anything that I wanted, even touring those artists who didn't make money. I could take a Joe Turner on tour because I like to hear Joe sing."

This appreciation would be a partial explanation for the numerous recording sessions, on his Pablo label, which Granz arranged for the singer towards the end of his career.[6]

When Val Wilmer visited Turner in 1976 Joe had a new green Cadillac "a present – against royalties, no doubt - from Pablo boss, Norman Granz".[7]

The few known June dates include, in Florida, the 23rd, at the Patio Club in Orlando; the 27th, when Joe and the Choker Campbell Band played the Manhattan Casino in St. Petersburg; and the 28th, when Joe was part of a show at the Municipal Auditorium in Tampa.

Joe Turner at the Newport Jazz Festival, July 5, 1958. Pete Johnson, piano, Jack Teagarden, trombone

On July 5th Joe appeared at the Newport Jazz Festival for the Saturday evening concert, which was entitled "Blues in the Night". He worked with an all-star Newport Blues Band, Buck Clayton, trumpet, Jack Teagarden, trombone, Tony Scott, clarinet, George Auld, Buddy Tate and Rudy Rutherford, reeds, Pete Johnson, piano Kenny Burrell, guitar, Tommy Bryant, bass, and Jo Jones, drums. The Phontastic CD-issue of Newport 1958 has Turner performing *Feeling Happy, Corrine, Corrina, Honey Hush* and *Shake, Rattle and Roll.*

An all-star grouping does not necessarily make an ideal accompaniment. Nat Hentoff wrote,

"Saturday night was the controversial blues evening, John Hammond - associate producer .... Joe Turner came on, backed by a band so mixed in styles and so under-rehearsed that he would have been better helped by rhythm section alone. Joe was a commanding spirit, but his repertory could have been better selected - again no planning - with less of his r&b hits."[8]

A long report in a July *Billboard* said very much the same as Hentoff. It praised the singers (Joe Turner, Chuck Berry, Ray Charles, Big Maybelle - "they performed splendidly"), but deplored their choice of material and the inappropriateness of the all-star band. In the *San Francisco Chronicle*, Ralph J. Gleason singled out Turner, writing, "The only really satisfactory moment came when Joe Turner took over."[9]

Saturday afternoon, July 19th, Big Joe Turner, Pete Johnson and Mary Lou Williams were featured in a program of Kansas City Jazz at the Berkshire Music Barn in Lenox, Massachusetts.

There was a television appearance on July 24th for WNTA-TV in New York. He was featured on the Art Ford Jazz Party, alongside a ten-piece band which included Max Kaminsky, trumpet, Bud Freeman, tenor, Herb Hall, clarinet, Stuff Smith, violin, and Johnny Guarnieri, piano. He sang *Exactly Like You, Low Down Dog* and an untitled blues, later given the title *Joe Turner Blues*.

Two days later he was at the Great South Bay Festival on Long Island, N.Y. His accompaniment here was by the South Bay Seven, including Rex Stewart, cornet, Benny Morton, trombone, Garvin Bushell, clarinet, and Dick Cary, piano. His song-list differed from his customary "best of my Atlantic hits"; it included *Baby Blues, Roll 'Em Pete, Red Sails in the Sunset, Pennies from Heaven*, and *Don't Get Around Much Anymore*.

In August he was the headliner at the Forest Theater in Dallas on the 8th and at the Rainbow Room in Monroe, Louisiana, on the 28th (with Bill Harvey and Orchestra). Then for September , the Shaw Artists Agency was arranging a series on engagements on the West Coast.

Three dates with vocal group The Midnighters and Carl Green and his Orchestra have been located, on September 19th at the Eagles Ballroom, Seattle, WA, on the 20th at the Palais Royale, Portland, OR, and on the 21st at the Evergreen Ballroom, Tacoma, WA. One other date, September 25th, at the Harmony Gardens in Bakersfield, had a very promising partnership on offer with Turner joining altoist Louis Jordan and his Tympany Five.

Known engagements for the remainder of the year number just two, October 10th at the Uak Bowl (University of Arkansas), Fayettville, AK and November 5th with Earl King and his Orchestra, at Club La Louisiane, New Iberia, LA.

The *Down Beat* polls for the year were published in October and December. The Critics Poll had Turner fourth in the Singers section, while the Readers voted him fourth in the R&B Personalities of the Year. (Ray Charles, Joe Williams and Fats Domino were ahead of him.)

An article in *Down Beat*, echoing the *Ebony* piece of 1954, told something of Turner's home life in 1958:

"These days, when Turner isn't on the road, he lives with his wife (Lou Willie) in an impressive brick home in Chicago. He drives a late model Cadillac; his wife drives a new Pontiac. (She) is a restraining influence on the blues singer. She has invested his income judiciously; the Turners own an apartment building and have paid off the mortgage on their luxurious home. Mrs Turner spends much of her time answering her husband's mail, which averages 50 letters each week."[10]

In the same article, by Frank London Brown, Turner is quoted saying:

"The nicest thing that ever happened to me was when I married my wife. It took the wind out of my sails. I was a pretty jumpy cat. I wouldn't let the grass grow under my feet. I was real nervous. It took a little while for me to realize that when you get married, you have to cool down."

No doubt it was this Chicago period to which Joe was referring when he told Peter Guralnick,

"I had two cooks, one bottle washer and one chauffeur wherever I travelled. I had four cats to help me with my clothes on, help me with my clothes off, and help themselves to my money."[11]

Published in 1958, *The Real Cool Killers*, a novel by Chester Himes, opens with a blues verse and we are told that Big Joe Turner is singing a rock-and-roll adaptation of *Dink's Blues*, with the "rhythm blasted from the jukebox with enough heat to melt bones"!

1959

The lack of press coverage during this year may have been because Turner was taking time off after a busy 1958 or perhaps he was touring away from the major cities. Another consideration is that his importance in the rock 'n' roll charts was waning, though he did have a recording session for Atlantic in New York on June 18th which produced a nice version of *Careless Love*.

Joe was at Don Albert's Keynote Club in San Antonio on January 13, then all is silence until May, when he did some touring with Roscoe Gordon's Band. On the 9th they appeared at the Delta Tau Delta Fraternity's Arabian Night party in Tallahassee, Florida, the 15th at the Manhattan Casino, in St. Petersburg, Florida and the 29th at the Municipal Auditorium in Charleston, West Virginia.

For one week, commencing June 5th he was part of a "Rock & Rave!" show at the Howard Theatre in Washington, D.C., which also included singers The Skyliners, The Shirelles, The Heartbeats, Bobby Hendricks, Gloria Jean and

Rick Henderson's All Stars. He broadcast on the Alan Freed Show from New Jersey on June 20th, but by July he was in Texas, appearing at the Pink Derby in Fort Worth on July 31st and August 1st.

The *Chicago Defender* for Friday, September 5th included an advertisement for a "Sox Review" at Roberts Show Club at 6620 South Parkway, with an Extra Added Attraction, Friday and Saturday only, Big Joe Turner.

He was back in New York for three Atlantic recording sessions on September 9th, 10th and 29th. The first two were for a follow-up album to the critically acclaimed "The Boss of the Blues".

It was called "Big Joe Rides Again", though the accompaniments were not as assured as on the first album. Pete Johnson was absent on piano, no doubt due to illness, and his replacement, Jimmy Jones, was not the most suitable. As that discerning critic Stanley Dance wrote in *Jazz Journal* when reviewing "the second unsatisfactory Atlantic LP," ".... but there is still the great voice to be savoured".

The September 29th date included remakes, with a string section and vocal group, of *Chains of Love* and *Honey Hush*, the latter reaching number 53 in the *Billboard* Hot 100 listing.

In October he had three nights, 10th, 11th and 12th, at the Celebrity Club in Providence, Rhode Island, while on November 26th he had a repeat appearance at the Pink Derby in Forth Worth, Texas.

Of uncertain date, but probably from the late 1950s, was the following appearance, recalled by collector Paul Garon, who was living in Louisville, Kentucky at the time.

> "I saw Joe Turner several years ago at a colored dance at a National Guard Armory. He mostly did his Atlantic stuff, *Honey Hush*, *Corrine Corrina*, *Chains of Love*, etc. It was monotonous because the little combo he had with him played the rhythm from Bill Doggett's *Honky Tonk* for every song; but Big Joe was still Big Joe, so it was a pretty good dance."[12]

Garon's comment on Turner's programme, combined with the criticism of his 1958 Newport Jazz Festival appearance, confirms that Joe was already restricting himself to the hit songs he thought his audiences wanted to hear, a habit he continued throughout the rest of his life.

As Turner was always himself on stage, his rich voice booming out, always worth hearing, always swinging, so the overall quality of any session or concert depended upon the suitability of the accompanying musicians. They needed to know the style and the beat that suited him. It was not always the best jazz players who provided the right backing. Is it sacrilege to suggest that Turner felt more at home with Bill Haley and his Comets than with some of the star-studded groups that Norman Granz and others selected?

On this subject, Turner said

> .... I have learned how to adjust myself with other things. All I want to do is if it get the good beat. They play halfway rock 'n' roll, I got it and gone.

I ain't too hard to please. Other people out there pull all their music out
.... but I carry mine in my head, what I want to do .... I can start singin'
and sing for an hour or two, never sing the same verse twice .... Guess I
learned that from the old-timers. Long as it sounds good.[13]

The singer expressed his opinions on his style and his part in the rock and roll
era during several interviews:

"Rock and roll is not something new, as many think. We have seen a lot
of new ideas applied lately but rock and roll gets its basic from what used
to be called 'rhythm and blues' and that has been here a long time. It is
true that it is new to many people and it has won them over because it
furnished something missing in popular music."[14]

On another occasion Joe said, "It wasn't but a different name for the same
music I been singing all my life".[15] Or, "This rock 'n' roll is nothing new. It's the
same as I've been singing since 1936 in Kansas City"[16]
And to Peter Guralnick he said,

"Doing blues was a kick. I just do it different. Most people sing blues slow
and draggy-like, but I put the beat to it. I've sung the blues all over the
world and I always got a good response. I never changed my style ever
since I started in to singing. I been in the same style all my life."[17]

Or to put it another way,

"I originated that style myself. Everybody was singing slow blues when I
was young and I'd thought I'd put a beat to it and sing it up tempo. Pete
Johnson and I got together and we worked at that for a long time and we
finally got pretty good at it. We used to do it in a nightclub and it went
over so good we just kept it up".[18]

Asked in 1956 how he liked being a rock 'n' roll star, he quipped,

"Rock 'n' roll? Hell, I've been singing the same thing for the last twenty-
eight years under different names, and I hope to go on singing it for
twenty-eight more!"[19]

Down Beat's Readers' Poll had Turner in 20th position in the Male Singer
slot and eighth in the R&B Personality Poll.

1960

There were no recordings for Atlantic in 1960, a confirmation perhaps that
his time with that company was running short.

"Frequently worked club dates, New Orleans, LA. Early 60s" is how *Blues
Who's Who* summarises this period in Turner's career, though a few more
appearances during 1960 are now known.

A booking at Jack's Place in Fort Worth on January 2nd was advertised as
a Battle of the Blues with Jimmy Nelson, and on the 22nd he was due to sing,

with his band (sic), at the Catholic Youth Organization Center in Baton Rouge, Louisiana, for the weekly teen-age dance. "Anyone wearing blue jeans will be denied entry. The dance will be well-chaperoned."

In April he was part of another package tour by "The Biggest Show of Stars for 1960 (Spring edition)". He was low man on the totem pole behind Lloyd Price, Clyde McPhatter, The Coasters, Bo Diddley, LaVern Baker, and others.

Known dates are:

April 1960
17	The Mosque, Richmond, VA
19	Memorial Auditorium, Greenville, SC
20	War Memorial Auditorium, Greensboro, NC
21	Reynolds Coliseum, Raleigh, NC
22	Bell Auditorium, Augusta, GA
24	Municipal Auditorium, New Orleans, LA
25	Robinson Auditorium, Little Rock, TX
26	College Park Auditorium, Jackson, MS
28	Auditorium, Atlanta, GA
29	Municipal Auditorium, Columbus, GA
30	Auditorium, Columbia, SC

May 1960
1	Auditorium, Birmingham, AL
2	Chattanooga, TN
?	Sulphur Dell, Nashville, TN
6	Municipal Auditorium, San Antonio, TX
10	Auditorium, Lubbock, TX
11	Municipal Auditorium, Oklahoma City, OK
13	Municipal Auditorium, Kansas City, MO
15	Kiel Auditorium, St. Louis, MO
17	Orpheum Theatre, Madison WI
19	Indiana Theater, Indianapolis, IN
21	Freedom Hall, Louisville KY
23	Graystone Ballroom, Detroit, MI
24	Canton Memorial Auditorium, New Philadelphia, OH
25	Syria Mosque, Pittsburgh, PA
26	Stambaugh Auditorium, Youngstown, OH
30	Sparrow's Beach, Annapolis, MD

The May 6th date clashes with an appearance, reported on the Setlists website, at the University of North Carolina, Chapel Hill, NC.

The May 8th edition of *The Tennessean*, of Nashville, carried a news story that 'The Biggest Show of Stars' had appeared "last week" at the Sulphur Dell. There was an attendance of about 8,000, with the reporter estimating that 60%

were white, of whom two-thirds were young men. There was a brief mention of the performers.

Turner was back in Texas at the end of June, appearing at the Skyliner Ballroom in Fort Worth on the 24th and the Club Riviera in Corpus Christi on the 30th.

In July Joe was in New York, then Chicago. In the first city he was at the Jazz Gallery from July 12th to 18th. In Chicago, from July 22th for one week, he was part of Al Benson's 'Rhythm and Blues, Rock 'n' Roll Star Parade' at the Regal theater, 4719 South Parkway. The other acts included Larry Darnell, Screamin' Jay Hawkins, Ben E. King, Faye Adams, Gene Ammons' Quintet and Red Prysock's Orchestra.

Some of the above details are from *The Chicago Defender* for July 9th and 23rd, and the *Chicago Tribune*, July 17th and 26th, though these reports only confirm that details can vary from paper to paper. The *Defender*, for example, quotes the show as starting on July 23rd, the *Tribune* on the more likely 22nd. The *Defender* reported that the 'All-New Rhythm & Blues Rock'n'Roll Star Parade' would play two weeks at the Regal, the first commencing July 9th with Joe Turner and a similar cast. Such a booking would have clashed with Joe's stay at the Jazz Gallery, as given in *Down Beat*, and does not seem to have been mentioned by the *Chicago Tribune*.

A show, which was due to run from 9:30 pm to 2:00 am, headlined by Dakota Staton, together with The Coasters, Joe Turner, Little Walter, and Sir (sic) John Lee Hooker, appeared at the Windsor Arena in Detroit on the Tuesday evening. The next morning's news story was not the one which the performers and producers had hoped for.

"Jazz Fans Battle Police in Windsor" was the headline in the *Detroit Times* for Wednesday, August 3rd. The continuation on another page was titled, "RIOT: 40 Injured In Windsor Melee," stating that 5,000 fans rioted and that there were three stabbing victims. Fighting had broken out sometime after midnight, said to be between rival gangs, there was a rush for the exits, and chaos ensued.

In September Turner was part of another package tour, this one called the 'The Lucky "7" Blues Show', with Jerry Butler, Billy Bland, Bobby Peterson, his electric piano and Orchestra, and Roscoe Gordon and his Orchestra. Again, known dates are:

September 1960
24	Municipal Auditorium, Charleston, WV
30	Coliseum, Evansville, IN

October 1960
1	Freedom Hall, Exposition Center, Louisville KY
2	Skatemoor Arena, Dayton, OH

Unusually, Joe was part of a show scheduled for a ten-day run at the Uptown Theater in Philadelphia, commencing October 7th. Also on the bill were Sonny Boy Williamson, The Bobettes, Screaming Jay Hawkins, Billy Massey and his Rock and Blue Orchestra, "and 10 beautiful dancing girls". Joe Turner "and his Orchestra" were at the Riviera Club in Corpus Christi for an October 21st appearance, while on October 31st he starred at a Halloween Dance at the M-B Corral in Wichita Falls, Texas, with the Alfred Braggs Orchestra.

On November 19th he featured at a dance, unknown location in Tampa Bay, Florida.

Down Beat for September 1st, 1960 reported that Joe Turner was "being sent on a tour abroad in November" but nothing further was heard of this.

1961

Information for this year is even scantier. On February 3rd, with the Rocking Shadows, Turner was at the M-B Corral in Wichita Falls, Texas, and at the end of that month he was in New Orleans to record his penultimate session for Atlantic, on the 28th. Five titles were made, including a two-part version of *Lucille*, but all remain unissued. He was in Phoenix, Arizona, on March 10th, for a gig at The Elk's Club, while the 17th he appeared at the Pacific Ballroom in San Diego, California, and in June he was playing one-nighters in the San Francisco area. including a gig at the Salinas Armory on June 2nd, with Freddy King and the Jimmy Norman Orchestra. An "early 1960s" appearance at the Five-Four Ballroom in Los Angeles is listed in *Blues Who's Who*.

In August Joe was back in Texas, including an appearance at The Tiffany Lounge in San Antonio on the 11th and in September he had a one week booking, alongside singer Lula Reed, at the Club 20 Grand in Detroit. A known date for October was the 26th at Perry's Danceland in Greensboro, North Carolina.

November found him in Chicago for one week from the 10th, singing at the Regal in a show entitled "Varieties of 1962". The cast of 40 included Christine Kittrell, Gene Miller, Jimmy Jones, The Sensations, The Clovers, The Vibrations and the orchestras of Arthur Prysock and Red Saunders.

An indication of the mutual benefit which Joe Turner and Atlantic Records derived from their association can be found in the number of hit recordings that Joe contributed to the company's catalogue.

Between 1951 and 1956 Joe Turner was featured regularly in the *Billboard* rhythm-and-blues charts, often in all three; Best Sellers In Stores (BSIS), Most Played By Jockeys (MPJ), and Most Played in Juke Boxes (MPJB). Starting with *Chains of Love* (25 weeks, reaching number 2), others with appearances in the Best Sellers in Stores charts were *Sweet Sixteen; Honey Hush* (25 weeks, reaching number 2, and (MPJ) 20 weeks, including 8 weeks at number 1); *TV Mama; Shake, Rattle and Roll* (27 weeks, peaking at number 3, and (MPJ) 33 weeks, reaching number 2); *Flip, Flop and Fly* (14 weeks, reaching number 3, as well as number 2 in MPJB).

Midnight Cannonball was number 11 (BSIS) and 3 (MPJB); *Morning, Noon and Night,* 7 (BSIS), 8 (MPJ); *The Chicken and the Hawk,* 7 (BSIS); *Corrine, Corrina,* 10 weeks, number 2, (BSIS), 8 weeks, number 2 (MPJ), 10 weeks, number 2 (MPJB); *Lipstick, Powder and Paint*, 8 (BSIS); *Jump For Joy* (15, MPJ). *Jump for Joy* was the final entry into the r&b charts, but it was *Corrine, Corrina* which achieved the uncertain distinction of entering the Top 100 (the pop charts) for 7 weeks, reaching number 43. The re-recorded version of *Honey Hush* also made a brief entry into the Top 100, at number 53.

It has been reported that Turner had several hits (including *Chains of Love*, *Honey Hush*, *Flip, Flop and Fly*, *Corrine Corrina*) which sold a million copies, though Nesuhi Ertegun, in a letter dated July 25th, 1963, was rather more conservative. He commented

> "Let me tell you, however, that when Joe Turner was very popular, his big hits sold in the hundreds of thousands: I would say that sales of his singles were between 50,000 and 200,000, unless the record was a flop. On the other hand, the 'Boss of the Blues' LP had very disappointing sales, under 15,000."

It seems fitting that this chapter should close as Big Joe Turner's association with Atlantic Records ended. His final session for the company was again in New Orleans, on May 31st, 1962, when he recorded four titles, though none was released. Ironically, the very last title made to mark his decade with Atlantic was *The Party's Over*.

13

"That's what it takes today, daddy"

(1962-1968)

1962

January found Turner again touring down Texas way. He was in a package entitled "Stars of '62". Chuck Berry was top of the bill, together with Bobby Hendricks, The Original Drifters, Ernie K-Doe and Gene and the Blue Aces. The known dates are:

January 1962

19	City Auditorium, Big Spring, TX
20	Floyd Gwin Auditorium, Odessa, TX
21	Coliseum, El Paso, TX
22	Civic Auditorium, Albuquerque, NM
25	Coliseum, Corpus Christi, TX
27	National Guard Armory, McAllen, TX
28	V.F.W. Hall, Alice, TX

During February he had a solo engagement at the Eastwood Country Club in San Antonio, Texas, and in March *The Pittsburgh Courier* reported that he was making headlines at the Dew Drop Inn in New Orleans, with vibraphonist Pete Diggs, exotic Ethel Kidd and Patsy Valder, female impersonator.

In April he was back in Texas. On the 12th he was at The Red Lion Club in Beaumont, while on Friday the 13th he was booked for the student party-dance as part of SMU's "Wild Weekend," in Dallas.

No other bookings have been traced until September, when he seems to have been on another extended tour of the South. On the 17th he opened the "all new" Peppermint Lounge in Shreveport, Louisiana, with a one week engagement and on October 5th he headlined on the Negro Day at the Gregg County Fair. He was back at The Red Lion Club in Beaumont, Texas, on October 25

An entry in *The Illustrated Encyclopedia of Jazz* includes, ".... in 1962 played a residency at Las Calvados, a Parisian club." There is no confirmation that Turner visited Europe in this year, so one can only conjecture that it was Joe Turner the pianist who played the club.

This was a year of mixed fortune, with one happy event followed by a serious mishap.

It is not clear when Joe married again, nor when the separation from Lou Willie took place, though re-marry he did. Born in 1922, Geraldine Brown had previously been Mrs. (Wilmot) Francois. In a 1964 letter Joe spoke of being married twice; and that his present wife was Mrs Geraldine Beaux Turner.[1]

Turner had been living at 7654 Calumet Avenue in Chicago but moved to New Orleans, Geraldine's hometown. Their address was 4 Marlborough Gate, New Orleans, Louisiana 70115.

Big Joe Turner

Mrs. Geraldine Turner

No 4 Marlborough Gate

New Orleans 15, La.   **Ph. 891-1807**

Then, in November, Joe had his serious accident. To quote Turner, "I'd had a fall November 1962 which kept me incapacitated late in 1963. My leg was broken in two places, which called for surgery. OK now."[2]

A report from New Orleans in *The Pittsburgh Courier* of December 15, 1962, advised that "A galaxy of entertainers and musicians are pooling their talents for a gigantic Benefit Show for ailing Big Joe Turner .... Joe, now living in the Crescent City, was injured in an accident recently." The benefit was to be held in the Dew Drop Inn on December 17th.

1963

Surprisingly, Turner still made some appearances early in 1963, both in Longview, Texas. He was advertised at The Embers Club for January 19th and 20th, and the Loop De Loop Club on March 31st. Then five months later, on August 29th, he was at The Red Lion Club in Beaumont, Texas.

Nesuhi Ertegun probably did not know of the accident when he wrote in July; "Joe Turner is still travelling constantly. He is always on the move, appearing usually in clubs in Southern cities. I think he has moved to New Orleans, which is now his home base, but I don't think he is home too often."[3]

Breaking his leg, with the resulting medical costs and loss of income, led to financial difficulties. In a letter written by Pete Johnson to collector Hans Mauerer in October 1963, he commented, "I heard from an old friend (Murl Johnson) of mine that played drums with Joe and me, he said that Joe wasn't doing so good and has lost a lot in the past years. Joe at one time had a car of his own but things made it so that he doesn't have any now."[4]

However, a short report from New Orleans in *The Pittsburgh Courier* for November 16th, 1963, states: "Blues king Big Joe Turner, now living here, all smiles last week on receiving news that he is destined to come in possession of a reported $75,000 as the result of a recent legal settlement". If this is correct, then the accident must have been more than a simple fall – and the resultant cheque would have been very welcome.

Down Beat's International Jazz Critics Poll for 1963 showed, in the Male Singer section, that Turner still had his supporters. He came fifth, after Ray Charles, Louis Armstrong, Jimmy Rushing and Mel Torme.

1964

Big Joe continued to be booked by Shaw Artists in New York and he listed bookings during this period in the Safari Room, Peppermint Lounge and the Dew Drop Inn, in New Orleans, plus several auditorium dates.[5]

Pianist Willie 'The Lion' Smith was scornful of the big booking agencies such as the Music Corporation of America (MCA) or the William Morris office, and Shaw Artists probably fell into this category. Smith stated,

> "Some big organisations have never cared or known anything about jazz music. All they have ever cared about was a buck - for themselves. They'd send Big Joe Turner out to sing the Whiskey Blues (I've Got To Have My Whiskey) to a bunch of blue-nosed old ladies at an anti-saloon league meeting if there was a commission in it."[6]

It may have been early in this year that Joe sang at the Moulin Rouge in Los Angeles with Duke Ellington. Stanley Dance, quoting reminiscences by members of the Duke's orchestra, said that Rex Stewart borrowed Nat Woodward's horn to play an obligato. Presumably Turner was visiting the nightclub and was invited to sing a number or two with the band.[7]

His trip to Texas in January this year included a booking at The Mecca in Beaumont. The advertisement is a little vague, but he may have played there on January 10th and 11th, with singer Barbara Lynn as the headline act. On Sunday, the 12th, The Mecca featured him as a solo artist.

Down Beat for April 8 reported, "Joe Turner made some of his rare New York appearances when he did two weekends at Birdland with the King Curtis Quintet." These weekends were February 15th/16th and 22nd/23rd. Jack Hutton described the Curtis band as "a sort of R&B-rock type group. Joe was in devastating form .... He belted out the words with fantastic drive and energy and sounded like a vocal version of the Basie band in toto."[8]

In *Jazz Journal*, Stanley Dance's view was, "He sounded utterly undiminished and terrific, hollering and singing with a nonchalance that somehow curiously increases his physical stature". Dance quoted the personnel as Curtis, tenor, George Stubbs, piano, Cornell Dupree, guitar, Jimmy Lewis, fender bass, Ray Lucas, drums.

Oscar Goldstein, the Birdland manager, told the *Las Vegas Sun* (February 28th, 1964), "I don't go for that far-out jazz. It's ruining the nightclub business. How can you bring them in when they have to go to a music school before they can understand what's going on?". The journalist commented, "Ironically, as he said this, Birdland was three-fourths empty, on a Sunday night."

After the Birdland weekends Turner travelled to Boston for a week at Louie's Showcase Lounge, opening on February 28th. He indicated that a record date was due on March 17th[9], though Decca have stated that it was the 19th when he made four titles which were subsequently issued on the Coral label, a Decca subsidiary.

Billboard for May 9th, 1964, had a news item headed:

Big Joe Turner Inked by Decca.

"New York – Big Joe Turner has signed an exclusive recording contract with Decca Records according to an announcement made this week by Leonard Schneider, Decca executive vice-president .... the artist's first Coral sides, *I'm Packin' Up*, coupled with *I Walk A Lonely Mile*, were released last week."

Two sides recorded in November 1963 and three or four in March 1964, were the only outcome from the "exclusive contract" and it is believed that these were made "on spec" and subsequently sold to Decca/Coral.

Jack Hutton, writing in the *Melody Maker*, reported that for the past two years Turner had been "hibernating in New Orleans where he has a house and a car". He quoted Joe saying, "Man, I've been getting fat, there ain't nothing else to do all day, but sit in the sun and eat. Sometimes I'd wash the car if I was feeling especially energetic".[10]

Joe was back in Texas in April. There was a repeat visit to The Mecca on April 12th, while on May 22nd and 23rd he was at Louanns in Dallas. Three months later he was also advertised at Louanns for a Sunday jazz session in August.

On September 19th singer Jon Hendricks, who had conceived and organised the programme, compered a Saturday afternoon at the Monterey Jazz Festival entitled "The Blues - Right Now!" Appearing with Big Joe were Joe Williams, Lou Rawls, Big Mama Thornton, Homesick James and the Hank Crawford Orchestra. Dizzy Gillespie and Gerry Mulligan made guest appearances.

Down Beat for December 17th, from San Francisco, reported: "Veteran blues singer Joe Turner made his first club appearance in the area in some time with a five-night gig at the Showcase in Oakland". This was probably late news. The San Francisco Chronicle of October 28th, 1964, stated that "Big Joe Turner opens tonight at the Showcase for five nights".

This may have been the occasion when a seriously ill Joe Sullivan called the club manager, suggesting he could fill the vacancy for a pianist to accompany Joe Turner. Told to come right over, "walking with a cane and looking closer to 80 than 60, he approached the manager and was quickly told that the job was taken, leaving the manager wondering who this strange character was". And so the opportunity to re-unite these two names from Cafe Society's heyday was lost.[11]

Turner's name continued to be a favourite with jazz fans. In the 1964 *Melody Maker* Critics Poll he came third, tying with Ray Charles.

1965

This year was highlighted by a British tour, arranged by trumpeter-bandleader Humphrey Lyttelton. The Lyttelton band was a fine, swinging septet of skilled musicians, well versed in the classic and mainstream tradition. Trumpeter Buck Clayton, who had a musical affinity with Humph, was also on the tour.

Turner arrived in the U.K. on May 5th, but without his work permit. When told by the immigration official, "You've got a nerve," his reply was, "That's what it takes these days, daddy."[12] There was a long delay until Jack Higgins from the Harold Davison Agency resolved the permit problem, but Joe had time that evening to sit in, with Buck Clayton, at Annie's Room, singer Annie Ross' club in Great Russell Street.

The first engagement, the following day, was a rehearsal and an appearance on the BBC's "Tonight" television show. Turner's accompaniment was Lyttelton and just the rhythm section (Eddie Harvey, piano, Dave Green, bass, Johnny Butts, drums). Then the tour got underway:

May 1965
7	Osterley Jazz Club (Rugby FC)
8	Royal Festival Hall, London
9	Redcar
10	Birmingham
12	100 Club, London
14	Bath
15	Dancing Slipper, Nottingham
16	BBC Television, Jazz 625, London

17	Black Prince Hotel, Bexley
18 (day)	Granada Television, Manchester
18 (eve)	Reece's, Liverpool
19	Aylesbury
21	Chelsea College of Art, London
22	Sports Guild, Manchester
23	Sports Guild, Manchester
24	BBC "Jazz Club" recording
26	Concorde Club, Eastleigh (originally scheduled for the 28th)
29	Nottingham University
31	Birmingham

June 1965

| 5 | 100 Club, London |
| 7 | Birmingham |

Left to right, Buck Clayton, Steve Voce, Joe Turner, Manchester Sports Guild, May 1965

The Royal Festival Hall concerts (there were two performances) were called "Jazz From Kansas City," in a programme devised by Humphrey Lyttelton and built around the Lyttelton band and pianist Stan Tracey's Trio. Guests that evening were Joe Turner, vocal, Buck Clayton, trumpet, Vic Dickenson, trombone, Ben Webster, tenor, Ruby Braff, cornet and Bruce Turner, alto. The two shows were virtually identical, with Turner singing *Flip, Flop and Fly, Wee Baby Blues* and *Hide and Go Seek* at both houses, plus *Feelin' Happy* at the first and *Do You Wanna Jump Children* and *Chains of Love* at the second. *Roll 'Em, Pete* was the grand finale, with all the musicians, except Ben Webster, on stage.

Left to right, Buck Clayton, Johnny Parker, Joe Turner, Beryl Bryden, Champion Jack Dupree, 100 Club, London, May 1965. Photograph courtesy of Blues & Rhythm

The Nottingham (15th) and Liverpool gigs were in ballrooms. The missing dates in the schedule were rest days. The recording on May 24th, for BBC's radio show, Jazz Club, was broadcast on the 31st. Dave Green, who kindly confirmed the tour dates from his diary, has a recollection that Turner and Clayton were present on June 7th in Birmingham, the final date of this tour.

Joe and Buck flew to Paris on May 13th to appear alongside trombonist Vic Dickenson in a concert at the Maison de la Radio for an ORTF Studio broadcast. Titles from this programme were subsequently released on Europa Jazz albums.

Between June 1st and 5th Joe and Buck were in Zagreb, Yugoslavia, recording for Black Lion on the 2nd, while on the 3rd and 4th they appeared at the Bled Jazz Festival. On each date they were accompanied by the Zagreb Jazz Quartet. They flew back to the U.K. on the 5th, with Alan Bates, owner of the Black Lion label, though it is not known if they made the advertised gig at 100 Oxford

Street that evening. (Alan Bates had fond memories of the trip, recalling, "Two hours with Joe and you are friends for life!".[13]) The afternoon of Sunday the 6th they attended a party at Joe Temperley's home. Temperley played baritone saxophone in the Lyttelton band, alongside tenor man, Tony Coe. Other guests included Val Wilmer and Beryl Bryden. Dave Green does not recall the two stars appearing at the Crawley gig in Sussex that evening.

Reviewing the first engagement on May 6th, Max Jones wrote,

> "The Rugby Football Club pavilion at Norwood Green where Osterley Jazz Club holds its meeting shook and practically swayed under the influence of a one-and-a-half-hour's blues session …. the accompaniment by Buck and the Lytteltons was little short of prodigious."[14]

Writing about the Yugoslavian trip, which was arranged by vibes player Bosko Petrovic of the Zagreb Jazz Quartet. Clayton goes into detail in his autobiography about the terrible hangover he suffered after imbibing too liberally of slivovitz, a damson plum brandy. He comments that "Joe Turner had quit drinking the slivovitz a long time ago because he only liked Scotch whiskey and the slivovitz was too tame in taste for him".

Buck Clayton clearly meant it when he wrote that it was "a quite enjoyable tour" and "a great tour". People in Britain had difficulty with Joe's accent, so Buck tried to act as interpreter, but there were times when he couldn't understand what Joe was saying either! Clayton continued, "I enjoyed working with Joe as it reminded me of Kansas City …. (Joe) kept us laughing all the time and traveling with him was a great experience".[15]

Dave Green recalls that

> "Humph drove Big Joe and Buck to all the gigs in his large Volvo (it needed to be large to accommodate Big Joe's massive frame). Humph acted as Joe's minder for the tour and consequently the band tended to do its own thing in terms of hanging out together. Joe referred to drummer Johnny Butts as 'Young blood' and would frequently say on the gigs, 'We're in a whole world of trouble,' said with a huge grin. We tended to play the same tunes every night – sometimes repeating the same tune, such as *Cherry Red*, in the same set."[16]

As one would expect, Humphrey Lyttelton too was greatly entertained by Joe Turner's part in the tour. On BBC radio's "Jazz Score" he said,

> "Other American musicians like Ben Webster and Buck Clayton, when I said that Joe Turner was coming here, said to me, 'You"ll find that he plays every number in C'. And sure enough, when he got here, every blues number he played in C, for <u>most</u> of the evening. He'd play, say, seven numbers in the key of C, and the eighth number we'd start off in the key of C and he'd turn round and say, 'Wrong key, wrong key'. And he'd tell us what key he wanted, and it was C."[17]

Joe Turner and Buck Clayton, Concorde Club, The Basset Hotel, Southampton, U.K. 1965. Photo courtesy of The Concorde Club Archive

Required reading is the chapter "Big Joe" in Humphrey Lyttelton's *Take It From The Top*, in which he explores Turner's innocence, gullibility, insecurity and the big penetrating voice that assumed a massive air of authority. Humph closed the chapter thus,

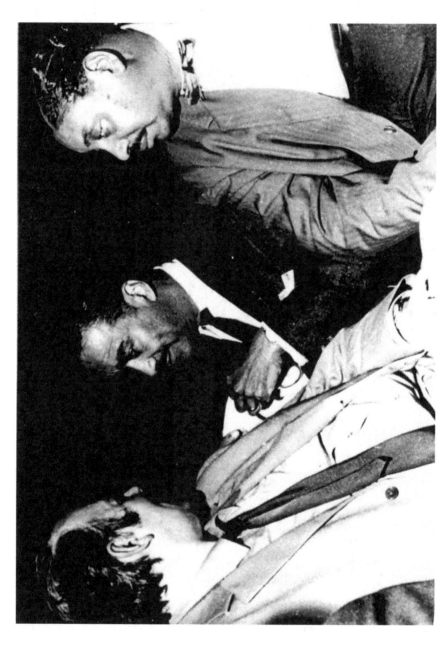

Left to right, Humphrey Lyttelton, Buck Clayton, Joe Turner, Concorde Club, The Basset Hotel, Southampton, UK. May 1965. Photograph courtesy of The Concorde Club Archive

"Joe Turner, the singer of powerful, sexually assertive, sometimes quite cynical blues .... personifies for me the jazz fans' perennial problem – how to reconcile two often irreconcilable halves of a musician, his music and his overt personality. For me there are still two Joe Turners, and I love them both".[18]

Valerie (Val) Wilmer, eminent jazz and blues writer/photographer, interviewed Turner during his visit, resulting in articles in *JazzBeat* and *Down Beat* and, later, her book *Jazz People*. She recalled,

"I was quite friendly with Joe when he was here and we hung out together, including going to Joe Temperley's place in Kent on a Sunday afternoon with Buck Clayton and Beryl Bryden."

After mentioning that Buck was in trouble with his slivovitz problem she continued,

"One of the best nights of my life was when I took Joe and Memphis Slim to Ronnie Scott's in Gerard Street. Ben Webster was the resident attraction and Joe and Slim sat in, to be joined by Gerry Mulligan, who was present as well. The audience included a number of the South Africans who came over with the show King Kong and stayed, together with Madeline Bell and possibly a couple of other gospel singers. All I remember about that night was that the club turned into a juke joint, a shebeen and a speakeasy all in one. It was a real Pan-African experience and a night I would not have missed for the world."[19]

Johnny Parker replaced Eddie Harvey as pianist for the Joe Turner sets with the Lyttelton band for the Royal Festival Hall concert on May 8th and the Jazz 625 telecast on the 16th and perhaps even at the 100 Club. His style was better attuned to Turner's; Harvey, who played in a more modern manner, switched to his other instrument, the trombone.

Fortunately, because many of the BBC's Jazz 625 tapes were wiped for re-use, the two television shows have been released on video tape and on DVD, in addition to being available on YouTube. These telecasts are an invaluable showcase for Big Joe Turner. He is in excellent form and has an accompaniment befitting his talent.

The jazz critics were enthused by the appearances of Joe Turner and Buck Clayton. After the May 12th gig at the Jazzshows Club, 100 Oxford Street, editor Albert McCarthy wrote in *Jazz Monthly*,

"The highspot of this session was undoubtedly the magnificent singing of Turner, without question the finest jazz blues vocalist of our era. Although the verses he sings are familiar ones, the controlled power of his voice is immensely impressive and this timing is in some ways the basis of his art. This was jazz singing in its finest sense...."

After the Festival Hall concert, George Ellis, in *JazzBeat*, proclaimed,

"That remarkable voice is just as fine as ever and he proved during a swiftly moving foursome that he is undoubtedly the greatest of all the city blues singers."

Of the Manchester Sports Guild gig, G.E. Lambert said in *Jazz Monthly*, "His voice …. is quite perfect for the style, his rhythmic sense and great swing incomparable." Lambert also referred to "…. his beautiful phrasing, perfect pitching and superb rhythmic control."

Steve Voce in *Jazz Journal* commented,

"Joe sings like the bark from a cannon and, as far as I was concerned, more than fulfilled all my hopes." He also remarked that Turner talked in the key of C, as well as sitting down with a sigh and saying, "We in a whole world of trouble. Somebody took the pin and burst the bubble."

Of the Maison de la Radio broadcast, Jacques Pescheux in the *Bulletin du Hot Club de France* called Big Joe Turner, "triumphant and exuberant"!

There was a rumour that Turner returned home after this tour with empty pockets, having spent all his money on a young lady who promised to show him a good time. It is a possibility, considering Joe's free and easy attitude to dollars and pounds.

An item in *The Pittsburgh Courier* (June 26th, 1965) reported,

"Blues singer Big Joe Turner, back from his short sojourn into merrie ole England, bar-b-queing with jest at his king-sized bar-b-que pit in the rear yard of his Marlborough Gate home uptown. Joe has made New Orleans his home, and has added more weight".

Mississippi was a port-of-call after the barbecue. On June 17th he starred at the Magnolia Inn in Hattiesburg, with backing by Cozy Corley and his Blue Gardenia Orchestra.

Earlier in the year Joe's two-volume album on Realm, "Sings the Blues," was sixth in the *Jazz Journal* (February issue) twenty best jazz records poll and first in the Blues section. Joe did not feature in the *Melody Maker* polls for 1965, but his subsequent British tour ensured fresh recognition the following year.

1966

Towards the end of January Turner was on tour again, this time in Mexico with Bill Haley and his Comets. Although Haley's fan base in the States had disappeared, he was still very popular in Mexico and for a time he lived there, with his Mexican wife. Haley recorded a hundred sides for the Orfeon label over a five year period, but the association came to an end in 1966 after a disagreement about the non-payment of royalties. Fortunately, not long before this split occurred, Turner recorded with Haley. The session took place in Mexico City on January 24th.

With Bil Haley and his Comets

Another souvenir of Big Joe in Mexico can be found on YouTube, where a version of *Well, Oh, Well* can be seen and heard, with the singer in full vocal flight, and the Comets rocking behind.

In February the *Melody Maker*'s Readers Poll had Turner tenth in the Male Singer category (Frank Sinatra was first), though the Critics had him first, with Sinatra fifth. In the Blues Artist section the readers placed him third (Jimmy Witherspoon was first), but the Critics had him second, with Witherspoon still first.

Two known engagements suggest that Turner was touring the South in the spring. He had a Thursday to Sunday booking at the Beach House in Biloxi, Mississippi, March 10th to 13th, 1966, and perhaps ten-days at Kitten's Korner in Atlanta, Georgia, commencing April 4th. At the Beach House the band was George Woods and the Royal Rockers; at Kitten's Korner there were "35 Beautiful Kittens to serve you".

There was a diversion on March 25th. This was the day after Pete Johnson's 62nd birthday, when there was a special concert at Kleinhan's Music Hall in

Buffalo, New Jersey, where Pete had lived since 1950. At this celebration Joe Turner sang with pianist Ray Bryant's trio, while the Buffalo Philharmonic Orchestra played Sy Oliver and Luther Henderson arrangements of *Wee Baby Blues* and *Roll 'Em Pete*.[20]

It is possible that Turner had his own bar in New Orleans for a time, where he did more tending than singing. Pianist Lars Edegran, a longtime Crescent City resident, believes that he did.[21] This might explain a verse in Joe's *Poor House*

recorded in 1967 for BluesWay, in which he sings of "hang around in a joint way down in New Orleans .... called Big Joe's Joint". The City Directory for 1964 and 1965 lists a Joe's Bar at 1303 Feliciana Street, proprietress Mrs Cletus S. Arroyo. This may, of course, be irrelevant.

Howlin' Wolf was the headliner when Joe had a booking for the Memphis Blues Spectacular at the Ellis Memorial Auditorium in Memphis, Tennessee, on Saturday, August 6th.

European Tour, 1966

Highlight of the year was another European tour. This was with the American Folk Blues Festival, an annual event promoted by two German enthusiasts, Horst Lippmann and Fritz Rau. Between 1962 and 1970 it featured an astounding number of blues singers and musicians, illustrious names such as T-Bone Walker, Brownie McGhee, Sonny Terry, Skip James, Bukka White, Son House, Sonny Boy Williamson, Big Joe Williams, John Henry Barbee, Victoria Spivey, Mississippi Fred McDowell, Little Walter, Muddy Waters, Howlin' Wolf, John Lee Hooker, Lightning Hopkins, and Memphis Slim.

The 1966 tour comprised, in addition to Turner, singer Sippie Wallace, singer/guitarists Sleepy John Estes, Robert Pete Williams and Otis Rush, singer/pianists Little Brother Montgomery and Roosevelt Sykes, and singer/harmonica player, Junior Wells. The rhythm section players were Jack Myers, bass guitar, and Freddie Below, drums. (On the whole, the British writers liked Joe Turner's singing but were unimpressed by the accompaniment he was given.)

Turner arrived in the U.K. on September 27, for the start of the tour the following day, the itinerary including:

September 1966
28   Royal Albert Hall, London
29   Free Trade Hall, Manchester
30   Recording for Granada TV, Manchester

October 1966
1   Theatre des Champs-Elysees, Paris
2   Stuttgart, Germany
3   Kurhaus, Baden-Baden, Germany
5   Liedertafel, Mainz, Germany (SWF TV recording)
6   Volkhaus, Zurich, Switzerland
7   Victoria Hall, Geneva, Switzerland
8   Stadtcasino, Basel, Switzerland
9   Prague Festival, Poland
10   Lucerne, Switzerland
11   Konzerthaus, Vienna, Austria
12   Theatre an der Brienner Strasse, Munich, Germany
13   Congresshalle, Frankfurt, Germany
14   Musikhalle, Hamburg, Germany
15   Kongresshalle, West Berlin, West Germany
16   Friedrichsstadtpalast, East Berlin, East Germany
17   Niedersachsenhalle, Hannover, Germany
18   Stadthalle, Kiel, Germany
19   Saalbau, Essen, Germany
20   University, Lille, France
21   Concertgebouw, Amsterdam, The Netherlands
23   Tivoli, Denmark
24   Konserthuset, Stockholm, Sweden
25   Kulturhaus, Helsinki, Finland

There were just four rest days apparently. The East Berlin concert was recorded and titles released on Amiga, Fontana and Bellaphon. Joe's tracks were *Flip, Flop and Fly* and *Roll 'Em Pete*, both of which can be found on YouTube and Spotify, as can *Well, Oh, Well* and *Hide and Seek* from the Granada television show.

At the Royal Albert Hall Turner, who had the final set of the concert, sang *Feelin' Happy, Chains of Love, Hide and Seek, TV Mama* and, the finale number, *Roll 'Em Pete*. George Melly commented that Joe was a "slight disappointment".

"The trouble was that he is used to cutting through a whole powerhouse band in full riff and here, backed only by guitars and a rhythm section, the great voice seemed to shadow box."[22]

Sadly, this writer never had the pleasure of meeting Big Joe Turner. The "nearly moment" was when Paul Oliver arranged with promoter Jack Higgins for my admission backstage at the Royal Albert Hall. Somehow our lines got crossed and the opportunity was missed.

During the tour Joe told Paul Oliver that he had appeared at U.S. Army and depots in Texas, around San Antonio, though it is not clear when this was.

In his article "Joe Turner", written for *Whiskey, Women and ...* Doc Pomus recalled Joe telling him that, "He had departed New Orleans in about 1969 for Los Angeles, leaving everything behind, including his address and an ex-wife."[23] However, it is possible that the break-up of Turner's second marriage took place as earlier, otherwise it is difficult to explain the significance of a song recorded for Bluesway in April 1967.

The verses of *Mrs. Geraldine* are full of mixed emotions, as the following extracts indicate:

Let me tell you what happened to me, way down yonder in New Orleans
Let me tell you what happened to me, way down yonder in New Orleans
I got married to a Louisiana queen.

She used to love me in the mornin', love me late at night
She used to love me in the mornin', love me late at night
I was happy and everything was going all right.

My Louisiana woman is as fine as she can be
My Louisiana woman is as fine as she can be
I got news for you, sure made a monkey out of me.

And there are lines such as "... that mean woman, Geraldine, I'm crazy about the baby way down in New Orleans", "I open my mouth and she wants a doggone fight," and "She's a mean mistreater but I love her so," before concluding "I'm leaving, I'm leaving that girl and I'm getting out, getting out of New Orleans."

After Joe left, Geraldine was somehow able to cash record company cheques and it was some years before the problem was resolved. One catalyst for this seems to have been a larger-than-usual royalty cheque, which Turner spoke of to Steve Propes:

"She had a brother named Joe Brown, he was a prize fighter, lightweight champion of the world .... She tried to pass off (her brother) that he was me, they told the bank manager they'd made a mistake [on the cheque] in the name. Instead of Joe Turner it should've been Joe Brown".

Fortunately the bank manager was not to be fooled.[24]

[Brown's success as a black boxer in the mid-1900s typically was not matched by equivalent financial success. Born in Baton Rouge in 1926, he became lightweight world champion in 1956, not losing the title until 1962. He died in 1997.]

Regardless of love, Turner headed for the West Coast, though leaving everything behind was to have its financial cost. But as he recorded in 1946,

Don't like to brag, don't like to boast
But I'm pretty sharp when I hit the coast.

1967

This was the year when Carnegie Hall celebrated its Diamond Jubilee and among the special events was the presentation, by John Hammond, of another From Spirituals To Swing concert. The date was January 15. Featured were the Count Basie Orchestra, guitarist George Benson's Quartet, and John Handy's Quintet, with Joe Turner and Big Mama Thornton singing the blues and Marion Williams the spirituals. Turner's set had backing by a Cafe Society All-Star band, Buck Clayton, trumpet, Buddy Tate, tenor, Ed Hall, clarinet, Ray Bryant, piano, Milt Hinton, bass and Jo Jones, drums. Canadian magazine *Coda*[25] reported, "Joe Turner had the nostalgia funky feeling going ...." Pete Johnson, who was far from well, was a special guest. He died just two months later, on March 23rd.

Writer Stanley Dance noted comments that Turner lacked showmanship and supposed that it was true.

"Joe just stood there and sang the blues, comfortable, almost nonchalant, letting the words tell the story, but swinging with marvellous time. .... When they led Pete Johnson on stage, there was a touching scene. He and Pete just stood there, hand in hand like a pair of kids, very happy to be together, but quite unaware of any need for spoken declaration and, eh, showmanship .... their faces said everything that was necessary. Then Pete sat down at the piano and played the treble on *Roll 'Em Pete* while Ray Bryant played the bass."[26]

Joe was in New York, recording for the ABC subsidiary, BluesWay, on May 12th and 13th, when the previously noted *Mrs Geraldine* was made, and he was in Chicago in early May, playing an engagement at the Golden Peacock. At the end of the month he was appearing at the Spot 77 night club in Denton, Texas.

In the sleeve notes for the BluesWay album, Frank Kofsky comments that Joe Turner is living in a modest but comfortable house in South-Central Los Angeles.

The summer of 1967 found him in New Orleans for an appearance at the Dew Drop Inn. It is not known if he saw Mrs. Geraldine during his stay.

For the week beginning November 10, the show at the Apollo Theatre in New York starred Odetta. T-Bone Walker, Jimmy Witherspoon, Big Mama Thornton, the Chambers Brothers, and Big Joe Turner were the supporting acts. Nine years earlier he had been top of the bill!

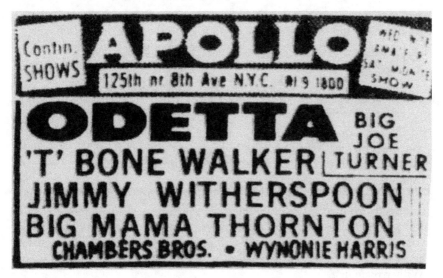

A late addition to the programme was Wynonie Harris, making it a special blues shouter gathering. In a review. Pete Lowry wrote of Turner, "Joe Turner followed them (the Chambers Brothers) with *Well, Oh, Well* and *Chains of Love* - even stoned this man comes on strong as hell and was well received."[27]

Turner was still in New York at the end of November when, on the 23rd, he played a Princeton Thanksgiving Dance, with a 7-piece band, at the Colosseum.

Joe continued to be featured in the *Melody Maker* polls. In the Readers Poll for Blues Artist he was fifth, while the Critics Poll showed him second as both Male Singer and Blues Artist.

1968

Yet another year where information is in short supply. The entry in Wikipedia for the 1960s refers to him living in the Los Angeles Adams District and playing clubs on Central Avenue, while *Blues Who's Who* tells us that Turner "in the late '60s toured with Johnny Otis Show, concerts on West Coast".

It is likely that this was the year that he recorded in Los Angeles for the Ronn label which was part of Jewel Records, operated by Stan Lewis from his record store in Shreveport, Louisiana. There were two Ronn singles, followed later by a CD and cassette on Jewel.

In August he would have been on another Texas tour, starring on the 15th at the Cow Bayou Club in Beaumont, but by October he was on the West Coast, his first local visit in some five years, according to reviewer Leonard Feather. He was at the Redd Foxx Club in late September, early October. Pianist James Wiggins and his trio were the house group.

To quote Feather,

> "If your vision of the blues is 11 electric guitars, five Fender basses, echo chambers and overdubbed voices, don't go to the Redd Foxx Club. The man at the microphone is Big Joe Turner, the original boss of the blues. He couldn't care less about rock n' roll (though, ironically, he was the first to bring that phrase to prominence as part of a 30-year-old blues lyric.) He doesn't compromise with rhythm and blues. What Joe sings is the plain, unadulterated tell-it-like-it-used-to-be blues".[28]

Joe had a one-night-stand at The Limit in Long Beach on November 7th and a two-nighter, November 15th and 16th, at the Nite Life club in Van Nuys, the advertisement for which states "Big Joe Turner & Ray Sharp". The house band was led by C. C. Ryder.

Jazz Expo 68 was a festival held in Britain in October, with Turner being incorrectly reported as one of the guests, but British fans had not forgotten him. In the 1969 *Melody Maker* polls its readers placed him seventh as Male Singer and fifth as Blues Artist, while the Critics had him joint third as Blues Artist, along side Son House and Skip James, with Muddy Waters second and Jimmy Witherspoon first.

14

"My sister got on my case"

(1969-1976)

1969

For the first half of the year just two engagements have been traced. On February 14th he was due at the Lazy X in North Hollywood, with Little Johnnie Taylor the headliner, but he was the main act at The Pink Poodle in Atlanta, Georgia, for nine days, April 18th-26th.

There were reports that Turner was to appear at the 1969 Newport Jazz Festival (on July 6th), but they proved to be premature. That same month he was signed by producer Bob Thiele, the resulting album, recorded in August, appearing on the Blues Time label. There was also an album of uncertain date for Kent, as well as titles with Pee Wee Crayton and T-Bone Walker released on L.M.I.

In July Turner was in California. He supported B.B. King at a concert at the Long Beach Arena on the 13th and then, on the 17th, he was among the mourners at Wynonie Harris' funeral. Harris had died on June 14th and was buried at the North Hollywood Memorial Park Cemetery. Other singers present were Jimmy Witherspoon and Lowell Fulson.

During 1969, according to the notes to a Fuel CD, Joe was heard at the Atlanta "Super Blues Festival". In addition, he made at least two television appearances, one on the Johnny Otis Show on KNET-TV in Los Angeles and "Jazz on Stage," intended mainly for overseas sale.

"Jazz on Stage" was produced in the fall of 1969 by Jack Lewerke, President of Vault Recording Corp. It was a series of twelve half-hour television programmes for Erua-Films Corporation, with pianist Hampton Hawes appearing each week with guest musicians. The episodes were shot at the Melody Lane club, "located on the edge of the black belt in Los Angeles." It was probably in October that Hampton Hawes was partnered with Harry Edison, trumpet, Sonny Criss, alto, Leroy Vinnegar, bass, Bobby Thompson, drums, and Joe Turner, vocals on *Feelin' Happy* and *Shake, Rattle and Roll*.[1] These titles were issued on a Jasmine LP and a Fresh Sounds CD.

The *San Francisco Chronicle* for October 6th had an item probably written by Ralph Gleason. It began, "This week a package of blues artists is beginning a night club tour of the country". The tour was to start at Mr. D's club on October 10 for three nights. It was certainly an all-star package, with Big Joe Turner, T-Bone Walker, Eddie 'Cleanhead' Vinson, Harmonica George Smith, Otis Spann and Rod Piazza.

A review by Bob Porter, using the alias Gene Gray, in *Down Beat* for November 13th, 1969, concerned a Celebrity Night at the Tiki Island club in Los Angeles, probably towards the end of October. Joe Turner was the celebrity for this particular Monday "off-night" accompanied by Charles Kynard, organ, Leo Blevins, guitar, and an unidentified drummer. Bob Porter caught only the opening set, missing a later appearance by singer/guitarist T-Bone Walker, but he did hear *Flip, Flop and Fly*, then "A brief *Honey Hush* set the stage for an incredible 35-minute version of *Chains of Love*. Obviously enjoying his instrumental support, Turner got as far into the blues as one can go. I don't know how many choruses he sang, but at the end of the tune there was tumultuous applause".

Bob Porter mentions that Turner was also there to help promote what might become an indefinite run of Tuesday night gigs, that Joe probably weighed around 280-lbs, and that he "has been hanging out in L.A. recently".

This may have been the year that pianist Jim Turner took his then girlfriend to the Tiki Island Cocktail Lounge on La Brea and Washington Boulevard to hear Joe Turner.

"It was a big, loud, crowded room. Ours were the only white faces in the place. The gin and tonic I ordered was at least 90% gin. They had a two drink maximum. Yes, maximum. Big Joe Turner sounded fantastic to me. I don't remember the names of any of the musicians in the band but they were all fine."

Joe Turner, Shuggie Otis, guitar, PBS-TV, A Night At The Barrelhouse, 1969. Photograph by Steve LaVere.

November 21st found him at the San Fernando State College in Northridge, California.

Sometime in 1969, in Los Angeles, photographer/collector Steve LaVere took photos during the filming of "A Night at the Barrelhouse," a PBS-TV production in its "Homewood" series. Joe Turner and T-Bone Walker were featured. It is not clear if this was a live broadcast or a recording or if the resulting programme is the same one mentioned during 1970.

The *Melody Maker* Critics Poll showed Big Joe improving his position in the "Male Singer" section to fifth place.

1970

California seems to have been Turner's base for the early months of 1970. On January 18th he supported Jimmy Witherspoon at The Factory on North LaPeer Drive in Los Angeles, while on February 3rd he was in Canada for two shows (9 and 11 p.m.) on the Riverqueen in Vancouver. Four days later he was due to be part of the musical entertainment at the Long Beach Municipal Auditorium. This was a benefit show in aid of the Community Improvement League, featuring stars of TV and music, also including T-Bone Walker, Eddie Vinson, and The Platters.

Under the heading "Big Joe Turner Still Singin' Those City Blues," the *Omaha World-Herald* reported on Joe's appearance at the Show Case in Omaha for three nights, March 13th-15th.

On May 2nd "B.B. King and Friends" were featured at Carnegie Hall. Among the blues man's singing "friends" were Joe Turner, T-Bone Walker, Eddie Vinson, Big Mama Thornton and Leon Thomas. Backing musicians included Russ Andrews, tenor, Wynton Kelly, piano, Lawrence Lucie, guitar, and Elvin Jones, drums. The *Down Beat* review stated that Turner sang three numbers "seemingly accompanied by Elvin Jones' drums alone," noting that the accompaniment was unsatisfactory and the sound system poor.[2] Presumably that was why Flying Dutchman, who recorded the concert, released only a portion on Blues Time.

The Johnny Otis Show began a two-week booking at the Ash Grove in Los Angeles on June 2. Joe Turner, T-Bone Walker, and Eddie 'Cleanhead' Vinson, were part of the revue and they also featured when the Show had a sixty-minute slot on TV station KCET. Band musicians mentioned were Melvin Moore, trumpet, Gene Connors, trombone, vocal, Plas Johnson, tenor, Preston Love, baritone, Johnny Otis, piano, vibes, vocal, Shuggie Otis, guitar, Wilton Felder, bass guitar, Paul Lagos, drums.

Leonard Feather in his review of the Otis Show in the *Los Angeles Times* (June 4th, 1970) mentions a seven-piece band, but no trumpeter, and Jim Bradshaw switching from bass to guitar. Other singers in the show were Delmar Evans, Margie Evans, and Esther Phillips.

Joe Turner and B.B. King, backstage at Carnegie Hall, May 2, 1970

Mary Katherine Aldin first became friends with Joe Turner when she was working at the Ash Grove, a blues and folk music club in Los Angeles - "It was your basic office job except for the fact that at night I got to hear terrific music all the time". As she recalled,

".... The Ash Grove did not do single night bookings; it booked all artists for a six-night run Tuesday through Sunday. Therefore I was able to spend a fair amount of time getting to know the musicians. Joe played there several times.

"Some of those engagements were with the Johnny Otis Show but these weren't so frequent as the gigs where Big Joe fronted a band. Johnny Otis Shows were done revue style, where Johnny and his band were on stage throughout and he would call guest singers up on the stage to do two or three numbers during each set. In one performance I might have seen Big Joe, Margie Evans, or earlier Esther Phillips (there was always a woman vocalist) and then he would spotlight instrumentalists like Big Jim Wynn, and Cleanhead Vinson (and Roy Milton)."

Mrs Aldin continued

"Many of the times that I saw Big Joe he would be playing with Pee Wee Crayton's band. Joe and Pee Wee were very good friend, as were their wives Pat and Esther. Pee Wee had more gigs than Joe did, so it was possible for Pee Wee to keep a fairly regular band together, whereas Joe had to use whatever backup band was available, and some of them were pretty awful. One of the best, other than Pee Wee's, was the James Harman band, because those guys had actually studied Joe's music, listened to his records and knew most of his material, so he could just count it off and they were right there with him."[3]

Down Beat for July 23rd, 1970 reported that the Ash Grove suffered a serious fire, but the Johnny Otis Show, with Big Joe, played the last week of its two-week booking.

June also saw the Joe Turner, T-Bone Walker, Eddie 'Cleanhead' Vinson package at the Exit Club in Palo Alto, California. They were accompanied by Dave Alexander, piano, Al King, bass, and Roy Milton, drums.[4]

Turner, together with Eddie Vinson, Marjorie and Delmar Evans, was in the Johnny Otis Show which played a one-week engagement, starting July 14, at Shelly's Manne-Hole, drummer Shelly Manne's club in L.A.

On Saturday afternoon, August 8th, Turner appeared at the three-day Ann Arbor Blues Festival in Michigan. He was scheduled to participate alongside T-Bone Walker, Eddie 'Cleanhead' Vinson, Sunnyland Slim, Otis Rush, Johnny Shine and Robert Pete Williams.

Two days later, Walker, Vinson and Turner appeared in a PBS-TV show entitled "A Night at the Barrelhouse". The *San Francisco Chronicle* stated:

"8:00 p.m. HOMEWOOD. The stirring atmosphere of 'The Barrelhouse,' one time Los Angeles mecca of rhythm and blues is recreated with the sounds of the pioneers of the rousing style."

The club, located in Watts, was originally founded by Johnny Otis in 1948. A couple of years later a *Billboard* report called the Barrelhouse a "perpetual 'hot spot' at the Southeast district". A Wolf CD, perhaps from this Show, has Turner singing his perennials, *Shake, Rattle and Roll* and *Chains of Love*, plus tracks by Roy Milton, Esther Phillips, Eddie Vinson, Lowell Fulson, T-Bone Walker and others. It is not certain if the KCET show was live or recorded, with the Wolf insert suggesting it came from early in 1970. A possibility is that it was a recording from 1969, as mentioned earlier. Musicians on the show included Melvin Moore, trumpet, Gene Connors, trombone, Plas Johnson, tenor, Preston Love, baritone, Wilton Felder, bass-guitar, and Paul Lagos, drums. *Down Beat* showed Johnny Otis and his son, Shuggie, on guitars.

Left to right; Gene Connors, Roy Brown, Roy Milton, Eddie Vinson, Pee Wee Crayton, Johnny Otis, Delmar Evans, Shuggie Otis. Los Angeles, fall 1970. Photograph by Ed Careaff.

The Johnny Otis show, "with Shuggie Otis, Big Joe Turner and others," opened at Fillmore West in San Francisco on August 14th, presumably for one week.

Under the heading, "Rhythm and Blues Hall of Fame All Stars," the Otis Show appeared at the 13th Monterey Jazz Festival on Saturday afternoon, September 19th, 1970. In addition to Joe Turner, the galaxy of singers included, among others, Little Esther Phillips, Jimmy Rushing, Pee Wee Crayton, Roy Brown, Ivory Joe Hunter, Roy Milton, Charles Brown, Eddie 'Cleanhead' Vinson, 'Sugarcane' Harris, Margie Evans and Delmar Evans. Otis announced, sang, played piano, vibes and drums. Part of this concert, with Joe singing *Hide and Seek* and *Roll 'Em, Pete*, was included in the documentary film "Monterey Jazz," which was released in 1973, and Epic issued a double album which contained *I Got A Gal* and *Plastic Man.*

The Otis band personnel was Melvin Moore, trumpet, Gene 'Mighty Flea' Connors, trombone, Jim Wynn, Richard Alpenalt, Clifford Solomon, Preston Love, reeds, 'Shuggie' Otis, Jim Bradshaw, guitar, Lawrence 'Slim' Dickens, bass, and Paul Lagos, drums.

Big Joe, Eddie Vinson and Lowell Fulson were among others who participated in a benefit concert for T-Bone Walker at an unnamed club in L.A. late August/early September. Walker was in hospital, suffering from tuberculosis.

Among the undated citations in *Blues Who's Who* is an engagement at Basin Street West in San Francisco, and a reference to an appearance by Turner on "Della," the Della Reese Show, on WOR-TV in New York City. (In a 1973 entry it states that Joe recorded with the singer for the Trojan label. No information has yet been traced about this recording, but one wonders if it was taken from the television show.) Reese and Turner were both managed by Lee Magid, who issued a Turner album on his LMI label. (Collector John Breckow said that no one had a good word to say for Magid.[5])

In the fall of 1970, Ross Russell, writer and one-time owner of Dial Records, held a series of concerts in connection with an Extension Course on the blues tradition that he ran at the University of California in San Diego. Big Joe Turner appeared on at least one occasion, in the Recital Hall, on Tuesday, November 17th. He was supported by Jesse Price and his Blues Band, Wallace 'Wiley' Huff, trombone, Julian Brooks, tenor, Jimmy Bunn, piano, Chuck Norris, guitar, bass-guitar, Price, drums, vocal.[6]

Plans were announced for Joe to tour France and the U.K. in October/November and as late as its November 14th issue, the *Melody Maker* announced "Big Joe Turner tour starts Monday," which was the 16th. In fact the tour was cancelled. In the following week's issue the *M.M.* advised that the tour was postponed until next year "due to increased work on the West Coast with the Johnny Otis Show and a recent mild illness."

Joe was to be part of an entertainment for children, under the auspices of Project We Care, on the afternoon of Saturday, November 21st, at the Central Juvenile Hall in Los Angeles. The many other artists appearing included singer Lorez Alexandria and saxophonist Red Holloway's Trio.

Christmas and the New Year were spent at the Ash Grove with the Johnny Otis Show, along with Margie Evans, Eddie Vinson, Delmar Evans and Shuggie Otis.[7] The opening was on Christmas Day and due to last until January 3rd. A poster for the Ash Grove lists Turner, Shuggie Otis, Vinson, Delmar Evans, The Mighty Flea [trombonist/singer Gene Connors] and saxophonist Big Jim Wynn as part of the programme. It does not give the year, only December 25th - January 4th, which suggests 1970.

Joe was still named in the 1970 *Melody Maker*'s Jazz Critics Poll. He was fifth in the Male Singer section and third in the Blues Artist.

1971

The West Coast was Turner's sphere during the early months of 1971. A dance-concert at the Hollywood Palladium on Friday, March 5 featured Chuck Berry, Little Richard and the Johnny Otis Show, which included Joe Turner and Eddie 'Cleanhead' Vinson. Otis was also at the Zellerbach Hall, University of California on Saturday, March 29th. Eddie 'Cleanhead' Vinson "with his band" was scheduled to play a concert at the Elks Hall, on Central Avenue in Los Angeles, on April 11th. The Ambassadors, Joe Turner and Roy Milton were also on the bill. Six days later, the 17th, "Joe Turner and his Band" were to play at the Harvest Hall, of the Kern County Fairgrounds in Bakersfield - "Ten Allied Clubs to Sponsor Annual Spring Formal Dance". The year's theme was "Fragrance in Spring".

The postponed 1970 trip to France took place in April 1971, but did not extend to Britain. Joe travelled with Milt Buckner, piano, Slam Stewart, bass, and Jo Jones, drums. The itinerary included a radio appearance at Maison de la Radio in Paris on April 19th and, on the 26th, a recording session for Black and Blue "au Studio Herouville," the resulting album being subtitled 'Texas Style'. Two titles from Paris, *Low Down Dog* and *I've Got A Pocketful of Pencil* can be seen on YouTube.

Joe was back with Eddie Vinson in the Johnny Otis show when it played a Saturday night concert, as part of a jazz weekend, at the UCD Coffee House of the University of California at Davis, Sacramento on May 8th. The *Hollywood Reporter* is quoted as saying of the Otis Show, "[it is] ...funky, free and, best of all, joyous".

Turner was at the City Auditorium in Atlanta, Georgia, on May 16th, 1971, when WAOX presented a "Super Heavy Blues Festival". On the bill were John Lee Hooker, Joe Turner, Al Hibbler, T-Bone Walker, Big Mama Thornton, Eddie Vinson, "plus Atlanta's own Billy Wright and Piano Red".

A "Salute to the Blues" was scheduled for the Newport Jazz Festival on July 4th, with Joe to be present, but this was the year when several thousand rioters gatecrashed the festival site on July 3rd, causing the remaining two days of the festival to be cancelled.

On July 31st a package was reported at the Theatre Antique for the Festival

D'Orange in France. Joe Turner was listed as one of the vocalists appearing, but it seems more likely that it was the pianist, rather than the singer.

In September, on the 18th, Joe was back at the Monterey Jazz Festival, singing the blues in a set entitled 'Kansas City Revisited', accompanied by Jesse Price's seven-piece Blues Band, with Harry 'Sweets' Edison, trumpet, Wallace 'Wiley' Huff, trombone, Preston Love, alto, Jimmy Forrest, tenor, Chester Lane, piano, Billy Hadnott, bass, Jesse Price, drums. Other K.C. veterans who appeared, though not with Turner, were Mary Lou Williams and Jay McShann's Kansas City Six. Leonard Feather commented, "Now 60 and large to the point of obesity, (Turner) had the audience with him from the very first ...."[7]

The film crew for the long-running television Western series "Gunsmoke" included "blues freak" Link Wyler. In October 1971 Wyler, hearing of a package tour featuring the Muddy Waters Blues Band, Big Mama Thornton, George 'Harmonica' Smith and Big Joe, encouraged the crew to put their gear into a car and head for the University of Oregon, located in Eugene, Oregon. They filmed the concert and in the resulting documentary, "Gunsmoke Blues," Joe is seen singing *Hide and Seek* and an interrupted *Shake, Rattle and Roll.* There are also noisy interviews in the back of a car with Waters, Thornton and Turner. Joe is on crutches for the finale on stage and is drinking and smoking during the 'interview'. The students are an enthusiastic audience and the DVD is another excellent opportunity to see Big Joe in his later years.

Other stops on this Pacific Westcoast tour are believed to have included Monroe State Prison, Monroe, WA, and Washington State University, Pullman, WA.

Undated 1971 engagements given in *Blues Who's Who* are at the Palladium in Hollywood, the Nite Life club in Van Nuys, California, and the Ebonee Ballroom in Seattle, Washington. Another undocumented appearance in the early seventies was in Oakland, CA, at Ruthie's Inn. Reference is also made to concert dates throughout Europe.

On the back cover of the Dave and Phil Alvin "Lost Time" yepROC CD, there is a photograph which shows Big Joe with the Alvin brothers, outside Rick's Blues Bar in 1971. Phil and Dave Alvin were to become keen advocates of Turner's music during the last decade or so of his life, offering him encouragement and learning from him. Later, their group The Blasters, would play gigs with him.

In 2015 Dave recalled,

> "When we saw Big Joe Turner for the first time, he was at the tail end of his prime, but still in it. He taught my brother a lot about singing and there were certain, almost Zen-like qualities to things he would say, advice he would give, rules I live by to this day."[8]

As customary, the year closed with a small-scale version of the Johnny Otis Show appearing at the Ash Grove for five days over the New Year period. Joe Turner was there, "as well as a new group of singing and dancing girls known as the Otisettes." Others present were Margie Evans and Eddie Vinson, with the musicians including Gene Connors, trombone, Big Jim Wynn, baritone, Shuggie Otis, Fred Robinson, guitars, and Jimmy Smith, Jr., bass.[9]

Turner may have been overlooked by other polls but the *Melody Maker* Jazz Critics remained constant. Their top Blues Artists for 1971 were 1. B.B. King, 2. Muddy Waters, 3. Joe Turner.

Phil and Dave Alvin, Joe Turner, Happy Hopkins, (other unidentified), Rick's Blues Bar, 1971

1972

At the end of January Joe Turner appeared at Esther's Orbit Room in Oakland, backed by the four-piece Oakland Blues Band, with Steve Freitas on lead guitar. This was probably a one-night stand. The review in *Living Blues* 8, Spring 1972, also referred to "an upcoming series of dates with the still legendary Johnny Otis Show". One of these was at the Golden Bear in Huntington Beach resort for the weekend of January 21st-22nd, when Eddie 'Cleanhead' Vinson and Shuggie Otis were also featured.

On February 14th, Turner was married in a Baptist ceremony to Patricia P. Sims at his home in the Cimarron district of Los Angeles. The bride, maiden name Harris, born in 1923, was the widow of Robert 'Snake' Sims, drummer with T-Bone Walker and other blues performers. The honeymoon was to have been spent in Europe in April, but was delayed.

Mary Katherine Aldin noted that Patricia (Pat) "nursed Snake through his final illness (cancer) and then married Joe and nursed him until he died".[10] Pat was to prove a true partner and companion throughout their thirteen-year marriage.

About this time Turner recorded an album for United Records, which included the song, *Good Mornin' Miss Patricia*. Whether it was an engagement or wedding gift, the lyric praises the lady of the title, ending "I want to thank you, baby, for showing me a wonderful time".

The Johnny Otis Show, with Joe Turner and Sugar Cane Harris, played at Claremont High School in Pomona, CA on March 11th. Then, on Easter Sunday, April 2nd, Turner appeared in "A History of Rock and Roll," headlined by Chuck Berry at the Coliseum Arena in Oakland.

"The History of Rock 'n' Roll, Volume 2," was also held at the Oakland Coliseum. On this occasion, Sunday, July 2nd, the show featured, among others, Bill Haley and the Comets, the Shirelles, The Coasters, Chubby Checker, and Joe Turner.

Count Basie and his Orchestra began another European tour on April 17th in Paris, which ended on May 14th in London. Joe Turner should have taken part alongside singers Eddie Vinson and Joe Williams. But as he told Leonard Feather, "I was all set to go …. But a few weeks ago, I was having trouble with my leg – a little arthritis – and I decided to go to the doctor for a check up. I mentioned to him that I'd been going to the bathroom an awful lot, and he thought he's (sic) better test me for sugar in my blood."[11]

The Basie tour was to be followed by one with Jazz at the Philharmonic, but as *Stars and Stripes* reported, Big Joe Turner "took sick in the States and had to be left behind".

Diabetes was diagnosed and he was advised against making the Basie tour or anything out-of-town until his condition was stabilised.

> "I've been going back and forth for treatments …. I played a couple of dates here around Los Angeles with Johnny Otis, but aside from that I've been staying pretty close to home."

Feather comments that Joe walks with a cane and is obviously very much overweight. Turner himself said, "Yes, right now I weigh 299 pounds. I lost six pounds a couple of weeks ago, but then I got carried away, ate too much I guess, and put it right back on." This minor weight loss is put in context by Feather saying that Joe "needs to lose at least 40 or 50 pounds, for the sake of his general well-being."

Asked if there was any income from his compositions, Turner replied, "Just a little bit. Ain't nobody making none of my tunes like they used to. I belong to BMI and I get a little money from them now and then, but its kinda petered out."

During the interview with Feather, Big Joe said he had the diabetes under control and was doing pretty good, and was waiting for something to turn up. Clearly his financial situation was not a satisfactory one, with little or no income and medical expenses to be paid.

The sleeve of the Pablo album 'Flip, Flop and Fly' gives 1972 as the year of the concerts from which the Turner/Basie titles are taken, but this has to be incorrect. It is probable that the concerts were recorded in October 1974, when Turner did tour Europe with the Basie orchestra.

Back in action in May, but staying close to home, Joe was the headliner at the Carousel in Oxnard, CA, on the 4th and, two days later, part of "A Story of

Rock and Roll" show at the Forum in Los Angeles, together with Frankie Valli, The Chantels, Jackie Williams and others.

In the summer of 1972 Johnny Otis had been scathing about the treatment of so many of the pioneers of blues and rock and roll. He referred to

"some of the glory that is due Big Joe Turner and Roy Milton and Eddie Vinson. These people are languishing in their old age and it's not fair. They're national treasures, but the way they're treated is a national disgrace. These people, and there are many others, are almost without exception very creative people who could contribute wonderfully well today, and should be allowed to, to sustain their dignity as human beings. We have no other trade and when you get that old you can't get a job, and if you did it'd be as a janitor or something. There's nothing wrong with that, it's an honourable profession, but there's something about Joe Turner sweeping a floor that breaks my heart".[12]

(Otis is not saying that Joe Turner had been working as a janitor, but is posing a possible scenario.)

Turner had been scheduled to appear at the Newport Jazz Festival on July 4th, but did not so do. If his non-appearance was due to illness, it may also account, at least in part, for a three month gap in his schedule. He was advertised for the Lowell Fulson Blues Review at the Armadillo World Headquarters and Beer Garden for three nights, October 11th-13th. By November he was back on the West Coast, due to play The Topanga Canyon Corral in Van Nuys on November 15th.

1972 was also the year that Lou Willie, his first wife, died.

1973

Turner did not stray far from California during the early months of 1973. He was scheduled to appear in a "Rock'n Roll Nostalgia Weekend" during February 17th, 18th and 19th, at the Magic Mountain in Los Angeles. Bo Diddley was the headline act for the first two days. Other acts included The Coasters, The Medallions, Cleave Duncan, et al. Diddley and Turner were also advertised in a "1950s Oldies Shower of Stars" concert at the Hollywood Palladium, with different groups, including The Crests, The Clovers, and The Chantels.

On March 4th he was top-of-the-bill, alongside Margie Evans, at the Ash Grove in Northridge, Los Angeles. The accompaniment was by the Ice House Blues Band, a trio, led by James Harman, harmonica, Walter Coretti, piano, and Larry Williams, guitar. The engagement was for one week, at least, but on the opening night the backing for Turner and Evans included star sitters-in Freddy King, guitar, and T-Bone Walker, unexpectedly, on piano.

Mary Katherine Aldin's career continued with work in a traditional record store, producing and hosting radio shows, and writing liner notes and later producing albums. She commented, "The Ash Grove burned down three times … all arson. The last one was in 1973."[13]

Johnny Otis, 1975

Singer Jimmy McCracklin opened his Continental Club with an Oakland Blues Festival the weekend of March 17th/18th, featuring Joe Turner and Lowell Fulson, as well as Little Joe Blue, B.B. Junior and other local singers and musicians. Joel Selvin commented in the *San Francisco Chronicle* (March 20th, 1973),

> "Over a thousand fans filled the spacious nitery - half whites and half blacks, with a surprising number of young blacks who supposedly reject blues as part of the old ways.
> "Though singing suffered from an inadequate p.a. system and equally inadequate house band, more than a few performers overcame the difficulties anyway. After all, most of them are veterans."

"Volume 2" of the "1950s Oldies But Goodies, Shower of Stars", a dance concert, was held at the Hollywood Palladium on Saturday, April 7th. In addition to Joe Turner there were twenty other acts, including Jimmy Reed, Joe Houston, and several vocal groups. Also in April, on the 18th and 19th, Joe was to appear, with Grayson Street, at the Long Branch Saloon in San Francisco, while on the 22nd the *Oakland Tribune* reported that "Big Joe Turner's great performance at the recent Oakland Blues and Rock Festival is featured on 'All Together Now,' Sunday, 10:30 pm on KPIX". (An Oakland Blues Festival was held February/March, 1973.)

Joe Turner and Lowell Fulson were back at Jimmy McCracklin's Continental Club in Oakland on June 15th/16th, alongside Big Mama Thornton, Etta James, Irma Thomas, Jimmy Witherspoon, and the Odessa Perkins Jubilee Singers. Each artist was restricted to two numbers and the accompanying Victor Green band failed to impress reviewer "J.H.".

On June 20th the Johnny Otis Show again appeared on the PBS-TV "Homewood" series. Big Joe Turner is quoted as singing *Shake, Rattle and Roll*, and the musicians noted were Otis, Melvin Moore, trumpet, Gene Connors, trombone. Preston Love, baritone, Shuggie Otis, guitar, and Wilton Felder, bass. It is uncertain if this is a repeat of the show broadcast in 1970.

The Newport Jazz Festival had moved to New York by 1973 and on June 29th there were two performances by a blues package at the Philharmonic Hall in the Lincoln Center. The usual suspects included Joe Turner, Eddie 'Cleanhead' Vinson, Big Mama Thornton, Gatemouth Brown, Arthur Crudup, Lloyd Glenn, the Jay McShann Trio and Muddy Waters with his Blues Band.

Back on the West Coast, on July 12th, Joe played a one-niter, with the Rocky Brown band, at Don Juan's in Lakewood. Joe Houston and The Penguins were also on the bill.

More undated engagements listed in *Blues Who's Who* include the Continental Club in Oakland, CA, and, in Los Angeles, the Topanga Corral and the Parisian Room. There is a photograph of Turner at the Parisian Room dated August 1973.[14] This was perhaps the month when writer Harry Milner reported in the *Sunday Gleaner* of Kingston, Jamaica, October 14th, 1973; "To my pleasure and surprise I saw that Big Joe Turner was appearing .... at the Parisian Club, a small but popular nightspot .... in the smarter black quarter of Los Angeles".

Mary Katherine Aldin too recalled the club.

"Besides the Ash Grove, Joe most often played at the Parisian Room, a black club located at the corner of Crenshaw Blvd and Washington Blvd. It later went out of business and is now a post office. It was an upscale 'dress to impress' club. I saw Joe there frequently. His usual accompaniment was Pee Wee Crayton and his band. This would be Pee Wee on guitar, plus bass, drums and one or two horns. One of the horn players was Pee Wee's grandson, Marshall, sometimes [tenor sax] Don Wilkerson.

"Joe and Pee Wee Crayton [1914-1985] were very close friends, as were their wives. Esther Crayton, Pat Turner, Lola Wynn (Big Jim Wynn's wife) and I spent many, many nights together in a booth at the Parisian Room watching as their husbands played on stage. It was an honor to be part of their sisterhood. When Pee Wee died Joe broke down completely and was unable to be at the funeral."

On the subject of Joe's friendships, Mary Katherine Aldin also recalled,

"Joe and Pat's house in LA had a small rec room out in the backyard. There was a table and chairs and a mini fridge. Joe had his friends out there mostly, playing cards, drinking and talking. Pat would cook and take food out there for everybody".[15]

At the Ann Arbors Blues and Jazz Fest on Sunday, September 2nd, Turner was part of the Johnny Otis Show, with Eddie 'Cleanhead' Vinson, Pee Wee Crayton, Louis Jordan, Marie Adams, and Gene 'Mighty Flea' Connors in an afternoon which also included Victoria Spivey with the Brooklyn Blues Chasers, Joe Willie Wilkins and Ornette Coleman. On Tuesday, September 11th, Joe was in Otis' Show at Paul's Mall in Boston for one week and on the 28th he was in a "Rock and Roll Revival II" package at the Selland Arena in Fresno. Also in the show were The Penguins, The Coasters, The Drifters and others.

Both Joe Turner and Joe Houston were back at Don Juan's in Lakewood, CA, for the "Old But Goodie Night" on Friday, December 7th.

To see out the year, Joe was one of ten acts to appear at the Fox Theatre in Redwood City, CA, December 29th, 30th and 31st, part of 'Rock and Roll Revival Volume 3'. Joe Houston, Bobby Day, The Coasters, and Shirley and Lee were others on the bill. There were two shows a day on Saturday and Sunday, and three on New Year's Eve.

This was the year when Norman Granz (1918-2001) began to record Joe Turner for his Pablo label, a series which continued into 1985, the year when Turner died. Granz featured him with Count Basie and his Orchestra, with blues groups and with all-star jazz combinations. The first of these albums was called 'The Bosses,' recorded in Los Angeles on December 11th, 1973. Joe sang with Count Basie and a small jazz combo, including Harry Edison, trumpet, J.J. Johnson, trombone, and the tenors of Zoot Sims and Eddie Davis.

Big Joe Turner. Pablo Records promotional photograph, 1970s, courtesy Peter Vacher collection

1974

The Mint Julep Room of George's Plantation in San Bernardino, California featured Big Joe Turner on January 13th, Sunday Night Only, and on February 3rd, with a cast including The Coasters and The Penguins, he sang at an All Ages Dance (2pm start, no liquor served, specially for those under 21) at Laboe's on the Sunset Strip, West Hollywood. February 9th he was paired with Joe Houston again, plus The Knickerbockers, at the Valley Cat Fifties, a young adult spot in Panorama City, and the weekend of George Washington's birthday (Saturday, Sunday, Monday, February 16th, 17th and 18th) we find him one of the "bevy of rock'n roll immortals" appearing in Santa Valencia, at the Magic Mountain amusement park's second annual 1950s Festival of Rock'n Roll.

On March 20th, 1974, there was a reunion of Kansas City jazzmen at the Musician's Foundation Building in Kansas City. More than thirty musicians attended, 16 of whom were interviewed, including Joe Turner, Count Basie, Jay McShann, Budd Johnson, Baby Lovett and Eddie Durham. Jay McShann led a big band for the occasion, as well as a piano-bass-drums trio. The evening's proceedings were filmed by director Bruce Ricker. The resulting documentary was released in 1978 and more details will be found in the next chapter.[16]

Back on the West Coast, Joe appeared at Don Juan's in Lakewood on March 29th in a show which included Joe Houston, The Penguins and The Chantels. He was there again on May 31st, with Gene & Eunice and The Coasters. Both appearances were under the title of "Oldie But Goodie".

In Vancouver, starting on March 11th, 1974, British Columbia (Canada) TV taped an eight part series of thirty-minute programmes entitled 'Oscar Peterson Presents'. The series premiered on the CTV network on June 23rd, 1974, with one of the programmes featuring Big Joe Turner as the pianist's guest. Joe sang *Flip, Flop and Fly*, *Wee Baby Blues*, and *Honey Hush*, accompanied by Oscar Peterson, piano, Niels-Henning Pedersen, bass, Louis Bellson, drums.[17]

On Saturday, May 11th, Pat Turner planned a celebration for her husband's fiftieth year in show business. It was held at the Oldies But Goodies Club in Hollywood, with Joe receiving a trophy and flowers. He sang, what else, *Shake, Rattle and Roll*, backed by the house band and the vocal group The Coasters. The club's owner, Art Laboe, interviewed Turner on his radio show. And Tom Bradley, Mayor of Los Angeles, made a presentation to Joe for outstanding achievement in the field of entertainment.[18]

A follow-up session for Pablo Records was held in Los Angeles on June 3rd, 1974. The album was entitled 'Life Ain't Easy,' again with a small jazz group, including Roy Eldridge, trumpet, Al Grey, trombone, and Lee Allen, tenor. In his Eldridge biography, John Chilton is scathing about the rhythm section and some of Joe's singing. To quote,

> "The album's issue undoubtedly dented Big Joe Turner's massive and deserved reputation. Roy's role in the musical mayhem is a subsidiary one: he simply co-exists alongside the sounds of an electric organ, a powerful guitar, and some pulverizing off-beat drumming .... Joe was in a strange mood that day and on the title track *Life Ain't Easy* offers some stream of conscious lyrics, issuing his brand of philosophy in unconnected stanzas - none of which make any sense.[19]

Don Juan's club in Lakewood had another "Oldie But Goodie Night" on May 31st, with Turner in the show. The Coasters were top of the bill. In June, on Sunday the 16th, we find him at The Joker Room in Van Nuys, together with The Shirelles, while on the 22nd, along with John Lee Hooker and his Coast-to-Coast Blues Band, and a group called Slamhammer, he played at the San Gabriel Auditorium. On July 3rd he was at The Orphanage club in San Francisco.

The fifth annual "Summer Festival" presented at the Robert Mondavi Winery in Oakville was held on five successive Sunday evenings, June 30th to July 28th. The 14th of July was an "All Blues" night, with Big Joe Turner, Alexander and Eddie 'Cleanhead' Vinson. Featured artists on the other evenings included guitarist Charlie Byrd, the Preservation Hall Jazz Band, pianist Max Morath and Sarah Vaughan.

Still in California, on August 1st, along with Jimmy Reed and Joe Houston, he played the Rock Bottom in Van Nuys, while on the 25th he joined singer Big Miller for a concert organised by the Edmonton Jazz Society at the SUB Theatre in Edmonton, Canada. The following day, he and Big Miller, who was then a resident of Edmonton, played a concert for Jazz Calgary at the MacEwan Hall Ballroom.

Joe was back in Van Nuys on Sunday, September 15th, for a gig at the Blue Max. The stars were The Chantels, with Joe Houston and Vernon Green also appearing. On the 23rd he, Houston and Green were part of more "Oldies But Goodies," this time at The Tiffany Club in Pomona, together with The Coasters and Shirley and Lee.

Pablo Records next session in Los Angeles, 'The Trumpet Kings Meet Joe Turner,' took place on September 19th, 1974, with rather better results than the June date. The Trumpet Kings were Dizzy Gillespie, Roy Eldridge, Clark Terry and Harry Edison.

The 17th Annual Monterey Jazz Festival was to be held at the Monterey County Fairgrounds the weekend of September 20th-22nd, with Turner scheduled to appear in an 'Afternoon of the Blues' on the 21st, with Dizzy Gillespie, Eddie Vinson, Bo Diddley and Sunnyland Slim.

Norman Granz promoted another European tour by Count Basie and his Orchestra, co-starring Oscar Peterson, with Joe Turner the featured singer. In brief, the itinerary was:

September 1974
28	Royal Festival Hall, London, England
29	Antwerp, Belgium
30	Fores-National Auditorium, Brussels, Belgium

October 1974
1	Philips-Halle, Dusselddorf, Germany
2-3	France (rest days)
4	Salle-Pleyel, Paris, France
5	Victoria Hall, Geneva, Switzerland
6	Stadt Casino, Basle, Switzerland
7	Kongresshaus, Zurich, Switzerland

8	Saarbrucken, Germany
9/10	Congresszentrum, Hamburg, Germany
11/12	Kuppelsaal, Hanover, Germany
13	Jahrhunderthalle, Frankfurt-Am-Main, Germany
14/15	Deutsches Museum, Munich, Germany
16-17	Austria
18	Philharmonie, Berlin, Germany
19	Stockholm, Sweden
20	Umea Jazz Festival, Sweden
21	Folketahus, Stockhom, Sweden
22-23	Helsinki, Finland
24	Amsterdam, Holland
25	travel day
26	Lucerne Hall, Prague, Czechoslovakia
27	fly to New York

This tour was the opportunity for Turner and his wife, Pat, to enjoy the European honeymoon, albeit a working one, they had planned and lost in 1972.

Joe made some use of a walking stick and was seated while singing, but at London's Royal Festival Hall, on Saturday, September 28th, second house, these problems had little impact on his vocals. He shouted his blues just as powerfully as ever, though perhaps his articulation was affected slightly. It seemed that no matter his age, his health or his accompaniment, Big Joe continued to shout the blues in his own time-honoured way.

Max Jones in the *Melody Maker* was not impressed by Joe's accompaniment, a Count Basie octet (Sonny Cohn, trumpet, Jigs Whigham, trombone (subbing for a delayed Al Grey), Curtis Pegler, alto, Eddie 'Lockjaw' Davis, tenor, Basie, piano, Freddie Green, guitar, William Davis, bass, Skeets Marsh, drums), partly due to poor amplification, but he affirmed that "Turner sang beefily, even nobly in places, and was one of the pleasures of the evening."[20]

Jones did criticise, as many others have, Joe's limited choice of material, the usual Atlantic hits, including *Flip, Flop and Fly* and *Shake, Rattle and Roll*, plus *Roll 'Em, Pete*. An exception was the less often heard *Since I Fell For You*.

As noted earlier, it is believed that the Pablo album, *Flip, Flop and Fly*, the sleeve of which gives recording dates in 1972, came from two Basie concerts during the October 1974 tour. Joe Turner could not make the 1972 trip due to his diabetes diagnosis.

In November, possibly on the 8th and 9th, Turner was in a show at the Anaheim Convention Center. This was another "Oldies But Goodies;" but the Christmas Day show at Don Juan's in Long Beach was an "Oldie But Goodie Christmas Special". In addition to Turner, The Chantels, The Penguins and Joe Houston were among the participants.

Engagements, for which dates are not known, were also at the Golden Bear in Los Angeles.

1975

"After a four-year absence, the Berkeley Blues Festival will return Thursday and Friday, January 16th and 17th, with panel discussion workshops and two evening concerts at Pauley Ballroom on the UC-Berkeley campus. Big Mama Thornton, Dave Alexander, Big Joe Turner, George (Harmonica) Smith and a surprise appearance by an unnamed world-famous blues duo will comprise the programme on January 16th."

This was the news item in the *San Francisco Chronicle* for December 14th, 1974.

Over the weekend of February 15th-17th, The 3rd Annual 50's Festival of Rock'n Roll was held at the Magic Mountain park in Los Angeles. The Coasters, The Olympics, The Penguins and Joe Turner were among the stars advertised. Joe and the last two vocal groups were also heard in "Oldies But Goodies" on Friday and Saturday nights at the L.A. Convention Center around this time.

One date known to have been cancelled was that scheduled for February 21st, when Turner was to have supported the headliner, Albert King, at the San Gabriel Civic Auditorium. The *L.A. Times* reporter, Dennis Hunt, wrote,

"The biggest disappointment was that Turner had to cancel. So it was necessary to endure an earnest but uninteresting set by his replacement, Pee Wee Crayton. It was like expecting a ride in a Rolls Royce and having to settle for a spin in a Pinto. Neither Crayton's band nor the opening group, Rod Piazza and the Dirty Blues Band, had any superior performers or showed any particular promise".

The first of two recording dates this year for Pablo took place on March 3rd, featuring Sonny Stitt on alto and tenor, and Pee Wee Crayton on guitar. Issued as *Every Day I Have The Blues,* the unidentified sleeve note writer, possibly Norman Granz, comments on Joe Turner's health, stating that it

"isn't what it used to be. He suffers from diabetes and carries more than 300 pounds on his 6-foot, 1½-inch frame. He walks with a cane and finds it more comfortable singing while sitting in a chair.
"The singer considers his weight a sensitive issue and won't discuss the exact figures. 'That's personal,' he declares, turning his palms face up. 'I used to be skinny. People called me TV Joe.' …. Nevertheless, his rich baritone is still strong enough to shake a room. It jumps and booms with a power that carries it into every nook and corner without benefit of a microphone, much like the old days when he stood flat-footed roaring out waves of lyrics."

On March 15th Joe was due to feature, along with The Penguins, in a "Rock & Roll Revival, a live dance concert," to be held in the Northridge Gym in the California State University.

Blues singer and guitarist Aaron 'T-Bone' Walker died in Los Angeles on March 16th. A memorial concert was held at the Musicians' Union Auditorium at which Big Joe was present.

The San Gabriel Civic Auditorium had a "Blues for a Night" on May 29th, to feature B.B. King and Joe Turner. *Blues Who's Who* lists two other engagements for this year, all on the West Coast; the Parisian Room in Los Angeles and the Cat's Cradle in San Francisco.

Two dates are noted for July. An advert. for The Channel Club in San Pedro on the 6th, states, "Return Engagement from Hollywood The Ever Popular Big Joe Turner, The Crests and Joe Houston", and on the 19th, The Hillside Cocktails in Long Beach presented Turner, Houston and The Coasters. Turner was coupled with an unidentified "Mark Anthony".

The "Big Joe Turner Quartet" appeared at The Times Restaurant in Studio City on August 1st and 2nd, with an unidentified quartet. On Monday, the 18th, Joe, plus The Olympics, was at the Playgirl Club in Santa Ana.

Pee Wee Crayton was again the guitarist on the second Pablo album of 1975, featuring with Roy Eldridge on trumpet and Milt Jackson on vibes. Recorded in L.A. on August 27th, 'Nobody In Mind' highlights Joe on eight titles, mainly his standards, but including a remake of *Red Sails In The Sunset*, plus two originals, *I Just Didn't Have The Price* and *Juke Joint Blues*.

A few more dates in September and October find Turner still working on the West Coast. On September 17th he was back with The Coasters and Joe Houston, playing at California West, in the Rosemead district of Los Angeles. The following Sunday, the 21st, he starred at Billy Jack's in Van Nuys. Next, a free "all star blues festival" was presented by Berkeley University on the evening of October 8th. Held in the campus gymnasium, Contra Costa College, San Pablo, it also featured singer Mississippi Slim and pianist Mark Naftalin.

This level of activity confirms Peter Guralnick's summary a year or two later, "In recent years he has lived in California in semi-retirement with his wife Pat and 'our dog Rhythm,' as his business card proclaims."[21]

1976

A news item in the *Melody Maker* for February 28th, 1976, stated, "Joe Turner is reported to be seriously ill in a Los Angeles hospital". However, this particular hospitalisation was not for any immediately obvious reason.

During an April 1976 interview with Valerie Wilmer at his home on Cimarron Boulevard, Turner admitted

"For three or four days I was drinking day and night - when I wasn't asleep. …. my sister got on my case. I had been drinking pretty heavy about six or seven months, but it was just routine. It was my sister who brought up this mess. She said, 'You ought to go into the hospital, you're getting to be an alcoholic'." Joe denied he was an alcoholic but was persuaded to go to hospital for treatment, which appeared to be successful.[22]

Looking back, Valerie Wilmer recalled

"When I saw Joe again in L.A., he was far more subdued. He was not in the best of health, terribly overweight and could only walk with a stick. I met his wife, who was friendly enough, but we didn't spend much time together, just did the interview, had an iced tea or something similar and then I left them to it."[23]

Bob Hite, of the white blues band, Canned Heat, confirmed Joe's comments about his drinking problem. Interviewed by Max Jones in *Melody Maker* (June 5th, 1976), he said, "Joe's off the sauce and he's alright. He doesn't drink any more, and that was his main problem.

"He's a great man but he's hard to work with. The way he'll stop you, he'll sit down on the stage – and he's twice as big as I am – and when he's done, he just holds his cane up in the air. When you don't see the cane in the air that's the end of the song."

Bob gave a deep-voiced imitation of Big Joe:

"Give the boys in the band a big hand now … well, we're gonna sing a little blues now.' And he starts singing and you'd better be there. Every number's in C. We once tried to change keys on him and he knew at once it wasn't in C. I guess the reason is that most people who back him don't know how to back him, so if he keeps everything in the same key, they'll at least have that in common."

There were two Los Angeles sessions for Pablo this year. The first, on March 10th, 1976, produced an album called 'In The Evening', and had accompaniment by Bob Smith on alto and Pee Wee Crayton again, with another guitarist, Herman Bennett. The second, on May 27th, had a front-line of Jake Porter, trumpet, Roy Brewster, baritone horn, and Curtis Kirk, harmonica. This was entitled 'The Midnight Special'. These varying instrumental backings are a far cry from the Kansas City days and even those at Atlantic.

Turner was listed in early announcements for the New Orleans Jazz and Heritage Festival. He was to sing in a show entitled "The Rhythm and the Blues" on board the S.S. President on April 9, 1976. However, his name is not included in the Festival's printed programme and it must be assumed that he cancelled, due to continued ill-health.[24]

The Oldies and Goodies Club, formerly Ciro's, at 8433 Sunset Boulevard, is mentioned again, suggesting that Turner had made at least one recent appearance. Open only at the weekends, the club seated 400, with admission $3.00 and drinks $1.00. The report in the *Melody Maker* for April 17th, 1976 suggests that Turner, among several others, "perform all the time"!

By now Joe was well enough to participate in a Norman Granz promotion called the "Pablo Jazz Festival," along with pianist Oscar Peterson, guitarist Joe Pass, and the Count Basie orchestra. The festival was called "a road show" by the

San Diego Union when it reviewed the May 2nd programme at the San Diego Civic Theater. Its critic referred to, ".... Joe Turner, a blues singer not so strong as he once was." and "Turner romped satisfactorily, if not brilliantly, through a couple of basic blues things, winding up on *Shake, Rattle and Roll* ...."

For the week of June 9th-13th Turner was featured at Hungry Joes in the seaside resort of Huntingdon Beach, south of L.A., while on Saturday, June 19th, he was with Joe Houston at The Iron Mask in Long Beach. It is possible that Joe spent a second week at Hungry Joes, when it was also "Featuring The Hollywood Fats Band".

The Monterey Jazz Festival included The Johnny Otis Show on Saturday afternoon, September 17th, with Turner a surprise guest, flying in "at the last minute". Another September date was at the Lighthouse in Hermosa Beach, where reedman Sonny Stitt was the headliner. Turner joined him for the weekend of the 25th and 26th. Then the East Coast beckoned, with a scheduled "The Blues" concert in Washington, D.C. for the Smithsonian Institute on October 3rd, accompanied by a sextet led by altoist Rick Henderson.

Barney Josephson, who had opened Cafe Society in New York in December 1938, had retired from the jazz business. Since 1955 he had been running a restaurant in Greenwich Village, but when Mary Lou Williams needed a gig he could not refuse her. The Cookery became a jazz restaurant as of November 20th, 1970, Williams' opening night.

Of Joe Turner's 1976 engagement, Josephson told Dan Morgenstern that

" .... it took considerable persuasive powers to lure the huge singer from his Los Angeles lair. Joe's health hasn't been good of late, but we hope it holds up for this date."

Turner, booked for four weeks, November 8th to December 4th, worked with "that fine blues pianist from the West Coast via Texas", Lloyd Glenn, and guitarist Wayne Wright.[25]

Morgenstern began his very complimentary report of The Cookery engagement, in the January 1977 issue of *Jazz Journal*, with this paragraph,

"Joe Turner's month long-sojourn at the Cookery caused quite a stir in the press. Whitney Ballett, John S. Wilson and Gary Giddins heaped praise upon the big man in the *New Yorker*, *New York Times* and *Village Voice*. As a result, Barney Josephson's pleasant Greenwich Village cafe did capacity business. Even on the coldest December 3rd in New York history, people were standing on line waiting to get in."

Wayne Wright was quoted as saying that it was a pleasure to watch Big Joe eat - "He's earned that stomach" and "He's so down home, it's unbelievable." Asked if he was enjoying the gig, Wright said, "Yeah, but we haven't gotten out of the key of C all week!"[26]

One result of this engagement was that a visit from Doc Pomus renewed his friendship with Joe, which was to strengthen from then on, proving a true benefit to Joe in his later, difficult years.

Another was that after the publicity generated by his stay at The Cookery, offers of bookings increased and he began to work more regularly.

Lloyd Glenn

15

"a voice to stop an army in its tracks."

(1977-1985)

"Blues giant Big Joe Turner performed three nights [January 20th-22nd] at The Palms, a tiny club [at 1406] Polk Street in San Francisco, where he was accompanied by guitarist Mike Bloomfield and pianist Mark Naftalin, both alumni of the Paul Butterfield Blues Band, along with drummer Tom Dolinger, bassist Pat Campbell (on acoustic upright) and saxophonist Phil Smith. Producer Norman Dayron captured the shows on tape for a possible future release on Pablo."

So read a report by Joel Selvin in the *Melody Maker* for February 5th, 1977. Mr. Selvin wrote a longer account for the *San Francisco Chronicle* (January 22nd, 1977), which included the comment,

"At The Palms he sang songs in only two tempos – fast and slow – and all in the same key. His foghorn baritone roared out of his lungs with inhuman volume. He alternated jump tunes with slower blues pieces, mixing many similar lyrics into all his songs".
"Calling Big Joe Turner a living legend is too simple a generalization. He is the last survivor of an important American musical era, and he is unique in his field. The combination of his soporific (sic) singing style and musical style creates a total musical picture that is far more than just the sum of its parts".

Joe's next known booking was on February 26th when he was featured at the Robert Mondavi Winery in the Napa Valley.

There was a second gig at The Palms for March 4th-5th, with Bob Scott on drums and a saxophonist listed as "unknown". Pat Campbell later identified two saxophonists, John Stafford, alto, and Phil Smith, tenor and baritone. A Rock Beat 2-CD issue contains 23 tracks, the insert giving a recording date of March 5th.

Whether the tapes were even offered to Norman Granz seems doubtful, but many titles from The Palms engagement have appeared on numerous small label CDs.

Pianist Mark Naftalin told Jan Mark Wolkin,

"The Big Joe Turner records are all bootleg, no matter what label they are on. The original release of this material was unauthorised and all other releases follow from that. Permission was never granted by Big Joe Turner or by any of the musicians for the use of our performances.
"On some of the recordings with Big Joe the rhythm section was Bob

Scott, drums, and Pat Campbell, bass. There may have been a different rhythm section on some of the songs; we did about six nights altogether with Big Joe. I don't remember who the sax player was."[1]

Blues Who's Who lists a "concert tour with Lloyd Glenn across U.S.A.," and such a tour could have been part of the route to New York City for another long booking at The Cookery, from March 20th to May 7th, 1977, again with Lloyd Glenn and Wayne Wright. In the same period he sang at three "free concerts" arranged for Sunday afternoons at County Libraries in New Jersey, with the same accompaniment. On March 13th they were at Plainfield, on the 20th, Shrewsbury and the 27th, Mount Holly.

"Joe Turner's blues roar like a K.C. locomotive" was the headline for a report on the 20th date, written by George Kanzler, Jr. for the *Newark Star-Ledger* of March 24th, 1977, in the course of which he wrote, "When Joe Turner begins a blues chorus it's like the blast from an open furnace on a locomotive".

During the tour, sometime in May, Turner and Glenn broadcast on WBFO-FM, with Ronald Weinstock as m.c. This would have been during the duo's booking at the Tralfamadore Cafe in Buffalo, NY.

Making his way back to the West Coast, Turner had a booking, May 12th-22th, at Sandy's Jazz Revival in Boston, with drummer Jo Jones a member of the backing group, followed by an appearance, June 1st-5th, at the Jazz Showcase on Rush Street in Chicago. It is likely that the house rhythm section (George Freeman, guitar, Eddie Calhoun, bass, Phil Thomas, drums) worked with Turner.

Back on the West Coast, Joe sang with pianist Dorothy Donegan's Trio, for two nights, June 10th-11th, at Lee Magid's Cafe Concert in Tarzana. A fortnight later, June 24th-25th, he had another gig at The Palms in San Francisco. Joe also recorded for the soundtrack of the ABC-TV series, "Roots", though heard only briefly.

July was scheduled to be a month of Festivals, but the previous four-months travelling and performing took its toll and Turner was less busy for the remainder of the year. He was due to feature at the Newport Jazz Festival (3rd), at a Blues Picnic in Stanhope, N.J. (4th), during the Nice Jazz Festival in France (7th-17th), the Beaulieu Jazz Festival in Britain (9th/10th), the North Sea Jazz Festival in Holland (16th), and perhaps also the Montreux Jazz Festival. He was unable to appear at any of these events.

Presumably he was still able to accept gigs on the West Coast, which would explain the subsequent advertisements for appearances at The Palms in San Francisco, July 15th-16th, with tenor-player Ben 'King' Perkoff's band, and another date with the Dorothy Donegan Trio, at the Cafe Concert in Tanzania.

Further dates advertised were two nights, August 26th/27th at the Gaslight District in San Diego, another two nights, December 16th/17th, with Mike Bloomfield at The Palms in San Francisco, and dates with singer Spanky Wilson at the Parisian Room in Los Angeles, December 24th, plus New Year's Eve and New Year's Day

Turner was scheduled to be part of the "Quaker City Jazz Festival" to be held in the Tower Theatre in Philadelphia, appearing in a "Blues in Jazz" show on October 6th, alongside singer-pianist Mose Allison, tenor player Hank Crawford, Eddie 'Cleanhead' Vinson and the band Roomful of Blues. This is another booking which has not been confirmed.

Undated engagements, given in *Blues Who's Who*, include the Starwood in Hollywood, and the Fox Venice Theatre in Los Angeles.

1978

The first known date after the New Year's Day at the Parisian Room was on Sunday, February 19th when, along with the Hollywood Fats Band, Big Joe Turner played at the Forum Theater, as part of the Laguna Beach Winter Festival. (Hollywood Fats, alias Michael Mann, a guitarist, led his five-piece blues band from 1974 until his death in 1986.) Joe is next mentioned as one of fifty stars, celebrities and performers (including Steven Spielberg, Sylvester Stallone, Rod Stewart and Fleetwood Mac) who attended the premiere of the Paramount movie "American Hot Wax," on March 10th. The film was based on the career of Alan Freed.

German pianist Axel Zwingenberger, a boogie woogie specialist, persuaded Joe to record an album with him and they went into the Johnny Otis studio in Los Angeles, with Otis as engineer on May 22th. The release on the Telefunken label was named, "Let's Boogie Woogie All Night Long".

In June Turner was in San Francisco, appearing on the 16th and 17th (Friday and Saturday) at the Coffee Gallery on Grant Avenue. The following week, on June 22nd, in Hollywood, he recorded for Pablo with a small band backing, including Lloyd Glenn. Five titles made up an album called "Have No Fear, Big Joe Is Here" and a further three were in a compilation entitled "Stormy Monday".

The weekend of July 7th found Turner starring at The Lighthouse in Hermosa Beach, with the Pee Wee Crayton Blues Band, plus Smokey Wilson and Rod Piazza's Blues Band, while on Sunday, August 6th, he was part of "The Original Oldies But Goodies Stars" appearing at The Channel Club in San Pedro. His co-stars were The Shirelles and Joe Houston. At the end of the month he was in San Francisco, making repeat visits to the Coffee Gallery on Friday, the 25th, and The Palms the following day. A reporter for the *San Francisco Chronicle* (September 1st, 1978) wrote of the Coffee Gallery gig,

> "Big Joe Turner, the immortal Kansas City blues shouter, came through town last weekend …. and appeared, alack, very mortal, indeed. Turner, now 67, and among the last of the breed now supplanted by the Jimmy Witherspoon and B.B. King schools of the blues, sits on a chair now as he hollers *Flip, Flop and Fly* or *Shake, Rattle and Roll* and walks with the aid of crutches."

Turner had two bookings at the Stage #1 cocktail lounge, Los Angeles, in September. For the weekend of the 8th, 9th and 10th he worked with singer Margie Evans, and for that of the 22nd, 23rd, 24th he was with Ms Evans and Percy Mayfield. Still in L.A. in October, on the 3rd, he was at The White House at Laguna Beach, backed by Lloyd Glenn's quartet, finishing the month with a one week engagement at The Lighthouse, Hermosa Beach, Tuesday October 24th through Sunday, October 29th. His accompaniment was by the Hollywood Fats Blues Band.

Joe Turner. promotional photograph for movie, The Last of The Blue Devils, 1974. Courtesy Malcolm Walker

"The Last of the Blue Devils" (sub-titled 'The Kansas City Jazz Story'), directed by Bruce Ricker and based around the reunion of Kansas City musicians in K.C. on March 20th, 1974, premiered in New York City on November 9th, 1978. Turner is prominently featured, alongside Count Basie, Jay McShann, Budd Johnson and many other K.C. veterans. This is a unique documentary. In an early, moving sequence, as the musicians start to arrive at the Hall, Joe struggles out of a car, meets a few of the other musicians, then walks up the steps into the old union building. There is snow on the ground and, clearly overweight, he has difficulty walking, despite using a stick. In the course of the film he sings with backing by pianist Jay McShann's big band and by McShann's trio (McShann, piano, James Whitcomb, bass, Paul Gunther, drums), as well as being seen in conversation and generally enjoying himself. He sings all or parts of *Piney Brown Blues, Shake, Rattle and Roll, Roll 'Em Pete,* and *New Kansas City Blues.* The DVD also includes audio out-takes of *Honey Hush, Rose Garden, Chains of Love* and another *Shake, Rattle and Roll, plus* an extract from the 'Soundie' version of *Shake, Rattle and Roll.* The film is a fine tribute to all the musicians and to Big Joe Turner in particular. More detail can be found in the discography.

The Count Basie Orchestra appears in the movie but this section was filmed at a concert on the following day. Joe Turner was not involved. It was reported that the film, which runs for 85 minutes, was edited from thirty hours of original footage.

The New Orleans newspaper, the *Times-Picayune*, in its October 31, 1978 issue, reported, "'Kansas City Revisited' is the title of a stellar nostalgia trip November 18 at 8 p.m. in the Hyatt-Regency's Grand Ballroom. 'Together again' will be Count Basie and his orchestra, vocalists Big Joe Turner and Helen Humes, and the Clark Terry Quintet." (The Basie-Turner-Humes package was to have been featured at the Tampa Bay Jazzfest to be held in St. Petersburg, Florida, in mid-November but the festival was cancelled shortly before the November 10th opening.)

In late November or early December, Joe Turner played a ten-day gig at Sandy's Jazz Revival in Boston, with Lloyd Glenn on piano and a local guitarist. During this booking he told Peter Guralnick that in recent years he had lived in California in semi-retirement, which seems a fair comment, also suggesting that since the weeks at The Cookery he had been working steadily, which does not. Another of his remarks was, "Since I got off my diet, I'm as big as a house again."[2]

1979

George Thorogood and the Destroyers had billing over Big Joe when they played at the Zellerbach Auditorium of the University campus in San Francisco on April 10th, while on the weekend of April 27th-29th he was backed by the Pee Wee Crayton Blues Band at The Lighthouse, Hermosa Beach.

The *Boston Herald* for August 21st, 1979, reported, "Blues and rock'n'roll legend Big Joe Turner settles into Lulu White's tonight for a six-day stand ..." This booking conflicts with one announced for August 25th, when Turner, The Shirelles, Joe Houston and the T.J. Walker Band were scheduled to play at the Newporter Hotel, Newport Beach, for a Banning High School (classes of 1959) Reunion.

In September, on the 20th, he was partnered again with pianist Lloyd Glenn, plus tenor player Jimmy Tyler for an engagement at the Lone Star Cafe in New York's Greenwich Village. It is surprising that no other bookings have been traced for an apparently extensive Eastern tour.

The Texas Rock 'n' Roll Reunion for 1979 was held in the Palladium in Dallas on Friday, October 19th and Saturday, the 20th. There were reports in two local papers, one headlined "Turner's an oldie, but goodie", the other "Big Joe Turner highlight of rock'n'roll shows". Other acts in the show included The Coasters, Jimmy Velvet, Jewel Aikens and Ray Sharpe. The papers also said that

Turner was "reportedly making his last tour," and that he closed the show with a three-tune set. Roger Kaye stated, "He is in ill-health and barely able to walk, even with the aid of crutches," and Pete Oppel concluded with, "This indeed may be Joe Turner's last tour, but his untiring spirit, his dedication to his craft, his love of the art, will always remain."

1980

Talk of Turner's final tour was exaggerated, for on Friday, February 22nd he is found in the company of The Clovers, The Flamingos and other acts, appearing at the Memorial Auditorium in Greenville, South Carolina.

On Sunday, April 13th, Joe was advertised at the Topanga Corral in Los Angeles, and the following Sunday, the 20th, he appeared at the Belly Up Tavern in Solana Beach. The musicians involved included Louis Gasca, trumpet, Lee Allen, Mark Lessman, reeds; Lowell Fulson, guitar, and Happy Hopkins, harmonica. The *San Diego Reunion* reviewer, Ken Leighton, briefly summarises Turner's career, gives his weight as 450 pounds and notes that *TV Mama* was dedicated to Sophie Tucker. Big Mama Thornton was originally advertised to appear but is not mentioned in the review.

Big Mama Thornton was again due to appear alongside Turner for a "Big Blues Night" at The New Ice House in Pasadena, on Friday and Saturday, April 25th-26th. Two weeks later, May 9th, 10th and 11th, Big Joe starred at The Lighthouse, 30 Pier Avenue, Hermosa Beach, with Pee Wee Crayton's Blues Band.

Health problems continued to restrict Joe's ability to accept engagements, but a special event held in Kansas City could not be resisted. In May members of the Mutual Musicians Foundation in Kansas City celebrated the fiftieth anniversary of the black musicians union, with a concert on Saturday, May 24th, as part of the occasion. Local groups competed in a 'Battle of the Bands' and Joe sang with Jay McShann's All-Stars; Eddie 'Lockjaw' Davis, tenor, Claude Williams, violin, McShann, piano, LaVern Barber, bass, Paul Gunther, drums, and Priscilla Bowman, vocals.[3] The day also marked the opening of "Goin' To Kansas City," a travelling museum exhibit which toured, mainly in the Midwest, for nearly three years.

By the following day, May 25th, Joe had returned to Los Angeles in time to appear with singer and writer Ian Whitcomb, at the Variety Arts Center.

Turner was back at the Belly Up Tavern in Solana Beach on Sunday, July 6th, where he was to perform with the English All-Star Blues Band, while on the 19th there was another engagement at The New Ice House in Pasadena. The following day, the 20th, a "Blues & Gospel Festival" took place at the Veterans Memorial Stadium in Long Beach, with The Chambers Brothers, Big Joe Turner, Lowell Fulson, Margie Evans and Pee Wee Crayton as part of the blues contingent. Station KLON sponsored the festival. Don Snowden reported in the *Los Angeles Times* (July 23rd, 1980), "Big Joe Turner may be getting on in

years but his voice was in fine shape as he belted out a half-dozen of his hits, ...
backed by guitarist Pee Wee Crayton and the Doug MacLeod band".

Down Beat reported in its August 1st, 1980 issue, that both Joe Turner, from
Los Angeles, and Jay McShann, from Kansas, had been in New York City to
attend a July showing of "The Last of the Blue Devils".

The *L.A. Weekly* for July 18th, 1980 listed a forthcoming programme for the
Parisian Room on La Brea and Washington. It included: "Opening Tues., July
22nd - a week of the blues from giants Big Joe Turner, who used to sing with
Count Basie, Jimmy Witherspoon, who's enhanced the work of several jazz players
with his ruby-rich voice, and Pee Wee Crayton, a superlative blues guitarist".

Two dates are known for August. An appearance on the 17th at the Belly Up
Tavern in Solana Beach and three nights at The Lighthouse in Hermosa Beach,
29th-31st. At the latter club he was to be accompanied by James Harman's Blues
Band.

In his memoir, "A Date with Joe Turner," published in the *Broadside* magazine
for December 2000, tenor player Tony Kisch reminisced:

"In 1980 I had the privilege of backing up Joe and Lloyd Glenn for about
a week of gigs along with a band I was with at the time. Nothing much
had changed. Joe still sang every song in the key of C, he still sang the
entire set slumped in a chair, he was still as 'big as a house'. Maybe bigger.
Joe was ailing pretty bad most nights. One particularly bad night, during
one particularly bad set, he called off *Shake, Rattle & Roll* three times. A
couple of nights though, the old magic shined through and made the rest
worthwhile and then some".

George Wein's promotion, "Jazz at the Hollywood Bowl," part of the Los
Angeles Philharmonic's summer schedule concluded on September 10th with
a "Bicentennial Blues" concert featuring B.B. King, Joe Turner, Lloyd Glenn,
and Big Mama Thornton. A report in the *Los Angeles Times* (September 12th,
1980) noted, "Pianist Lloyd Glenn's quartet kicked off the show with a jazzy
instrumental, then accompanied Big Joe Turner, whose brief four-song segment
wasn't quite up to his usual standard".

Ten days later, on Saturday, the 20th, a "Back to the Blues" show was featured
at the Monterey Jazz Festival. This afternoon session was to star the James
Cotton and Hollywood Fats Bands, Eddie "Cleanhead" Vinson, Big Joe Turner
and Jay McShann with The Monterey Jazz Festival All Stars.

Another young musician who worked with Turner during the 1980s was
guitarist and singer Bernie Pearl, leader of his own Blues Band. Three of those
occasions he recalled in particular:

"I played a benefit Xmas show for KPFK - Pacifica Radio – at the Santa
Monica Civic Auditorium. I had called Pee Wee Crayton to do it with
me and he suggested I also call Big Joe .... as it was no pay, I assumed he
wouldn't be interested. I was wrong. He didn't want to be excluded and
told Pee Wee so. Joe was an outgoing, accessible, and really good man, as
I found out.

"I did a weekly Sunday show at a nice lounge (Ms. Whis) in Long Beach, with vocalist Barbara Morrison. We often called on some of our local artists to come in and do a set – it was a paid gig, even if it wasn't a lot of money. Most everyone accepted, including Big Joe.

"I was asked to be the back-up for several L.A. artists at a small festival in Fresno. I probably contacted some of them, although I had no involvement with the payment and cannot recall the exact way they were booked. I had a Ford van at the time and packed the whole contingent in, including Big Joe. The festival headliner was to be Albert King, who cancelled at the last minute. I have no idea of the cause. By the time we got there local interest had died and we played - I believe it was a two-day event - to largely empty bleachers outdoors. The producer did pay my band what we were promised and I heard no one else complain that they weren't paid. I asked Joe what he thought and he said something like, 'What we have here is a flop. I played plenty of them'."

Bernie Pearl also has a memory of playing with Turner on a Jules Bihari recording session for Kent Records, though he can recall few details.[5] In 1980 he was hosting a "Nothing But The Blues" show on radio station KLON (later KKJZ), when the station decided he should direct the "KLON Blues and Gospel Festival" which would help fund its activities. The first event, on July 20th, 1980, at the Veteran's Stadium, Long Beach featured Joe Turner, Pee Wee Crayton, Lowell Fulson, the Chambers Brothers, the Hollywood Fats band and others.

Bernie Pearl remembered,

"I largely booked people I knew and who lived locally, that first year. I had booked Pee Wee Crayton. He asked, "What about Big Joe?" I didn't know Joe personally and was, frankly, shocked that such a high-profile performer (as I saw him) might be interested in playing a low-budget, first-time local event. ….I called him and he readily agreed to play".[6]

Another young singer/guitarist who worked with Joe Turner in this period was Doug MacLeod, who was only thirteen or fourteen when he first heard Joe at the Brooklyn Fox Theatre, when the MacLeod family lived in New York. Thirty years later, when Doug knew and accompanied him, it was towards the end of his life, when he was not well, but still had so much energy, that joy of entertaining people. "It was an honour to work behind him."

Doug recalled that from late 1970s until Joe's death in 1985 his backing musicians were like a family. Everybody played with everybody else.

"I had two bands. The first band in 1979 was The Gravy Bros. Band with George 'Harmonica' Smith, Gilbert Hansen on bass and Sam Canzona, drums. We played at Hollahan's (later called The Starboard Attitude) on the Redondo Beach Pier. (The club had a seating capacity of fifty and was always packed.) On those Saturday and Sunday afternoons people like Joe, Big Mama, Lowell Fulson, Shakey Jake, Johnny Dyer, and

Cleanhead Vinson played, darn near every blues musician that was living in the L.A. area.

"In 1980 or so George encouraged me to start my own band because I was writing all original songs. The first band was Llew Matthews on piano, Eric Ajaye on bass, and Lee Spath on drums.

"Others in the "family" were Pee Wee Crayton, guitar, Eddie 'Cleanhead' Vinson, alto, Freddy Clark, tenor, Bill Clark, tenor, Teddy de Rouen, guitar, Soko Richardson, drums. Often there were three guitars in the backing group, with Crayton, MacLeod and de Rouen. Gigs were played all over, at spots like The Lighthouse, the Parisian Room, Shakey Jake's Safari Club, Smokey Wilson's Pioneer Club, and the Redondo Beach Pier.

"One night at the Lighthouse Jazz and Blues Club Turner went on stage, only to realise he had left his teeth in the dressing room. Or, as Pee Wee Crayton commented, gone on 'with a mouthful of empty'. There followed a protracted plot to retrieve the teeth and smuggle them to Joe!"[7]

1981

David Driver and Joe Turner, 6121 Cimarron Street, L.A., April 21, 1981. Photograph courtesy Liz and David Driver

"It was late in 1980 [recalled David Driver] that we discovered that (Turner) was dangerously ill in a Los Angeles hospital with blood clots on his lungs, diabetes and pneumonia." This news was also reported by the *Austin-American Statesman for* February 7th,1981, "Big Joe Turner described as 'critically ill' at Cedars-Sinai in L.A. ..." and in Britain by the *Melody Maker,* February 14th, 1981, "Blues singer Big Joe Turner is reported in serious condition at Cedars Sinai Hospital in Los Angeles".

One cancelled date would have been a return visit to The Lighthouse in Hermosa Beach on December 4th - "opening night for a wonderful blues show with Big Joe Turner, Jimmy Witherspoon and the band of guitarist Pee Wee Crayton".

Left to right, Liz Driver, Joe Turner, Pat Turner, 5121 Cimarron Street, L.A., April 21, 1981. Photograph courtesy Liz and David Driver

Another undoubted cancellation was the January 27th opening night at the Parisian Room on La Brea and Washington for a "rip-roaring Blues Festival, with greats Big Joe Turner, Big Mama Thornton and the Pee Wee Crayton band. Hooray for the immortal twelve bars". This was the announcement in the *Los Angeles Weekly* of January 23, 1981.

In April David and Liz Driver made the journey from the U.K. to L.A., visiting the Turners on April 21st. Joe was still poorly but progressing. After the visit, David Driver wrote to *Jazz Journal* to confirm that Turner "had recovered from his illness – in fact, it was more like a series of illnesses."[8]

Joe Turner putting on a brave face. 6121 Cimarron Street, L.A. April 21, 1981.
Photograph courtesy of Liz and David Driver

On May 22nd, four days after his birthday, Turner was sufficiently recovered to record a second album with Axel Zwingenberger, entitled "Boogie Woogie Jubilee". The pianist said,

> "Joe and Pat and myself stayed in contact and in 1981, following a difficult period of Joe's health, we recorded a second album on the occasion of Joe's seventieth birthday, at his home with his friends partying with us"[9]

He also commented that Turner was depressed and hid in his bedroom for a time, because he believed that his voice was gone, though he soon emerged when he heard Zwingenberger and drummer Roy Milton settling into a rocking groove. *Cimarron Street Boogie* was a solo piano tribute to the location, 6121 Cimarron Street, Inglewood.

An even more dramatic story unfolded thus in *Jazz Singers* -

> "In 1981, at the age of 70, Big Joe Turner discharged himself from a Los Angeles hospital where he had been treated for pneumonia and blood clots and made his way across several states to take the stage at a celebrated nightclub in New York".[10]

JoeTurner and Axel Zwingenberger 1981

The "celebrated" nightclub was at 125 E.15th Street and was called Tramps. It was perhaps July 3rd when Joe was scheduled to start a two-week engagement there, four nights a week, Wednesday through Saturday, though later newspaper reports suggest the actual days were flexible.

Turner's initial backing was led by pianist Sammy Price, with Percy Francis, tenor, Bill Davis, bass, and Ronnie Cole, drums.[11] When Gary Giddins visited the club he noted Percy France (not Francis), tenor, and Wes Landers, drums.[12] Stanley Dance stated that Tramps made Turner so comfortable he had extended his engagement to the end of the year and his backing unit then included Charlie Brown, tenor, and Charles Otis, drums.[13] Towards the end of December the personnel was, in addition to Brown and Otis, probably Chris Tonens, piano, Mike Barnett, guitar, and Jesse 'Preacher' Fairman, bass.

Six months after their trip to Los Angeles, David and Liz Driver made the pilgrimage to New York to hear Joe Turner, catching him at Tramps on October 21st and 24th, as well as having lunch with Joe and Pat on Sunday, the 25th. Driver agreed with other reports, writing that "Joe was in fine voice, as strong and powerful as you could want. Off stage he is monosyllabic and his gait was unsteady but he came alive on stage." He also commented that on the Saturday the Percy France band, who had a previous booking, were replaced by a band led by the overloud Charlie Otis.[14]

Joe Turner, Pat Turner, Liz Driver, Tramps, NYC, October 24, 1981

Big Joe Turner at Tramps, New York, October 21, 1981. Charles Otis may be drummer. Photographs courtesy of Liz and David Driver

Other known dates for Turner's weekend appearances at Tramps at this time, Friday and Saturday nights, are October 30th/31st, November 6th/7th, December 11th/12th, 18th/19th, then Thursday, 31st, and no doubt January 1st. Giddins also reported Joe sitting in at the Greene Street club where Jay McShann, piano, Claude Williams, violin, and Paul West, bass, were playing.

At the time of Turner's appearance at Tramps, Stanley Dance wrote:

"Joe has been living on the West Coast and has been quite ill over the past half dozen years and his trips to New York, or anywhere for that matter, have been infrequent …. But what is most extraordinary about Big Joe Turner's engagement at Tramps is that, despite the fact that he is 70 years old and has been so sick that he must walk on crutches and looks rather wan and ashen, Joe Turner is singing with as much power and majesty as he ever has."

He continued

"Joe sits on a stool with a kingly presence and belts out his repertoire (you know it well – *Shake, Rattle and Roll, Cherry Red, Roll 'Em Pete*) with a voice so rich and clear and strong that the walls shake, the plates rattle and the tables rock."[15]

The Village Voice (October 20th, 1981) also mentioned that he looked a lot thinner and echoed Dance's comment, "After five years at home in L.A., when he was too ill to travel..." which raises concerns about the reported previous trips to New York, Kansas City and Boston in 1978, 1979 and 1980.

Similarly, Arnold Schwartz (in *Living Blues*, July/August 1994) reported,

"To reach the stage from his table he required the use of a walker and assistance from a club employee …. his facial expression sometimes seemed to say he wished he could be anywhere else …." "And then it was star time, and I do mean star time – all eyes were on this enormous man struggling to reach the stage, and there was an electric energy in the room not felt when other blues performers played Tramps.
"The best part of seeing him in this intimate setting was that he had lost none of his vocal ability, power or charisma – he just sat down, picked up the mike, and sang up a storm."

Another visitor to Tramps was Leslie Gourse, who said that Joe was reportedly very ill with diabetes, with his lower body stiffened by arthritis. His being thinner was obviously relative; Gourse wrote, "Over 235 pounds by most estimates, he had once weighed about 350".[16]

Big Joe Turner, with the ten-piece Roomful of Blues Band, played at Sandy's Jazz Revival in Boston on November 10th. Steve Morse of the *Boston Globe* (November 12th, 1981) wrote,

"But unlike many early legends whose gifts waned with age, Turner has continued to churn out the blues with authority. While he has been periodically sidelined in recent years – suffering from pneumonia and diabetes – he has never lost the fire. And though he needed crutches to get him on the stage on Tuesday night, he settled into his chair and eschewed sympathy".

Morse also noted that Big Joe "still has a voice that could stop an army in its tracks".

A further date with Roomful of Blues was scheduled for November 17th at Lupo's Heartbreak Hotel in Providence, Rhode Island. This was probably the occasion when the mayor of Providence awarded him the key to the city. While in the New York area he was also reported playing a gig at the Ginger Man club.

Tony Kisch, in his *Broadside* memoir, infers that it may have been the late 1970s, rather than the early 80s, when he was hanging out with the Roomful of Blues. He wrote,

"I was lucky enough to see them with Joe on a number of occasions, which ranged from the lethargic to the sublime, and offstage quite often to the surreal."

One evening he went with some band members to collect Turner for their gig. They found him in his hotel bedroom, and scattered around were insulin bottles, U-100 syringes, and empty bourbon bottles. Joe was lying on the bed, polishing off a pint of Pralines 'n' Cream ice cream.

1982

As Spring arrived, Turner became more active around the Los Angeles area. On March 8th he was at The Music Machine in West L.A. and on the 14th at the Tiki Island room. For the latter date he was featured alongside Percy Mayfield and Mickey Champion. Then, on Saturday, the 20th, he was due at the Club Lingerie in Hollywood, where his backing group was to be The Lee Allen Orchestra, with Phil Alvin, harmonica, Bill Bateman, drums, Gene Taylor, piano; Larry Taylor, bass-guitar and Steve Berlin, baritone.

"Turner continued to play club dates, drawing rave reviews for a 1982 Club Lingerie performance in Hollywood when he was backed by members of The Blasters and saxophone legend Lee Allen."[17] Larry Cohn said that Joe often sang in Los Angeles area "nu-wave niteries," accompanied by such retro-hip bands as the Blasters."[18]

Tenor player and occasional band leader, Lee Allen, first recorded with Joe Turner in 1953, around the time that Allen was a member of Fats Domino's group. That Atlantic session was followed by numerous meetings over the next thirty years, including recording sessions for Pablo.

The Blasters had been formed by Dave and Phil Alvin. Both sang and played guitar, usually with Dave on lead guitar and Phil as lead singer and occasional harmonica player. In the notes to their album, 'Lost Time,' recorded in 2015, Dave wrote,

"There is one artist, however, that we pay tribute to on this album who holds a very special place in my brother's heart and mine: the legendary blues shouter Big Joe Turner. Phil and I were barely teenagers when we were blessed to become friends with and be mentored by the decades older, larger than life Mr. Turner. We remained friends with him the rest of his life and we remain Big Joe's humble students to this day. In his memory we lovingly cut four of his songs for this record and I proudly believe not many other singers today can do Big Joe justice like my brother Phil can."

The four titles to which Dave Alvin refers are *Hide and Seek*, plus three of Joe's compositions, *Cherry Red Blues*, *Wee Baby Blues* and *Feeling Happy*.

Dave Alvin also wrote and recorded, in 2008, a song tribute to Joe Turner called *Boss of the Blues*. This was included on a CD entitled "Dave Alvin and the Guilty Women". Writing in *The Blasters Newsletter*, issue 59, about the songs on the CD [YepRoc YEP-2155], Alvin recalled

".... a true story that happened one night after a gig when Phil's band backed up Big Joe Turner. I was acting as Joe's manager – even wearing a suit. Usually after a gig, we would drive him home directly. But on this night he was feeling no pain and he said: 'Let's drive down Central Avenue." It was a ghost town at this point, but Joe pointed out where all the clubs were and where he sang and everybody played. It was one of the great memories of my life."

An advertisement in the *Los Angeles Times* (March 21st 1982) announced "Big Joe Turner's Blues Festival," which opened Tuesday, the 23rd, running until Sunday the 28th, in the Parisian Room at 4906 West Washington Boulevard. With Joe were singer Margie Evans and guitarist Pee Wee Crayton's band, consisting of three saxes, piano, second guitar, bass and drums. A report by Mark Humphrey in the *L.A. Weekly*, dated April 8th, 1982, stating that he saw the show on Monday, the 22nd, said:

"Then came Big Joe Turner – on crutches. Pale, stolid, at once massive and frail, Turner's moribund appearance didn't prepare you for what happened when he opened his mouth. He launched into *Everyday I Have The Blues*, head bobbing, eyes shut and sounded for all the world like one of his records from 30 years ago. As he sat impassively, his performance took on a mediumistic quality, as if this massive voice had taken possession of a frail old man. All that stentorian thunder issuing forth from someone who looked better suited to a hospital bed than a nightclub stage was startling, to say the least."

Mark Humphrey's review concluded, "It was one of the most amazing – and moving – performances imaginable."

The Cabaret on La Cienega Boulevard had a Grand Opening on Friday, April 2nd, with Joe headlining on the 3rd and 4th. He was again backed by Pee Wee Crayton's band. On the 12th he was with The Night Owls at the Music

Machine in West L.A., followed in May by another booking at the Parisian Room, 11th to 15th, alongside Margie Evans. Then, with Lowell Fulson, he returned to the Tiki Lounge for the weekend of May 28th-31st.

It was on May 3rd, 1982, that James Austin interviewed Joe for the November 1982 edition of *Goldmine* magazine, with the singer telling him, "... I've been having a little trouble with my eyes. I been seeing double, so I don't know how I'm going to get around too good". He then talked of his diabetes, of being off injections and tablets, but trying to control it by dieting.

On June 15th Turner was scheduled to give a concert as part of the four-day Basically American Music Festival, held in the Northrop Auditorium at the University of Minnesota, but one advertisement is over-stamped, "Big Joe Turner will not appear due to illness".

By July, however, he was fit enough to travel to New York, appearing at Tramps again, for an extended run of weekend bookings, starting on the second. There were two shows, 9 and 11:30 p.m. In September the gig was increased by two days, Wednesdays through Saturdays. The accompanying band had, in late August, become Eddie Chamblee, tenor, Ernest Hayes, piano, Billy Butler, guitar, Sonny Wellesley, bass; and Belton Evans, drums.

The Boss of the Blues is back

By SANDY INGHAM

Big Joe Turner is back in town. And if you like blues singing, you should go to town too — this is a rare opportunity to see one of the all-time greats.

Turner has been shouting down the house at Tramps, a downtown New York nightclub, on weekends for the past month. In September, he'll be working four nights a week — Wednesdays through Saturdays.

A giant of a man with a bullhorn of a voice, Turner, now 71 years old, learned his trade in Kansas City in the 1920s and '30s. It was a wide-open town back then, and its music, epitomized by Count Basie, roared out of every speakeasy. Turner was a bartender who also sang, and legend has it he would occasionally step outside to drum up business, and let loose a blast of music whose sound carried for blocks. At last hearing, the voice had lost none of its raw power.

Turner shows up in one New York club or another about once a year. I last saw him a few years ago at The Cookery. He blew listeners away with his stirring reworkings of old

blues classics like "Cherry Red," "How Long," "Roll 'em Pete" and "Shake, Rattle and Roll." The latter was his song before Bill Haley & The Comets popularized it in the early '50s — it was about as close as Turner ever came to a hit record.

Turner's baritone voice is devoid of tricks. He plunges straight into his songs, using almost no vibrato, ramming his notes home right on the beat, then lagging a bit behind it, then pushing up the tempo. His numbers are often amalgams of several old blues about women who do their men wrong, and he borrows a lyric here, a lyric there. But the words themselves mean little; what counts is that soaring, shouting, blue-note machine of a voice.

During his current engagement, Turner is backed by a five-piece band: Billy Butler, guitar; Ernest Hayes, piano; Eddie Chamblee, sax; Belton Evans, drums; and Sonny Wellesley, bass.

Tramps is at 125 E. 15th St. There's a $7 cover charge weeknights, $8 Fridays and Saturdays. Shows are at 9 and 11.30. Reservations are a must. (212-777-5077).

JOE TURNER
... K.C. shouter

Central New Jersey Home News, September 2, 1982

Other engagements while in the East included a gig with the Roomful of Blues band at Lupo's Heartbreak Hotel in Providence, Rhode Island. One track, *Shake Rattle and Roll*, recorded there on July 22nd, was included on a Rounder CD by the band. The singer continued to be in good voice, as the recording confirms. At the end of the month, July 30th/31st, Joe was at Sandy Berman's Jazz Blues Revival in Boston, with "an all-star line-up" of George Leh, singer, Ron Levy, piano, and the Luther 'Guitar' Johnson band".

Roomful of Blues: l-r, front, Ronnie Earl, Doc Pomus, Joe Turner; back Bob Eros, Bob Porter, Rich Lataille, Greg Piccolo, John Ros.

In October, on the 11th, he was with the Dicey Band (Bill Dicey, harmonica) at Jonathan Swift's in Cambridge, Mass., and on the 18th with the Billy Butler-Belton Evans Band at the Interlude in Blauvelt, N.Y. At the end of that month, probably the 28th, he appeared with Dr. John's Band at the Lone Star Cafe in New Jersey. Dr. John subsequently guested as a pianist on a Turner recording session a few weeks later.

Joe was still at Tramps for Christmas and to welcome in 1983.

1983

Remaining on the East coast, Turner was at The Lone Star Cafe in New Brunswick, NJ, on January 20th, where he teamed up with "Texas rock 'n' roller Delbert McClinton", while Roomful of Blues, led by tenor-man Greg Piccolo, and New York were the connection again when Turner recorded with this nine-piece band for Muse Records, January 26th, 1983. New Orleans pianist, Dr. John (Malcolm John Rebennack) was a special guest for one track on the resulting 'Blues Train' album. Bob Porter, who co-produced the session with Doc Pomus, confirmed that Doc rehearsed the new tunes with Joe. "He used a blind pianist (Al Copley) and despite the fact that the pianist couldn't see and that Joe could neither read nor write, Joe insisted on the sheet music."

Porter also recalled,

"After Joe finished his vocals, he was told he could leave if he wished. He said no, that he wanted to listen to 'these guys' play. At the end of the date, diabetic Joe had consumed an entire six-pack of beer and he passed out, falling atop [guitarist] Ronnie Earl."[19]

Doc Pomus with Shirley Hauser, his then lady friend. New York, 1980s. Photograph courtesy Liz and David Driver, and Sharyn Felder

Johnny Otis was at the Blue Room of the Fairmont Hotel in New Orleans from February 9th to 23rd. It is not known if Joe Turner was part of the show.

Joe was at the New Orleans Jazz Fest for two appearances, one on April 30th with trumpeter Dave Bartholomew's Orchestra and the following day with the big band of Luther Kent and Trick Bag. Bartholomew's band included the guitarist Justin Adams and one spectator recalled that Joe Turner was "magnificent – in excellent voice."[20] During his Sunday (May 1st) set, festival producer George Wein sat-in on piano.

On May 6th and 7th he was scheduled to sing at Dick Gibson's all-star Jazz Concerts at the Paramount Theatre in Denver, but there is no confirmation that he did appear.

It would seem that Turner spent most of the first half of the year on the Eastern side of the country. He recorded in New York again on May 18th, 1983, this time for the Southland label, part of the GHB Foundation, which has been releasing records on Jazzology, Circle and other labels since 1947. Joe's backing was by pianist Knocky Parker's Houserockers. Parker was perhaps a surprise choice to lead the group, being best known as a ragtime pianist, though Eddie Chamblee, playing alto and tenor in the quintet, was a noted blues player, who had also featured with the Lionel Hampton big band.

On May 29th Turner was due in Detroit for an appearance with drummer J.C. Heard's Quintet at the Stroh's Motor City Bluegrass and Traditional Music Festival in Meadow Brook. Perhaps this was the occasion recalled by Jim Gallert, when Big Joe sang at the WDET festival in Detroit's Eastwood Gardens, where his accompanying quartet included George Benson, tenor, Jeff Halsey, bass, J.C. Heard, drums, and an unidentified pianist.

The following month Joe was in New York for a week at Fat Tuesday's, supported by Jay McShann, piano, Major Holley, bass, and Joey Baron, drums. Lee Jeske reviewed in *Down Beat* (July 1983) and among his comments was,

> "...Big Joe settled himself onto a chair, opened up his toothless mouth and launched into *Hide And Go Seek*. The voice is massive - an undiminished American monument – and McShann shut his eyes, shook his jowls and dug into the boogie blues".

Another jazz date was at New York University's Loeb Student Center on June 10th, Turner appearing with Joe Newman, trumpet, Bob Wilber, reeds, Dave McKenna, piano, Major Holley, bass, and Oliver Jackson, drums. On the 18th he was to sing at Folk City on West 3rd Street, and on the 24th at the Red Creek's Harmonia Gardens, in Rochester, NY, where his accompaniment was to be "from the local band of the blues guitarist Joe Beard".

Reporting on the Rochester gig, Jack Garner wrote:

> "A worn 72-year-old hulk of a man continues to hobble on crutches each night onto a stage in a rock or jazz club or blues haven, most likely in New York City. He struggles with the arthritic pain in his legs and slumps painfully onto a stool at center stage.

But then the ageless music of the blues begins, and an equally ageless booming baritone voice bursts forth from Big Joe Turner. One recent night here, Joe Turner sang the classic blues couplets that have been part of his repertoire since he first got his reputation as a singing bartender in Prohibition speak-easies."[21]

The 1983 Kool Jazz Festival ran from June 24th to July 3rd. It is likely that a Kansas City Blues Reunion, Jay McShann and Big Joe Turner, with Major Holley and Oliver Jackson, scheduled for three nights, June 28th-30th were part of the Festival. Another, held in Carnegie Hall on July 1st, was called 'An Evening with Joe Williams and Friends,' with Barry McRae's review in *Jazz Journal* for September 1983 stating, "There were fine contributions from Frank Wess [tenor], Joe Wilder [trumpet] and Billy Mitchell [tenor] but the whole show was stolen by Big Joe Turner, who eagle rocked us all to oblivion". On July 3rd at Town Hall, the concert was titled, 'Good Times, Bad Times,' narrated by Studs Terkel, and included a set by Turner with Jay McShann, and drummer Panama Francis.

These concert dates were followed by a short booking, with Jay McShann and a rhythm section, at Fat Tuesday's, while on July 16th/17th Joe was scheduled to play with Roomful of Blues at Sandy's Jazz Revival in Boston.

August found Turner's stay on the East Coast coming to a close. On the 6th he was at a jazz festival (named for pianist and composer Eubie Blake) held at Heckscher State Park in Islip, when his accompanists were Buddy Tate, tenor, Jay McShann, piano, Major Holley, bass, and Oliver Jackson, drums. By the time of his next known engagement he is back on the West Coast; on August 14th, at the Tiki Island club in Los Angeles, a "Battle of the blues with Big Joe Turner and Lowell Fulson".

A news item in the *Los Angeles Sentinel*, August 30th, 1983, reported, "The wife of blues artist Big Joe Turner is in critical condition in the cardiac care unit of Cedars-Sinai Hospital, and Big Joe is not doing so well himself." Fortunately, Patricia did recover.

Two benefit performances followed, the first for George 'Harmonica' Smith at the Hall of Fame Club on Western Avenue. The second was for Roy Milton, who was in hospital having suffered a stroke, held at the Club Lingerie on September 4th. This last was an all-star affair, with Jimmy Witherspoon, Eddie 'Cleanhead' Vinson, Jay McNeely, Lowell Fulson, Percy Mayfield, Pee Wee Crayton and Joe Turner.

Joe was in Canada in September, playing an engagement in Ottowa at the Cock'n'Lion Room of the Chateau Laurier, with Wray Downes, followed by two-weeks, closing October 8th, at Bourbon Street in Toronto, accompanied by local musicians P.J. Perry, alto, tenor, Wray Downes, piano, Steve Wallace, bass, and Archie Alleyne, drums. Shortly afterwards Joe was admitted to a New York hospital, reportedly having suffered a stroke.[22]

If these dates are correct, then his stay in hospital was relatively brief, because on October 14th and 15th he was back in Los Angeles to appear at Club Lingerie in Los Angeles, where he was backed by The Blasters. An advertisement in the *L.A. Weekly* refers only to:

THE GRANDFATHER OF ROCK AND ROLL RETURNS
BIG JOE TURNER
with LEE ALLEN and guests

It was probably this engagement which Tony Kisch was recalling when he wrote,

> "The last time I saw Joe was in 1983 …. at Club Lingerie in Hollywood. By some miracle he was feeling good that night. It was probably because he was being backed by the Blasters, whose pianist, Gene Taylor, he had always especially liked. When he wanted to, Gene could play just like Pete Johnson. That night, Joe sang old favorites and requests and after almost every tune he'd point to Gene and bellow, 'The white Pete Johnson!'"

Bullmoose Jackson and Big Joe Turner, with a fan. Club Lingerie, Hollywood, 1980s. Photograph courtesy Mary Katherine Aldin.

Twelve days later, the 27th, Joe was at the Music Machine in Santa Monica, with Eddie Vinson and a band led by Lee Allen. John Breckow recalled that the club was as tacky as its name, saying "The show was typical of the later Joe 'mush mouth' Turner. That booming, rolling voice that had thrilled for decades was on its way out".[23] (Bob Porter's view was that the Music Machine was just another blues joint) A selection of titles recorded that evening was issued on a Floating World CD.

November was comparatively busy. Pat Turner had organised an all-star benefit at the Tiger Lounge for Sunday, November 6th, where the participants included Pee Wee Crayton, Charles Brown, Jimmy Witherspoon, Percy Mayfield, Ernie Andrews, Lowell Fulson, Margie Evans, Lee Allen, Red Hollway and more, plus her husband, of course. On the 11th and 12th Turner appeared at the Manhattan Supper Club in Santa Monica and on the 24th-26th he was in Fort Worth, Texas, at the Caravan of Dreams "avant-garde arts center". In between, on the 18th, he sang at The Nugget on the campus of Cal State Long Beach, featured alongside Eddie Vinson and the Lee Allen Orchestra.

Advertised for December were engagements, Sunday, the 11th, at Goodies in Fullerton, Orange County, Friday, the 16th, at Hop Singh's in Marina Del Rey, and Monday, the 19th at Mugsy Malone's in Anaheim. At Malone's he was billed with Will King and Guitar Shorty. He appeared again at Hop Singh's, with A Band Called Sam, seeing the old year out on December 31st. The band was led by singer/guitarist Sam 'Bluzman' Taylor, son of tenor player Sam 'The Man' Taylor, who had recorded with Turner several times in the 1950s.

During the year Joe Turner was inducted into the Blues Hall of Fame, located in Memphis, Tennessee.

Katie Bryant, Joe's sister, died in 1983 in Los Angeles, where she too had lived for many years. It was also about this time that Joe's mother passed.

1984

Hop Singh's was again the venue, with A Band Called Sam, for Turner's next known engagement on Saturday, January 21st, followed by a concert with the Lee Allen All Stars at The Last Nights of Pompeii in Palm Springs on February 12th.

In Hollywood, on February 14, Joe recorded his penultimate Pablo recording session. Tenor saxophonist Lee Allen was one of the octet, with electric guitars and a bass guitar prominent. The album, 'Kansas City Here I Come' has just six tracks, the shortest not quite four-and-half-minutes. One title is Joe's version of the Frank Sinatra hit, *Time After Time,* as surprising a choice as when he recorded it for Atlantic a quarter of a century before.

Also early in the year, singer Joe Williams was the subject of a one-hour television documentary. He had Joe Turner as a guest, recording two songs with him.[24] On YouTube they can be seen duetting on *Wee Baby Blues,* aided by Harry Edison, trumpet, Gerald Wiggins, piano, Monty Budwig, bass and Gerryck King, drums.

On Sunday afternoon, February 19th, Joe joined with Pee Wee Crayton and Percy Mayfield to play a union benefit, and on Saturday, March 3rd, the James

Harman Band played at Madame Wong's club in Los Angeles' Chinatown, with "very special guest," Big Joe Turner. Also, early in March, possibly the 8th, Turner and Lee Allen appeared at the Belly Up Tavern in Solana Beach. On March 16th he was due at the Music Machine, alongside Katie Webster and Charles Brown, followed on the 26th by an all-star gig at the Long Beach Hyatt Regency Hotel, with Jimmy Witherspoon, Pee Wee Crayton, Margie Evans, and Eddie Vinson.

Bassist Howard Rumsey was closely associated with the Lighthouse Cafe in Hermosa Beach for two decades as leader of the Lighthouse All Stars and later manager and co-owner. In 1972 he moved to Redondo Beach, opening at 100 Fisherman's Wharf (on the pier) a club he called Concerts By The Sea. One appearance there by Joe Turner was of three or four day duration, ending on Sunday, April 22nd. Six days later he was billed at the Blue Lagune (sic) Saloon, with no address given. The next known date is Saturday, May 12th, at Madame Wong's West, with the Mighty Flyers.

An All Star Blues Benefit for Percy Mayfield was held at the New Mint on Sunday, June 10th. The singers due to appear, in addition to Big Joe, included Jimmy Witherspoon, Lowell Fulson, Pee Wee Crayton and Charles Brown. Another June date was on Friday, the 29th, when he appeared with the James Harman band at the Music Machine in West L.A., while July gigs included, on the 6th, Hop Singh's in Marina Del Rey and, on the 7th, the Southern California Blues Society's second annual "Celebration of the Blues"at the Will Geer Theatricum in Topanga. In addition to Turner, others featured included Etta James, Richard Berry, Lee Allen, Bernie Pearl and a presumably recovered-from-illness Percy Mayfield. Another star-studded festival, commencing at 11 a.m., took place on the 15th at the California State University's athletic field in Long Beach, for which John Lee Hooker, Elvin Bishop, Buddy Guy, Junior Wells, Denise La Salle, Big Joe Turner, Pee Wee Crayton, and Brownie McGhee were booked. That same evening Turner, Crayton, Smokey Wilson, the James Harman band and others played a benefit evening for an ailing Shakey Jake Harris at The Music Machine.

The Olympic Jazz Festival was scheduled "for a mid-games August 2nd to 5th playtime at the John Anson Ford Theater". The headline acts were mainly jazz instrumentalists, but the singer's appearance was summarised in the *Los Angeles Times* for August 7th, "Big Joe Turner, the Kansas City paterfamilias of the blues, now 72 and grown huge, sang from a seated position just about every blues verse he would remember". Another "All Star Blues Revue," with Etta James, Eddie 'Cleanhead' Vinson, Esther Phillips, Big Joe Turner, Harry 'Sweets' Edison, Slappy White, Barbara Morrison and Leonard Reed, played at the Wilshire Ebell Theater on August 8th.

Big Mama Thornton had died on July 25th and on August 12th, "A Tribute to Big Mama Thornton" was held at The Music Machine, with Hank Ballard, Johnny Otis, Jimmy Witherspoon, the Clara Ward Singers, Lee Allen, Big Joe Turner and "others" advertised. Another all-star show that week, produced by the Southern California Blues Society, at an L.A. venue, featured Bo Diddley, with a support group including Dave Alvin, Phil Alvin and Bill Bateman of The Blasters. Also on the programme were Joe Turner, Percy Mayfield and John Lee Hooker. Then, to close the week, on the 17th and 18th, Joe was the featured artist at Carmelo's in Sherman Oaks, followed by a gig with the James Harman band at the Music Machine on the 25th. The following weekend, Friday to Sunday, August 31st-September 2nd, "the gravelly voiced, passionate blues singer" was at Concerts By The Sea ("a great room for jazz, with theater-style seats, though they're a little narrow") on Redondo Beach.

In the second week of September the Johnny Otis Show was again scheduled to appear at the Monterey Jazz Festival, with Turner set to participate, but he did not make it into the festival programme, one surmises for health reasons.

The fifth Long Beach Blues Festival was held the weekend of September 15th/16th at the California State University athletic field, noon to 6 p.m.. Scheduled to appear on Saturday, the 15th, were John Lee Hooker and the Coast to Coast Blues Band, Denise LaSalle, Big Joe, who was backed by Pee Wee Crayton and his Blues Orchestra (including Rod Piazza, harmonica, Honey Alexander, piano, and Doug MacLeod, guitar), Buddy Guy and Junior Wells, and Brownie McGhee. (Four tracks from Turner's set can be heard on YouTube.)

Joe travelled to Austin, Texas, the weekend of September 21/22, to appear at Antone's club. While there he received a write-up by Michael Point in the *Austin American-Statesman* for the 21st. The *Texas Monthly* (January 1985) reported that Turner was accompanied by the house band, Don Wilkerson, alto, Smokey Joe, tenor, Mel Brown, guitar, and Sarah Brown, bass.

During September Joe also made an appearance at the Oasis in San Francisco, while two known October gigs were on the 19th and 20th at Memory Lane ("Big Joe Turner shakes, rattles and rolls his way through a mountain of blues tunes. The Whodunit Band helps out.") and the 28th/29th at the Rainbow in Seattle, backed by Jr. Cadillac.

On an unknown date in 1984, in Los Angeles, Joe made a guest appearance on Tom Reed's television show and the year closed with news from Philip Elwood in the *San Francisco Examiner* that "The current issue of *Beano Magazine* (small, local, good) includes a rare informal interview with Merle Haggard and a good one with Big Joe Turner, too".

1985

Known engagements in the first months of the year were concentrated in the Los Angeles area. On January 21st the Santa Barbara Blues Society organised a 'Rent Party', 8p.m. to 11:30p.m. at La Casa de La Rosa in Santa Barbara. Among the all-stars on this occasion, in addition to Joe Turner, were Pee Wee Crayton, Eddie 'Cleanhead' Vinson, Jimmy Witherspoon, Phillip Walker, Tom Ball, Lloyd Glenn and the Pontiacs.

The *L.A. Weekly* had an item which told of a booking for February 14th/15th:

"He may be sittin' in his easy chair, taking it slow after his recent heart attack, but he's just gotta sing the blues for you. Backing up Big Joe is an all-star quintet featuring Henry Butler [piano] and Harold Battiste [reeds]. Joe plays the beautiful Palace Court, 1735 N. Vine St., tonight and tomorrow night".

The following month Joe was back on North Vine Street, at number 1610, the Vine St. Bar & Grill, where he played three nights, March 7th-9th. At the end of the month, on Saturday, the 22nd, he was the headliner for a blues concert at the CSUN Gymnasium in Northridge.

April found him back at the Vine St. Bar & Grill on a number of occasions, the 3rd, 15th, 22nd and the 28th. The last date was for another all-star concert, an 'Esther Phillips Tribute,' intended to raise donations for the Esther Phillips Scholarship Fund. Among those scheduled to appear were Carmen McRae, Etta James, Linda Hopkins, Big Joe Turner, Margie Evans, Johnny Otis, Ella Mae Morse and Leonard Feather. Between those dates, on April 6th, Joe was to work alongside Joe Liggins and the Honeydrippers at the Music Machine.

For Turner's last recording session for Pablo he was partnered with fellow blues shouter Jimmy Witherspoon. Held in Hollywood on April 11th, 1985, the same backing musicians were used as the previous year, except that altoist Red Holloway replaced one of the guitarists. Lee Allen was the tenor man and the resulting album, again with six titles, was called 'Patcha, Patcha, All Night Long: Joe Turner Meets Jimmy Witherspoon'.

On May 8th, Turner, along with Eddie Vinson, Joe Houston and the Barney McClure Quartet (Dave Peterson, guitar, Chuck Deardorf, bass, Dean Hodges, drums, the leader on piano) played the Mt. Baker Theatre, in Bellingham, Washington. His set contained *Hide and Seek, Call the Plumber, Sweet Little Angel, Kansas City* and *Corrine Corrina*. Barney McClure recalled in a 2021 e-mail

"Big Joe's performance was memorable, as he straddled a simple kitchen-type chair backwards and counted each tune off loudly and with a strong foot stomp. We had no rehearsal and our first time to play the tunes was on that stage that night."

On the 12th and 13th, Joe was scheduled at the Vine St. Bar & Grill in L.A., followed by the 25th/26th, probably at Hop Singh's. The *L.A. Weekly* news item for this gig declaimed

"Big Joe Turner, who has been shouting the blues ever since his wild youth in the free-for-all musical melting pot of Kansas City, MO., in the 1930s .... may be a septuagenarian, but his voice, with its ringing timbre and amazing gusto, is still young and fresh. Long Gone Miles also appears".

Joe was back at the Vine St. Bar & Grill on consecutive Mondays, June 3rd and 10th, and in-between he was booked to appear on the 7th and 8th at the Chicago Blues Festival. Other participants named included Koko Taylor, John Hammond, Pee Wee Crayton, Eddie 'Cleanhead' Vinson, Lowell Fulson and Otis Rush. A little over a week later, the 16th, he played a Father's Day gig at Ms.Whis Cocktail Lounge at Long Beach.

He was due to see the month out in the San Francisco area, the 28th at the Koncepts Cultural Gallery in Oakland and the Mendocino Brewery, Hopland, the following day, but both bookings were cancelled "because of illness". It is likely that such cancellations occurred more frequently during this period in Turner's life than these pages suggest. Bookings are advertised, cancellations rarely.

Another of Joe's now regular gigs at the Vine St. Bar & Grill was scheduled for July 5th-7th, followed by a concert on the 13th. The *Los Angeles Times* report (July 14th, 1985 issue) stated,

"A rollicking crowd of an estimated 1,000 people turned out Saturday for the Third Annual Southern California Blues Society concert. They were treated to the likes of 'blues shouter' Big Joe Turner ...."

This July 13th event, dedicated to the memory of Pee Wee Crayton, was held at the Will Geer Theatricum Botanicum in Topanga, with the cast including the Bernie Pearl Blues Band with Henry Butler, Harmonica Fats, the Cash McCall band and the Magic Blues Band.

Also due in July was an engagement for Turner with the Bernie Pearl Blues Band at Sardie's Cajun restaurant in Burbank on the 20th, followed by the Watts Music and Arts Festival on July 27th/28th at the Watts Towers Arts Center, featuring Bo Diddley, Johnny Otis, Buddy Collette, and the Clara Ward Singers.

Joe was to headline again at the Vine St. Bar & Grill on Monday, August 5th, then he was off to the Big Apple to appear at Tramps on August 8th and 9th. As David Hinckley, in the (New York) *Daily News* for August 16, 1985, reported:

"He's here in New York this month, for the first time in quite a while, playing at Tramps. Shows are 9:30 and 11:30 tonight and tomorrow night (16th and 17th), then Thursday, Friday and Saturday the next three weekends.and don't be surprised if partway through the show, you forget that Joe Turner is almost 74 years old."

Those three weekend dates were Aug 22nd, 23rd, 24th, August 29th, 30th, 31st and September 5th, 6th, 7th.

Mary Katherine Aldin confirmed that Turner played his final gig at Tramps nightclub in September, and one obituary reported, "That engagement was cut short by ill-health. He flew home, entered a local hospital for dialysis treatment and later transferred to Daniel Freeman." [25]

It is hard to believe that Turner, given his state of health, would even consider flying to New York to perform, but equally one can accept that that is just what he would do, almost regardless of any problems, inconvenience or pain.

During September he was to feature at the NAACP Blues Festival in Sacramento on the 9th, and at the San Francisco Blues Festival, with accompaniment by Roomful of Blues, on the 15th.

Also advertised were repeat shows at the Vine St. Bar & Grill in L.A., September 30th and October 7th. Unsurprisingly, the *San Francisco Examiner* for September 13 reported:

> The 13th Annual San Francisco Blues Festival will be a bit bluer without the presence of Big Joe Turner, 74, who last night cancelled his scheduled appearance because of a turn for the worse in his health.
>
> Festival producer Tim Mazzolini said he talked by phone to Turner in Los Angeles, and confirmed that Big Joe "is obviously very ill and in no condition to travel".

The original Blues Brother

Big Joe Turner, a true legend, and the man who first recorded "Shake, Rattle and Roll," will be appearing at Tramps, 125 E. 15th St., tonight and tomorrow, 9 and 11:30. For reservations: 777-5077.

New York Daily News, December 11, 1981

16

"Thank you, Joe Turner"

(1985)

Even the strongest, most powerful heart cannot beat forever and Big Joe Turner's gave out after 74 years. He died on Sunday, November 24, 1985, in the Daniel Freeman Hospital, Inglewood, California. A hospital spokeswoman quoted the cause of death as "kidney failure and complications resulting from a stroke two years ago".[1] And as we also know, Turner was excessively overweight, lived a far from healthy life-style and suffered from arthritis and diabetes.

He died impoverished and was buried at Roosevelt Memorial Park, Gardena, California. Mary Katherine Aldin recalled that to reduce the funeral costs Joe was interred with his sister Katie, who already occupied half of a double grave.

Pat, who was "a very, very heavy smoker," subsequently moved to New York, dying of lung cancer, in 1990. She was cremated and the urn with her ashes was laid in Joe's coffin next to him.[2]

Pallbearers at Joe's funeral service on November 30 at the Angelus Crenshaw Chapel in Los Angeles were Lee Allen, James Austin, Tony George, John Griffin, Michael Hughes, Dick Ludwig, Doug Macleod, Jack Miller, Renaldo Rey and Bill Walker. Honorary pallbearers were Steve Bull, Lowell Fulson, James Harman, Jimmy McCracklin, Red Holloway, Eddie Vinson, Jimmy Witherspoon, Johnny Otis, Bernie Pearl and Bernard Stone.

Being confined to a wheel-chair, causing problems with the airline, Doc Pomus was unable to fly to Los Angeles for the service. His taped tribute, "Joe Turner's Legacy," was played to the congregation.

Memorial service

IN LOVING MEMORY

Of

JOSEPH "Big Joe" TURNER

Saturday, November 30, 1985
1:00 P.M.

Angelus Crenshaw Chapel
3875 Crenshaw Blvd., Los Angeles, California

Reverend Dennis Woods
Officiant

ACTIVE PALLBEARERS

LEE ALLEN	DICK LUDWIG
JAMES AUSTIN	DOUG MACHEOD
TONY GEORGE	JACK MILLER
JOHN GRIFFIN	RENALDO REY
MICHAEL HUGHES	BILL WALKER

HONORARY PALLBEARERS

Jerome "Doc" Pomus - Steve Bull - Lowell Fulson
James Harman - Red Holloway - Jimmie McCracklin
Johnny Otis - Bernie Pearl - Bernard Stone
Eddie "Cleanhead" Vinson - Jimmy Witherspoon

ANGELUS FUNERAL HOME
Directors in Charge

Ahmet Ertegun

Pat Turner. Memorial Service photographs from Pat Turner, courtesy Liz and David Driver

Ernie Andrews

Justine Picardie and Dorothy Wade, in their book *Music Man, the story of Atlantic Records*, Ahmet Ertegun, and the record business at that time, tell of Joe Turner's string of hits for Atlantic and how

"…. long after age and arthritis should have dictated retirement," he carried on working. They continue, "Even so, he died flat broke, leaving a tangle of debts, and an impoverished widow who could not afford to pay for his funeral. That may have been because Joe Turner was not very good with money, but then he didn't earn very much money anyway; he never received the lucrative recording contracts that are commonplace today." .... "it was Ahmet Ertegun who paid for the funeral and paid off the mortgage on his widow's house; and he did so quietly, in such a way that his gesture was not reported in the columns of the musical press."

The writers state that Atlantic in more recent years had "recalculated" royalties on foreign sales and record reissues, paying out hundreds of thousands of dollars to the musicians and singers who made the company famous in the 1950s. It also established a two-million-dollar fund to make tax-free grants to needy r&b artists. They also point out that Ertegun, as a multi-millionaire, could well afford his generosity to Pat Turner, "whose company is merely paying a debt long overdue".

Mary Katherine Aldin believes that Ertegun possibly contributed to Joe's final expenses but, having seen the cheque, knows that the funeral was paid for by Doc Pomus.[3] Sharyn Felder, Doc's daughter, said that her father always felt that it was an honour and a privilege to be able to help Joe Turner.[4] He had planned a benefit show to help defray Joe's hospital costs and this was scheduled to take place at the Lone Star Cafe in New York on December 9th. It now became a tribute to the singer, with Dr. John and the Roomful of Blues among the artists performing.

The Joe Turner obituary in the trade paper *Cash Box* (December 7th, 1985), was one of so many printed in the major newspapers and jazz magazines around the world, but this editorial/obituary concentrated on Joe's final years, trying to apply a simple answer to a complex matter.

Under the heading "Let's Learn From The Life And Death of Big Joe Turner," it asked why Turner died penniless when he had contributed so much to modern music. It commented how he faced racial discrimination:

"The life and death of Joe Turner represents far more than one man's passing. He is representative of a breed of artists that can never be directly repaid for what they contributed and what they had to go through to contribute. There are facets of Joe Turner's career the industry would rather not remember. So it's important for an industry that has supposedly put its racial prejudices behind it to reflect on the extent and scope of those inadequacies that claimed Joe Turner and many others as victims".

In 1991, Akio Yamanaka, editor of the Japanese blues magazine *Juke*, visited Turner's grave and was horrified to discover there was no marker or any sign to indicate where Joe was buried. As a result of Yamanaka's visit, the Joe Turner Musician's Fund was established. The original but unsuccessful aim was to raise enough money to pay for the removal of Joe's body to Inglewood Park Cemetery so that a head stone could be erected. Roosevelt Memorial allowed only grave markers.

Thanks to a benefit held at the Music Machine club featuring, among others, Dave and Phil Alvin, Top Jimmy, Rosie Flores, and the Bernie Pearl Blues Band,

and other money-raising schemes, the Fund was able to arrange a special grave marker for Joe, his wife and his sister.

Grave marker for Joe, Pat and Kate Turner

The following are just a small selection from the many, many tributes which were made to Big Joe Turner both before and after his death:

When Joe Turner died, Doc Pomus sent this message to his old friend: "The angels are all going to have to sing a little louder to keep up with you."[5]

Joe was inducted into the Rock-and-Roll Hall of Fame (Cleveland, Ohio) in 1987, together with twenty other singers, writers and producers. These included Ahmet Ertegun, Jerry Wexler, Jerry Lieber, Mike Stoller, Bill Haley, Muddy Waters, Bo Diddley, Louis Jordan and Hank Williams.

Charlie Gracie, a veteran of country and western music, said in a BBC radio interview, that Joe Turner was one of the great blues artists of the 1950s "and that's where we get our ideas".[6]

On a 2004 CD recorded with pianist Jools Holland's orchestra, (Sir) Tom Jones sang Turner's *Sally Suzas* (*Sally Zu-Zazz*) and the same pairing welcomed in 2021 on BBC television with a version of *Flip, Flop and Fly*, together with a verbal and photographic tribute to Mr. Turner.

Singer Joe Williams, who made his name with the Count Basie orchestra, remarked during a set at the 1977 Nice Jazz Festival, "Joe Turner inspired me to sing the blues. I was in Chicago singing sweet and swing songs until I heard him".

A Canadian singer named Chuck Jackson, leader of his Big Bad Blues Band, heavily influenced by Joe Turner, released a CD on the Linus label 270147, as a tribute. Recorded in 2012 it is titled "A Cup of Joe," with twelve tracks associated with Joe, including *Cherry Red*, *Rebecca*, *The Chill Is On*, *Corrine Corrina* and *Goin' Away Blues*.

A similar CD is "Thank You, Joe Turner: a tribute to Big Joe Turner" by pianist and singer Rob Rio, on Boss BP012, recorded in 2008. Titles include the Rio composition, *Thank You, Joe Turner*, and nine from the Turner catalogue; *Corrine Corrina*, *Cherry Red*, *Wee Wee Baby*, *Shake Rattle & Roll* among them.

Dave Alvin's part in the Joe Turner story has been told earlier, but in his book of poetry, *Nana, Big Joe and the Fourth of July* (Liberatum, 1986) he included a fittingly lyrical tribute with which to conclude this saga of the Boss of the Blues Big Joe Turner.

> Every juke joint[7]
> boogie woogie pianist
> three day rent party
> 4 am tenor sax battle
> Kansas City black woman
> California white woman
> New Orleans creole
> every tapping foot
> every dress slit up the side
> every shot of whiskey, vodka and gin
> every blue song
> every song that ever swung
> every Chicago ballad
> and New York rhythm and blues shuffle
> every Saturday night kiss
> every Sunday night tear
> everything that was good and right
> everything that had love for the world
> is in a grave in Gardena.

Promotional photograph, probably 1970s, Los Angeles.

Appendix 1 - The Man

Did Joe Turner find the ideal way to journey through life? He seems to have calmly accepted whatever the fates, be they personal managers or booking agencies or promoters or even wives, might throw at him. His was a laissez-faire attitude, combined with a touch of indolence, as well as an "easy come, easy go" approach to money.

As he told his friend, Doc Pomus, "Too many people get sick today worrying about yesterday". To Val Wilmer he said, "So many things happened to me that I just sort of rolled with the tide". Or to Peter Guralnick, "I make it up as I go along. I don't plan nothing. I have no plans. I live my whole life in music and I don't tell nobody my secrets". And as he sang on *Oke-She-Moke-She-Pop*, "We can talk about the future and forget about the past."

In 1983 Pomus said,

> "Joe is shy and non-verbal. If he likes you he calls you 'cousin' and if he really, really likes you he'll quietly tell you stories about yesterday; they're always interesting and colorful. Joe doesn't read or write too well, but for someone who's never had formalized schooling or a manager, he's had an amazing career with uncanny instincts about people and life and show business."[1]

Humphrey Lyttelton, discussing the 1965 U.K. tour, considered that Joe, by comparison with Buck Clayton, was "an innocent". Certainly he was not a complicated man. He had accepted little schooling, hence his problems with reading and writing, yet he succeeded as a singer and wrote many of the songs he sang.

He was unconcerned about the billing on the blues package shows in which he appeared, nor did he show any animosity towards Bill Haley because of the latter's success with *Shake, Rattle and Roll*. Joe's interviews do not mention race, though he must have suffered his share of discrimination, especially when touring the Southern States. His size, perhaps, may have deterred some racists.

Asked by James Austin if he was offended by such labels as "race music" and "the way white people had the fear of black music," Turner by-passed the subject, saying, "No, it never bothered me, because I worked in the white nightclubs in my hometown lots of times and it wasn't nothin' new to me".[2]

Or as he told Michael Point, "I had my day and enjoyed it, I never expected to get real rich or famous and I'm not even sure I'd want to be in the situation that some of these modern rock stars are in. I don't mind people knowing who I am and what I've done, but I just don't think I could put up with all the craziness that goes on now".[3]

An editorial-cum-obituary in the trade magazine *Cash Box* commented,

> "Turner never admitted to any anger. He swallowed the hurt suffered over sour publishing deals, unauthorized covers, and a color-minded

industry that relegated black artists to merely originators of the material that designated white cover artists would take nationwide".[4]

In *Nothing But The Blues*, Mark Humphrey suggested,

".... [Turner's] ebullient nature steered him less towards the subtleties of jazz and more towards the elemental energies of boogie-woogie, rhythm and blues, rock 'n' roll – the labels changed with the decades, but Big Joe in essence did not."

The first part of that sentence is debatable. As suggested earlier, Turner took the work that was offered, whether headlining at a club, recording with a choir, or taking fourth place billing on a blues package tour. One doubts that he ever raised a query about the backing group he was given, though it was the jazz accompaniments which provided his voice with the right setting. Many will claim that the Atlantic recordings are his main legacy, and they are important, but for this writer the sessions with, for example, Pete Johnson, Art Tatum, and Hot Lips Page are the summit.

Turner had spoken of his nervousness prior to his first Carnegie Hall appearance, hardly surprising in the circumstances, but nearly thirty years on he was still anxious, as Humphrey Lyttelton discovered.

"On stage, Joe occasionally showed the insecurity which seemed to dog his incursions into unfamiliar surroundings. He had a stock phrase .... to express his periodical – and always unfounded – conviction that things had gone wrong. 'We're in a world of trouble,' he would say, 'Someone took a pin and burst the bubble'." But when he was confident and in congenial company, the big penetrating voice assumed an air of massive authority."

Lyttelton also wrote,

"It was hard, at first sight, to reconcile the huge, genial man with his eager boy's face and rather worried, insecure temperament with that forthright voice, full of masculine assertiveness, that belted out penetrating and quite sophisticated blues lyrics of his own devising on so many cherished records."[5]

Dimitri Wischnegradsky wrote of Joe Turner, "He is superstitious and believes in the influence of the stars on people; several times he told me, 'Don't miss your star when you see it in the sky'."[6]

This is borne out by the "magic bean story," as told by Turner to Doc Pomus and to Whitney Balliett. To the latter Joe said,

"I got the bean from an African who worked in a place where he walked on broken glass and swallowed fire and didn't hurt himself. He told me to rub it and say that mumbo-jumbo and the bean would do anything as long as I believed in it".

A mention of the magic bean on the Walter Winchell radio show meant that Turner was pestered about it -

"Finally, it scared me to death to have so much power and I put the bean in the toilet and pulled the chain. But I believed in anything in those days".[7]

At Cafe Society, Barney Josephson had first-hand experience of the magic bean. On one occasion he walked into the club feeling low. Big Joe produced the bean from his wallet and said, "In this hand is a bean and in this bean is a face, alive as you or me. You can tell it your troubles". He put the bean on the counter, covering it with his hand. He told Albert Ammons and Josephson to put their hands over his. "Then he makes a mumbo-jumbo, sasa-fasa-juba-jaba, breaks our hands apart". Turner puts the bean back in his wallet and tells Josephson that his worries are over. Josephson starts to laugh and Turner says, "You see, Pops. Everything's okay."[8]

Jimmy Witherspoon, a keen admirer of Turner's singing, told Val Wilmer that, in his opinion, Joe's laziness had been the main factor in retarding his progress in more commercial pastures.[9] Ms.Wilmer herself found Joe to be lethargic but good-natured off-stage.

It was probably the simple approach to life rather than any sense of humour which gave rise to stories from his 1965 British tour. Humphrey Lyttelton's include the instances when Joe wanted to buy a transistor radio and lawn-mower; the radio because he sure liked the programmes they got; the lawnmower because "I'm gonna be the only guy in my street who has a lawn-mower with an English accent"! Guitarist Nevil Skrimshire recalled that Turner, when asked his favourite British group, said "the Stepping Stones".[10]

Lyttelton also told the following story,

"On our tour Big Joe Turner asked me to help him buy a simple camera. On the way into Manchester we stopped at a camera shop and I asked the assistant for the simplest camera he had. He got out an Instamatic and was describing how all you had to do was load it, put it to your eye and shoot, when Joe headed for the door.
"Outside, I asked, 'What's the matter, Joe?' He said, 'Man, you gotta go to school to work one of those.'[11]

Researchers and discographers have expressed their frustration at trying to extract information from Joe Turner before finally accepting that it was not in his nature to remember the fine details of his recording sessions, his engagements or even his accompanying musicians. Interviewers asking him about the Kansas City period and the early days in New York seemed to have fared better. Talks with Whitney Balliett, Val Wilmer, Frank Brown, Max Jones, and others, appear to have been as frank and as detailed as Turner's memory would allow.

Paul Oliver had a view on this, writing,

"Took Joe Turner to buy a hat [size 7¼] – had a chat with him but he is pretty vague on most details – doubt if discographically he would be of any use at all; his increasingly unretentive memory (must be the reason why he sings the same verses over and over) ..."[12]

And on Turner's general manner:

"I don't know whether this is affectation, laziness or just the man. I feel the latter sometimes, for he seldom creates new verses and seems to me to be a bundle of stereotypes."[13]

Yannick Bruynoghe commented,

"After the [J.A.T.P.] concert, Turner and Johnson came home for supper. I tried to question him on some accompaniments but immediately noticed that it was useless. He doesn't care, doesn't remember and doesn't recognise the musicians. He asked me, 'Who's this Johnny Stitt who blowed with me tonight?'!"[14]

This failure to recall many of his accompanists is in contrast to his ability to remember so many blues verses. Bob Porter is another who recalls hearing Joe in a Los Angeles club, probably mid-to-late sixties, singing "*Chains of Love* for forty-five minutes without repeating a verse."[15]

In his piece in *The Observer* (May 16th, 1965), singer George Melly summed up Joe Turner as follows,

"Physically he's enormous, over six foot tall and very heavy. He carries himself with proper aldermanic solemnity. He's a sharp dresser and wears a neat hairline moustache. He watches what's going on from under half-closed coded eye-lids. When I bought him a drink, he said, "Break the money, honey, and keep on travelling."

"Turner is an impossible man to interview, but a pleasure to listen to. He talks pure blues all the time. He's hazy or deliberately obscurantist about facts and dates, but he loves images."

Appendix 2 - The Appetites

Joe Turner was large by any definition. Physically imposing, his height was usually given as six foot two inches and his weight as 250-pounds, though he was said to have reached 350-plus-pounds in the last years of his life. An item in the *Melody Maker* (June 1965) stated, "When Joe Turner weighed himself on [singer] Beryl Bryden's scales, the needle hit 20 stones [ie: a minimum of 280-pounds] and went back to zero!"

His attraction to alcohol has been evident throughout his biography – the 1950 Dew Drop Inn story and his 1976 problem which led to hospitalisation are prime examples. Mary Katherine Aldin said that Joe was a very heavy drinker when she knew him but that it did not seem to affect his ability to perform. (She also commented, "His weight was a burden to him but he did not seem to be able to do anything about it.)

Johnny Otis wrote,

"In my experience, drunks are a pathetic mess. They are a big headache to whoever hires them. Bone [T-Bone Walker], Cleanhead [Eddie 'Cleanhead' Vinson] and Joe Turner were exceptions. No matter how intoxicated they were, they could still go up to the mike and perform. In the end, though, no matter how well they balanced their drinking and performing, they weren't made of steel, and the alcohol took its toll".[1]

Saxophonist Jackie Kelso did a tour with Joe in the 1950s and has been quoted as saying,

"... I was just amazed how he could be just almost totally blind drunk, he would just get up and create new verses on the songs. You could hardly tell what he was saying, but you could recognize that he was rhyming things".

Then there was food. The following examples demonstrate how he indulged, over-indulged, himself.

Humphrey Lyttelton called Turner "One of the most prodigious eaters I ever met". He continued,

"When he toured with me, we stopped one morning in North London, on the way home, so that he could buy himself a steak for lunch. The butcher brought out a long strip of rump steak and, hovering over it with a knife, asked how big a steak he wanted. 'I'll take it all' was the reply, and this huge mattress of meat was rolled up and put in a bag. The story has an appalling sequel. Getting back to his apartment, he lit the electric stove and put the steak (folded three ways, no doubt) under the grill. He then lay on the bed and went to sleep for two hours, with results on which we need not dwell.[2]

Singer Freddie King told Max Jones,

"I once saw Joe eat nine pork chops and a dozen of eggs. And Lowell [Fulson] told me how he and Joe decided to share a treat one night. Joe bought a ham and a big cabbage head and put them in the pot. Lowell bought the booze, two fifths of Scotch, and set them up. By the time the food was ready the fifths were gone; they'd drunk about one each."

Fulson went to the tavern, returning with more Scotch.

"When he got back there was a savoury smell, and he went over to the stove and opened the pot. All he saw was a few cabbage leaves floating on the top. Joe had ate all that ham and most of the cabbage. Boy, Lowell cursed that night."[3]

In the biography there is a story of the singer, suffering from diabetes in the early 1980s, surrounded by bottles of insulin, empty bottles of bourbon, and eating a pint of ice cream.

Then, no doubt, there was the opposite sex. It does seem unlikely that he was immune to the temptations of the road caused by many weeks away from home and the nearness of adoring fans and attractive co-stars or chorus girls.

Add cigarette smoking into the mix and it is fair to say that Joe Turner failed to follow any plan for healthy living.

Appendix 3 - The Money

Humphrey Lyttelton shines some light on Turner's attitude to money, having seen Joe's excessive generosity, first to a down-and-out, and then to a young lady collecting on behalf of an amateur folk group. It is not surprising that Joe was reported to have returned home after the 1965 British tour with little or no money, especially as it was rumoured that another young lady had helped him with the spending.

Whitney Ballett quoted Turner as saying that, "Whatever money I've made, the wives about got it all".[1] Nick Tosches unflatteringly called Joe's first wife, Lou Willie, the "dark lady of the flip side".[2]

Until late in his career he had little regard for the complexities of recording payments, publication rights or royalties. "I didn't know nothing, all I got paid was money for making them [the records].[3]

Joe told Doc Pomus that he had written songs as "Lou Willie Turner" on the assumption that he would die first and to avoid any litigation the songs were published under her name. It was not until several years later, with his friend's help, that he began to receive the royalties he was due on those songs.

Asked about the success of *Lipstick, Powder and Paint* on Atlantic, Turner laughed, saying, "I wasn't getting that much money off that record. I was getting two cents for a record. You have to sell a whole lot of them to make some money.[4]

When, in 1969, he left his second wife, Geraldine, and moved to Los Angeles, leaving her in New Orleans, Turner did not advise Chappell Music Publishers of his change of address. No cheques were forwarded to him. "My ex-wife was getting them and cashing them."[5] It was nearly ten years later, again with the help of Doc Pomus, before the situation was rectified.[6]

Another story, which he told to Steve Propes, also concerned Doc Pomus, who was "talking about some bunch of boys had done the number (*Flip, Flop and Fly*) and sold a million, so he said, 'You oughta get a nice royalty cheque'". Joe found out who the un-named rock group recorded for and contacted the company, to discover that the royalty cheque had been sent to Geraldine, who had been trying unsuccessfully to cash it. It was one cheque that found its way to its rightful owner.[7]

In interviews Turner seemed contented with his wives at that time, no doubt pleased to have them looking after him and his finances. For a time Lou Willie was his agent and both she, then Geraldine, managed his income. We have seen the comfortable life he and Lou Willie were living in Chicago, though later Joe was to say, "I had two cooks, one bottle-washer and one chauffeur wherever I travelled. I had four cats to help me with my clothes on, help me with my clothes off and help themselves to my money".[8]

Given Turner's failure to save when times were good, especially during the Atlantic decade of the 1950s, combined with the dubious actions noted above and the bills incurred as his medical problems grew, the money problems at the end of his life are understandable.

Appendix 4 - The Voice

In an interview with jazz journalist Max Jones, blues singer Jimmy Witherspoon asked, "Have you noticed that about blues singers? They sing the way they talk, and talk the way they sing". Witherspoon was speaking of John Lee Hooker, but his observation was an accurate one. Two other examples which immediately spring to mind are Memphis Slim and Big Bill Broonzy.

Whitney Balliett noted, "Indeed, there is little difference between his (Turner's) speech and his singing; one walks, the other lopes", while Val Wilmer refers to "Turner's rambling, poetry-like speech".

Bob Hite said of Turner, "And when he talks, he talks in the key of C, so that's hard to know when he's stopped talking and started to sing."[1]

Similarities with the great classic blues singer Bessie Smith cannot be ignored. Writer Eddie Lambert noted,

"To compare (Joe Turner) with singers of the same style is like comparing Bessie Smith with other singers of the 'classic' school. As in all forms of art each blues singer has his or her special qualities, but Joe, like Bessie, emerges as the master, the archetype, the very matrix of the style". And in similar vein, he wrote, "His voice – here again the comparison with Bessie Smith is striking - is quite perfect for the style, his rhythmic sense and great swing incomparable".[2]

Humphrey Lyttelton too made the point,

"Bessie's way, taken up and carried forward right into the rock 'n' roll era by the great Kansas City blues singer, Big Joe Turner, was to restrict the range of a song to no more than five or six notes and to construct her phrases so economically that a change in direction of just one note could have a startling dramatic and emotive effect."[3]

Stanley Dance was another writer to link Joe Turner to The Empress of the Blues when he wrote,

"Unsuccessfully imitated by a few, he may perhaps be regarded more as an inspiration than an influence. His unquestionable authority, like Bessie Smith's, has had a galvanising effect on all kinds of groups, in all kinds of blues and jazz contexts."[4]

To begin his sleeve note to the "*Nobody In Mind*" album on Pablo, Benny Green refers to Joe Turner's limitations - few key variations, few vocal effects and "a highly specialised repertoire". But then Green talks of Turner in the jazz sense,

"his voice has a body to it, a certain aural succulence, which makes its impact very nearly a physical sensation .... he has an arsenal of vowel sounds and glottal shocks which you can very nearly reach out and touch.

Moreover, his range is ideally suited to the nature of his material and that material is perfectly adequate to express the essence of his personality. In other words, Joe Turner has done, no doubt by pure instinct, what every creative artist ought to do but what few ever manage; he has contrived an ideal marriage of form and content".

And George Melly wrote,

"Turner's voice has a limited range and a flinty cutting edge. He sticks to 12-bar blues most of the time, many of them up-tempo and all of them in the key of C, and yet he's never monotonous, always immediately identifiable".[5]

Leonard Feather, in Turner's entry in *The Encyclopedia of Jazz*, complimented the singer, I think, when he said,

"He is one of the most unspoiled of blues shouters in the great tradition in which sonority and conviction take precedence over clarity of diction".

Reviewing Turner's "Rockin' The Blues" album on Atlantic 8023, Mimi Clar wrote:

"Joe's voice is the kind that shouts even when he whispers, and does so effortlessly. He has a way of skimming over lines at an even level of dynamic volume and vocal texture and depending on undulating phrasing and unexpected rhythmic twists and stresses for variety. The characteristic linear scansion of Turner - shoving most of the text into the first half of the line so it ends a measure or so before it 'should' or slurring one word to dovetail into the next – emerges in extroverted display, not only in Joe's forte, *Jump for Joy*, but throughout the whole LP".[6]

Writing in *The Village Voice*, Gary Giddins described,

"The acoustic miracle that is Turner's voice is as cavernous and majestic as ever, almost a kind of human thunder. It makes all the points about fickle women and troubled nights quickly, dispassionately, and without fanfare, and it brooks no appeal."

Sandy Ingham, reviewing an appearance at Tramps wrote,

"Turner's baritone voice is devoid of tricks. He plunges straight into his songs, using almost no vibrato, ramming his notes home right on the beat, then lagging a bit behind it, then pushing up the tempo. His numbers are often amalgams of several old blues about women who do their men wrong, and he borrows a lyric here, a lyric there. But the words themselves mean little; what counts is that soaring, shouting blue-note machine of a voice."[7]

Blues historian Paul Oliver's view was,

"It is just his tremendous delivery which makes him what he is. When he sings he uses no actual mental effort at all."[8]

In a record review he put it differently,

"Here is Joe Turner in his full maturity, his voice round and strong, his words declaimed in confident, almost negligent ease which sometimes obscure their meaning but keeps the music swinging."[9]

Stanley Dance:

"One might say that Joe Turner was, in a sense, impervious to his accompaniment, that all he needed was a steady drum beat at an appropriate tempo, so unfailing was his rhythmic assurance in every context."[10]

In *Jazz Singers* it is claimed that "Big" refers to "the size of his (Turner's) voice, the full force of which was surely strong enough to register on the Richter scale."[11] This power has been touched upon many times, comparisons being made also with Sherman tanks and thunder, and not forgetting Gunther Schuller's comment, "what a great operatic baritone he could have been!"[12]

In *All What Jazz* Philip Larkin referred to him as a " knotty-voiced shouter".

Harnessing this unique voice with an innate sense of swing gave Turner the foundation to become the boss blues shouter that he was. As with so many of his generation, he had no special production or effects: no fireworks, no light show, no back projection, no lasers, no auto-tune, no dancers. Just his voice and an accompaniment were all that were needed.

Appendix 5 – The Songs

There is a treatise waiting to be written on the subject of Joe Turner's compositions and their relationship to the blues tradition. This appendix covers some of his thoughts on the matter, to which are added a few relevant points which could provide fuel for more extended research.

A starting point might be to query if his songs merit detailed study. Is it not enough to enjoy his singing without worrying about the source of his material? (That seems to have been Turner's view.) Is it pointless to seek answers in the lyrics, when often they seem so random, contradictory or even senseless? How many of the words were his own? How many were from the reservoir of traditional verses which accumulated during the last months of the 19th Century and the first thirty years of the 20th?

Blues historians Paul Oliver and Jacques Demetre were no doubt correct when they queried the extent to which Turner wrote his own lyrics. Oliver commented,

"This raises your point again – whether his blues are original at all. I don't know – a few .... like (Jimmy) Rushing he seems to draw from a very limited pool of material. The emphasis on performance makes these singers closer to jazz in my view".[1]

Michael Steinman, when looking back at the 1967 "Spirituals to Swing" concert album, made this reference to Joe Turner,

"In his later years he often appeared to be very little concerned with what verses he sang in what order (although he may have had a plan that I am not able to discern) and the result was a kind of swing autopilot, where I and others just listened to the majestic roar and holler of his voice. But here, on a blues called (perhaps after the fact) *I'm Going Away To Wear You Off My Mind*, his dramatic gift, his sadness, is lovely and powerful."[2]

To quote George Melly's opinion again,

"His subject matter is sex. He shouts the good times and rages against the bad. He is the most masculine of the great blues singers. He can be aggressive, violent, humorous and even tender, but never self-pitying. He can be crude, too, but because he is concerned with celebrating pleasure and exorcising pain, he is never pornographic".[3]

Ulf Carlsson suggested that,

"Mostly the male character in Turner's lyrics is unsuspicious and kindhearted, easily taken in by womanly cunning. There's always a romantic stroke in his artistry, a tenderness and innocence, that transformed even the pornographic imagery of a '50s masterpiece like *TV Mama*, 'the one with the big wide screen' ... Joe's strong point has never been irony or ambiguity or overstatement, but rather the joyful, undisguised praise of life as an adventure, full of promises, but also of "lovin' propositions that can get somebody killed."[4]

Turner told an interviewer,

"I owe my success to my creativity. I write most of my songs. I feed my creativity. It's an excitement. I enjoy it. I'm very sure of it I like to write catchy words, good expressions, with a meaning to tell a story."[5]

To Val Wilmer he said,

"Blues I did mainly for the fun of it. I didn't really give much thought to what was behind the songs. Most of the time I pick out the songs where I feel I can get the most emotion out of the people in the audience. I kind of work at the people in the audience and once I get them on my side, I let 'em have it!".[6]

And similarly to Peter Guralnick,

"I have been doing this all my life and I know how it goes, and I watch the response on people's faces, where I can tell when they're enjoying it and when they're not, and I keep working at them till I get 'em where they can be comfortable and where I can be comfortable and then I go from there".[7]

To Whitney Balliett, "I keep busy. Singing's all I know how to do,"[8] while quoted by Big Joe Laredo on the subject of music, he said, "It's one of the things that's the most fun in the world".[9]

When he was no longer recording for Atlantic, Joe said he lost interest in writing new songs or lyrics. In 1965 he said, "I used to write a lot of songs, most of the blues I sang were mine. I don't do it as much now. No, I don't know why. I guess I lost the urge."[10] Nine years later, on the same subject? "I just lost my touch. I got out of the habit."[11]

And about his later repertoire, he also told Val Wilmer,

"I'd rather do something that I like - else quit. If I do something I don't like, it won't sound like anything. And nobody brought me any stuff I appreciated in a long time".[12]

Appendix 6 – Joe's Songs, Other Singers

A partial, uncritical listing of Joe Turner songs/lyrics recorded by other singers.

Cherry Red	Dave & Phil Alvin (Yeproc), Count Basie/Joe Williams (Columbia), Ella Fitzgerald (Verve), Chuck Jackson (Linus), B.B. King (ABC-Paramount), Jimmy Reed (Vee Jay), Gary Richards (Crown), Rob Rio (Boss), Jimmy Witherspoon(Reprise), Eddie 'Cleanhead' Vinson/ Count Basie (Pablo)
Chill is On, The	Bill Haley (Decca), Chuck Jackson (Linus)
Crawdad Hole	Chuck Jackson (Linus)
Feeling Happy	Dave & Phil Alvin (Yeproc)
Flip, Flop and Fly	Rob Rio (Boss), Bill Haley (Warner Bros.)
Goin' Away Blues	Chuck Jackson (Linus)
Honey Hush (Rounder)	Jerry Lee Lewis (Mercury), Robert Nighthawk, Fleetwood Mac
Piney Brown Blues	Sammy Price (London), Muddy Waters (Chess), Jimmy Witherspoon (Victor)
Rebecca	Chuck Jackson (Linus)
Roll 'Em Pete	Long John Baldry (United Artists), Count Basie/Joe Williams (Clef), Ella Fitzgerald (Reelin' in the Years DVD), Richard Holmes (WarnerBros.), Harry James (Dot), Lou Rawls (Capitol), Jimmy Reed (Vee Jay), Sarah Vaughan (Roulette, as Jump For Joy) Mal Maldron (Music-Minus-One), Jimmy Witherspoon (Hi Fi Jazz)
Sally-Zu-Zass	Tom Jones & Jools Holland (Radar - as Sally Suzas)
Wee Baby Blues	Dave & Phil Alvin (Yeproc), Count Basie/Eddie 'Cleanhead' Vinson (Pablo), Bumble Bee Slim (Amos Easton) (Pacific Jazz), June Christy (Capitol), Nat 'King' Cole/Count Basie (Capitol), Shakey Horton (Chess), Albert King (King as Oo Wee Baby), B.B. King ((ABC-Paramount), Jack McVea (Apollo), Sammy Price (London), Rob Rio (Boss)

Wikipedia also names Jeff Beck, Chuck Berry, Eric Burden, Eddie Burns, Eric Clapton, Elvis Costello, Willie Dixon, Freddie King, The Kinks, Taj Mahal, Paul McCartney, Van Morrison, Muddy Waters, Robert Plant and Shakin' Stevens.

(Wikipedia includes non-Turner songs but ones associated with him)

Appendix 7 - "Hey cousin, how you doin'?"

An Appreciation of Big Joe Turner, by Mary Katherine Aldin

I first heard Joe Turner sing the blues in 1965. I was working then at a club on Melrose Avenue called The Ash Grove, and it was there that I learned the real feelings, emotions and validity of the music that would come to encompass my life. Till the Ash Grove and my time spent working there for Ed Pearl, "folk music" was something beatniks sang on the radio; "blues" was old black men lying in gutters, clutching bottles; "bluegrass" was a bunch of poorly-dressed hillbillies carrying banjos and fiddles, sawing away at them and telling corny jokes. When these musical traditions became real, and valued, to me, when the richness of my own musical heritage opened up to me and when the performers within these various traditions became living, breathing human beings, and my dear friends as time went on, I realized at last that what I wanted to do with my life was to spend it working to preserve and promote these traditions and the artists who explore them, and so it has been since then. In a variety of ways I try to keep the flame burning. I'm no museum-keeper, dusting cobwebs of dead-sea artifacts, but a fortunate participant in a vital and exciting body of American musical history.

Joe Turner was a perfect example of that continuing validity and vitality. If, as time passed and he grew older, heavier and more exhausted, he occasionally sang the same song twice in an evening, the two versions were never the same. If, as sometimes happened, he'd had more to drink than was good for him, his shows never faltered and his voice never failed. The older he got, the sicker he got and the more his physical strength left him, the louder he sang, as if to combat these ravages of time through sheer volume and force of will. Cursed with an ongoing series of incompetent backup bands, he'd shrug, grin, and count off the first song with an optimism never quenched by previous disasters; if they were absolutely hopeless, he'd fill in the gaps with a running commentary on life, death, music history, stories about his old days in Kansas City, philosophy dissertations and lectures to his captive and captivated audiences about the blues. His oldest friend, song-writer Doc Pomus, told me the day before the funeral that he had never met, or heard of, a single person anywhere who met Joe Turner and didn't like him. This reversal of the old Will Rogers joke tells a lot about the man; there was nothing about him to dislike. He lived for 74 years and never made an enemy; what a rare and wonderful quality in a human being these days!

I am not in favour of the current practice of immediately sanctifying anyone who dies by reeling off lists of his virtues - canonizing him, making an unreal image of him, denying his faults. Joe was a human being. He lived, as his wife Pat said, to make people happy through his music, and at the very canniest reckoning his life must be counted a success on that level. He was the despair of his friends and his long-suffering wife because he never believed that that the rules that applied to other people applied to him. He drank, he smoked (on one visit to his hospital bedside when he lay seriously ill, he said weakly, "Hey cousin, how you doin'?" and then showed me the pack of cigarettes and a bottle hidden under the corner of his mattress!!) and generally ruined his health. He was a diabetic, but only his wife's unceasing vigilance kept him alive in his last years; left to himself he would have ignored his dietary restrictions and forgotten his insulin. He had a bad heart, collapsed veins, no kidneys to speak of; he'd had heart attacks, strokes and dialysis treatments, but he kept on singing, stubbornly refusing to believe he was really sick. He dragged his aching, exhausted bulk around on crutches as long as he could; child-like in his faith, he reasoned that he was here to sing the blues, and sing he did. Whatever his virtues, whatever his faults, from the moment back in 1965 when he stepped on to the Ash Grove stage, I knew that I was privileged to be in the presence of a great talent, a wonderful person and a good friend.

As so often happens, his funeral brought forth numerous accolades from the public and his peers. Etta James, Ernie Andrews and Barbara Morrison sang at his service. Ahmet Ertegun, President of Atlantic Records, flew in to pay his respects. Fans jammed the small chapel and spilled outside into the street. The mayor of Kansas City sent a plaque ... but like so many blues singers, Joe Turner died alone. Since that great heart finally gave up its unequal battle, those of us who are left to mourn know we will never hear a voice like his again.

* * * *

First published in the Los Angeles Reader *(1985) and then in* Blues & Rhythm *No. 18, April 1986. Published here courtesy of Mary Katherine Aldin.*

Appendix 8 - The Recordings (a survey)

In a critique of Joe Turner's recordings, written for *Jazz On Record*, Alun Morgan stated:

"Joe Turner can take the most innocuous song and invest it with tremendous significance. He has a big, commanding voice which has served as the inspiration for many singers, from Jimmy Witherspoon down, and it is interesting to observe that when rock-'n'-roll became popular during the nineteen-fifties Joe was able to stage a comeback without any alteration to his basic singing style."[1]

Indications of the quality of Joe Turner's recordings have been given in the biography and readers have been advised that regardless of his accompaniments, they are all, with few exceptions, worth hearing for the quality of his voice and the swing he imparts to almost any song. And when the accompaniment is accomplished and sympathetic, the results are amongst the finest in jazz and blues recordings.

The Vocalion Period

With their first recordings Joe Turner and Pete Johnson, powerful earthy singing, combined with driving piano boogie accompaniment, made an immediate and lasting impact on the jazz scene. Their vocal and piano duets on the 1938 session for Vocalion (*Goin' Away Blues*/*Roll 'Em* Pete) and the two titles from Carnegie Hall and the three from Cafe Society, majestic singing, stunning piano playing, confirmed that they were one of the great partnerships in jazz.

Dan Morgenstern wrote,

"*Goin' Away Blues* is a medium tempo shout piece that features the singer's signature style. Big Joe sang in just one key and pretty much treated all his material in the same fashion, but he had a potent delivery and great propulsive time, and as his long and quite consistently successful career proved, the public loved him."[2]

The small band recordings made between June 30th, 1939 and October 15th, 1940 with Pete Johnson and his Boogie Woogie Boys, The Varsity Seven, Joe Sullivan and his Cafe Society Orchestra and Benny Carter and his All Star Orchestra are exemplary examples of exciting small band jazz of the time. Joe Turner is in fine form, as a listen to the Pete Johnson titles, *Cherry Red*, *Baby Look At You*, *Jump for Joy* and *Lovin' Mama Blues*, will confirm. They have superior backing by the leader himself, surging, powerful piano playing, and by Hot Lips Page, trumpet and Buster Smith, alto. If it is possible to fault the session, it might be that Page could have cut back on his use of a mute. But, mute in or out, this was music rocking mightily more than twenty years before rock and roll was born.

(*Cafe Society Rag* by the Boogie Woogie Trio is shown with a Joe Turner vocal, but his part in the proceedings is limited to shouting encouragement at the pianists.)

If the recordings with Pete Johnson provide a taste of Joe Turner in Kansas City, *Low Down Dirty Shame* and *I Can't Give You Anything But Love* by Joe Sullivan do the same for Joe in Cafe Society. Instrumental honours here go to the leader on piano and the underrated Eddie Anderson on trumpet. On the Benny Carter titles, *Joe Turner Blues* and *Beale Street Blues*, with the leader mainly playing clarinet, it is trumpeter Bill Coleman who shines alongside the singer.

Non-commercial recorded material from 1939 and 1940 includes broadcasts from the Cafe Society and from the Chamber Music Society of Lower Basin Street. Any material by the Joe Turner-Pete Johnson partnership is to be welcomed. The Document CD of 1938 and 1939 duets has three fine tracks with Johnson, plus an example of Turner singing a standard (*Sunny Side of the Street*) with the Frankie Newton band. There is a typically attractive trumpet solo by Newton. Taken from worn acetates, the sound quality on the Document is lo-fi, though better than on the two sides on Masters of Jazz.

From the 1940 Chamber Music Society of Lower Basin Street broadcast, we have Pete and Joe tearing into *Roll 'Em Pete* and *Goin' Away Blues* with undiminished vigour. making exciting companions to the Vocalion issue. These are on Storyville and Swing House LPs and the Masters of Jazz CD.

Other broadcast material which has found its way onto records many years later includes a version of *Low Down Dog* (labelled by Storyville as *Turner's Blues*) from a 1943 Jubilee broadcast. Albert Ammons is the pianist here, a happy substitute for Pete Johnson. A little later, but in the same vein, are the Turner/Ammons duets (*Roll 'Em* and *Low Down Dog*) from a soundie of 1944. As in 1943, it is to Ammons credit that Pete Johnson is hardly missed! *S.K. Blues* and *Love My Baby*, with the Johnny Otis big band, also from a Jubilee broadcast, are of lesser interest.

The Decca Period

Most important of the Decca sides are those with, again, Pete Johnson, and a handful of very impressive titles featuring pianist Art Tatum. There were also worthy sessions with pianists Willie 'The Lion' Smith, Freddy Slack, Sammy Price and Fred Skinner.

Dan Morgenstern believes that Turner ".... reached a peak with Art Tatum on Decca – on the face of it, an unlikely combination., but one that inspired Joe."[3] Very true, with the leads aided by the two peerless musicians Joe Thomas on trumpet and Ed Hall, clarinet.

And National and ....

Listening to the recordings made between the early 1940s and the early 1950s (National, Aladdin, M.G.M. Imperial, DownBeat, Freedom) one can detect the shift from small band swing accompaniments towards rhythm and blues. During this period Turner was mainly accompanied by a trumpet, two or three saxophones and a featured pianist. Often there is a big-toned, sometimes rasping tenor sax solo at the halfway point and all is carried along by a strong, powerful beat and riff backings.

In the series of recordings for National, between February 1945 and December 1947, the band can sometimes seem to be competing with the singer, rather than complementing. Despite this, Turner continues in fine voice and there are worthwhile, albeit short, contributions by trumpeter Frankie Newton, tenor man Don Byas, pianists Albert Ammons, Pete Johnson, Al Williams and Camille Howard, guitarist Teddy Bunn and the alto player, probably Porter Kilbert. All titles are worth hearing, with *Playboy Blues* (a retitling of *It's A Low Down Dirty Shame*), *Miss Brown Blues*, *S.K. Blues*, *Johnson and Turner Blues*, *Watch That Jive*, *Rocks In My Bed* and *Sally-Zu-Zazz*, good examples.

On Aladdin, favourites such as *Low Down Dog* and *Roll 'Em Pete*, uphold the standard, aided by tenor man Jack McVea's neat and spirited sextet, but those where Joe duets with Wynonie Harris (*Battle of the Blues*, etc) promise more than they deliver, though they do give a direct opportunity to compare their two voices.

Similarly, the Imperial session is successful, although *Jumpin' Tonight* is a fairly inconsequential "hepcats" dance song. An added bonus is Fats Domino at the piano making his presence felt.

Eight titles on *Down Beat*/Swingtime Records keep the standard at a satisfactory level, with both Joe Turner and Pete Johnson in top form, as are the two sessions, ten titles, for M-G-M Records, with a good jump band led by trumpeter Dootsie Williams and featuring more excellent Pete Johnson, as well as some worthy tenor solos by Maxwell Davis. Two titles for Coast can be linked with the M-G-M sessions.

The titles for Freedom maintain the standard, with some interesting songs - *Life Is Just A Card Game*, *Still In The Dark* and *Adam Bit The Apple* included. The first title is a gambler's lament, with Goree Carter's guitar work featured.

And Others

From this period Turner is also vocally strong on the two titles for Excelsior and the two for Rouge, although the balance favours his accompaniments; piano/guitar/bass trio for the former and a small band for the latter. The four songs *(I Don't Dig It; Ooh Ouch Stop; Wish I Had a Dollar; Fuzzy Wuzzy Honey)*, all credited to Turner, are of an inconsequential jive type. The dollar song ends with the strange line, "Wish I had a dollar, I would treat it like a piece of ginger bread" and the Honey number includes the deathless verse,

> One and one is two, two and two is four
> I never get enough, I always want some more.

Roll 'Em Pete, Kansas City Blues, Riding Blues, and *Playful Baby,* from a 1947 "Just Jazz" concert are another four exciting performances by Turner and Johnson. They are playing with a superfluous rhythm section, but the stars, spurred on by an enthusiastic audience, take no prisoners.

And Atlantic

Views of the Atlantic records may vary, but what must be kept in mind is that Joe Turner's "shouting" during this period continued to be strong, powerful, rhythmic and musical.

Atlantic 8023, "Rockin' The Blues," was one of the albums which placed Turner's singles for that label onto 12" microgroove and Mimi Clar's critique of the album in *The Jazz Review* could be taken as a summary of nearly all the singer's work for Atlantic.

Clar began by referring to "(1) Joe's position as head man in the blues field, to whom his contemporaries pay highest respects and newer singers like Joe Williams defer; (2) his epitomisation of the urbanized "wide-open," roaring-days-of-the-big-cities side of the blues; (3) his value as an entertainer for the let's-have-a-ball, party-time music; and, finally, (4) his recent enrichment and enlivening of the Rock and Roll scene.

> "'Rockin' the Blues' overlooks none of these aspects of Joe Turner. The entire album leans towards the dance and party-type blues, but offers good listening besides .... The majority of numbers are marked by fast boogie-woogie rhythms or rock-and-roll triplets; except for occasional piano comments and guitar obligato, not much subtle polyphony or antiphony occurs. the band laying down more of a rhythmic foundation from which Joe builds solid foundations."[4]

The bulk of Turner's Atlantic output, on 78s and 45s, was aimed at the rhythm-and-blues charts and the growing interest in the genre from white teenagers. Even allowing for the careful production of his recordings, it is still most surprising that a forty-year-old blues shouter could become so popular with that generation.

As a rule the singles run between two and three minutes. (The one exception is a five-minute version of Leroy Carr's *In The Evening,* which was released on an EP, though Joe's accompaniment marred this classic blues.) Also, as a rule, the singer's backing was by a small band, as Mimi Clar indicated, although not mentioned was the mandatory tenor sax between the vocal choruses. Generally the arrangements were to a pattern.

Instrumental solos appear occasionally. Examples, taken from the sessions for which personnels are known, include trombonist Pluma Davis with his tailgate riff on *Honey Hush,* guitarist Elmore James on *TV Mama,* and tenor players Sam 'The Man' Taylor on *Rock A While* and *Wee Baby Blues,* King Curtis on *Jump For Joy* and *Love Oh Careless Love,* plus Choker Campbell on *Love*

Roller Coaster. Pianist Johnny Jones can be heard accompanying on *Oke-She-Moke-She-Pop* and there are occasional baritone solos - Heywood Henry on *Shake, Rattle and Roll*, *In The Evening* and *The Chicken and the Hawk*, McKinley Easton on *Oke-She-Moke-She-Pop*; with a few bars of Hilton Jefferson's alto on *Blues in the Night*. A special mention goes to drummer Panama Francis for his contribution to the October 1957 session, particularly *Teen Age Letter*.

As to the issued titles, made between 1951 and 1959 (sessions in 1961 and 1962 were not released), the songs chosen can be placed in a number of categories. There are the originals, many by Ahmet Ertegun, Jesse Stone, Doc Pomus, or Turner himself, which made entries into the charts (*Chains of Love*, *Shake, Rattle and Roll*, *The Chill Is On*, *TV Mama*); classic blues (*Trouble In Mind*, *In The Evening*, *Love Oh Careless Love*); numerous novelty songs (*Ti-Ri-Lee*, *Oke-She-Moke-She-Pop*, *Hide and Seek*, *Lipstick, Powder and Paint*, *Bump Miss Susie*); and the recreation of a few old favourites, some successful (*Corrine, Corrina*, *Roll 'Em Pete* as *Jump For Joy*), others less so (*Wee Baby Blues*).

Joe puts his individual stamp on those ballads which he seems to enjoy singing, titles such as *After My Laughter Came Tears*, *Don't You Cry*, *My Reason For Living* (credited to Turner) and *Red Sails in the Sunset*. The last title, an unusual pop song from the 1930s, of British origin, has a fiancée praying that her fisherman lover will return safely from his final voyage, prior to their next-day wedding. An unlikely theme, but it clearly appealed to Turner (he recorded it on three further occasions) and he does it justice, overcoming the gender problem by substituting "we" for "he". Joe has less success with *Tomorrow Night* and *I'll Never Stop Loving You*. Another song he adapts well, though not a ballad, is *Sweet Sue*.

When we reach 1956 we find attempts to improve sales, with vocal groups, more musicians, and organists being added. *Honey Hush* and *Chains of Love* were re-recorded with strings, but the demand for Joe Turner records was declining.

One of the best of the "new" Atlantic songs was *Poor Lover Blues*, followed by *World of Trouble*, *Married Woman*, *Midnight Cannonball* and *You Know I Love You*. This last song is closer to a blues than the title might suggest. Of *Midnight Cannonball*, Dave Penny wrote,

> "... (it) really breaks the mould: although it is just the same old Joe Turner purveying the kind of jump blues he had been shouting for nearly 20 years, the backing turns this into one of his very first Rock and Roll recordings."[5]

"The Boss of the Blues: Joe Turner sings Kansas City Jazz" was one of two jazz LPs recorded for Atlantic. This 1956 album was the apex of Turner's Atlantic career and probably the finest he ever recorded; two sessions where everything came together, singer, ensemble, soloists and arranger. Joe is at his very best, Pete Johnson could not be bettered, while trombonist Lawrence Brown merits special mention for his solo work. A small complaint might be that drummer Cliff Leeman is sometimes too obtrusive, though one does wonder if he was playing to instructions. Another is the replacement of Joe Newman on trumpet by Jimmy Nottingham for the second session; though the latter contributes a nice solo on *I Want A Little Girl*. This is still a classic album.

It was an anti-climax that the 1958 follow-up, "Big Joe Rides Again", fell short of the standard set by "The Boss of the Blues". There were several reasons for this, a major one being the replacement of Pete Johnson by a very different type of pianist, Jimmy Jones. Other personnel changes did not help and the song selection was poor, The inconsequential *Switchin' In The Kitchen* and the Blue Lu Barker minor-hit *Don't You Feel My Leg* (here as *Don't You Make Me High*), plus four ballads, do not an exciting programme make. One also wonders if arranger Ernie Wilkins had been asked to tailor his charts towards the style of Turner's hit records for Atlantic. Even Joe does not seem entirely happy.

The Atlantic decade is a significant part of Turner's legacy, mainly for his exposure to a far larger audience than he had known previously. *Shake, Rattle and Roll* and his other hits were noteworthy factors in the pop music upheaval of the 1950s. In addition, his stay with Atlantic resulted in the magnificent "The Boss of the Blues" album.

And .....

Turner's set at the 1958 Newport Jazz Festival is of minor interest. Despite the illustrious names present in the Newport Blues Band and Joe being in good voice, the singer and the group do not gell. The choice of four Atlantic r&b hits may have contributed to this.

Five titles from 1963/64, four released at the time on Coral and one many years later in a Charly album, can safely be by-passed, unless vocal groups and unsuitable arrangements are acceptable.

When Joe and Buck Clayton flew to Yugoslavia in 1965 to appear at a festival, they also recorded an album for Black Lion records. Joe sings on four of the tracks. He is in his usual fine form, as is Clayton, one of the best and most consistent of the trumpet players of his era. What also makes the album a success is the contribution by the very effective Zagreb Jazz Quartet, vibes, piano, bass, drums.

Three interesting tracks from a 1965 Paris broadcast, issued on Europa Jazz albums, are by Big Joe Turner and his All Stars. The octet consists of American musicians, several ex-pats, and one major French player, tenor saxist Alix Combelle. Also present is Joe's namesake, the pianist Joe Turner. Trumpeter Buck Clayton is again in splendid form. The tune labelled as *Shake, Rattle and Roll* is actually *Roll 'Em* Pete, with additional verses, while *Cherry Red* is taken at a slower tempo than usual.

Joe's contributions to The American Folk Blues Festival '66 tour of Europe produced a few live recordings and a DVD. The latter is valuable as a sight of Turner at this time and it is interesting to hear him in a different setting, accompanied by just a rhythm section, with either Roosevelt Sykes or Little Brother Montgomery on piano. Surprisingly, neither veteran adds much to the proceedings.

It was south of the border, in Mexico in 1966, that Turner recorded with Bill Haley and his Comets, a pairing which proved more simpatico than many which followed thereafter. Unfortunately, the Orfeon recordings have not received a wide distribution.

The April 1967 titles for BluesWay are something of a curate's egg. Joe's voice is not at its best and the backing (harmonica or tenor sax, with prominent guitar) is a matter of preference. At times it seems that the band is trying to obscure rather than enhance. What is of interest is the inclusion, among the old favourites, of two rather unusual songs, *Poor House* and *Mrs. Geraldine*. Both are credited to Turner, though *Poor House* has earlier origins.

Bob Thiele produced the BluesWay album. He was another superior jazz record producer, both for Decca and for his own Signature and Flying Dutchman companies but, like others before him, failed to find the right setting when he signed Turner to his BluesTime label (1969). "The Real Boss of the Blues" album has boring rhythm patterns, unsuitable arrangements and soloists with no flair. Joe, needless to say, carries on regardless. Moreover, the Super Black Blues Band, despite the presence of T-Bone Walker and Otis Spann, also provides poor support. On *J.O.T.'s Blues* the drummer seems to be hammering in nails, while *Here I Am Broken Hearted* is another of Joe's generally unsuccessful ventures into ballad singing. The two 1970 titles from a Carnegie Hall concert add little to Joe's oeuvre.

Stanley Dance, in his sleeve notes for "Bosses of the Blues" phrases it tactfully, "Both sessions on this record were recorded as the turbulent '60s were coming to an end, a fact sometimes reflected in a heavy back beat, fender bass and unsophisticated harmonic underpinning." Dean Rudland, in his CD notes for Ace, talks of "the music being updated for a modern age ... with a burbling electric bass line and fatback drumming," referring to the album "as a worthy attempt at crossing-over...."

The Jewel recordings from the 1960s were made with a small band playing somewhat tedious arrangements, making it a pleasure to turn to the three 1967 titles recorded at the 'Spirituals To Swing' concert in Carnegie Hall. Joe is enjoying himself, with fine trumpet playing from Buck Clayton and a nice spot of Count Basie piano on *Blues For John*, a riff on *Well Oh Well*.

An album on L.M.I. contains tracks from 1969 and 1970. Here again, Joe is in fine fettle, with accompaniments typical of those he had during this period, prominent guitar, harmonica and tenor among them.

In the 1970s Turner sang on many occasions with the Johnny Otis Show, including the Monterey Jazz Festival of 1970. The three tracks with Big Joe are rumbustious, but good fun and swinging; worth hearing for the enthusiasm which the Johnny Otis Show generates in the audience. In 1974 Joe recorded a "Great Rhythm and Blues Oldies" album for the Otis label, Blues Spectrum. It is a good insight into Joe's work with the Show. He is singing well, with a satisfactory band of that period providing a suitably happy if repetitive accompaniment. *Wee*

Baby Blues deserves a mention. The Decca is the benchmark, but this version has a satisfying accompaniment by Mack Johnson playing muted trumpet, with Johnny Otis well featured on piano.

One can say the same of the few 1970 titles with Johnny Otis which appeared on the Wolf and Epic labels. Turner's excellent form is a constant, as are the songs; a generalisation which applies to much of his work in his later years.

Among television appearances in this period, there are three pleasant titles from 'Oscar Peterson Presents' with just piano, bass and drums, though Peterson is a little florid in his accompaniment. And three titles from an Art Ford Jazz Party make good listening. The unannounced blues (subsequently titled *Joe Turner Blues*) is referred to elsewhere and *Exactly Like You* is one of Joe's best versions of a standard popular song. His backing group, with a couple of exceptions, might have been the house band from Eddie Condon's Club, with the singer fitting into the jam session format as smoothly as one might have expected..

The Bihari brothers, Jules and Saul, had recorded Turner during their promotion of Modern Records (later including the labels R.P.M., Flair and Crown), which they had formed in 1945. Twenty-five years later, producer and label owner Jules Bihari followed in the wake of Bob Thiele, recording Turner with "music being updated for a modern age" for an album on Kent and United. Joe is again in good voice. George "Harmonica" Smith is reported to be the harmonica player and instrumentally he dominates most of the tracks. On *In The Evening* Joe twice says, "I want the guitar man to play a little blues," but it is the harmonica which solos. It is not until the final two titles on the LP that the pianist and guitarist assert themselves.

In 1978 a "Really The Blues" album was recorded for another of the Bihari labels, Big Town. This had a typical Turner backing for the time, with no harmonica but two guitars, bass-guitar and off-beat drumming inevitably present. The sleeve claims that all the tunes, including *In The Evening*, were "composed" by J. Turner.

The L.M.I. album and the Fuel CD follow the same pattern as the above, usually with the fender-bass over-prominent and the drummer lacking subtlety.

A recommended album is "Texas Style," recorded in France for the Black and Blue label during a 1971 tour. Joe is in powerful voice, Slam Stewart hums and bows on four tracks, Jo Jones is the drummer and Milt Buckner, not employing block chords here, was one of the better piano accompanists the singer had in his later years, particularly on the evidence of the first five titles. However, it should be noted that the anonymous reviewer in the Bulletin du Hot Club de France was not impressed with the timekeeping of this rhythm section.

About 1972 Turner made an album, "Still Boss of the Blues," for United Records, which was operating from Jules Bihari's address, 5810 S. Normandie Avenue, in Los Angeles. The sound here is similar to that on the Blues Time, Big Town and Kent releases, with piano, guitar, bass-guitar and prominent drums.

And for Pablo

Norman Granz was highly successful both as a jazz promoter (Jazz At The Philharmonic, Oscar Peterson, Ella Fitzgerald) and as a record label owner (Clef, Verve, Norgran and Pablo). He also became very wealthy, which enabled him to indulge his wishes, which included collecting paintings by Picasso as well as recording Joe Turner for his Pablo company. What was unfortunate was that the numerous Turner sessions for Pablo between 1974 and 1985 produced few releases of substance. Despite his admiration for Joe's work and his success as a producer, Granz failed to ensure that the singer received truly sympathetic accompaniments. Even the all-star units do not gell as they should.

A comment made by an anonymous reviewer, in the *Bulletin du Hot Club de France*, could be applied to so many of the Pablo releases. He ended his critical review of Pablo 2310.760, "*Nobody In Mind,*" by saying of Joe Turner: ".... despite all his talent, he cannot counterbalance the depressing atmosphere created by his accompanists .…. "In brief, a record which will only be of interest to the loyal fans of the great singer".[6]

Producer and recording engineer for some of the Pablo sessions, Eric Miller, has been quoted as saying, "Joe didn't really care, as long as he had guys around him. We'd pick guys who were in town... ."[7] And the problems seem to have started from there.

"Flip, Flop & Fly" is an album of concert recordings issued about 15 years after the event and is a typical example from the European tour which Turner and Basie made in the 1970s. That the concerts were enjoyable is illustrated by the enthusiasm of the audiences. Joe's singing is lusty, the Basie orchestra, not as singular as earlier versions, remained a powerful instrument and the repertoire may have been somewhat worn, but the customers were happy.

"The Bosses" was the first and best of Turner's Pablo albums. Recorded in December 1973, it starred Joe Turner with Count Basie and a small all-star group. As always, Joe is the star, with Basie providing quietly understated support. and they have quality backing in the rhythm section from Ray Brown on bass and Louis Bellson on drums.

Starting with the 1974 "Trumpet Kings" the decline begins. For example, *Stormy Monday* features relentless drumming and the 14-minutes of *TV Momma* seem endless. These are presumably head-arrangements so that no one has to take responsibility when, too often, the trumpets impede the singer. John Chilton is more generous towards the musicians than this writer.

1975 saw the release of two albums, "Everyday I Have The Blues" and "Nobody In Mind". The former has a repetitious rhythm on most tracks and a noisy Washington Rucker on drums. In this version of *Lucille*, surprisingly, Turner uses mainly new, though not fresh, lyrics; only two verses remain from his classic Decca versions. *Martin Luther King Southside* is another Turner composition difficult to fathom. It is a version of *Miss Brown Blues*, but with Martin Luther Avenue replacing South Park Avenue. There is no mention of the Southside.

On "Nobody In Mind" there is more heavy drumming, part of a rhythm section not suited to Eldridge and Jackson. John Chilton commented that the session:

"produced musical results that, at times, border on the ludicrous. This album's issue undoubtedly dented Big Joe Turner's massive and deserved reputation. Roy's (Eldridge) role in the musical mayhem is a subsidiary one; he simply co-exists alongside the sounds of an electric organ, a powerful guitar, and some pulverizing off-beat drumming.

.... Joe Turner, for whom that song [*Morning Glory*] was a triumph on his Boss Of The Blues album, chose not to get involved in any disputes, and sings his lines seemingly untroubled by the laughable mangling of the changes. Joe was in a strange mood that day, and on the title track, *Life Ain't Easy* offers some stream-of-consciousness lyrics, issuing his brand of philosophy in unconnected stanzas – none of which makes any sense.

"Having got away with singing whatever came into his head, Joe decided to try the same tactics on *For Growin' Up*, and makes unresolved comments about various people including his grandparents, linking these observations with mundane thoughts about nothing in particular."[8]

There were three albums released in 1976. "In The Evening" has Turner accompanied by an alto saxophonist plus rhythm section, including two guitars. The group is loud, but Joe sings well and the programming is different. There are three Turner "originals," two Turner favourites, one classic blues and four songs from Tin Pan Alley. *Two Loves Have I,* credited to L.W. Turner, is a reasonable attempt to write a popular song. The album is worth sampling if only for Turner's more than creditable singing of the standards, including *Summertime* and *Sweet Lorraine*.

"The Midnight Special" is one of the better Pablos, though that is faint praise. The album is a curate's egg, ranging from the raucous interpretation of the title song to respectable versions of *You're Driving Me Crazy* and *I'm Gonna Sit Right Down and Write Myself a Letter*, Joe sings well here, with the accompaniment on some titles more sympathetic. Other standards chosen are less suitable for Joe's voice, including *I Lost My Heart In San Francisco* (as Joe persists in singing) and *So Long*. This last song is credited to Woody Guthrie on both LP and CD. On the latter it is entitled *So Long (It's Been Good To Know You)*. However, it is James Brown's *So Long*. Why Turner would record three versions of the same James Brown song for Pablo is difficult to understand, as is the fact that all three are credited to Woody Guthrie.

Life Ain't Easy again has heavy drumming, plus an organ groaning, and is generally dreary.

The "Things That I Used To Do" album is another run-of-the-mill selection, with pianist Lloyd Glenn doing his best to raise the band's standard. Of the Joe Turner compositions, *Hey Little Girl* is a pedestrian effort and *My Train Rolled Up In Texas* is a promising title but tells the usual story of a loving woman, now with someone else. There are references to the engineer blowin' the whistle and to Miss Vida Lee. The drumming is loud and still unrelenting. Released later on "Stormy Monday" (a compilation album) was *Time After Time*: a hit for Frank Sinatra but a surprising and uncomfortable choice for Turner to sing. A short alto solo by Eddie Vinson is a pleasant respite.

"Have No Fear Joe Turner Is Here" (1978) has ten musicians with nothing to do but play loud. The comments above for the the drummer (Charles Randall) and Lloyd Glenn apply here as well. From the same session, but on the compilation "Stormy Weather, " *Somebody Loves Me*, by Turner, not Gershwin, has both singer and musicians going through the motions with no one seeming involved, while *Long Way From Home* is another song where the lyrics are thrown together with, apparently, a "that will do" attitude.

The six vocal tracks on the 1980 Pablo album by Count Basie, "Kansas City Shout," are shared by Joe Turner and Eddie 'Cleanhead' Vinson, though it is the latter who seems more comfortable in the big band setting. Joe is not in good voice, while his "original" (*Blues for Joe Turner*) is a limp compilation. Neither the band nor the arranger seemed to have made any concession to Joe's style, which might explain his lacklustre form. He is still in Kansas City; for the Basie orchestra that was fifty years ago.

During and After Pablo...

The Palms, 1977: Big Joe is in excellent form on these live recordings, which should be sampled for that fact alone. One's view of them, as in many other instances, will be coloured by the accompaniment. If you favour white blues revivalists, you should enjoy these. As one writer put it, "The piano and the sax player have lengthy solos throughout, sounding great. Mike Bloomfield plays beautiful guitar on some of the songs." Without doubt, an exciting evening for the audience.

Also 1977, in March that year, came an album on the Spivey label (named for singer Victoria Spivey). The quality of Turner's singing is revealed by comparison with the shouting of Brenda Bell, who mercifully only intrudes twice, on *T'ain't Nobody's Biz-ness*, but ruins *Red Sails In The Sunset*. There is one track (*Little Birdie Tweet-Tweet-Tweet*) where the band becomes obtrusive, but elsewhere it is comparatively subdued, though the presence of a washboard becomes rather wearing. An album worth auditioning for Joe's vocals and for Lloyd Glenn adding a spot of class to the proceedings.

In his lyric for *Boss of the House* Turner makes one of his rare family references when describing his lover. He sings that "she's a cutie like my old sister Kate" unless, that is, he is referring to the Kate who shimmies.

In 1978, and again in 1981, Turner was recorded with German pianist Axel Zwingenberger for Telefunken Records. Hearing the singer in this period with just boogie piano and drums accompaniment is an interesting variation, although these are just average Turner outings. (Of course, "average" for Joe

Turner is "excellent" for most blues singers.) Perhaps the track to pinpoint is the nearly 15-minute *Boogie Woogie Jubilee*, another amalgam, which also features Eddie 'Cleanhead' Vinson and Margie Evans, as well as Roy Milton on drums. This 1981 double album was recorded at a party to celebrate Joe's 70th birthday (Vinson includes "Happy birthday to you, Joe Turner" in his lyrics) and the atmosphere is congenial - and contagious.

The 1983 Muse album, "Blues Train," offers the listener the opportunity to hear Joe, backed by a medium-sized band called Roomful of Blues, another grouping of mainly young, white revivalists. Of its time and soul influenced, what it lacks in subtlety it makes up with spirit and enthusiasm. *Red Sails In The Sunset* remains an unusual choice, but it is well sung, if a little dramatic. *I Love The Way (My Baby Sings The Blues)* is a fitting finale, with pianist Al Copley valiantly following in Pete Johnson's footsteps and everyone falling into a good groove. This album is another reminder of how well Turner continued singing the blues until just before his death.

Also from 1983 came the Southland album with Knocky Parker and his Houserockers. This unlikely combination of a pianist (Parker) who specialised in ragtime and early jazz, an r&b tenor man (Eddie Chamblee), known for his work with Lionel Hampton, plus a trad band tuba player (David Ostwald) works far better than one might imagine. Parker does not venture into boogie woogie, but his playing fits, while Chamblee is obviously at home. Turner's voice is a little coarse on a few tracks, but vigorous on the majority. The programme is of tried and trusted favourites, some retitled, plus a curio, *Seventy-Two*, in which Joe sings happy birthday to himself, "I just made 72"! No finesse here and a pounding rhythm background, but deserves a hearing.

A set at The Music Machine in Santa Monica in October 1983, with accompaniment by tenor man Lee Allen's band, was recorded and released on RetroWorld. On the evidence of this CD the club was rocking that night, with an enthusiastic audience cheering Joe on. Despite this and the unsatisfactory acoustics, his voice remains as potent as ever, with no indication of health problems.

His final recordings, in 1984 and 1985, are of historical interest, but otherwise fail to do him justice. Ten years on from the "Trumpet Kings" album, the "Kansas City Here I Come" personnel is very different but the aim remains the same, everyone play fortissimo or turgid and slow. The version of *Time After Time* is even more uncomfortable than the one recorded in 1977.

In April 1985's "Patcha, Patcha, All Night Long," Joe duets with Jimmy Witherspoon on three tracks and has one solo outing. Joe is still singing well, with surprisingly little loss of power. It is unfortunate that the "original compositions" are of no consequence or consist of the same old stanzas, played by a band which flatters to deceive on *Patcha, Patcha*, then succumbs to pounding monotony on the remaining titles.

In the following month, he appears on what, at the time of writing, are his last known performances to find their way onto disc, four concert titles on a CD privately issued by pianist Barney McClure. These, including a nicely rocking

Corrina, Corrina (sic), confirm that even in his last few months, his voice was hardly diminished.

For over forty years Joe Turner was a frequent visitor to recording studios, so that now his voice can be heard and admired at every stage of his career. One's appreciation of each part of that recorded legacy will depend, as already said, upon the individual listener and his appreciation of the singer's accompaniments.

On The Screen...

There are opportunities to view Joe Turner in action via videos, DVDs and the Internet. Information and comments on the following appear in both the biography and discography, but the titles are listed here, in chronological order, for reference.

Swingtime Jamboree (1944) It is unfortunate that the two Soundies recorded in January 1944 only have Turner on the soundtrack, not on the screen, but *Roll 'Em/Low Down Dog* with Meade Lux Lewis on piano is a pairing not to miss.

Apollo Showtime (1955) It was not until the Atlantic period that Turner was on the screen, firstly in this television variety series, when *Shake, Rattle and Roll* (Stars Over Harlem episode) and *Oke-She-Moke-She-Pop* (Variety Time episode) were broadcast, then on the big screen when the titles were used in feature films, *Oke-She-Moke-She-Pop* in "Rock 'n' Roll Revue" ("Harlem Rock 'n' Roll" in the U.K.) and *Shake, Rattle and Roll* in "Rhythm and Blues Revue". This is an opportunity to see Joe's manner in performance, easy-going, light-footed, slightly awkward, a few hand gestures, yet still a presence.

Shake, Rattle & Rock! (1956) This was a 75-minute B feature, complete with actors and a script, though Turner's part was to sing *Feelin' Happy* and *Lipstick, Powder and Paint* in the same style and manner as those for the Apollo Showtime television films.

Jazz 625 (1965) A notable television appearance, alongside Buck Clayton, Vic Dickenson and the best British mainstream band of the period, led by Humphrey Lyttelton on trumpet. An important event in Joe Turner's career.

In Mexico (1966) Online, a version of *Oh Well Oh Well* can be found. This can be recommended for both the singer and for the spirited backing by Bill Haley and his Comets.

The American Folk Blues Festival (1966) is another good opportunity to see Turner in action, recorded for Granada Television in Manchester, and later in Germany. Veteran blues pianists Little Brother Montgomery or Roosevelt Sykes are among his accompanists.

Jazz On Stage (1969) This television series, starring pianist Hampton Hawes, was filmed in a dimly-lit club, but the Joe Turner episode is interesting viewing.

Monterey Jazz (1970) This film, which appeared in 1973, was a record of the 13th Annual Monterey Jazz Festival of 1970. It has Joe Turner singing *Hide and Seek* and *Roll 'Em Pete* with the Johnny Otis show.

Oscar Peterson Presents (1974) The Joe Turner episode from this series is another acceptable part of the singer's filmography.

Last of the Blue Devils (1974) This full-length documentary, filmed at a reunion of Kansas City musicians, had Count Basie, Jay McShann and Joe Turner as the well-featured guest stars, both playing and being interviewed. As stated in Chapter 14, the film is essential viewing. (A brief clip of Turner and McShann from this film is included in "Piano Blues: a film by Clint Eastwood" (2003) on SnapperMusic/Vulcan VD 036.)

To summarise, and to repeat the opening remarks to this brief film review, any opportunity to see and hear Big Joe Turner in action should be taken, with priority being given to "Last of The Blue Devils" and to the Jazz 625 broadcasts with Humphrey Lyttelton.

Film Soundtracks

Among the films which credit Joe Turner recordings on the soundtrack are the following, although their use is often minimal or hard to discern:

"The Big Town" (1987, with Matt Dillon, Tommy Lee Jones) using the Atlantic version of *Shake, Rattle and Roll*.

"Corrina, Corrina" (1994, Whoopi Goldberg) using the Atlantic version.

"Lone Star" (1996, reported to include a Joe Turner track)

"Malcolm X" (1992, Denzil Washington), the Atlantic version of *Roll 'Em, Pete* is heard over the opening scene, after the credits.

"Uncle Buck" (1989, John Candy) using the Atlantic version of *Lipstick, Powder and Paint*.

"The Rainmaker" (1997, Matt Dillon, Danny DeVito), using the Pablo version of *Woman, You Must Be Crazy*.

Appendix 9 -Letters and Cards from Joe and Geraldine Turner

UNiversity 6-3300

HOTEL **Theresa**

SEVENTH AVENUE at 125th STREET
NEW YORK 27, N. Y.

March 13th 1964

Dear Mr. Collier:

I rec'ived your letter and was delighted to know that the interview with Jack was published.

Well the engagement at Birdland was quite a success, and from there I did nine days. at Louie' Lounge in Boston, which was also a success. Just now I'm being groomed for another recording session dated for Tuesday 17th. The record scheduled for release this week is entitled "I stand accused" — and "I walk a lonely mile" on Decca I think it has possibilities.

Now the question of my coming over has been constantly being brought to my attention by

HOTEL **Theresa**

SEVENTH AVENUE at 125th STREET
NEW YORK 27, N. Y.

several writers, editors and etc.
but I'm seriously considering a tour
th + is if something could be worked
out for at least a couple of months.
So if you can lend an ear and
do a little speading in my behalf.
I do hope Jazz is being kept alive
in that area.

Presently I reside in New Orleans
a city of Jazz origin. I've played the
safari room, Peppermint Lounge,
DEW DropInn plus several auditorium
dates — although I'd had a fall Nov.
1962 which kept me incapacitated
late in 1963, my leg was broken
in two places — which called for
surgery. O.K. now.

Anyway I plan to be here in
N.Y. three this week before.
returning home. And if there is
any information, that you (over)

should pin point my wife
will be Glad to furnish such
at my bidding — as she is with
me most of the time.
I am still booked thru
Shaw Artists, 565 fifth ave.
Enclosed my card.
Best of luck to you on your
future articles.

Sincerely

Joe Turner

New Orleans, La.
May 7, 1965

My Dear Mr. Collev;
I am Mrs. Joe Turner,
as you probaly know Joe is in
London since Wednesday May 5th
However if possible, I would
certainly appreciate any matter
in advertisement about Joes,
engagements over there.
Which I shall have published
here prior to Joes' return to the
states; in hopes that the publicity
will be an asset to him in
the field of promotion.
Meantime allow me to thank you
in advance, and if in the future
I can be of any help to you on this
end, be sure and feel free to write.

Sincerely
Mrs. Geraldine B. Turner

New Orleans, La
Sept. 13, 1965

Dear Mr. Coeler:
Sorry to hear that you
were ill earlier, however I
do hope that all is well with
you at this writing.
Thanks a million for
the ~~~~ material etc, overall
the book (Pete Johnson Story)
which I'm sure you arranged
for me to recieve, it really
gave me a tremendous recall
I recently recieved a very
gratifying letter, autographs
and pottions that are being
compiled on a biography of
my life from Zurich, this
mail and material has
been following me since
January. New Jazz Club Zurch

headed by Jörg (George) Koran, However on my return to London maybe I can set in on one of their Wednesday sessions. The material I received was printed in a book called (Dig It) real great.

During this lull between now and then let me hear from you, my wife extends her best to you. Thanks again, be sure to call on me in any case that I can be of assistance.

Sincerely
Big Joe Turner

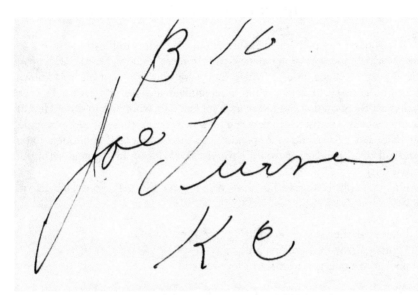

Big Joe Turner signature (source unknown)

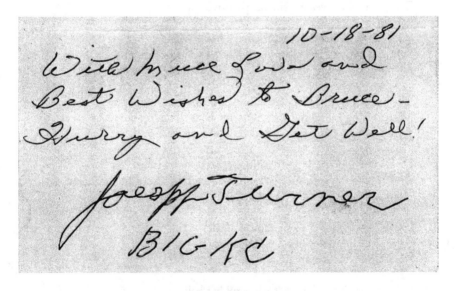

Big Joe Turner signature (courtesy Steve Adamson)

Appendix 10 - The Lyrics

This is not a comprehensive examination, but it aims to illustrate the casual way in which Joe Turner approached his songs, changing words, adding or deleting verses, or the order in which they were sung. Some of his best-known blues are discussed in detail, while other individual lines or verses have been singled out for quotation. A modest attempt has been made also to show a few of the more obvious connections between Joe's stanzas and those of earlier singers. Reference has been made in Appendix 5 to the innumerable traditional blues verses, all of which Turner would have absorbed during his apprenticeship in Kansas City.

One example is the ad-lib blues he sang on the "Art Ford Jazz Party" television broadcast of July 24, 1958:

I gotta gal, she lives up on a hill
I gotta gal, she lives up on a hill
Fool gonna quit me, Lord, but I love her still

She got ways like an angel, talks just like a baby child
She got ways like an angel, talks just like a baby child
Everytime she loves me she nearly drives me wild

I call her early in the morning, I call her way late at night
I call her early in the morning, I call her way late at night
No matter when I call my baby, she always talks just right

My little dog is barking, he knows my baby's coming home
My little dog is barking, he knows my baby's coming home
He gonna get fed regular, don't have to worry about being alone

Don't the moon look pretty shining through the trees
Don't the moon look pretty shining through the trees
Don't my baby look good walking along home with me

I wish I could holler like a mountain jack
I wish I could holler like a mountain jack
I'd go up on the mountain and call my baby back

It takes a rocking chair to rock, a rubber ball to roll
It takes a rocking chair to rock, a rubber ball to roll
A fine little girl to satisfy my soul

Baby, baby, ev'rything'll be alright
Baby, baby, ev'rything'll be alright
I'll see you today, baby, be back tomorrow night

I want to love you, I want to hold you tight
I want to love you, I want to hold you tight
Tell you pretty baby, everything's alright

Treat me baby, treat me all night
Treat me baby, treat me all night
I want to hold you baby, everything's alright

As suggested in Chapter 4, these lyrics, perhaps, illustrate how Turner kept the Kansas City nightclubs rocking, singing chorus after chorus. They are also an example of what Tony Burke and Dave Penny in "Big Joe Turner: Have No Fear, Big Joe Is Here, Part 1" (*Blues & Rhythm*, issue 11, 1983) called "an amalgam of Joe's favourite throwaway lines". Burke and Penny are describing *I Love Ya*, but their accurate portrait of his casual approach applies more generally.

This "amalgam" system is on display from the earliest of Joe's recordings. Formal blues songs and popular standards are treated alike. The lyrics as written are given some attention, but not for too long. *Beale Street Blues* and *Rocks In My Bed* are examples of this. Reasons for these variations could include a form of improvisation, selecting a verse to suit a mood or the fact that Turner, unable to read a song sheet, was reliant on his memory.

In later years a verse from any source might appear on any of his records. For example; his recorded versions of *St. Louis Blues* (Atlantic, Kent) add traditional stanzas "Blues jumped a rabbit, ran him for a solid mile" and "What makes grandma love old grandpa so?" to W.C. Handy's lyrics. And a version on Southland adds a third:

Mississippi river runs long, deep and wide
Mississippi river runs long, deep and wide
I've got to see my baby, she lives on the other side

George Kanzler, Jr. in the *Newark Star-Ledger* (March 24th, 1977), stated that "blues jumped a rabbit" was one of 150 (sic) verses that Turner interpolated into *St. Louis Blues*," When queried about its source, Turner told him, "That's old stuff, don't know where I heard that – I might even have made it up myself". It is telling that Turner is blasé about the long established "blues jumped a rabbit".

It was common practice for singers to adopt or adapt the lyrics of others. Paul Oliver has referred to "the common pool of traditional lyrics" and to the "images, phrases, even whole verses, which communicated effectively through many different social contexts within the Negro community".[1]

These then were the bricks with which Joe Turner built his house of blues, the sources from which he mixed his blues cocktails.

Turner's earlier recordings tend to be the most interesting for this purpose, with alternative takes available for comparison. They show how Turner would change lyrics or re-arrange the order of verses for four songs within the allotted three or four hours of a 78 rpm recording session. On them one can appreciate the way in which he uses the verses stored in his memory, a vast library of blues choruses from which he borrowed, sometimes aptly, but often with little regard for relevance.

Cherry Red (Vocalion 1939)
Run here, pretty baby, sit down on your daddy's knee
Run here, pretty baby, sit down on your daddy's knee
I want to tell everybody how you've been sendin' me

Now, if that's your secret, you can keep it to yourself
Now, if that's your secret, you can keep it to yourself
'Cos if you tell me I might tell somebody else

I never loved, I hope I never will
I never loved, I hope I never will
Because a lovin' proposition will get somebody killed

Now, you can take me baby, put me in your big brass bed
Now, you can take me baby, put me in your big brass bed
Eagle Rock me baby, until my face turns cherry red

Cherry Red remained in Turner's repertoire for the next forty-plus years, the basic lines remaining largely unchanged, but with additional verses. Frequently the "big brass bed" became the "Hollywood bed," which may refer to the Hollywood Bed & Spring Mfg. Co. of Commerce, CA, founded 1925.

In Thomas Dorsey's 1928 song, *Victim of the Blues*, Ma Rainey sang of "my cheeks turned cherry red," though this reference ("I cried about my daddy until my cheeks turned cherry red") was about loss of a lover, not sex. Around the same time Bessie Tucker sang, "Because love is a proposition that's got many a poor girl killed".

Roll 'Em, Pete (Vocalion 1938)

I got a gal lives up on the hill
I got a gal lives up on the hill
This woman's tryin to quit me, Lord, but I love her still

She's got eyes like diamonds, teeth shine like Klondike gold
She's got eyes like diamonds, teeth shine like Klondike gold
Every time she loves me, she sends my mellow soul

You're so beautiful, but you got to die someday
You're so beautiful, but you got to die someday
All I want's a little lovin', babe, just before you pass away

Roll it boy, let 'em jump for joy
Yes man, happy as a baby boy
My gal bought me a brand new choo-choo toy

Well, babe, goin' away and leave you by yourself
Well, babe, goin' away and leave you by yourself
You've mistreated me enough, baby, now you can mistreat somebody else.

The third verse is one of the most famous in jazz and blues. In 1932 Big Bill Broonzy recorded *Bull Cow Blues*, which includes the line "Babe you may be beautiful, you got to die someday" and Lee Green recorded for Decca a song entitled *You May Be Beautiful But You Got To Die*.

In a 1983 version he called *You Mighty Beautiful*, Turner added to the original verses, three which began: "My gal's a jockey, she teaches me how to ride," / "I cried, Rebecca, Rebecca, get your big leg off of me," / Don't talk me to death, I ain't ready to die", plus a fourth saying:

Crazy about you baby, but I just don't have the price
Crazy about you baby, but I just don't have the price
You're a high-class woman, so I guess it's no dice

"We wanna jump for joy, happy as a baby boy, who's got another brand new choo-choo toy" is one of Turner's favourite expressions. Perhaps he borrowed this from the Mitchell Parish opening verse for *Sweet Lorraine*, written in 1928:

I found joy, I'm as happy as a baby boy
Who has found a brand new choo-choo toy
When I'm with my sweet Lorraine.

As with so many of these early classics, *Roll 'Em, Pete* also remained a constant at Turner's performances, as did the blues it inspired, *Rebecca*, recorded for Decca in 1944.

Joe Turner Blues (OKeh 1940)
On occasion Turner would sing standard lyrics more or less as they were written, but this 1940 recording illustrates those times when he completely

disregards them. Although Okeh's label credited W.C. Handy with the song, Turner's version, with the exception of the very first verse, is quite different. The first line of the second stanza is from *Michigan Water Blues*, copyright composer Clarence Williams, but claimed as stolen from Jelly Roll Morton. (Morton refers to "sherry wine", but Turner is closer to "cherry wine".)

You never miss your water 'til your well run dry
You never miss your water 'til your well run dry
You never miss Joe Turner until he says his last goodbye

That there Michigan water tastes just like cherry wine
That there Michigan water tastes just like cherry wine
And the reason I love you baby, 'cos you so swell and fine

Have you ever heard the song I'm singing to you
Have you ever heard the song I'm singing to you
I'm a hip cat, baby, and we call it the Joe Turner blues

So take it easy, Joe Turner's knocking on your door
So take it easy, Joe Turner's knocking on your door
You can tell the way he knocks, that's he's been here before
Joe Turner knockin' on your door

Joe Turner (or Turney) ran a chain gang for profit, but Handy turned him into a victim of unrequited love, while Big Bill Broonzy made him a hero of an 1892 Mississippi flood. Handy's original lyric included two traditional verses, used by Big Joe elsewhere, including "Sorry to your heart .... when you and I must part" and "I bought a bulldog for to watch you while you sleep".

Beale Street Blues (Okeh 1940)

This was another W.C. Handy composition recorded at the 1940 Benny Carter Okeh session. In these two takes Turner is quite free with Handy's lyrics, in addition to quoting *Basin Street Blues*, presumably in error. The first two verses are approximately according to Handy and the third according to Turner. The following is from take -2.

If Beale Street could walk, if Beale Street could talk
Married men would pick up their beds and walk
Except one or two, left with the blues
The blind man on the corner tryin' to shine some shoes

Hear me talkin', baby, I'm only talking to you

I'd rather be here than any place I know
I'd rather be here than any place I know

'Cos I love you baby, love you 'cos you so and so

Baby's feet is just so neat, everybody's mellow on the street
Everything is just so fine, you always swingin' take your time

Hear me talkin'bout the fine wine, Basin, Basin Street Blues

Beale Street Blues (Okeh 1940)
On the originally issued take -1 the first verse is as above, except that the blind man on the corner is "hollerin' I'm looking out for you".

The second verse is as above, but last line is: "Hear me talkin' baby, talkin' 'bout your so and so"

The third verse is: Beale Street blues, so just as fine as wine
I just can't remember anything's on my mind
Beale Street is so fine as wine

Rocks in My Bed (Decca 1941)
This is a composition by Duke Ellington, written for Turner to sing in the revue "Jump for Joy". Turner says he contributed to the lyrics. Certainly there is a marked difference between Ellington's recorded version, with an Ivie Anderson vocal, and Turner's for Decca.

Take -A of the Turner record has the following stanzas which are not Ellington:

Now ain't but two people in this world I just can't stand
Now ain't but two people in this world I just can't stand
That's a two-faced woman and jealous hearted man
But she's got eyes like diamonds, every time she smiles
she makes my blood run cold
But she's got eyes like diamonds, every time she smiles
she makes my blood run cold
And I love my baby, I want the whole world to know

So I'm gonna call up to China, because I want to see
if my baby's over there
So I'm gonna call up to China, because I want to see
if my baby's over there
Say, I've got a feeling, my good gal's in this world somewhere

On take -B the "eyes like diamonds" verse is dropped, substituted with:

Says she's long, she's tall, she's shaped just like a willow tree
Says she's long, she's tall, she's shaped just like a willow tree
I'll tell the world, my baby's all right with me

Minor variations are not shown, though on take -B Turner reverses adjectives by referring to "a jealous hearted woman and a two-faced man". Typical Turner lyrics, although rather distant from the theme of *Rocks in My Bed*!

When Turner recorded *Rocks in My Bed* again in 1947 for National, he followed, more or less, the original Duke Ellington/Ivie Anderson version, but inserted the "I'm gonna call up China...." verse he used on the Decca take -B. For the Pablo recording he added a verse which tells us that his woman has a black cat's bone.

Low Down Dirty Shame (Vocalion 1940)

There are numerous variations on this song title. They are not always the same blues and numerous composer credits are given. For the 1940 Vocalion recording the credits name Joe Turner and bandleader Joe Sullivan. Two of the verses are:

I was standing in my window, I saw a poor boy walking in the rain
I was standing in my window, I saw a poor boy walking in the rain
I can hear him say, it's a low down dirty shame

I was standing in my window. 'til my feets is soaking wet
I was standing in my window. 'til my feets is soaking wet
I never seen nobody looks like my baby yet
It's a low down dirty shame

One assumes that the repetition of "standing in my window" is an error on Joe's part. The reference to "feet is soaking wet," which Chris Smith has traced to a 1925 recording by Papa Charlie Jackson, is usually preceded by someone "walking in the rain".

The above two verses were slightly amended when used in his version for National, where it became:

Playboy Blues (National 1946)

Some people call me a pimp, some people call me a gambler, I'm neither one
Some people call me a pimp, some people call me a gambler, I'm neither one
I'm just a hip little playboy out to have my fun

I was standing by my window, I saw a poor boy walking in the rain
I was standing by my window, I saw a poor boy walking in the rain
I can hear him say, it's a low down dirty shame

I walk the streets all night long, 'til my feets is soaking wet
I walk the streets all night long, 'til my feets is soaking wet
I never seen nobody look like my baby yet
It's a low down dirty shame

I give up, I want my baby home
I give up, I want my baby home
I'm just doggone tired, sleeping all alone

Yes, give it up, give it up, I want my baby back home
I'm doggone tired, sleeping all alone

Rebecca (Decca 1944)

On take -A Joe gives us four verses, plus his trade mark repetition of "yes, yes; alright then, alright then; bye bye".

I got a gal lives up on the hill	verse 1
I got a gal lives up on the hill	
Well the fool's trying to quit me, but Lord, I love her still	

She got eyes like diamonds, teeth shine like Klondike gold	verse 2
She got eyes like diamonds, teeth shine like Klondike gold	
Every time she loves me, she sends my mellow soul	

My baby's a jockey, she teaches me how to ride	verse 3
My baby's a jockey, she teaches me how to ride	
She says twice in the middle, then daddy from side to side	

Well, Rebecca get your basket, let's go down to the woods	verse 4
Well, Rebecca get your basket, let's go down to the woods	
We may not pick no berries, but we'll come back feelin' good	

On an originally unissued and unidentified take, Turner sings the first three verses above, adds verses 5 and 6, then inserts verse 4, and ends with verse 7!

Three and three is six, six and three is nine	verse 5
Three and three is six, six and three is nine	
You give me some of yours and I'll give you some of mine	

Well, Rebecca, Rebecca, get your big leg off of me	verse 6
Well, Rebecca, Rebecca, get your big leg off of me	
Might be sending you, babe, but it's worryin' the hell out of me	

Cried last night, cried the night before	verse 7
Cried the night before	
Change my way of living, won't have to cry no more	

Rebecca Take -B

Here he sings the verses in this order: 1, 2, 3, 6, 4 and 8:

Babe, what's the matter now   verse 8
Babe, what's the matter now
Tryin' to quit me baby, swear you don't know how

"Rebecca, Rebecca, get your big leg off of me" is a line Turner inserted into numerous songs.

Lucille (Luther Williams) is another classic number from this Decca period, closely associated with Turner. Over the years Joe did change and add to the lyrics, sometimes being credited with the original composition. One of the extra verses he added, with a name change, came from *Louise Louise*, written by Johnnie Temple:
Lucille, Lucille, you're the sweetest gal I know
Lucille, Lucille, you're the sweetest gal I know
She made me walk from Chicago to the Gulf of Mexico

*　*　*　*　*

A few of Joe Turner's lyrics have been quoted in the biography. For example, *Miss Brown Blues, Fun in Chicago, Mrs Geraldine, Good Mornin' Miss Patricia* etc, which may just have some biographical relevance.

Also quoted in part in the biography is *Piney Brown Blues*, an illustration of his haphazard approach to lyrics. One verse is a tribute to Brown, another mentions Kansas City and the other two are concerned with affairs of the heart.

Piney Brown Blues (Decca 1940)

Well, I've been to Kansas City, girls, and everything is really all right
Well, I've been to Kansas City, girls, and everything is really all right
Where the boys jump and swing until the broad daylight

Yes, I dreamed last night I was standing on 18th and Vine
Yes, I dreamed last night I was standing on 18th and Vine
I shook hands with Piney Brown and I could hardly keep from crying

Now come to me baby, I want to tell you I'm in love with you
Now come to me baby, I want to tell you I'm in love with you
Because you understand every thing I do

I wanna rock you baby, while the tears run down your cheek
I wanna rock you baby, while the tears run down your cheek
I wanna hold your hand, tell you that you can't be beat

Joe's 1948 version mentions Piney Brown in every verse:

Old Piney Brown's Gone (Down Beat/Swingtime 1948)

Well, I went back to Kansas City, old Piney Brown was gone
 Well, I went back to Kansas City, old Piney Brown was gone
This is a mean old world, hope he's got a better home

Down on 18th and Vine, where old Piney Brown got his start
Down on 18th and Vine, where old Piney Brown got his start
He was a goodtimer, was a playboy from his heart

He went to California, stood on Hollywood and Vine
He went to California, soon everything got around
Little girls jumped and shout, here comes Mr. Piney Brown

The last time I saw old Piney he was standing on 18th and Vine
The last time I saw old Piney he was standing on 18th and Vine
I'll tell the world, sure was a friend of mine

Another example is *Martin Luther King Southside*. This odd song with its odd title appears to have no direct connection with the civil rights activist, but rather to Dr. Martin Luther King Jr. Drive in Chicago. It is an offshoot of *Miss Brown Blues*.
    I've Got Love For Sale, no connection with Cole Porter's *Love For Sale*, seems to quote Mae West, "Don't mind me, baby, come up and see me some time". And perhaps Turner raided Ira Gershwin for the title *Somebody Loves Me*? To cause further confusion, there are two versions of *Howlin' Winds* (National), with very different lyrics, and three of *(I'm) Still In The Dark*.

I'm Still In The Dark (National 1947)
    Two versions of this title were issued, with matrix NSC 143 having five verses, NSC 172 only four.
    The missing verse was:

Yes, I met a civilian, yes, and he was from old New York
Yes, I met a civilian, yes, and he was from old New York
He said, "Sucker, sucker, sucker, don't go home 'cos you still in the dark"

As this suggests, Turner had servicemen returning from the war in mind, the first verse setting the scene:

My boat landed in San Pedro and my wife is in New York
My boat landed in San Pedro and my wife is in New York
I'm going ashore and have me a ball, 'cos I spent two years in the dark

Still In The Dark (Freedom 1949)

This version utilises the same four verses as NSC 172, the main difference being that, with the war four years in the past, the very first line has been amended:

My train rolled up in Texas and my wife is in old New York

For no apparent reason, other than the use of the word 'Texas,' a similar verse is used in Joe's 1971 *Texas Style*:

We roll up in Texas where they know who we are
We're years away from home, I'm still in the dark

It is rare for Turner to mention skin colour , but he does so in *Tell Me, Pretty Baby*, even though it is out of context with the song's other verses:

Brownskin women are evil, yellow girls are worse
I got myself a mulatto, boy, I'm playing it safety first

And in *Miss Brown Blues* on National, Joe sings that, "she's a real fine yellow".

An unusual line used in *Cry Baby Blues* and *Empty Pocket Blues* is "Everybody's crying 'mercy,' but what does 'mercy' mean?" In his "new" version of *Wee Wee Baby Blues* for National Turner sings "I gotta soundproof room, baby," leaving its purpose to the imagination of the listener. Then there is the imagery of "She still is pretty, she can make a blind man see" (or perhaps it is "She smells so pretty, she can make a blind man see") (*Nothin' From Nothin' Blues*) and "I'm in the land of sunshine, standing on Central Avenue" (*Blues on Central Avenue*) or "I got the blues so bad, it hurts my feet to walk" (*Let Me Be Your Dog*).

Even hair and hairdressing find their way into some verses. Length, curls and colour ("She's a real pretty woman and she's got coal black hair") (*Boss of the House*) are important, and there is the contradictory "She's got bobbed hair, boys, but she's got great long curls" (*Mardi Gras Boogie*) plus "I don't want no lady uses a straightening comb" (*Married Woman Blues*).

He feels sorry for himself in *Life Is Just A Card Game*, when he starts to complain that "Life is like a card game, I always get a bad deal," then follows with:

I'm so unlucky, I was born with a losing hand
I'm so unlucky, I was born with a losing hand
I'm behind the eight-ball, but I'm doing the best I can

Aces are high, low cards is all I got
Aces are high, low cards is all I got)
I play the game, pretty baby, whether you like it or not

I know my luck is bound to change, 'cos they change every draw
I know my luck is bound to change, 'cos they change every draw
I know my luck is going to change if I try hard enough

And in *Whistle Stop Blues* he repeatedly tells us "My life is full of misery"!

A few of the other traditional lines used by Turner in any context include:

"Sail on, little girl, sail on" *(Jump for Joy, Sun Risin' Blues)*.
Title of blues recorded by Bumble Bee Slim (Amos Easton) in 1934.

"It takes a rocking chair to rock, a rubber ball to roll" (*ad lib blues*).
Found in Ma Rainey's *Jealous Hearted Blues* of 1924, composer Lovie Austin.

"Love is like water, it turns off and on" (*Lovin' Mama Blues, You're So Damn Mean, Baby, Love Is Like A Faucet*).
Earlier occurrences are from 1923, in Hannah Sylvester's *Down South Blues* and Ethel Waters' *Ethel Sings 'Em.* (The line also appears in Billie Holiday's *Fine and Mellow.*)

"You never miss the water until the well runs dry" (*Back Breaking Blues, Joe Turner Blues*).
Paul Oliver traced this to a song copyrighted in 1874. Also refer to earlier *Joe Turner Blues* note.

"I'm going away babe, to wear you off my mind" (*Back Breaking Blues, Goin' Away Blues, Blues For Joe Turner, Howlin' Winds* and title song).
This title was recorded as an instrumental by King Oliver and his Creole Jazz Band in 1923. There were also vocal versions that year by Edna Hicks, Alberta Hunter and Eva Taylor.

"Sun's gonna shine in my back door someday" (*Last Goodbye Blues*).
Perhaps from Chippie Hill's *Trouble In Mind* (1926) or even the later hit by Georgia White, *New Trouble In Mind* (1937).

"I was standing in my window, I saw a poor boy walking in the rain" and "I walk the streets all night long, 'til my feets is soaking wet" (*Playboy Blues, Rainy Weather Blues, World of Trouble, Low Down Dirty Shame, Trouble Blues*).

"feet (or "feets") soaking wet" appear in Bessie Smith's *Homeless Blues* (1927) and Jelly Roll Morton's *Mamie's Blues*. The last was recorded in 1939, but Morton claimed the song was played by Mamie Desdoumes (Desdume/Desdune) in 1902.

"Did you ever dream lucky, wake up cold in hand?" (*World of Trouble, I'm In A World of Trouble, Trouble Blues*).

Bessie Smith recorded *Cold In Hand Blues* in January 1925 and Barbecue Bob (Robert Hicks) used the phrase in his *Barbecue Blues* in 1927.

"Blues jumped a rabbit, ran him for a solid mile" (*Blues Jumped The Rabbit, Love My Baby, St. Louis Blues*).

Used by Blind Lemon Jefferson, *Rabbit Foot Blues*, 1926. Another source, also 1926, could be Tommy Johnson's *Cool Drink of Water Blues*.

"I don't know why she's so pretty, don't know why she's so doggone mean I asked her for a drink of water and she gave me gasoline" (*Story To Tell*).
Used by Ishman Bracey, *Saturday Blues*, 1928.

Other standard phrases Turner used include:
"It's raining here, baby, stormin' on the sea."
"The sun is shining, but it's raining in my heart"
"How come my dog don't bark when you come knocking at my door"
"Buy me a bulldog, watch you while you sleep"
"I've been your dog ever since I've been your man"
"Let me be your little dog until the big dog comes"
"Take me back, baby, try me one more time"
"She's mine, she's yours, she's somebody else's too"
"Don't the moon look lonesome shining through the trees".

Occasionally he will use a rural allusion, such as "Let 'em roll like a big wheel in a Georgia cotton field" (*Honey Hush, Yakety Yak, Flying All Day, I Love You Baby*) or, as in *Flip, Flop and Fly*, "Like a Mississippi bullfrog sittin' on a hollow stump, got so many women don't know which way to jump". On one occasion he is feeling low, "lower than a wagon wheel" (*I'm In A World of Trouble*).

In 1939 Cafe Society advertised Joe Turner singing about "no butter since my cow been gone," but later Joe was singing "I ain't had no milk and butter since my girl's been gone" (*Milk and Butter Blues*). This is related to Kokomo Arnold's *Milk Cow Blues*, from 1934.

A frequent theme is the manner in which the singer is mistreated by his lover, whether by neglect, cheating, desertion, theft or abuse, physical and verbal.

However, just once or twice, Joe himself threatens violence, as in: "Don't make me nervous when I'm holding a baseball bat" (*Honey Hush, Money First, Yack, Yack, This and That, Yakety Yak*) and "Gonna catch me a picket, right off my back fence...." (*That's When It Really Hurts*).

Sex is, of course, a common blues theme, often with mentions of kitchen men, chauffeurs, ice men, mechanics and all the other handy men. Turner sometimes offers such innuendo as in *Rose Garden, Plant Your Garden, One Hour in Your Garden, You've Been Squeezin' My Lemons,* and *Stoop Down Baby*. Sometimes he is more direct, as with *Cherry Red, Riding Blues, Jockey Blues* and *Back Breaking Blues*.

That then is a sampling from the blues of Big Joe Turner. A virtual history of the blues embodied in one man and his magnificent voice.

Appendix 11 - Compositions credited to Joe Turner

This listing is based upon composer credits shown on Joe Turner's recordings, though using record label information for such a purpose has its limitations. The same song can be "(Joe Turner") on one label and ("Public Domain") on another. There is an example of one composer listed on the label of a first release, only for another composer to be credited on a second pressing.

Turner seems to have been little affected by the dubious practices used many managers, a&r men and agents, to claim a share of royalties by adding their names as co-composers, perhaps because there were few or no royalties to worry about. However, there were record producers aiming for further sales by reissuing songs under changed titles, or even engineering two new songs, with new titles, by mixing verses from two recordings.

Songs by other composers colonised by Turner included *Low Down Dog Blues* (Leroy Carr) which became *Doggin' The Dog* (Joe Turner); *When The Morning Glories (traditional)* became *Early Morning Blues* or *Cocka-Doodle Doe* (Joe Turner); *Don't You Feel My Leg* (Barker) became *Lovely Party* (Turner).

In Turner's case there are also the compositions which have been incorrectly credited to him, whether by design or by accident. On the Kent album "Big Joe Turner Turns On The Blues," for example, famous blues such as *In The Evening* (Leroy Carr) and *Good Morning Blues* (Count Basie-Jimmy Rushing), another amalgam, are credited to (Turner). Duke Ellington's *Rocks In My Bed,* Saunders King's *S.K. Blues* and Charles Calhoun's (Jesse Stone) *Morning, Noon and Night* have, on occasion, suffered the same fate.

Another example would be *Lucille*. Originally credited to Luther Williams, the song became so associated with Joe Turner that it is assumed that he was the composer. *Nobody In Mind*, claimed by J. Mayo Williams, was credited to Turner on a Pablo LP.

In the listing, when co-writers are involved, their names are shown in brackets after the song title. "No c.c." indicates "no composer credit," but it is presumed that Joe Turner is the source.

10-20-25-30

Adam Bit The Apple
After A While

Baby, Look At You (Pete Johnson)
Baby, Won't You Marry Me
Back-Breaking Blues (Wynonie Harris)
B & O Blues
Big Joe's Lonesome Blues (no cc)
Big Leg Woman
Big Wheel
Bluer Than Blue
Blues (Wynonie Harris)
Blues For Joe Turner
Blues Jump The Rabbit
Blues Lament (Jimmy Witherspoon)
Blues On Central Avenue
Boss of the House
Bring It On Home

Cherry Red (Pete Johnson)
Chewed Up Grass
Christmas Date
Christmas Date Boogie
Chill Is On, The
Cimarron Street Breakdown (Axel Zwingenberger)
Crawdad Hole (Lou Willie Turner)

Dawn Is Breaking Through (originally Midnight Is Here Again)
Don't Talk Me To Death (no c.c.)
Don't Love You No More

Empty Pocket Blues

Feeling Happy
Feel So Fine
Feelin' So Sad
Flip Flop and Fly (C. Calhoun/L.W. Turner)

Flying All Day
For Growin' Up
Front Door In, Back Door Out
Fun In Chicago (no c.c)
Fuzzy Wuzzy Honey

Get Me A Rockin' Chair
Going Home (Wynonie Harris)
Good Morning Miss Patricia (no cc)
Hanging On The Wall
Hey Little Girl
Hide and Seek (Winley Byrd - Pablo)
Hollywood Bed
Honey Hush (Lou Willie Turner)
How Come My Dog Don't Bark
Howd'ya Want Your Rollin' Done
Howlin' Winds

I Got A Gal (Roll 'Em Pete) (Pete Johnson)
I Got A Gal For Every Day In The Week
I Got Love For Sale
I Got My Discharge Papers (no cc)
I Just Didn't Have The Price
I Know You Love Me Baby
I Love You Baby
I'm Going Away To Wear You Off My Mind
I'm In A World of Trouble (see World of Trouble)
I'm On My Way To Denver (no cc)
I'm Sharp When I Hit The Coast
I'm Still In The Dark
It's The Same Old Story
I've Been Up On The Mountain
I've Got A Pocketful of Pencils
I Want My Baby (retitled When The Rooster Crows)

Jelly On My Mind
Johnson and Turner Blues (Pete Johnson)

J.T.'s Blues
Juke Joint Blues
Jump For Joy (Pete Johnson)
Jumpin' At The Jubilee
Jumpin' Tonight
Just A Travellin' Man

Kansas City Blues
Kansas City On My Mind
Kick The Front Door In

Last Goodbye Blues
Let Me Be Your Dog
Life Ain't Easy
Life Is (Like) A Card Game
Little Birdie Tweet-Tweet-Tweet
Little Bittie Gal's Blues
Little Bitty Baby
Little Girl
Long Way From Home
Love Ain't Nothin'
Love Is Like A Faucet
Love My Baby
Love Oh Careless Love
Love Roller Coaster (Pomus, Shuman)
Lovin' Mama Blues (Pete Johnson)
Low Down Dirty Shame Blues (J. Sullivan)
Low Down Dog

Mad Blues
Mardi Gras Boogie
Married Woman Blues (Jackson)
Married Woman (Lou Willie Turner)
Martin Luther King Southside
Midnight Cannon Ball (Lou WillieTurner)
Midnight Rockin'
Milk and Butter Blues
Miss Brown Blues
Money First
Moody Baby

My Gal's A Jockey
My Train Rolled Up In Texas

New Ooh Wee Baby Blues (Pete Johnson)
Nothin' From Nothin' Blues (J. Otis)

Oke-She-Moke-She-Pop (Lou Willie Turner)
One Hour In Your Garden
Ooo-Ouch-Stop (no c.c.)

Patcha, Patcha
Piney Brown Blues (Pete Johnson)
Plant Your Garden
Playboy Blues (Pete Johnson)
Playful Baby
Poor Lover Blues
Rainy Day Blues (W. Smith)
Rainy Weather Blues
Rebecca
Riding Blues
Rock Me Baby
Rock of Gibralter
Rocks In My Bed
Roll 'Em Hawk (Pete Johnson)
Roll 'Em Pete (Pete Johnson)
Roll 'Em Boys
Rolling Into Your Big Town

Sally-Zu-Zazz
Shout
Since I Was Your Man
So Many Women Blues
Somebody Loves Me
Squeeze Me, Baby
Stoop Down Baby
Story To Tell
Sunday Morning Blues
Sun Is Shining, The
Sun Risin' Blues

Tell Me Pretty Baby
Texas Style

That's When It Really Hurts
Ti-Ri-Lee (Ahmet Ertegun-Gerald
   Wexler)
Too Late, Too Late
TV Mama/Momma (Lou Willie
   Turner)
Two Loves Have I (Lou Willie
   Turner)

Watch That Jive (Pete Johnson)
Wee Baby Blues (Pete Johnson)
Well Oh Well
When The Rooster Crows
   (originally I Want My Baby)
Whistle Stop Blues
Wine-O-Baby Boogie   (no c.c.)
Wish I Had a Dollar
Woman You Must Be Crazy
World of Trouble

Yack Yack This And That
You Know I Love You   (Lou
   Willie Turner)
You're So Damn Mean, Baby (no
   c.c.)
You've Been Squeezin' My Lemons

Label Photographs

1. Vocalion 4607
Joe Turner and Pete Johnson
Roll 'Em Pete
New York City - December 30, 1938

2. Vocalion 4997
Pete Johnson and his Boogie Woogie Boys
Cherry Red
New York City - June 30, 1939

3. Elite 5012
The New Orleans Seven Orchestra
How Long, How Long Blues
New York City - January 15, 1940

4. Decca 7824
Big Joe Turner with Willie 'The Lion' Smith At The Piano
Doggin' The Dog
New York City - November 26 , 1940

5. Decca 7856
Big Joe Turner
Ice Man
New York City - July 17, 1941

6. AFRS Jubilee No. 17 - radio show
various
no detail
Los Angeles - 1943

7. Decca 48042
Big Joe Turner and Pete Johnson Trio
Little Bittie Gal's Blues
Chicago - October 30, 1944

8. National 9011
Joe Turner with Pete Johnson's All Stars
Johnson & Turner Blues
New York City - February 2, 1945

9. National 4009
Joe Turner with Bill Moore's Lucky Seven
Mad Blues
Los Angeles - January 30, 1946

10. National 4017
Joe Turner and his Boogie-Woogie Boys
That's What Really Hurts
Chicago - October 12, 1946

11. Stag 509
Big Vernon (Joe Turner)
Steady Grinder
San Francisco - November 1947

12. Aladdin 3013
Joe Turner and his Band
Low Down Dog
San Francisco - November 6, 1947

13. RPM 331
Joe Turner and Pete Johnson
Kansas City Blues
Los Angeles - December 27, 1947

14. Modern 20-691
Joe Turner with Pete Johnson
Don't Talk Me To Death (I Ain't Ready To Die)
Los Angeles - December 27, 1947

15. Down Beat 153
Joe Turner's Orchestra with Pete Johnson at the "88"
Tell Me Pretty Baby
Los Angeles - mid-1948

16. M-G-M 10397
Joe Turner
Rainy Weather Blues
Los Angeles - c. July 1948

Joe Turner
Married Woman Blues
Los Angeles - late1948/early 1949

18. Rouge ROU-105
Joe Turner :
Music by Joe Houston
Fuzzy Wuzzy Honey
Baton Rouge ? - early 1949

19. Freedom F 1546
Joe Turner Combo
Lonely World
Houston, TX - early 1950

20. Freedom F 1546
Joe Turner with Orchestra
Jumpin' At The Jubilee
Houston, TX - early 1950

21. London 45-HLK 9119
Joe Turner
Chains of Love
New York City - April 19, 1951

22. Atlantic 45-2072
Joe Turner
Sweet Sue
New York City - January 22, 1958

23. Coral 62429
Big Joe Turner
There'll Be Some Tears Fallin'
New York City - March 17, 1964

24. Ronn 28
Joe Turner
I've Been Up On The Mountain
Los Angeles - 1966

Big Joe Turner
Love Ain't Nothin'
Los Angeles - c. 1969/1970

26. Atlantic 45-1026
Joe Turner and his Blues Kings
Shake, Rattle and Roll
New York City - February 15, 1954

ATLANTIC EP 565

SHAKE, RATTLE AND ROLL
FLIP, FLOP AND FLY
IN THE EVENIN' WHEN
THE SUN GOES DOWN

JOE TURNER

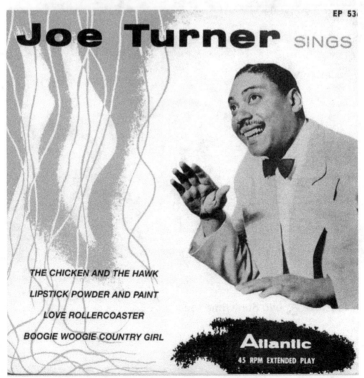

Joe Turner SINGS

EP 53

THE CHICKEN AND THE HAWK

LIPSTICK POWDER AND PAINT

LOVE ROLLERCOASTER

BOOGIE WOOGIE COUNTRY GIRL

Atlantic
45 RPM EXTENDED PLAY

Movie, 1955. See 'Apollo Showtime'" on page 267

The Discography

Introduction

A combined editorial and obituary for Joe Turner appeared in the entertainment journal, *Cash Box*, for December 7, 1985. It included the following sentence, "In fact, Joe Turner recorded so many cuts for so many labels that a complete and accurate discography would be virtually impossible to compile."

What follows is unlikely to disprove that paper's claim. This listing will not be truly complete, because it does not try to cover every reissue. Only original releases are shown, plus a selection of reissue LPs and CDs. If written today the *Cash Box* editorial would have referred to the multitude of titles by Joe Turner, available on innumerable reissue labels. The early recordings on Vocalion and Decca have appeared on numerous occasions, often in anthologies ('Kansas City', 'Boogie Woogie', etc) and these have been followed by a veritable deluge of reissues from the Atlantic label.

Consider just a few of the CD sets which have appeared: Avid (2-CD), Factory (2-CD), Rhino/Atlantic (3-CD). Big Three (3-CD), Jasmine (2-CD), Properbox (4-CD), JSP (5-CD), Real Gone (5-CD), Disky (5-CD).

An attempt has been made to indicate variations between different takes or versions of the same title. Examples from the Decca period can be found in Appendix 6, The Lyrics, while others are given herewith.

Details of radio broadcasts are shown if one or more of the titles have found their way onto a commercial record, whether or not it is a pirate release. Radio transcriptions are included where details are known. Reference is made to a few private recordings when they seem of particular relevance.

Most recordings were made for and released by U.S.A. companies. Appendix 2 to the Discography lists the country of origin for other labels.

Despite these reservations, it is hoped that this listing will be an informative guide to the recordings of Big Joe Turner.

References:

Walter C. Allen, *Hendersonia: The Music of Fletcher Henderson and his Musicians, A bio-discography*, self published, 1973

Ray Astbury, *Big Joe Turner Discography*, unpublished

Tony Biggs, *The Recordings of Big Joe Turner*, self-published, 2011

Tony Burke and Dave Penny, "Big Joe Turner, Have No Fear, Big Joe Is Here," (part 1) *Blues & Rhythm*, No. 11 (July 1985), (part 2) *Blues & Rhythm*, No. 12 (September 1985)

Robert M. W. Dixon, John Godrich, Howard W. Rye, *Blues and Gospel Records 1890-1943*, Oxford University Press, 1997

Frank Dutton, Joe Turner on National, (Jazz Information 346), *Jazz Journal*, October 1963

Les Fancourt & Bob McGrath, *The Blues Discography 1943-1970, The Classic Years*, Eyeball Productions, Inc. 2019

Robert Ford & Bob McGrath, *The Blues Discography, 1971-2000, The Later Years*, Eyeball Productions, Inc. 2011

Chris Sheridan, *Count Basie, a bio-discography*, Greenwood Press, 1986

Jan Van Leeuwen: Jazz 625 on YouTube

https://groups.io/g/jazz-research
www.thediscographer.dk/vinyl/bloomfield
Other reference works which have been consulted include *Jazz Records 1942-1968* by Jorgen G. Jepsen, *The Jazz Discography* by Tom Lord, *Jazz Records 1897-1942* by Brian Rust, and *New Hot Discography* by Charles Delauney.

Acknowledgements

My special thanks to the many friends, collectors, writers and researchers who have provided information over the years, copying or loaning records, checking their files, so typical of the generous, cooperative spirit shown by discographers the world over.

Ray Astbury
Tony Biggs
Tony Burke
Ron Clough
Martin Colvill
Mark Cantor
Stanley Dance
Charlie Crump
Frank Dutton
Lars Edegran
Colin Escott
Rob Ford
Bill Greensmith
George Hulme

Trevor Huyton
Len Kunstadt
Mike Leadbitter
Barney McClure
Kurt Mohr
Dave Penny
Bob Porter
Anthony Rotante
Michel Ruppli
Paul Sheatsley
Peter Vacher
Gary Von Tersch
Bert Whyatt

Thanks to Anne and Dave Bennett, Tony Biggs, Tony Burke, Steve Newland and, especially, Bob McGrath, for their help with label photo quality.

Label Photograph Credits:
3, 5, 8, 9, 16-19, 22-25, author's collection:
7, courtesy Franz Hoffman;
16, courtesy Bob McGrath;
all others, courtesy Tony Biggs.

Abbreviations

Instruments abbreviations used include:
- a-h   alto-horn
- arr   arranger
- as   alto saxophone
- b   string bass
- b-cl bass clarinet
- b-sax bass saxophone
- bar   baritone saxophone
- bj   banjo
- cel   celeste
- cga   conga drum
- cl   clarinet
- co   cornet
- d   drum
- e-g   electric guitar
- fl   flute
- fr   french horn
- g   guitar
- hca   harmonica
- kbd   keyboard
- org   organ
- p   piano
- ss   soprano saxophone
- tb   trombone
- tp   trumpet
- ts   tenor saxophone
- tu   tuba
- vl   violin
- vo   vocalist
- vtb   valve trombone

Other:
alt = alternative take; inc. = incomplete;
TBD refers to *The Blues Discography*.

Abbreviations for the types of record issues are:
- (78)   78 r.p.m recording, 10" or 12"
- (45)   45 r.p.m. Recording, 7"
- (CD)   Compact Disc
- (EP)   45 r.p.m. recording, extended play, 7"
- (ET)   33&1/3rd r.p.m. electric transcription, 12" or 16", produced for use by radio stations
- (LP)   33&1/3rd r.p.m. recordings, microgroove long-play, 10" or 12"
- (AC)   audio cassette tape
- (VC)   video cassette tape
- (DVD   digital video disc
- (FST) film soundtrack

JOE TURNER (vo, Pete Johnson, p).
"From Spirituals To Swing" concert, Carnegie Hall, New York City
December 23, 1938
(a)　　It's All Right Baby　　　　　　(LP)　　Vanguard　　VRS8524
(b)　　Low Down Dog　　　　　　　(LP)　　Magpie　　　PY4421
PY4421 title: Jump For Joy, Unissued Boogie 1938-1945 (with Meade Lux
Lewis, Albert Ammons)
Other issues include: (a) on (LP) Fontana TFL5187, (a) on (CD) Magpie
PYCD21, Vanguard VCD2-48, Rhino R2-71550(a)(b) on (CD) Music
Memories 88048-2.

JOE TURNER and PETE JOHNSON (Turner, vo, Johnson, p).
New York City December 30, 1938
23891-1　　Goin' Away Blues　　　　　(78)　　　　　　Vocalion　4607
23892-1　　Roll 'Em Pete　　　　　　　(78)　　　　　　Vocalion　4607
both titles on (LP) Official 6028, (CD) Mosaic Select MS-030, Classics 656
(Pete Johnson), Masters of Jazz MJCD 134, Rhino R2-71550

JOE TURNER with PETE JOHNSON (Turner, vo; Johnson, p).
NBC broadcast, Cafe Society, Sheridan Square, New York City
January 31, 1939
(a)　　Low Down Dog　　　　　　　(CD)　　Document DOCD 1003

(same). NBC broadcast, Cafe Society, Sheridan Square, New York City
February 1, 1939
(b)　　Honey Dripper　　　　　　　(CD)　　Document DOCD 1003

(same). NBC broadcast, Cafe Society, Sheridan Square, New York City
February 21, 1939
(c)　　Early Morning Blues　(When The Morning Glories)
　　　　　　　　　　　　　　　　　(CD)　　Document DOCD 1003
Other issues: (a)(b) also on (CD) Masters of Jazz MJCD 134, on which (b) is
shown as *Risin' Sun Blues*, with both titles given a broadcast date of February
11, 1939.

JOE TURNER with FRANKIE NEWTON ORCHESTRA (Turner, vo;
Frankie Newton, tp; with (probably) Tab Smith, Stanley Payne, as; Kenneth
Hollon, ts; Ken Kersey, p; Ulysses Livingston, g; Johnny Williams, b; Eddie
Dougherty, d; Joe Turner, vo).
NBC broadcast, Cafe Society, Sheridan Square, New York City
February 22, 1939
On The Sunny Side of the Street　vJT　(CD) Document DOCD 1003
Document DOCD 1003 album title: Rare Live Cuts.

PETE JOHNSON and his BOOGIE WOOGIE BOYS (Oran 'Hot Lips' Page, tp; Henry 'Buster' Smith, as; Pete Johnson, p; Lawrence Lucie, g; Abe Bolar, b; Eddie Dougherty, d, Joe Turner vo; band vo-1)

New York City June 30, 1939

25023-1	Cherry Red vJT	(78)	Vocalion	4997
25024-1	Baby Look At You vJT	(78)	Vocalion	4997
25025-1	Lovin' Mama Blues vJT	(78)	Vocalion	5186
- 0 -	Jump For Joy -1	vJT	CD) Columbia CK65631	

Mosaic states that *Jump For Joy*, which was originally on the same side of a lacquer disc as *Lovin' Mama Blues*, was not assigned a matrix or take number. It has been claimed that an alternative take of 25023 was issued on Meritt LP19, but *Cherry Red* is not on that LP.

Other issues include: 25023/24/25 on (CD) Classics 656; Masters of Jazz MJCD 134; all titles on (CD) Mosaic Select MS-030. 25024-1, 25025-1 also on (CD) Columbia 503282 2 (Hot Lips Page anthology); 25023-1 on (CD) Rhino R2-71550

ALBERT, MEADE, PETE and THEIR THREE PIANOS (Albert Ammons, Meade Lux Lewis, Pete Johnson, p; Abe Bolar, b; Eddie Dougherty, d; Joe Turner, vo).

same session

25026-1	Cafe Society Rag vJT	(78)	Vocalion	5186

Other issues include: (CD) Mosaic Select MS-030, Classics 656 (as Pete Johnson), Masters of Jazz MJCD 134.

THE VARSITY SEVEN (Benny Carter, tp, as; Danny Polo, cl; Coleman Hawkins, ts; Joe Sullivan, p; Ulysses Livingston, g; Artie Shapiro, b; George Wettling, d; Joe Turner, vo).

New York City January 15, 1940

US 1284-1	How Long, How Long Blues JT	(78)	Varsity	8173
US 1285-1	Shake It and Break It vJT	(78)	Varsity	8179

The reverse of the Varsity issues are non-vocal.
Other issues include: both titles on (LP) Official 6028, (CD) Masters of Jazz MJCD 134

JOE SULLIVAN and his CAFE SOCIETY ORCHESTRA (Eddie Anderson, tp; Benny Morton, tb; Edmond Hall, cl; Danny Polo, ts; Joe Sullivan, p; Freddie Green, g; Henry Turner, b; Johnny Wells, d; Joe Turner, vo).

New York City February 9, 1940

26502-A	Low Down Dirty Shame vJT	(78)	Vocalion	5531
26503-A	I Can't Give You Anything But Love vJT	(78) Vocalion	5496	
26503-B	I Can't Give You Anything But Love vJT	(LP) Meritt LP19		

reverse of the Vocalion issues are non-vocal.
Other issues include: 26502-A on (LP) Official 6028; 26502-A/26503-A on (LP) Blu-Disc T-1005 and all three takes on (CD) Mosaic Select MS-030; (CD) Masters of Jazz MJCD 134.

PETE JOHNSON and JOE TURNER (Joe Turner, vo; Pete Johnson, p; unknown, d).

NBC broadcast, "Chamber Music Society of Lower Basin Street," New York, City
August 11, 1940

| (a) | Goin' Away Blues | (LP) | Swing | House | SWH-43 |
| (b) | Roll 'Em Pete | (LP) | Swing | House | SWH-43 |

Some sources give a date of August 18, 1940. album title: R&B and Boogie Woogie, volume 3.
Other issues include: both on (LP) Storyville 28469, SLP229; and (CD) Masters of Jazz MJCD 134.

BENNY CARTER and his ALL STAR ORCHESTRA (Bill Coleman, tp; Benny Morton, tb; Benny Carter, cl; George Auld, ts; Ellerton 'Sonny' White, p; Ulysses Livingstone, g; Wilson Meyers, b; Allen 'Yank' Porter, d; Joe Turner, vo).

New York City October 15, 1940

28876-1	Joe Turner Blues vJT	(78)	Okeh	6001
28876-2	Joe Turner Blues vJT	(LP)	Meritt	LP10
28877-1	Beale Street Bluev v JT	(78)	Okeh	6001
28877-2	Beale Street Blues vJT	(LP)	Meritt	LP10

Other issues include: 28876-1/28877-1 on (LP) Official 6028. all takes on (CD) Mosaic Select MS-030, Masters of Jazz MJCD 134; .28876-2/28877-2 on (CD) Neatwork RP2030.

JOE TURNER and his FLY CATS (Joe Turner, vo; Hot Lips Page, tp; Pete Johnson, p; John Collins, g; Abe Bolar, b; A.G. Godley, d).

New York City November 11, 1940

| 68333-A | Piney Brown Blues | (78) | Decca 18121 |

Non-vocal title (*627 Stomp*) from this session issued as Pete Johnson's Band.
Other issues include: (CD) MCA MCAD42351; Masters of Jazz MJCD146, Avid AMSC701X, Rhino R2-71550

BIG JOE TURNER (vo, with Willie 'The Lion' Smith, p).

New York City November 26, 1940

68394-A	Doggin' The Dog	(78)	Decca	7824
68395-B	Careless Love	(78)	Decca	7827
68396-A	Jumpin' Down Blues	(78)	Decca	7827
68397-A	Rainy Day Blues	(78)	Decca	7824

Other issues include: all on (CD) MCA MCAD42351; Classics 692 (Willie 'The Lion' Smith), Masters of Jazz MJCD 146; 68395-B on Rhino R2-71550

ART TATUM and his BAND (Joe Thomas, tp; Edmond Hall, cl; Art Tatum, p; John Collins, g; Billy Taylor, b; Ed Dougherty, d; Joe Turner, vo).

New York City January 21, 1941

| 68605-A | Wee Baby Blues | vJT | (78) Decca 8526 |
| 68607-A | Last Goodbye Blues | vJT | (78) Decca 8536 |

68606/68608 are non-vocal titles.
Other issues include: both on (CD) MCA MCAD 42351; (CD) Classics 800*, Affinity AFS1035-3*, Masters of Jazz MJCD146. * Art Tatum anthologies.

ART TATUM and his Band (Joe Thomas, tp; Art Tatum, p; Oscar Moore, g; Billy Taylor, b; Allen 'Yank' Porter, d; Joe Turner, vo, all titles)

New York City June 13, 1941

69356-AA	Lucille	(LP) Collectors Item 011
69356-B	Lucille	(78)	Decca	8577
69357-A	Rock Me Mama	(78)	Decca	8577
69358-A	Corrine Corrina	(78)	Decca	8563
69359-A	Lonesome Graveyard	(78)	Decca	8563
69359-B	Lonesome Graveyard	(78)	Decca	8563

69359-A has also been labelled *Lonesome Graveyard Blues* on Decca 8563.
Other issues include: 69356-B/69357-A/69358-A/69359-B on (CD) Classics 800*; all takes on (CD) MCA MCAD42351, AffinityAFS 1035-3*. * Art Tatum anthologies

BIG JOE TURNER (vo; Sammy Price, p; Leonard Ware, g; Billy Taylor, b; ensemble vocal -1).

New York City July 17, 1941

69523-A	Nobody In Mind	(78)	Decca	7868
69524-A	Somebody's Got To Go	(78)	Decca	7856
69525-A	Ice Man	(78)	Decca	7856
69526-A	Chewed Up Grass -1	(78)	Decca	7868

Other issues include: all on (CD) Classics 940, Masters of Jazz MJCD146. All, except 69526, on (CD) MCA MCAD42351. MCA MCAD42351 also (AC) MCA MCAC42351.

JUMP FOR JOY (Joe Turner, vo; Duke Ellington, p).

"Salute To Labor" radio show, KFI, Los Angeles September 1, 1941

| Rocks In My Bed | (AC) | Azure | CA22 |

four other 'Jump For Joy' titles are included in this issue; one vocal by Ivie Anderson, one by Herb Jeffries and two by the chorus.
cassette title, "At the end of 1997".
Other issue: (CD) Rhino R2-75872 ("Central Avenue Sounds"). Reported to have been issued originally by KLON (Long Beach) radio station on a free promotional CD.

JOE TURNER (vo; Freddy Slack, p; Al Hendrickson, g; Jud deNaut, b).

Los Angeles September 8, 1941

DLA 2738-A	Rocks In My Bed	(78)	Decca	4093
DLA 2738-B	Rocks In My Bed	(78)	Decca	4093
DLA 2739-A	Blues On Central Avenue	(78)	Decca	7889
DLA 2740-A	Goin'To Chicago Blues	(78)	Decca	4093
DLA 2741-A	Sun Risin' Blues	(78)	Decca	7889

Decca 4093 labelled as Joe Turner with Freddie Slack Trio.
Other issues include: all -A takes on (CD) Classics 940; all -A takes,
except 2740, on (CD) Rhino R2-715550; all takes on (CD) Masters of Jazz
MJCD146.

(vo; Fred Skinner, p; Clifford McTyner, g; Johnny Miller, b; trio vocal -1).

Los Angeles January 28, 1942

DLA 2865-A	Blues In The Night -1	(CD)	Decca	Jazz	GRD-621
DLA 2865-B	Blues In The Night -1	(78)	Decca		7885
DLA 2866-A	Cry Baby Blues	(78)	Decca		7885
DLA 2866-B	Cry Baby Blues	(CD)	Decca	Jazz	GRD-621

Other issues include: DLA2865-B/2866-A on (CD) Classics 940;
DLA2866-A on (78) Decca 86056, (CD) Magnum Music CDMF098; all
takes on (CD) MCA GRP16212

Joe Turner sang on a "Jubilee" broadcast in January 1943, but his contribution
was not included on the AFRS transcription (Program No. 17) of the show.

JOE TURNER (vo; Pete Johnson, Albert Ammons, p; unknown d).

"Jubilee" broadcast, Hollywood c. November (15?), 1943

Low Down Dog	(ET)	AFRS	Jubilee	52

Other issues: on (LP) Storyville SLP229 and 28469, labelled as *Joe Turner's
Blues*.
(DVD) Charly 'Soundie 2,' Idem IDVD1055.

TURNER and LEWIS (Joe Turner, vo; Meade Lux Lewis, p).

soundie" soundtrack, Los Angeles January 24, 1944

(a)	Roll 'Em	'Soundie'	16008
(b)	Low Down Dog	'Soundie'	16508

Other issue: (LP) Magpie PY 4421. album title: Jump For Joy: The Piano
Blues, Volume 21.

BIG JOE TURNER and PETE JOHNSON TRIO (Turner, vo; Johnson, p; Ernest Ashley, g; Dallas Bartley, b).

Chicago October 30, 1944

C25230-A	It's The Same Old Story	(78)	Decca			11001
C25231-A	Rebecca	(78)	Decca			11001
C25231-	Rebecca (inc.)	(CD)	Decca	Jazz	GRD-621	
C25231-B	Rebecca	(CD)	MCA	GRP	16212	
C25231-C	Rebecca	(CD)	MCA	GRP	16212	
C25232-A	Little Bittie Gal's Blues	(78)	Decca			48042
C25232-	Little Bittie Gal's Blues	CD)	Decca	Jazz	GRD-621	
C25233-A	I Got A Gal (For Every Day of the Week)					
		(78)	Decca			48042
C25233-B	I Got A Gal (For Every Day of the Week)					
		(CD)	Decca	Jazz	GRD-621	

Recording details were originally shown in *The New Hot Discography* as New York City, November 13, 1944. The master numbers above are those originally allocated; master numbers 72523-26 were assigned later; (source: notes to GRP-16212). Decca CD title: Every Day In The Week.
Other issues include: C25230-A/C25233-A on (LP) Official 6028. all -A takes on (CD) Classics 940. all takes on (CD) MCA GRP 16212.

In 2023 Lars Edegran, Vice President of the GHB Foundation in New Orleans, found World Broadcasting test pressings for Big Joe Turner in the GHB New Orleans warehouse. On examination the titles proved to be those recorded for Decca on October 30, 1944, including the alternatives listed above.

A 1945 session by the Flennoy Trio has long been in query as a Joe Turner date, but Dave Penny has been able to confirm that Turner is not present. The musicians are Lorenzo Flennoy, p; Jimmie Edwards, g, vo; and Robert Lewis, g. The titles are *Somebody's Got To Go, Mr. Jones/Now That You Know* (Excelsior 119) and *My Love/That's The Wrong Gal, Brother* (Excelsior 140).

JOE TURNER with PETE JOHNSON'S ALL STARS (Turner, vo; Frankie Newton, tp; Don Byas, ts; Pete Johnson, p; Leonard Ware, g; Al Hall, b; Harold 'Doc' West, d).

New York City February 2, 1945

NSC 33	S.K. Blues (Part I)	(78)	National	9010
NSC 34	S.K. Blues (Part II)	(78)	National	9010
NSC 35A	Johnson & Turner Blues	(LP)	Savoy	SJL2223
NSC 35	Johnson & Turner Blues	(78)	National	9011
NSC 36	Watch That Jive	(78)	National	9011

NSC 35A is quite different to NSC 35; for NSC 35A, the meaning of one verse is changed and in another, "Here comes my baby and I'm jumpin' for joy ...." replaces one in NSC 35 which ends "If I can't have you, baby, I don't want nobody else".
Other issues include: all, except NSC 35A on (LP) EmArcy MG36014, Savoy MG14016, and (CD) Classics 940. All except NSC35 on (CD) JSP 7709B, Avid AMSC1142. All takes on (CD) Savoy SV-0265; NSC35A on (CD) Rhino R2-71550

(Turner, vo; with (possibly) Bill Martin, tp; John 'Flaps' Dungee, as; Josh Jackson, ts; Joe Liggins p; unknown, g; Dallas Bartley, b; unknown, d)

Chicago May 10, 1945

NSC 60A	Howlin' Winds	(LP)	Savoy SJL 2223
NSC 60B	Doggin' The Blues	(LP)	Savoy SJL 2223

Master NSC 60 is by Dallas Bartley and NSC 61 is by Billy Eckstine. The master numbering for the Joe Turner titles is unexplained. Liggins suggested by Pete Johnson. *Howlin' Winds* was initially rejected and remade as master NSC 340, with very different lyrics, on December 9, 1947.
Other issues include: NSC 60A on (LP) Savoy MG14012; both on (LP) EmArcy MG36014, Savoy SJL 2223, (CD) Classics 940, Avid AMSC1142

JOE TURNER (vo, with unknown, tp; cl; ts; p; Allan Reuss, g; b, d).
broadcast, Lamplighter Jazz Session, Station KPAS, Pasadena, CA July 4, 1945

When I Was Young		(CD)	Vogue 655.004

CD title: Lamplighter's All Star Jazz. July 4 was a Wednesday; show usually held Sundays.

JOE TURNER with Johnny Otis and His Orchestra (Turner, vo; Lester Current, Lloyd Walker, Eddie Preston, Billy Jones, tp; John Pettigrew, Jap Jones, George Washington, tb; Kenneth Pope, Bob Harris, as; Paul Quinichette, James Von Streeter, ts; Leon Beck, bar; Henry Owens, p; Bernie Cobbs, g; Curtis Lee Counce, b; Johnny Otis, d; Ernie 'Bubbles' Whitman, mc).

broadcast, Jubilee show, Hollywood October 15, 1945

(a)	S.K. Blues		vJT	(ET) AFRS Jubilee 152

(same, plus the Jubilee All Stars: Harry Parr Jones, tp; Willie Smith, as; Corky Corcoran, ts; Cal Jackson, p; Oscar Pettiford, b; perhaps Johnny Otis, d; Miguelito Valdez and his Cuban rhythm section, including Pepe Marrero, congas).

same broadcast

(b)   *Love My Baby*   vJT   (ET) AFRS Jubilee 152

(b) is part of a "Jam Session Blues" medley, which also includes *Empty Bed Blues* by Ivie Anderson and a band instrumental.

In 2002 Otis suggested that the personnel for this broadcast was probably: Teddy Buckner, Lloyd Walker, Harry Parr Jones, Bobby Jones, tp; John Pettigrew, Jay Jones, Henry Coker, Eli Robinson, tb; Rene Bloch, Bob Harris, as; Paul Quinichette, James Von Streeter, ts; Leon Beck, bar;Bill Doggett, p; Bernie Cobbs, g; Curtis Lee Counce, b; Otis, d.

Other issues: (a)(b) on (LP) Swingtime ST 1009.

JOE TURNER with Bill Moore's Lucky Seven Band (Turner, vo; Warren Brocken, tp; Wild Bill Moore, Lloyd Harrison, ts; Al Williams, p; Teddy Bunn, g; John 'Shifty' Henry, b; Alray Kidd, d).

Los Angeles January 23, 1946

NSC 140	Miss Brown Blues	(LP) Savoy SJL2223
NSC 141	I Got My Discharge Papers	(LP) Savoy SJL 2223
NSC 142	My Gal's A Jockey	(78) National 4002
NSC 143	I'm Still In The Dark	(LP) Savoy SJL 2223
NSC 144	I Got Love For Sale	(78) National 4002

Miss Brown Blues and *I'm Still In The Dark* were originally rejected. They were remade as NSC173 and NSC 172 respectively on October 11, 1946.

NSC 140 lyrics have several variations; verse two refers to "walked down South Park Avenue"; in NSC 173 it becomes "walked down 42nd Avenue".

NSC 143 has five verses (the fifth has a civilian calling Joe 'sucker, sucker, sucker'), NSC 172 only four. NSC142 also on (78) National 9106 (reverse, NSC172).

Other issues include: NSC140 & 143 on (LP) Savoy MG14012; NSC144 on (LP) Savoy MG14016; all titles on (CD) Savoy Jazz SV-0265, JSP 7709B. NSC140 & 141 on Classics 940; NSC142/143/144 on (CD) Classics 1034; NSC142 on Rhino R2-7110

JOE TURNER with **Bill Moore's Lucky Seven** (Turner, vo; Russell Jacquet, tp; Wild Bill Moore, Lou 'Freddie' Simon, ts; Camille Howard, p; Teddy Bunn, g; John 'Shifty' Henry, b; Walter Murden, d).

Los Angeles January 30, 1946

NSC 145	Sunday Morning Blues	(78)	National	4009
NSC 146	Mad Blues	(78)	National	4009
NSC 147	It's A Low Down Dirty Shame	(78)	National	9099

Other issues include: all on on (LP) Savoy MG14016; NSC147 also on (CD) Savoy Jazz SJL 2223; all titles on (CD) Savoy SV-0265, Classics 1034, JSP 7709B. NSC147 on some issues as *Playboy Blues*.

JOE TURNER (vo; Teddy Buckner, tp; unknown, ts; Eddie Beal p; Red Callender, b; Zutty Singleton, d).

Lamplighter Jazz Session broadcast, Station KPAS, Pasadena, CA June 23, 1946

	Lovin' Man		(CD)	Vogue	655.004

CD title: Lamplighter's All Star Jazz.
Other issue: on (CD) Atlantic/Rhino R2-71550 as *I'm A Lovin' Man*.

JOE TURNER and his **Boogie Woogie Boys** (Turner, vo; with possible personnel: Sonny Cohn, tp; Porter Kilbert, as; Leon Washington, ts; Albert Ammons, p; perhaps Ike Perkins, g; unknown, b; Theodore 'Red' Saunders, d).

Chicago October 11, 1946

NSC 172	Still In The Dark	(78)	National	9106
NSC 173	Miss Brown Blues	(78)	National	4011
NSC 174	Sally-Zu-Zazz	(78)	National	4016
NSC 175	Rock O' Gibralter (sic)	(78)	National	4016
NSC 175 (alt)	Rock of Gibraltar Blues	(LP)	Savoy	MG14012

NSC 175 has 3 verses, with the piano solo after the second verse, the alternative has 4 verses, with variations, and the piano solo after the third verse. Joe Turner told Jacques Demetre that Ammons was the pianist for this session and aurally there seems no reason to doubt this identification. Sonny Cohn recalled recording with Turner when he was in the Red Saunders band. Tab Smith has been quoted as possibly the alto player, though he was New York based. Some issues give NSC 172 title as *I'm Still In The Dark*.
NSC 172 and NSC 173 titles previously recorded on January 23, 1946. For lyric variations, see notes for that session.
Other issues include: NSC172/173/174 on (LP) Savoy MG14012; all except NSC175 (alt).(CD) Savoy SV-0265, Classics 1034, JSP 7709B; NSC172/173 on (CD) Avid AMSC1142 ; NSC174 on (CD) Rhino R2-71550

JOE TURNER and his Boogie Woogie Boys (Turner, vo; with same or similar personnel, except possibly Porter Derico or Rudy Martin, p; replaces Ammons).

Chicago October 12, 1946

NSC 176	Milk and Butter Blues	(LP)	Savoy	SJL2223
NSC 177	That's When It Really Hurts	(78)	National	4017
NSC 178	I'm Sharp When I Hit The Coast	(78)	National	4011
NSC 179	Ooh Wee Baby Blues	(78)	National	9100

Other possible members could be Nat Jones or Antonio Cosey, as; Leon Washington, ts; Mickey Simms, b.
Other issues include: all on (LP) Savoy MG14012; (CD) Savoy SV-0265, Classics 1034, Avid AMSC1142; NSC179 on (CD) Rhino R2-71550

JOE TURNER and WYNONIE HARRIS (Turner, Harris, vo; possible personnel: Pat Jenkins, Joe Newman, tp; Tab Smith, as; Allan Eager, ts; Larry Belton, bar; Bill Doggett, p; Mary Osbourne, g; Al McGibbon, b; Walter Johnson, d; ensemble vocal -1).

New York City July 1947

A4077-3	Battle of the Blues (Part 1) -1	(78)	Aladdin	3036
A4077B	Battle of the Blues (Part 1)	(LP) Imperial LM 94002		
A4078-1	Battle of the Blues (Part 2) -1	(78)	Aladdin	3036
A4079-1	Going Home	(LP) Imperial F 1561431		
A4080-2	Blues	(LP) Imperial F 1561431		

A4077/A4080 and A4078/A4079 were remastered by Imperial as IM 5046/7 and IM 4785/6 respectively. Aladdin files, which gave only instrumentation, listed one trumpet.
Other issues include: all, except A4077B, on (LP) Imperial F 1561431; (CD) Classics 1013 (Wynonie Harris). A4077B on (LP) Liberty LBL83215E, (CD) Rhino R2-7155o; All takes on (CD) EMI E2 99293

BIG VERNON (Joe Turner, vo; Pete Johnson, p).

San Francisco November 1947

(a)	Around The Clock Blues (part 1)	(78)	Stag	508
(b)	Around The Clock Blues (part 2)	(78)	Stag	508
(c)	Steady Grinder	(78)	Stag	509
(d)	Hot Nuts	(78)	Stag	509
(e)	Don't You Feel My Leg			unissued

Other issues include: (a) on (CD) Sunset Boulevard SBR-7009. (a)(b) on (LP) Official 6038, (CD) Arhoolie CD 333, Classics 1034

JOE TURNER and His Band (Turner, vo; Sammy Yates, tp; Jack McVea, ts; Pete Johnson, p; Pee Wee Crayton, g; Frank Clarke, b; Rabon Tarrant, d).

KFSO, Mark Hopkins Hotel, San Francisco November 6, 1947

1000-2	Morning Glory	(78)	Aladdin	3013

1001-1	Nobody In Mind	(LP)	Imperial	1561431
1002-2	Low Down Dog	(78)	Aladdin	3013
1003-1	Back-Breaking Blues	(78)	Aladdin	3070
1004-2	Empty Pocket Blues	(78)	Aladdin	3070

No tp, ts, bar on 25-1001-1. The above personnel came from the Aladdin/
Imperial files. The same personnel, but with Gene Phillips on guitar, was given
by Jack McVea to Swiss researcher Johnny Simmen. The above were remastered
by Imperial as IM-4779/80/81/82/78
Other issues include: 1001/02/03 on (LP) Imperial F 1561431: all on (CD)
EMI E2 99293; 1003-1 on (CD) Acrobat ADDCD3275

(possibly from the above session)

IM-4783	Roll 'Em Pete	(LP)	Imperial	1561431
IM-4784	Ice-Man Blues	(LP)	Imperial	1561431

Other issues: both on (LP) Imperial F 1561431; (CD) EMI E2 99293

JOE TURNER with orch. acc. (Turner. vo; Charles Gray, tp; Riley
Hampton, as; Otis Finch, ts; Joe Liggins, p, harpsichord-1; Ike Perkins, g;
Robert Moore, b; James Adams, d).

Chicago November 29, 1947

NSC 311-3	Nobody In Mind	-1	(78)	National	9099
NSC 312	Lucille, Lucille	-1	(LP)	Savoy	MG14016
NSC 313	Rocks In My Bed		(78)	National	9144
NSC 314	Careless Love		(LP)	EmArcy	MG36014

Turner suggested Ellsworth Liggett as pianist for this session, but he was
probably a bass player. Pete Johnson later cited Joe Liggins for some of the
National sessions from this period.
Other issues include: NSC 311/313 on (LP) EmArcy MG36014; NSC 312 &
NSC 313 on (CD) Savoy SV-0265. All titles on (LP) Savoy MG14016; (CD)
Classics 1094, Avid AMSC1142.

(same or similar, but probably Lloyd Glenn, p; replacing Liggins).

Chicago December 9, 1947

NSC 337	Last Goodbye Blues	(LP)	EmArcy	MG36014
NSC 338	Whistle Stop Blues	(78)	National	4017
NSC 339	Hollywood Bed	(78)	National	9100
NSC 340	Howlin' Winds	(78)	National	9144

Burke & Penny give Meade Lux Lewis, p; but Lloyd Glenn told Axel
Zwingenberger that he was the pianist.
Other issues include: NSC 338 on (LP) EmArcy MG 36014; NSC 337/338
on (LP) Savoy MG14012; all on (CD) Classics 1094, Avid AMSC1142;
NSC339 on (CD) Rhino R2-71550

JOE TURNER and PETE JOHNSON (Turner, vo; Pete Johnson, p; with Barney Kessel, g; Harry Babasin, b; Don Lamond, d).

Just Jazz concert, Shrine Auditorium, Los Angeles December 27, 1947

MM 1627	Roll 'Em Boys	(78)	RPM	331
MM 1628	Kansas City Blues	(78)	RPM	331
MM 1746	Riding Blues	(78)	RPM	345
MM 1747	Playful Baby	(78)	RPM	345

RPM 345 labelled as JOE TURNER.

The suggested rhythm section is the one which played with the All Star Band on this show.

MM 1627 was reissued on (78) Modern 20-691. It was allotted matrix number MM 1113-3A and retitled *Don't Talk Me To Death*, with a tenor sax, possibly Maxwell Davis, dubbed onto the recording.

MM 1746/47 have also been listed with master numbers MM1629/30.

Turner was not included in the excerpts which appeared on an AFRS transcription, Jubilee 271, from this concert.

MM 1627 as *I Got A Gal* on Crown and United, and as a severely curtailed *Roll 'Em Pete* on Ace.

MM 1746 as *Jockey Blues* on Ace. *Kansas City Blues* is a retitling of *Piney Brown Blues*.

December 27 date confirmed on original acetate and by *Down Beat*, December 31, 1947, news item.

Other issues include: MM 1627/28 on (LP) Crown CLP5383, United 7794; all titles on (LP) Jackson LP 1207, Ace CHD-243; (CD) Classics 1094.

PETE JOHNSON and his ORCHESTRA (James Ross, Art Farmer, tp; Frank Sleet, as; Pete Peterson, ts; Milburn Newman, bar; Pete Johnson, p; Addison Farmer, b; Robert Brady, d; Joe Turner, vo).

Los Angeles June 28, 1948

4005	Radar Blues	(78)	SwingTime 151

Other issues include: (LP) Arhoolie 2004, (CD) Classics 1094, Arhoolie CD 333, Rhino R2-71550, Sunset Boulevard SBR-7009.

JOE TURNER and PETE Johnson with Orchestral Accompaniment (same personnel, plus unknown g).

Los Angeles - mid-1948

4127	Trouble Blues	(78)	SwingTime 151
4128	Wine-O-Baby	(78)	Down Beat 152
4129-1	B & O Blues	(78)	Down Beat 152
4129-2	B & O Blues	(LP)	Arhoolie F1012
4130	Christmas Date Boogie	(78)	Down Beat 153
4131	Tell Me Pretty Baby	(78)	Down Beat 153
	Baby Won't You Marry Me	(78)	Down Beat 154
4170	Old Piney Brown Is Gone	(78)	Down Beat 154

(78) Swing Time 269 coupled master 4130 (titled *Christmas Date*) with master 4131 (re-titled *How D'Ya Want Your Rollin' Done*). A guitarist solos on 4130. All titles possibly recorded on June 28, 1948.

Label credits vary: Swing Time 151 (also on Swing Beat 151 & Swing Records 151) is "Joe Turner's Orchestra featuring Pete Johnson at the Piano," 152 is "Joe Turner with orchestral accompaniment featuring Pete Johnson at the '88'," 153 is as the heading for this session; 154 is "Joe Turner's Orchestra with Pete Johnson".

Other issues include: all titles, except 4129-2, on (LP) Arhoolie R2004 and (CD) Arhoolie CD 333, Classics 1094; all except 4127/29/70 on (CD) Sunset Boulevard SBR-7009. 4128/31 on (CD) Rhino R2-71550

JOE TURNER with instrumental accompaniment (Turner, vo; Walter 'Dootsie' Williams, tp; Kirtland Bradford, as; Jewel Grant, as, bar; Maxwell Davis, ts; Pete Johnson, b; Herman Mitchell, g; Ralph Hamilton, b; Jesse Sailes, d).

Los Angeles - c. July 1948

48-S-81	Messin' Around	(78)	MGM	10321
48-S-82	Mardi Gras Boogie	(78)	MGM	10274
48-S-83	My Heart Belongs To You	(78)	MGM	10274
48-S-84	So Many Women Blues	(78)	MGM	10321
48-S-85	I Don't Dig It	(78)	MGM	10397
48-S-86	Rainy Weather Blues	(78)	MGM	10397

Other issues include: all titles on (CD) Arhoolie CD333, Classics 1180

(probably same personnel, less Mitchell).

Los Angeles – late 1948/early 1949

48-S-214	Feelin' So Sad	(78)	MGM	10719
48-S-215	Boogie Woogie Baby	(78)	MGM	10492
48-S-216	Married Woman Blues	(78)	MGM	10492
48-S-217	Moody Baby	(78)	MGM	10719

As Williams was probably the contractor for the MGM sessions, he is the likeliest candidate for the trumpet chair. There is also a "Williams" listed as co-composer for three of the MGM titles.

Other issues include: 48-S-216 on (LP) Official 6028. all titles on (CD) Arhoolie CD333, Classics 1180

DOOTSIE WILLIAMS & HIS ORCHESTRA (Williams, tp; rest perhaps as for previous MGM session; Joe Turner, vo).

Los Angeles - October 28, 1948

(a)	I Love Ya, I Love Ya, I Love Ya	(78)	Coast	8064
(b)	Born To Gamble	(78)	Coast	8064
(c)	Everybody's Jumpin' Tonight	(78)	Blue	107

(b) was later retitled *Gamblin' Blues* and issued on another Williams label, Blue 107.

Nick Tosches, in *Unsung Heroes of Rock 'n' Roll* incorrectly gives *When I'm Gone/No, There Ain't No News Today* on (78) Dootone 341 as a Joe Turner item. Other issues include: (a) on (78) Dootone 305 as "vocal by Big Joe Turner : Pete Johnson and his Orchestra", reverse, Betty Hall Jones. (a)(b) on (CD) Ace CDCHD 1115, Magnum Music ARB 011.

JOE TURNER (vo; with Loumell Morgan Trio: Morgan, p; unknown, g; b; Al Wichard, d)

broadcast, "Jubilee", Hollywood - c. November 1948

      Cherry Red   (ET)   AFRS   'Jubilee'   306

James 'Ham' Jackson, g; Jimmy Smith, b; have been suggested for this date. The broadcast date has also been given as c. September 1948.

JOE TURNER with FLENNOY TRIO (Turner, vo; Lorenzo Flennoy, p; and possibly, Leonard 'Lucky' Enois, g; Winston Williams, b; ensemble vo -1).

Los Angeles – late 1947 or January 1949

(a)   I Don't Dig It -1   (78)   Excelsior OR 533
(b)   Ooh-Ouch-Stop -1   (78)   Excelsior OR 533

Reverse of (a)(b) are non-vocals. (b) see also August 1954.
Other issues: (b) on (CD) Stash STB 516/517; (a)(b) Magnum Music ARB 011.

JOE TURNER: Music by Joe Houston (Turner, vo; possibly Nelson Pitts or Russell 'Fats' Emory. tp; Joe Houston, Sam Wilson, ts; James Hurdle, p; J.P. Mosely, b; Allison Tucker or James Byrd, d)

Baton Rouge - late 1949

(a)   Wish I Had A Dollar   (78)   Rouge ROU-105
(b)   Fuzzy Wuzzy Honey   (78)   Rouge ROU-105

Recording location stated to be the home of Joe Houston's girl friend in Baton Rouge: Joe Turner in correspondence with Richard J. Johnson (*Blues & Rhythm* 15). Label states: "Rouge Records with studios in Baton Rouge, LA". Turner had a residency at the Ace Club in Baton Rouge in late 1949. (b) see also August 1954.
Other issues include: (a)(b) on (CD) Classics 1180, Magnum Music ARB 011.

JOE TURNER and ORCHESTRA (vo; unknown, tp; Conrad Johnson, as; probably Sam Williams, ts; Lonnie Lyons, p; Goree Carter, g; Louis Pitts, b; Allison Tucker, d).

ACA Studio, Houston, Texas - December 22, 1949

SMK 1342 Adam Bit The Apple   (78)   Freedom F 1531
SMK 1343 Still In The Dark   (78)   Freedom F 1531

Other issues include: both on (LP) Ace CHD 243, (CD) Classics 1180, JSP 7709E, Acrobat ADDCD3275; SMK1343 on Rhino R2-71550, Sunset Boulevard SBR-7009

Master numbering for Freedom records is variable. Sometimes ACA is scratched into the wax, sometimes not. On occasion different numbers have been quoted; eg: 1563 below as ACA 1396 and 1844 as ACA 1397.

(Turner, vo; Joe Bridgewater, tp; Conrad Johnson, as; Vernon Bates, ts; James Toliver, p; Goree Carter, g; unknown, b, d).

ACA Studio, Houston, Texas – early 1950

1561	Just A Travellin' Man	(78) Freedom F 1537	
1562	Feelin' Blue	unissued	
1563	Life Is Like A Card Game	(78) Freedom F 1537	

Other issues: 1561/63 on (LP) Ace CHD 243, (CD) JSP 7709E, Sunset Boulevard SBR-7009. 1561 on (CD) Acrobat ADDCD3275 1563 on (CD) Classics 1180 (as *Life Is Just A Card Game*).

(vo; same or similar personnel; ensemble vocal -1)

ACA Studio, Houston, Texas - early 1950

ACA 1647	'While You'll Be Sorry	(78)	Freedom F 1540
ACA 1648	I Want My Baby	(78)	Freedom F 1545
ACA 1649	Midnight Is Here Again	(78)	Freedom F 1545
ACA 1650	Feelin' Happy -1	(78)	Freedom F 1540
ACA1650 (alt)	Feeling Happy -1	(LP)	Ace CHD 243
1844	Jumpin' At The Jubilee	(78)	Freedom F 1546

JOE TURNER COMBO (same, less tp & as: "with Goree Carter, vocal")

same location and date

1845	Lonely World	(78)	Freedom F 1546

Joe Turner does not sing on this title.

ACA 1650: alternative version on Ace contains a trumpet solo and the vocal refers to "... a big fat mama, she weighs 300 pound." The original issue tells us she is skinny & weighs 90 pound.
Other issues include: ACA1647 on (78) Fidelity 3007 as *After A While*; ACA1648 on Fidelity 3000 as *When The Rooster Crows*. ACA 1647/48/49 (the last as *Dawn Is Breaking Through*) on (LP) Ace CHD 243.
ACA 1647/48/49/50/1844 on (CD) JSP 7709E (1648 as *I Want My Baby (When The Rooster Crows)*. 1644/47/48/50 (alt) on (CD) Sunset Boulevard SBR-7009. 1844 on (CD) Classics 1180, Proper P1456, Acrobat ADDCD3275, Rhino R2-71550

Pianist Lloyd Glenn told Whitney Balliett he was positive he recorded with Joe Turner in Los Angeles, in the 1950s, in an upstairs studio, for a label that had a picture of Liberty on it. The Freedom label shows the Statue of Liberty, but is not known to have recorded outside Houston.

JOE TURNER accompanied by Dave Bartholomew and his Orchestra
(Turner, vo; Dave Bartholomew, tp; Waldron 'Frog' Joseph, tb; Joe Harris, as;
Clarence Hall, Herb Hardesty, ts; Fats Domino, p; Ernest McLean, g; Pete
Badie, b; Thomas Morris, d.

J&M Studios, New Orleans - April 1950

IM 190	Story To Tell	(78)	Imperial	5000
IM 191	Jumpin' Tonight	(78)	Imperial	5000
IM 192	Lucille	(78)	Imperial	5093
IM 193	Love My Baby	(78) Imperial 5093		

IM 191, retitled *Midnight Rocking,* and IM 193, retitled *Little Bitty Baby,* were
issued on (78) Colony 108. IM 631 *Blues Jumped A Rabbit (*assembled from
parts of IM 191/193) and IM 632 *The Sun Is Shining (*assembled from IM
190/192) were issued on Bayou 015.
(Personnel as given in TBD. The rhythm section has previously been listed as
Justin Adams, g; Frank Fields, b; Earl Palmer, d).
Other issues: all, including IM 631/632, on (LP) ImperialF 1561431; (CD)
Classics 1180, JSP 7709E, EMI E2 99293; IM190/191/192/193 on (CD)
Proper P1456; IM192/193 on Acrobat ADDCD3275

An unissued session for Mercury, recorded in New York , circa 1950, with
accompaniment by Art Farmer, tp; Budd Johnson, ts; Pete Johnson, p;
Tiny Grimes, g; Chris Powell, b; Panama Francis, d, has been listed in
print, but is unconfirmed. Farmer lived in Los Angeles between 1945
and 1952. No mention of the session has been found in any available
Mercury files.

The next session is Joe Turner's first recording for Atlantic, the start of
a partnership which was to last throughout the decade. The tracks were
re-issued in numerous versions by Atlantic and in all formats – 78, 45,
EP, LP and CD. Many reissues appeared subsequently on other labels.
Appendix 3 to the discography gives a representative listing of some of
these reissues. Turner's recordings for Atlantic were originally issued
on 78rpm discs, but for a time, during the changeover from 78rpm to
45rpm, they were issued in both formats.

JOE TURNER with Van 'Piano Man' Walls and his Orchestra (Turner,
vo; unknown, tp; as; ts; Harry Van Walls, p; unknown, g; b; d; ensemble vo-1).

New York City - April 19, 1951

A600	The Chill Is On	(78)	Atlantic 949
A601	After My Laughter Came Tears	(78)	Atlantic 939
A602	Bump Miss Susie -1	(78)	Atlantic 949
A603	Chains of Love	(78)	Atlantic 939

(Turner, vo; James 'Taft' Jordan, tp; Albert 'Budd' Johnson, Freddie Mitchell, ts; Arlem Kareen (Ernest 'Pinky' Williams), bar; Harry Van Walls, p; Rector Bailey, g; Leonard Gaskin, b; Connie Kay, d).

New York City - January 20, 1952

A786	I'll Never Stop Loving You	(78)	Atlantic	960
A786 (alt)	I'll Never Stop Loving You	(LP)	Atlantic	8033
A787	Sweet Sixteen	(78)	Atlantic	960
A788	J.T. Blues			unissued
A789	Don't You Cry	(78)	Atlantic	970
A790	Poor Lover's Blues	(78)	Atlantic	970

It appears that the 78rpm version of A786 has not been reissued. The microgroove and CD issues heard are all from the alternative take. There are numerous variations between the lyrics, in typical Joe Turner fashion. The 78rpm issue runs 3;10; the LP/CD issues 3:15.

(Turner, vo; Joe Morris, tp; Salvatore Davis, tb; William Burchett, Arlem Kareem, as; Freddie Mitchell, ts; Dave McRae, bar; Harry Van Walls, p; perhaps Sheb Hobbs, g; unknown, b; d).

New York City - September 23, 1952

A906	Still In Love	(78)	Atlantic	982
A907	Baby, I Still Want You	(78)	Atlantic	982
A908	Feel Like Having Some Sport			unissued
A909	What Is Your Secret?			unissued

JOE TURNER and His Band (Turner, vo; Frank Mitchell, tp; Pluma Davis, tb; August 'Dimes' Dupont, as; Warren Hebrand, ts; Alvin 'Red' Tyler, bar; perhaps Johnny Fernandez, p; Edgar Blanchard, g; perhaps Stewart Davis, b; Alonzo Stewart, d; band vo-1).

J&M Studio, New Orleans - May 12, 1953

A1071	This'll Make You Laugh			unissued
A1072	Oke-She-Moke-She-Pop	(LP)	Atlantic	4586
A1073	Honey Hush -1	(78)	Atlantic	1001
A1074	Crawdad Hole	(78)	Atlantic	1001

Personnel based upon statements by drummer Alonzo Stewart ("We did the *Honey Hush* session") in *Wavelength*, October 1985 and *New Orleans Music*, December 2006. Other pianists mentioned for this session are Edward Santino, who played in the Edgar Blanchard band in 1953, and Kathy Thomas, who is named in an Atlantic CD insert note. Fernandez has also been listed as a bassist, but this is believed to be an error. TBD lists Tommy Sheldon as a second tp. In his autobiography, *Rhythm and the Blues*, Jerry Wexler mentions, in addition to Pluma Davis and Red Tyler, Lee Allen, tenor; and Fats Domino, piano. On A1072 (2:59), originally issued in Japan, Turner sings "Step into my Roadmaster, baby". When remade on October 7, 1953, in Chicago, Joe sang, "Step into my Cadillac, baby".
Honey Hush (A1073) was also labelled on 45-1001 as *Yakity-Yak*.

JOE TURNER and his BLUES KINGS (Turner, vo; Sonny Cohn, tp; Harlan Floyd or John Arant, tb; Grady Jackson, Joe Tillman, ts; McKinley Easton, bar; Johnny Jones, p; Elmore James, g; Jimmy Richardson, b; Red Saunders, d).

Universal Studios, Chicago - October 7, 1953

A1125	Love To Spare		unissued
A1126	Ti-Ri-Lee	(78)	Atlantic 1053
A1127	Oke-She-Moke-She-Pop	(78)	Atlantic 1016
A1128	TV Mama	(78)	Atlantic 1016

Joe Turner told Steve Propes that he recorded with Elmore James on this one occasion only. A1127 *Oke-She-Moke-She-Pop* runs 2:43. Elmore James is to the fore, there is a baritone solo and Turner sings, "Step into my Cadillac, baby".
Refer to notes to May 12, 1953 session.
Ti-Ri-Lee was remade on January 28, 1955 in New York City, though apparently unissued.

(Turner, vo; John Girard, tp; Worthia 'Showboy' Thomas, tb; Gus Fontanette, as; Joe Tillman, ts; Alvin 'Red' Tyler, bar; Edward Frank, p; Lloyd Lambert, b; Oscar Moore, d).

J&M Studio, New Orleans - December 3, 1953

A1220	You Know I Love You	(78)	Atlantic	1026
A1225	Married Woman	(78)	Atlantic	1040
A1226	Midnight Cannonball	(78)	Atlantic	1069

C1221-1224 were allocated to a Rose Marie McCoy session for the Cat label.
It is believed that master number A1227 was unused.

(Turner, vo; (possibly) unknown, tp; Wilbur DeParis, tb; Sam Taylor, ts; Frank 'Heywood' Henry, bar; Harry Van Walls, p; Mickey Baker, g; Lloyd Trotman, b; Connie Kay, d; Ahmet Ertegun, Jerry Wexler, & possibly Van Walls, vo trio-1)

. *New York City - February 15, 1954*

A1209	Shake, Rattle and Roll -1	(78)	Atlantic	1026
A1210	Time After Time			rejected
A1211	In The Evening	(EP)	Atlantic	EP565
A1212	Well All Right -1	(78)	Atlantic	1040
A1213	How Deep Is The Ocean			unissued

Turner told Steve Propes, "Jesse Stone wasn't even on that", ie: *Shake, Rattle and Roll.*

(vo; with Paul Williams' Band: Jimmy Brown, tp; Noble Watt or Eddie Silver, ts; Paul Williams, bar; Freddie Johnson, p; Steve Cooper, b; Belton Evans, d).

Studio Films, Hollywood - August 1954

(a)	Shake, Rattle and Roll	(VHS)	Storyville SV-6016
(b)	Oke-She-Moke-She-Pop	(VHS)	Storyville SV-6016

Storyville title: "Rhythm and Blues at the Apollo Theatre":

Other issues:(a)(b) on (DVD) Idem DVD1026, title: "Swing Era: Count Basie".
On YouTube these two clips can be found, labelled as *Ooh-Ouch-Stop* and
Fuzzy Wuzzy Honey, dubbed (badly) from the recordings by Joe Turner with
the Flennoy Trio (Excelsior; 1949) and with Music by Joe Houston (Rouge:
1949).

(vo; with unknown accompaniment).

New York City - October 19, 1954

A1328	Morning, Noon and Night	Atlantic	rejected
A1329	Country Love	Atlantic	unissued
A1330	Hide and Seek	Atlantic	rejected
A1331	Heavy Hittin' Mama	Atlantic	unissued

JOE TURNER and his BLUES KINGS (Turner, vo; unknown tp; Al Sears,
ts; unknown bar; Jesse Stone, p; unknown g, b, d; Connie Kay, d; duo vo-1).

New York City - January 28, 1955

A1424	Morning, Noon and Night	(78)	Atlantic 1080
A1425	Hide and Seek -1	(78)	Atlantic 1069
A1426	Ti-Ri-Lee		unissued
A1427	Flip Flop and Fly	(78)	Atlantic 1053

Hide and Seek incorrectly listed on label of Atlantic 1069 as A1426. Charly
CRB1070 contains A1126 *Ti-Ri-Lee*, not A1426 as suggested in the notes.

JOE TURNER and his BLUES KINGS (vo, with unknown, tp; Wilbur
DeParis, tb; unknown ts; Heywood Henry, bar; Harry Van Walls, p; unknown, g;
b; Connie Kay, d; band vo -1).

New York City - November 3, 1955

A1687	The Chicken and The Hawk (Up, Up And Away) -1		
		(78)	Atlantic 1080
A1688	Boogie Woogie Country Girl	(78)	Atlantic 1088
A1688*	Boogie Woogie Country Girl	(LP)	Atlantic 8005

A1688 has been edited; it fades out at 2:38. A1688* fades out at 2:54, the
closing piano solo running longer. It does not appear to be an alternative take.

JOE TURNER (vo; with (probably) Charles Gillum, tp; Jack Kelso, as;
Clifford Scott, ts; Floyd Turnham, bar; Camille Howard, p; Jimmy Davis, g;
Lawrence Cato, b; Roy Milton, d, leader)

Blues Jubilee concert, Shrine Auditorium, Los Angeles - December 31, 1955

(a)	Flip, Flop and Fly	(LP) GNPD 2261
(b)	Three O'Clock in the Morning (Chains of Love)	(LP) GNPD 2261
(c)	Up, Up and Away (The Chicken and the Hawk)	(LP) GNPD 2261
(d)	Blues	(LP) GNPD 2261

Turner says, "Let the piano lady play a little boogie for me," which is part
confirmation that the pianist is Camille Howard and the band Roy Milton's.

The listed LP/CD issues would be from promoter Gene Norman's sponsored recordings.
Other issues include: (a)(b)(c) on (LP) Vogue LDM 30.220; (a)(b) on (CD) Sunset Boulevard SBR-7009; all on (CD) Vogue 600171.

JOE TURNER with Chorus & Orchestra (Turner, vo; Dick Vance Jimmy Nottingham, tp; Earl Warren, as; Sam 'The Man' Taylor, ts; Ernie Hayes, p; Billy Mure, George Barnes, g; Lloyd Trotman, b; David 'Panama' Francis, d; The Cookies, vo).

New York City - February 24, 1956

A1884	Corrine Corrina vTC	(78)	Atlantic	1088
A1885	Lipstick, Powder and Paint vTC	(78)	Atlantic	1100
A1886	Rock A While	(78)	Atlantic	1100
A1887	Nothing In Mind			unissued

An unidentified baritone, possibly Taylor, can be heard on A1886.

JOE TURNER (vo; Joe Newman, tp; Lawrence Brown, tb; James 'Pete' Brown, as; Frank Wess, ts; Pete Johnson, p; Freddie Green, g; Walter Page, b; Cliff Leeman, d; Ernie Wilkins, arr).

New York City - March 6, 1956

A1915	Low Down Dog	(LP)	Atlantic	SD 1234
A1915-4	Low Down Dog	(LP)	KC	108
A1916	Roll 'Em Pete	(LP)	Atlantic	SD1234
A1916-4	Roll 'Em Pete	(LP)	KC	108
A1916-5	Roll 'Em Pete	(LP)	KC	108
A1917	Cherry Red	(LP)	Atlantic	D1234
A1917-1	Cherry Red	(LP)	KC	108
A1917-2	Cherry Red (incomplete)	(LP)	KC	108
A1917-3	Cherry Red	(LP)	KC	108
A1918	How Long Blues	(LP)	Atlantic	SD 1234
A1919	Piney Brown Blues	(LP)	Atlantic	SD 1234
A1920	Morning Glories	(LP)	Atlantic	SD 1234
A1920-1	Morning Glories	(LP)	KC	108
A1920-4	Morning Glories	(LP)	KC	108

Newman and Wess are omitted from A1920.
An instrumental, *Testing The Blues*, was issued on (LP) KC 108 & (CD) Bear Family BCD17505.
A1917-2 breaks down at 52 seconds. Take numbers for original SD1234 issue are not known.
Colin Escott understood that Nesuhi Ertegun made copies of the out-takes for a friend who ran a festival in Switzerland. The friend may have been the late Claude Nobs of the Montreux Jazz Festival. The tapes are presumed destroyed in February 1978, during a fire at the Atlantic warehouse in Long Bridge, New Jersey.

Other issues include: SD 1234 titles on (LP) Atlantic Special 590.006. all takes, both mono and stereo, on (CD) Bear Family B17505. All takes, except A1917-2, on (CD) Avid AMSC1142; A1915/A1920 on (CD) Rhino R2 71550

(same personnel, except Jimmy Nottingham, tp; Seldon Powell, ts; replace Newman and Wess; Ernie Wilkins, arr).

New York City - March 7, 1956

A1921	I Want A Little Girl	(LP) Atlantic SD	1234
A1921-2	I Want A Little Girl (incomplete)	(LP)		KC108
A1921-3	I Want A Little Girl	(LP)		KC	108
A1922	St. Louis Blues	(LP) Atlantic SD	1234
A1922-1	St. Louis Blues	(LP)		KC	108
A1923	You're Driving Me Crazy	(LP) Atlantic SD	1234
A1923-1	You're Driving Me Crazy	(LP)		KC	108
A1924	Pennies From Heaven	(LP) Atlantic SD	1332
A1925	Wee Baby Blues	(LP) Atlantic SD1234

Notes to the Bear Family CD B17505 suggest both March sessions were taped at the Carnegie Hall recording studio, located in the Hall. A1924 appeared on a British release of SD1234 but was not shown on label or sleeve. Take details for the original SD1234 issue are not known.
Other issues include: SD 1234 titles on (LP) Atlantic Special 590.006 (stereo), plus (unlisted on label or sleeve), matrix A1924. All takes, both mono and stereo, on (CD) Bear Family B17505, except that A1921-2 is shown as A1921-1. All stereo takes are on (CD) Avid AMSC1142, except A1917-2 and A1924. A1921/A1923 on (CD) Rhino R2 71550

JOE TURNER (vo, with Choker Campbell and his Band: unknown tp; tb; Campbell, ts; unknown bar; p; b; d).
"Shake, Rattle and Rock!" film soundtrack, Los Angeles – c. September 1956
Lipstick, Powder and Paint
Feelin' Happy
Film title: "Shake, Rattle and Rock!" (can be viewed on YouTube).

JOE TURNER and his BLUES KINGS (Turner, vo; unknown - 2 tp; Sam Taylor & unknown, ts; p/org; Mickey Baker, g; unknown b & d; vo group -1, band vo-2).

New York City - November 20, 1956

A2219	After A While -1	(78)	Atlantic 1131
A2220	Midnight Special Train -1	(78)	Atlantic 1122
A2221	Red Sails In The Sunset -1	(78) Atlantic1131
A2222	Feeling Happy -2	(78)	Atlantic 1122

Michel Ruppli advises that A2222 was wrongly shown as A2223 on Atlantic. A2223 is a Ray Charles track.

JOE TURNER with CHOKER CAMPBELL and his Orchestra (Turner, vo; Phil Guilbeau, tp; Melvin Juanza, Edward O'Connor, tb; Chuck Reeves, ts; Choker Campbell, ts; Freddie Johnson, p; Allen Hanlon, Al Caiola, g; Bobby Nicholson, b; David 'Chick' Booth, d).

New York City - May 13, 1957

A2533	Trouble In Mind	(78)	Atlantic 1155
A2534	Blues In My Heart		unissued
A2535	World of Trouble	(78)	Atlantic 1146
A2536	Love Roller Coaster	(78)	Atlantic 1146
A2537	I Need A Girl	(78)	Atlantic 1155

JOE TURNER: orchestra & chorus directed by Jesse Stone (Turner, vo; Jerome Richardson, as; Sam Taylor, ts; Mike Stoller, p-1; Ray Charles, p-2; Allen Hanlon, Mundell Lowe, g; Lloyd Trotman, b; Panama Francis, d; vo group-3).

New York City - October 2, 1957

A2802	Teen Age Letter -1, -3	(78)	Atlantic 1167
A2803	Wee Baby Blues -2, -3	(78)	Atlantic 1167
A2804	Blue Moon		unissued
A2805	Howling Winds		unissued

JOE TURNER: arranged & conducted by Howard Biggs (Turner, vo; Hilton Jefferson, as; King Curtis, ts; Billy Mure, George Barnes, g; Howard Biggs, p; Lloyd Trotman, b; Panama Francis, d; Mike Chimes, hca-1; The Bobbettes -2).

New York City - January 22, 1958

A2927	Sweet Sue -2	(45)	Atlantic 2072
A2928	Switchin'		unissued
A2929	Go Red Go		unissued
A2930	Jump For Joy	(45)	Atlantic 1184
A2931	Blues In The Night -1, -2	(45)	Atlantic 1184

Atlantic 1184 label as "Joe Turner with Howard Biggs Orchestra & Chorus". Reissues of A2930 were labelled *We're Gonna Jump For Joy*. Joe Marshall has been cited as a second drummer for this session.

JOE TURNER (vo; Roy Eldridge, tp; Sonny Stitt, as; Pete Johnson, p; Herb Ellis, g; Max Bennett, b; Gus Johnson, d).

Jazz at the Philharmonic, concert, Zurich, Switzerland - June 2, 1958

(a)	I Want A Little Girl	private tape
(b)	St. Louis Blues	private tape

(same, but omit Eldridge; Stitt plays ts).

Alhambra, Paris - June 3, 1958

(c)	Cherry Red	(CD) Sunset Boulevard SBR-7009

JOE TURNER with Pete Johnson and the Newport Blues Band: (Wilbur 'Buck' Clayton, tp; Jack Teagarden, tb; Tony Scott, cl; George Auld, George 'Buddy' Tate, ts; Rudy Rutherford, bar; Pete Johnson, p; Kenny Burrell, g; Tommy Bryant, b; Jonathan 'Jo' Jones, d, ensemble vo-1).

Newport Jazz Festival, Newport, R.I. - July 5, 1958

(a)	Feelin' Happy -1	(LP) Jackson	LP 1206
(b)	Corrine Corrina	(LP) Jackson	LP 1206
(c)	Honey Hush	(CD) Phontastic NCD8815	
(d)	Shake, Rattle and Roll -1	(CD) Phontastic NCD8815	

Let The Good Times Roll has been given as an unissued track from this concert, but is probably a mis-titling for *Feelin' Happy*, which includes "Let the good times roll" in its lyrics.
Other issues include: (b) on (LP) IAJRC 44; (a)(b) on (CD) Phontastic NCD8815; (a) on (CD) Magnum Music CDMF098; (a)(b)(c) on(CD) Avid AMSC1142.

ART FORD JAZZ PARTY (Max Kaminsky, tp; Cutty Cutshall, tb; Herbie Hall, cl; Bud Freeman, ts; Stuff Smith, vl; Johnny Rae, vb; Johnny Guarnieri, p; Danny Barker, g; Vinnie Burke, b; George Wettling, d; Joe Turner, vo).

radio & TV broadcast, WNTA, Newark New Jersey - July 24, 1958

(a)	Low Down Dog	(AC) Jazz Connoisseur Cassettes AFJP 3
(b)	Exactly Like You	(AC) Jazz Connoisseur Cassettes AFJP 3
(c)	Joe Turner Blues	(AC) Jazz Connoisseur Cassettes AFJP 3

(c) no title was announced on the broadcast; the title was given by the cassette producer.
Other issues: all titles on (AC) Jazz Connoisseur Cassettes JCC98; (b) on (AC) JCC 104.

JOE TURNER with the South Bay Seven (Turner, vo; Rex Stewart, tp; Benny Morton, tb; Garvin Bushell, cl; Dick Cary, p; unknown rhythm section).

concert, Great South Bay Festival, Long Island, New York – July 26, 1958

(a)	Baby Blues	unissued
(b)	Roll 'Em Pete	unissued
(c)	Red Sails In The Sunset	unissued
(d)	Pennies From Heaven	unissued
(e)	Don't Get Around Much Anymore	unissued

United Artists recorded some or all of the Great South Bay Festival, though only one album is known to have been issued, "Rex Stewart leads the Fletcher Henderson Alumni".

JOE TURNER (vo; Joe Bridgewater, tp; Sammy Harris, Isadore Pollard, Richard Waters, Richard Little, unknown instruments; Clarence Holloman, g; Clayton Mitchell, Richard Dell Thomas, unknown instruments).

ACA Studio, Houston – January 28, 1959

four unissued titles

Discographer Kurt Mohr reported these as Atlantic recordings, but Michel Ruppli advises they are untraced in the Atlantic files.

JOE TURNER (vo; King Curtis, Leon Cohen, ts; Marlow Morris, p, org-1; Bill Suyker, g; Abie Baker, b; Sammy 'Sticks' Evans, d; Reggie Obrecht, arr-2; vo quintet-3).

New York City - June 18, 1959

A3554	My Reason For Living -1	(45)	Atlantic	2072
A3555	Love Oh Careless Love -2,-3	(45)	Atlantic	2034
A3556	Got You On My Mind -2,-3	(45)	Atlantic	2034
A3557	Whatcha Gonna Do			unissued

JOE TURNER and his All Stars (Turner, vo; Paul Ricard, tp; Vic Dickenson, tb; Jerome Richardson, as; Coleman Hawkins, ts; Jimmy Jones, p; Jim Hall, g; Doug Watkins, b; Charlie Persip, d; Ernie Wilkins, arr).

New York City - September 9, 1959

A3735	Until The Real Thing Comes Along	(LP)	Atlantic SD1332
A3736	Nobody In Mind	(LP)	Atlantic SD1332
A3737	I Get The Blues When It Rains	(LP)	Atlantic SD1332
A3738	I Got The World On A String		unissued
A3739	Rebecca	(LP)	Atlantic SD1332

Note: masters 59C-3740/3741 are by Robert Hutch Davie (Atco 6149)
Other issues include: all on (LP) London LTK-Z 15205; (CD) Real Gone Music RGMCD200, Sequel RSACD810; A3736/A3739 on (CD) Rhino R2 71550

(same, except Ernie Royal, tp; replaces Ricard).

New York City - September 10, 1959

A3742	Time After Time	(LP)	Atlantic SD1332
A3743	When I Was Young	(LP)	Atlantic SD1332
A3744	Switchin' In The Kitchen	(LP)	Atlantic SD1332
A3745	Here Comes Your Iceman	(LP)	Atlantic SD1332
A3746	Don't You Make Me High	(LP)	Atlantic SD1332

SD1332 album title: Big Joe Rides Again
Other issues include: (LP) London LTK-Z 15205; (CD) Real Gone Music RGMCD200, Sequel RSACD810; A3742/A3746 on (CD) Rhino R2 71550

JOE TURNER (vo; Taft Jordan, tp; King Curtis, Al Sears, ts; Budd Johnson, bar; Ernie Hayes, p; Mickey Baker, Wally Richardson, Paul Winter, g;

Lloyd Trotman, b; Belton Evans, d; string section; Helen Way, Doryce Brown, Christine Spenser, vo trio -1; Jesse Stone, arr).

New York City – September 29, 1959

A3809	Chains of Love -1	(45)	Atlantic	2054
A3810	My Little Honey Dripper	(45)	Atlantic	2054
A3811	Tomorrow Night -1	(45)	Atlantic	2044
A3812	Honey Hush	(45)	Atlantic	2044

(Turner, vo; personnel unknown)

New Orleans – February 21, 1961

A5381	I Get The Blues	unissued
A5382	You Busted My Bubble	unissued
A5383	Good Loving	unissued
A5384	Lucille, Part 1	unissued
A5385	Lucille, Part 2	unissued

(Turner, vo; John Brunious, tp; Nat Perilliat, ts; Alvin "Red" Tyler, bar; James Booker, p; Eskew Reeder, org?; Justin Adams, g; Peter Badie, e-b; John Boudreaux, d; James Black, d).

New Orleans – May 31, 1962

A6253	Howling Winds	unissued
A6254	Laura Lee	unissued
A6255	untitled	unissued
A6256	The Party's Over	unissued

Personnel given by Michel Ruppli.

BIG JOE TURNER (vo; 8-piece band, tp; tb; 2 saxes; p; g; b; d; vo group).

New York City – November 1963

| 114499 | I Stand Accused | (LP) | Charly | CR30237 |
| 114500 | I Walk A Lonely Mile | (45) | Coral | 62408 |

Other issues include: 114500 on (LP) Charly CR30237; both on (CD) Decca Jazz GRD-621, MCA GRP16212

(with chorus and instrumental accompaniment: similar instrumentation, except 2 fl and bss, -1).

New York City – March 17, 1964

114757	I'm Packin' Up	(45)	Coral	62408
114758	Shake, Rattle and Roll -1	(45)	Coral	62429
114759	There'll Be Some Tears Fallin'	(45)	Coral	62429
	Sad Night		unissued	

The Blues Discography adds an organ for this session.
John Inman, in *The Golden Age* 16, p17, says these titles were purchased by Decca; 114499/500 on February 6, 1964; 114757/758/759 on April 6, 1964.
Label refers to "An Award Music Production". This is given credence by a

February 17, 1965 letter from Coral Records Inc. which provided the 114500 and 11457/8/9 master numbers but no recording dates or personnels. The existence of the unissued *Sad Night,* which is listed in Jepsen's *Jazz Records,* volume 8, published c. 1964, has not been confirmed.
Other issues include: 114757 on (45) Hipshakin' HS-45-012 (rev: Roy Brown); 114757/758 on (CD) Decca Jazz GRD-621, MCA GRP16212

BIG JOE TURNER and his ALL STARS (vo; Buck Clayton, tp; Vic Dickenson, tb; Benny Waters, Alix Combelle, ts; Stuff Smith, vl; Joe Turner, p; Jimmy Woode, b; Kenny Clarke, d).
Studio 102, Maison de la Radio, ORTF broadcast, Paris - May 13, 1965
(a)   Shake Rattle and Roll   (LP)   Europa   Jazz   EJ-1014

(omit Clayton, Dickenson, Combelle, Smith).

same broadcast
(b)   Flip, Flop and Fly   (LP) Europa Jazz EJ-1026
(c)   Cherry Red   (LP) Europa Jazz EJ-1026
(a)   is actually Roll 'Em Pete.
Other issues: (a) on (LP) I Giganti Del Jazz GJ-17, Curcio 17; (b)(c) on (LP) I Giganti Del Jazz GJ-33; (b) on (CD) Denon DC8530.

BIG JOE TURNER (vo; Humphrey Lyttelton, tp; Eddie Harvey, tb; Tony Coe, ts; Joe Temperley, bar; Johnny Parker, p; Dave Green, b; Johnny Butts, d).
BBC Television Centre, London - May 16, 1965
(a)   I Feel So Happy   (VC) Green Line Video Vidjazz 40
(b)   I Want A Little Girl   (VC) Green Line Video Vidjazz 40
(c)   Wee Baby Blues   (VC) Green Line Video Vidjazz 40
(d)   Shake, Rattle and Roll   (VC) Green Line Video Vidjazz 40

(same, plus Buck Clayton, tp; Vic Dickenson, tb).
(e)   Low Down Dog   (VC) Green Line Video Vidjazz 40

(Clayton, tp; Dickenson, tb; same rhythm section)   .
(f)   Morning Glories   (VC) Green Line Video Vidjazz 40

(same, plus Coe, ts; Temperley, bar).
(g)   Cherry Red   (VC) Green Line Video Vidjazz 40

(same, plus Humphrey Lyttelton, tp)
(h)   Roll 'Em Pete   (VC) Green Line Video Vidjazz 40
(i)   Bye, Baby, Bye (incomplete) (VC) Green Line Video Vidjazz 40

(Lyttelton, tp; Dickenson, tb; same rhythm section)
(j)   Chains of Love   (VC) Green Line Video Vidjazz 40

In the above listing, the titles are grouped according to personnels, and not in the order they were played on the telecasts.

Vidjazz 40 ("Big Joe Turner: The English Concert") is an Italian bootleg, with a partially incorrect personnel listed.

These titles were taped for two transmissions (June 16/November 3, 1965) in the BBC's "Jazz 625" series.

Other issues: (c)(d)(e)(i) are on (VC) PNV Video PNV1043; (c)(d)(e)(j) on (DVD) PNE (no number); all on (DVD) Impro-Jazz IJ528. Can be viewed on YouTube.

BIG JOE TURNER (vo; with Buck Clayton and the Humphrey Lyttelton Band, as above).

Tapes from Joe Turner's appearances at the Osterley Jazz Club on May 7, the Royal Festival Hall, London, on May 8, the 100 Club, London, on May 12, and the Dancing Slipper, Nottingham, on May 15, have been circulated by collectors.

BUCK CLAYTON & JOE TURNER with the Zagreb Jazz Quartet: (Turner, vo; Bosko Petrovic, vb; Davor Kafjes, p; Kresimir Remata, b; Silvije Glojnaric, d; band vo-1).

Zagreb, Yugoslavia - June 2, 1965

(a)	I'm In A World Of Trouble	(LP) Black Lion BLP 30145
(b)	Feel So Fine -1	(LP) Black Lion BLP 30145
(c)	I Want A Little Girl	(LP) Black Lion BLP 30145

(add Buck Clayton, tp).

same location and date

(d)	Too Late, Too Late	(LP) Black Lion BLP 30145

Three other tracks are without Turner.

Album title: Joe Turner/Buck Clayton: Feel So Fine.

Other issues include: all on (LP) Black Lion 2460-202, Fontana 826200, Audio Fidelity 202; (CD) Black Lion BLCD 760170. (b)(d)   on Alta ATLP105, unless, as Lord's *The Jazz Discography* indicates, they are from a separate session.

(same):

Yugoslavia Jazz Festival, Bled, Slovenia - June 3 & 4, 1965

Tapes of two half-hour broadcasts are in the Radio Slovenia Music Archive.

BIG JOE TURNER (Turner, vo; Rudy Pompilli, Mike Shay, ts; Bill Haley, Johnny Kay, g; Al Rappa, b; Johnny Lane, d; band vo-1)

9445	Me siento feliz (Feelin' Happy)	(45)	Orfeon	1842
9446	Corine Corina (Corrine, Corrina)	(45)	Orfeon	1842
9457	Tiempo de Amar (Chains of Love)	(EP)	Orfeon	EP-550
9458	Hombre mono (Monkey Man)	(EP)	Orfeon	EP-550
9460	Tormenta en Lunes (Stormy Monday)	(EP)	Orfeon	EP-533
9461	Callate vidita (Honey Hush) -1	(EP)	Orfeon	EP-550
9462	Tren solitario (Lonesome Train)	(EP)	Orfeon	EP-533
9463	Perro lento (Low Down Dog)	(EP)	Orfeon	EP-550
	Night Time Is The Right Time			unissued
	Flip, Flop and Fly			unissued
	Hide and Seek			unissued
	Morning, Noon and Night			unissued

Mexico City - January 24, 1966

Other issues include: 9445 on (EP) Orfeon 533; 9446 on (EP) Orfeon EP533, EP-1341; 9457/58/62 on (EP) Orfeon EP-1431

JOE TURNER (vo; same accompaniment).

Discoteca Orfeon A Go-Go, TV show, Mexico City - January 1966

Oh Well, Oh Well -1   (CD) Rock Beat ROC-3388

This track appears on the CD but is not shown on label or insert. The other tracks on the CD are from March 1977. A film clip of the Turner/Haley performance can be seen on YouTube.

(vo; with Little Brother Montgomery, p; Otis Rush, g; Jack Myers, b-g; Fred Below, d).

television show, American Folk Blues Festival, Granada TV Centre,
Manchester, UK   September 30, 1966

(a)	Oh Well, Oh Well	(DVD) Hip-O Records 0008353-09
(b)	Hide and Seek	unissued

(b) can be seen on YouTube.

DVD title: The American Folk Blues Festival - The British Tours 1963-1966

(Joe Turner, vo; Little Brother Montgomery, p; Otis Rush, g; Jack Myers, e-b; Freddie Below, d).

concert, Stuttgart, Germany - October 2, 1966

Chains of Love	private tape
TV Mama	private tape
Feelin' Happy	private tape
Hide and Seek	private tape
Flip, Flop and Fly	private tape

(add Junior Wells, hca; Roosevelt Sykes, p; Sleepy John Estes, Robert Pete Williams, g; Yank Rachell, mandolin).

Roll 'Em Pete   private tape

(Turner, vo; Montgomery, p; Otis Rush, g; Myers, b-g; Below, d).
> *concert, American Folk Blues Festival, Kurhaus, Baden-Baden, Germany -*
> *October 3, 1966*

(a)	Low Down Dog	(CD) Sunset Boulevard SBR-7009
(b)	Honey Hush	(CD) Sunset Boulevard SBR-7009
(c)	Feelin' Happy	private tape
(d)	Chains of Love	private tape
(e)	Hide and Seek	private tape

(vo; with Montgomery, p; Rush, g; Myers, b-g; Below, d).
> *television show, American Folk Blues Festival, Süd westfunk TV station,*
> *Mainz, Germany - October 5, 1966*

Flip, Flop and Fly(DVD) Hip-O Records 06024982 17832
DVD title: The American Folks Blues Festival 1962-1969 - Volume 3

(same personnel)
> *concert, Congresshall, Frankfurt, Germany - October 13, 1966*

(a)	Feelin' Happy	private tape
(b)	Hide and Seek	private tape
(c)	Chains of Love	private tape
(d)	Flip, Flop and Fly	private tape

(vo; Little Brother Montgomery, p-1; Roosevelt Sykes, p-2; Otis Rush, g;
Jack Myers, b-g; Fred Below, d):
> *concert, American Folk Blues Festival Friedrichsstadt-Palast,*
> *East Berlin, Germany - October 16, 1966*

(a)	Flip, Flop and Fly -1	(LP) Fontana 885 431D
(b)	Roll 'Em Pete -2	(LP) Fontana 885 431D
(c)	Feeling Happy -1	(LP) Amiga 885126
(d)	Come On Baby (Hide and Seek) -1	(LP) Scout Sc-2
(e)	Chains of Love -1	(LP) Scout Sc-3
(f)	Well Oh Well -1	(LP) Scout Sc-3

Other issues: (a)(b) on (LP) Amiga 855114, Fontana TL5389. (a)(b) on
(CD) Bellaphon CDLR726222, CDLR42069, Amiga 82876-63060-2. (a) on
(DVD) Hip-O Records 0602 4982 1783 Z (The American Folk Blues Festival
1962-1969, Volume 3). (b)(c) on (CD) Sunset Boulevard Records SBR-7009.
(b) on SBR-7009 is unedited, but on Fontana TFL5389 is edited with a fade.

(vo; possible instrumentation, 2 tp; tb; 2 ts; p-1, org-2; g; b-g; d; George
Davis, arr-3).

Los Angeles - c. 1966

SL 1414	I've Been Up On The Mountain -1, -3	(45) Ronn 28
SL 1414 (alt)	I've Been Up On The Mountain -1, -3	(CD) Jewel JCD 5059
SL 1415	I Love You Baby -2, -3	(45) Ronn 28
SL 1561	Night Time Is The Right Time -1,-3	(45) Ronn 35
SL 1561 (alt?)	Night Time Is The Right Time -1,-3	(CD) Jewel JCD 5059
SL 1562	Morning Glory -1	(45) Ronn 35
(a)	Honey Hush -1	(CD) Jewel JCD 5059
(b)	Honey Hush -1	(CD) Jewel JCD 5059
(c)	Hello Joe -1	(CD) Jewel JCD 5059
(d)	Movin' On Down -2,-3	(CD) Jewel JCD 5059
(e)	B Flat Blues -1	(CD) Jewel JCD 5059

Another mysterious set, with even the location and year of recording uncertain. SL1414 on Ronn 28 runs 3:42; SL1414 (alt) runs 2;20, but seems to be an edited version of an alternative take. SL 1561 on Ronn 35 runs 2:58. On Jewel one version of SL1561 is faded out at 2:37, the other, apparently an alternative, ends at 2:07. (a) one version of *Honey Hush* is edited to 2:02, losing two verses, compared with (b) at 2:42.

(d)*Movin' On Down* is a retitling of SL1415 *I Love You Baby*. (e) *B Flat Blues* is a retitling of (c) *Hello Joe*.

Other issues: SL 1414/1415/1561/1562 also on (CD) Jewel JCD 5059, Fuel 302 062 008 8; SL 1414 also on (CD) Charly CRB 1149. (SL = Stan Lewis.)

(vo; with the Cafe Society All Stars: Buck Clayton, tp; Ed Hall, cl; Buddy Tate, ts; Ray Bryant, p; Pete Johnson, p-1; Milt Hinton, b; Jo Jones, d).
concert, Carnegie Hall, New York City - January 15, 1967

(a)	I'm Going Away To Wear You Off My Mind	(LP) Columbia G30776
(b)	Hide and Go Seek	unissued
(c)	Roll 'Em Pete -1	(LP) Columbia G30776

-1 Pete Johnson plays the right hand part.

(vo; with Count Basie and his Orchestra: Buck Clayton, Al Aarons, Sonny Cohn, Harry Edison, tp; Richard Boone, Harlan Floyd, Grover Mitchell, Bill Hughes, tb; Ed Hall, cl; Marshall Royal, Bobby Plater, as; Buddy Tate, Eric Dixon, Billy Mitchell, ts; Charlie Fowlkes, bar; Count Basie, p, org; Freddie Green, g; Norman Keenan, b; Jo Jones, d).
concert, Carnegie Hall, New York City - January 15, 1967

| (d) | Blues for John (edited) | (LP) Columbia LP G30776 |

Album title: John Hammond's Spiritual To Swing.

(vo; Buddy Lucas, hca-1, ts-2; Patti Bown, p; Wally Richardson, Thornel Schwartz, g; Bob Bushnell, b-g; Herbie Lovelle, d; band vo-3).
New York City - April 12, 1967

| 13968 | Since I Was Your Man -1 | (LP) BluesWay BL-6006 |
| 13969 | Roll 'Em Pete -1,-3 | (LP) BluesWay BL-6006 |

13970	Ballad Blues	unissued
13971	Well Oh Well -2,-3	(LP) BluesWay BL-6006
13972	Joe's Blues -2	(LP) BluesWay BL-6006
13973	Lonesome Train	unissued

(same personnel, except Lucas omitted -4; Panama Francis, d; replaces Lovelle).

New York City - April 13, 1967

13986	Piney Brown Blues -1	(LP) BluesWay BL-6006
13987	Mrs Geraldine -4	(LP) BluesWay BL-6006
13988	Cherry Red -4	(LP) BluesWay BL-6006
13989	Lonesome Train	unissued
13990	Big Wheel -1,-3	(LP) BluesWay BL-6006
13991	Poor House -1	(LP) BluesWay BL-6006
13992	Bluer Than Blue -1	(LP) BluesWay BL-6006

Other issues include: 13986 on (CD) MCA GRP 16212: 13990?13992 on (45) BluesWay 61009; BL-6006 also on (LP) StatesideE SL10226 and (CD) MCA MFCD 780.
Album title: Joe Turner Singing the Blues

SUPER BLACK BLUES BAND (Joe Turner, vo; Ernie Watts, ts; George Smith, hca; Otis Spann, p, vo; T-Bone Walker, g, vo; Arthur Wright, g; Ron Brown, b; Paul Humphrey, d)

Los Angeles - August 14, 1969

(a)	Paris Blues vTBW	(LP) BluesTime BTS-9003
(b)	Here Am I Broken Hearted vJT	(LP) BluesTime BTS-9003
(c)	J.O.T's Blues vJT, vOS, vTBW	(LP) BluesTime BTS-9003
(d)	Blues Jam vJT, vTBW	(LP) BluesTime BTS-9003

(a) includes a spoken interjection by Turner. Album title: Super Black Blues. Other issues include: all titles on (LP) Philips 6369 416, (CD) RCA Victor 85164-2.

JOE TURNER (vo; Buddy Brisbois, Marion Childers, tp; Jack Nimitz, ts, fl-1; Gary Coleman, vb; James Carmichael, p; Jim Burton, David Cohen, David Walker, Don Peake, g; Max Bennett, b; Paul Humphrey, d; Gene Page, arr & conductor).

Los Angeles - August 18, 1969

(a)	Shake, Rattle and Roll	(LP)	BluesTime	BTS-9002
(b)	Lonesome Train	(LP)	BluesTime	BTS-9002
(c)	How Long, How Long Blues	(LP)	BluesTime	BTS-9002
(d)	Careless Love -1	(LP)	BluesTime	BTS-9002
(e)	Two Loves Have I	(LP)	BluesTime	BTS-9002

(vo; with: probably Tom Scott, ts-3; George "Harmonica" Smith, hca; Artie Butler, p; Louie Shelton, g; probably Max Bennett, b; Paul Humphrey, d).*

same date

(f)	Corrine, Corrina		(LP)	BluesTime	BTS-9002
(g)	Honey Hush	-3	(LP)	BluesTime	BTS-9002
(h)	Plastic Man	-3	(LP)	BluesTime	BTS-9002

* personnel based upon Bluebird notes and Stanley Dance mention of Tom Scott, who also recorded with T-Bone Walker the following day.

album title: The Real Boss of the Blues. On Bluebird the title is: Joe Turner and T-Bone Walker: Bosses of the Blues - Vol. 1.

Other issues include: (a) to (e) on (LP) Philips SBL 7911, RCA NL88311. (a)(c)(f) on (LP) RCA SF8427; all on (CD) Bluebird ND88311, Ace CDCHM 1394.

HAMPTON HAWES ALL STARS (guest Big Joe Turner) (Harry Edison, tp; Sonny Criss, as; Hampton Hawes, p; Leroy Vinnegar, b; Chuck Thompson, d; Joe Turner, vo.

telecast, "Jazz on Stage," Memory Lane club, Los Angeles - c. October 1969

(a)	Feelin' Happy	(LP)	Jas	JAS-4005
(b)	Shake, Rattle and Roll	(LP)	Jas	JAS-4005

Album title: Hampton Hawes: Melody Lane Live; other titles are non-vocal.

(a)alias *Hide and (Go) Seek*.

Other issues: (a)(b) on (LP) Fresh Sounds FSR 406; (CD) Fresh Sounds FSR-CD406; (DVD) Rhapsody R1130 (as L.A. All Stars).

BIG JOE TURNER (vo; with, reportedly, Paul Mitchell, p; unknown 2g; b; d.)

live, Atlanta, GA - 1969

(a)	Honey Hush	(LP)	LMI	LP1004
(b)	I've Been Up On The Mountain	(LP)	LMI	LP1004

Notes to the CDs state these titles recorded at the Super Blues Festival, Atlanta. T-Bone Walker, Pee Wee Crayton possibly the guitarists. Perhaps from the WAOX "Super Heavy Blues Festival" of May 16, 1971?

Other issues: (b) on (CD) Sunset Boulevard SBR-7009; both on (CD) Fuel 302 062 008 8

BIG JOE TURNER (vo; George 'Harmonica' Smith, hca; unknown, p; g; b-g; d).

Los Angeles - c. 1969/1970

(a)	T.V. Mama	(LP)	Kent	KST-542
(b)	Everyday I Have The Blues	(LP)	Kent	KST-542
(c)	Good Morning Blues	(LP)	Kent	KST-542
(d)	St. Louis Blues	(LP)	Kent	KST-542
(e)	Chains of Love	(LP)	Kent	KST-542
(f)	In The Evening	(LP)	Kent	KST-542
(g)	Night Time Is The Right Time	(LP)	Kent	KST-542
(h)	Don't Love You No More	(LP)	Kent	KST-542

(i)	Little Girl		(LP)	Kent	KST-542
(j)	Kansas City Blues		(LP)	Kent	KST-542

Album title: Big Joe Turner Turns On The Blues.
Other issues: (e) on (45) Kent 4561; all on (LP/AC) Kent KLP/KLC-2012,
United US-7759.

(vo; with perhaps unknown p, g, b, d).

possibly same location and period

(a)	10-20-25-30	(45)	Kent	K	512
(b)	Love Ain't Nothin'	(45)	Kent	K	512
(c)	Battle Hymn of the Republic	(45)	Kent		4561
(d)	One Hour In Your Garden	(45)	Kent	KS	4569
(e)	You've Been Squeezin' My Lemons (Cause The Juice Is All On The Floor)	(45)	Kent	KS	4569

(c) horns and strings added. (e) hca added.
(The titles for Kent may be from a later period. Bernie Pearl, g; states he
recorded with Joe Turner for Kent in the early 1980s, though he does not
know if the results were issued. Also present were Everett Minor, sax; George
"Harmonica" Smith, hca; and probably Curtis Tillman, b. "I recall that at one
point [George Smith] sat at the drums to show the drummer how to play a
shuffle.")

BIG JOE TURNER (vo; Jimmy Forrest, ts; Rod Piazza, hca; Mark Leonard,
p; George Phelps, g; Jerry Smith, b; Dick Innes, d).

Eldorado Studios, Hollywood - 1970

(a)	Flip, Flop and Fly		(LP)	LMI	1004
(b)	29 Ways		(LP)	LMI	1004
(c)	Big Joe's Lonesome Blues		(LP)	LMI	1004
(d)	Can't Read, Can't Write Blues		(LP)	LMI	1004
(e)	Matchbox Blues		(LP)	LMI	1004
(f)	Chains of Love	no ts or hca	(CD) Sunset Boulevard SBR-7009
(g)	Wee Baby Blues	no ts	(CD) Sunset Boulevard SBR-7009
(h)	You've Been Squeezin' My Lemons	no ts	(CD) Sunset Boulevard SBR-7009

Details for this session are uncertain. Fuel and Sunset Boulevard CD notes
suggest recorded at Eldorado Studios, Hollywood, 1970. Rod Piazza
confirmed the Eldorado but thought the date was 1973. Rhino CD notes
quote "early 1974". For other titles on LMI, see 1969.
Other issues: (b) on (CD) Sunset Boulevard SBR-7009 as *Twenty-Nine Ways
To Get To My Baby's Door*. (b)(d)(e) on (CD) Fuel 302 062 008 8, album title:
Bossman of the Blues. (d) on (CD) Atlantic/Rhino R2-71550.

(vo; Russ Andrews, ts; Wynton Kelly, p; Lawrence Lucie, g; Al Hall, b; Elvin Jones, d):

concert, Carnegie Hall, New York City - May 2, 1970

(a)	Honey Hush	(LP)	BluesTime BST-9009
(b)	Yakety Yak	(LP)	BluesTime BST-9009

Other titles on the album by T-Bone Walker, EddieVinson, Big Mama Thornton and Leon Thomas. *Down Beat* reported that Turner sang three songs at this "B.B. King and Friends" concert.   other issues: both titles on (CD) Ace CDCHM 1394.

THE JOHNNY OTIS SHOW (Joe Turner with possible instrumentation: tp; ts; bar; Johnny Otis, p; Shuggie Otis, g; b-g; d).

possible telecast, Los Angeles – early 1970

(a)	Shake, Rattle and Roll	(CD)	Wolf 120.612
(b)	Chains of Love	(CD)	Wolf 120.612

Album title: Johnny Otis Show: Live 1970.
Other titles have Roy Milton, Esther Phillips, Johnny Otis, Eddie Vinson, Charles Brown, Lowell Fulson and T-Bone Walker.
In June 1970 a Johnny Otis personnel was: Melvin Moore, tp; Gene Connors, tb; Plas Johnson, ts; Preston Love, bar; Johnny Otis, p; Shuggie Otis, g; Wilton Felder, b-g; Paul Lagos, d. This line-up is a possible for the above session.

THE JOHNNY OTIS SHOW (Joe Turner, vo; Melvin Moore, tp; Gene 'The Mighty Flea' Connors, tb; Richard Aplenalp, Clifford Solomon, Big Jim Wynn, reeds; Johnny Otis, vb-1; Roger Spotts, p; Jim Bradshaw, Shuggie Otis, g; Lawrence 'Slim' Dickens, b; Paul Lagos, d). band vo-1).

Monterey Jazz Festival - September 19, 1970

(a)	I Got A Gal	(LP)	Epic EG30473
(b)	Plastic Man	(LP)	Epic EG30473

(finale, with Roy Brown, Margie Evans, Esther Phillips, Eddie Vinson, Delmar Evans, Roy Milton, vo).

same concert

(c)	Boogie Woogie Bye Bye -1	(LP)	Epic EG30473

(c) only Turner and Phillips solo on this title. other tracks are without Turner.
Album title: The Johnny Otis Show Live at Monterey (Volumes 1 and 2)
Other issues: all titles on (LP) Epic S64441/S64442; (a)(b)(c) on (CD) Edsel DED266

BIG JOE TURNER (vo; with Milt Buckner, p; Slam Stewart, b; Jo Jones, d).

live, Paris, France – April 19, 1971

(a)	Hide and Go Seek With Me	(CD)	Blue Jazz BJ029
(b)	Cherry Red	(CD)	Blue Jazz BJ029

(c)	Flip, Flop and Fly	(CD)	Blue Jazz BJ029
(d)	Honey Hush	(CD)	Blue Jazz BJ029
(e)	Shake, Rattle and Roll	(CD)	Blue Jazz BJ029
(f)	I've Got A Pocketful of Pencils	(CD) Sunset Boulevard SBR-7009	
(g)	Mad Blues	(CD) Sunset Boulevard SBR-7009	
(h)	Every Day I Have The Blues	(CD) Sunset Boulevard SBR-7009	
(i)	Corrine, Corrina	(CD) Sunset Boulevard SBR-7009	
(j)	The Chicken and the Hawk	(CD) Sunset Boulevard SBR-7009	

Other titles on Blue Jazz BJ029 are instrumentals. The CD is titled: Milt
Buckner, Slam Stewart, Jo Jones, Big Joe Turner. It is not known if (a) to (e)
were taped at the same or separate concerts or broadcasts to (f) to (k).
Other issue: (e) on (CD) Sunset Boulevard SBR-7009

BIG JOE TURNER (vo; Milt Buckner, p; Slam Stewart, b, vo*; Jo Jones, d;
trio vo-1).

Hérouville, France - April 26, 1971

71-013-1 Rock Me Baby *	(LP)	Black and Blue	33.028
71-013-2 Rock Me Baby *	(CD)	Black and Blue	BB903-2
71-014 Texas Style *	(LP)	Black and Blue	33.028
71-015 I've Got A Pocket Full of Pencils*	(LP)	Black and Blue	33.028
71-016 Money First -1	(LP)	Black and Blue	33.028
71-017 'T Ain't Nobody Business	(LP)	Black and Blue	33.028
71-018-1 Morning Glory	(CD)	Black and Blue	BB903-2
71-019 Cherry Red	(LP)	Black and Blue	33.028
71-020 T.V. Mama	(LP)	Black and Blue	33.028
71-021 Hide and Seek -1*	(LP)	Black and Blue	33.028

*indicates Slam Stewart's bowing and humming.
Rock Me Baby, take -1, is 6:05 mins: on LP it runs 4:21. Album title: Texas Style.
Other issues include: 33.028 titles on (LP) Black and Blue 33.547 (small
variations in titles, *Pencils/Pencil*, *Tain't Nobody Business*) and (CD) Black and
Blue BB903.2 ND215, Evidence ECD-26013-2.

BIG JOE TURNER: refer to Atlanta, GA , 1969, for note re: WAOX
Super Heavy Blues Festival of May 16, 1971,

PAPA JOHN CREACH (Joe Turner, vo; Blue Mitchell, tp; Henry Coker,
John Ewing, tb; John Lane Davis, Jerry Jumonville, ts; Papa John Creach, vl;
Harmonica Fats, hca; John 'Knocky' Parker, kbd; Kevin Moore, g; Sam Williams,
b-g; Holden 'Hoagy' Rapheal, percussion).

Give Me An Hour In Your Garden and I'll Show You How To Plant A Rose
(LP/CD)   Grunt   FTR-1009
Turner sings just the one title. album title: Filthy

GUNSMOKE BLUES (Joe Turner, vo; Bill Potter, ts-1; J.D. Nicholson, p;
Steve Wachsman, g; Bruce Sieverson, b-g; Todd Nelson, d).
University of Oregon, Eugene, OR - October 1971
(a)	Hide and Seek -1	(DVD) Dreyfus EDV725
(b)	Shake, Rattle and Roll (incomplete) -1	(DVD) Dreyfus EDV725
(c)	The Night Time Is The Right Time *	(DVD) Dreyfus EDV725
(d)	Who Shot My Baby/Rebecca -1 *	(DVD) Dreyfus EDV725

* audio only. Turner is on stage for the closing ad-lib *So Long*, but cannot be
heard.
Other issues: (a)on (CD) Magnum Music CDBM 141; (a)(b) on (CD) Top
Cat TCO3012
DVD title: Gunsmoke Blues

(Joe Turner, vo; Bill Potter, ts; J.D. Nicholson, p; Steve Wachsman, g; Bruce
Sieverson, b-g; Todd Nelson, d.)
same concert
(a)	Hide and Seek	(CD) TopCat TCO3012
(b)	Shake, Rattle and Roll	(CD) Top Cat TCO3012

Both titles on (CD) TKO Magnum Music CDBM 141

JOE TURNER (vo; with unknown p; g; b-g; d)
Los Angeles - c. 1972
(a)	One Hour In Your Garden -1	(LP)	United US-7790
(b)	Front Door In, Back Door Out	(LP)	United US-7790
(c)	Fun In Chicago	(LP)	United US-7790
(d)	Lovely Party	(LP)	United US-7790
(e)	Good Mornin', Miss Patricia	(LP)	United US-7790
(f)	You've Been Squeezin' My Lemons -1	(LP)	United US-7790
(g)	Shout	(LP)	United US-7790
(h)	You're So Damn Mean, Baby -1	(LP)	United US-7790
(I)	Mornin', Noon and Night -1	(LP)	United US-7790

Album title: Still Boss of the Blues.

When 2310-937, *Flip, Flop & Fly*, by Joe Turner, with Count   Basie
and his Orchestra, was released in 1989, the sleeve   notes stated that the
contents were recorded at two concert in Europe in 1972; in Paris on
April 17 and in Frankfurt on April 24. Joe Turner was scheduled to be

part of this "Caravan of Blues" tour but his diabetes was confirmed just prior to its start. As a result he remained in Los Angeles for treatment. It is assumed that the recordings were made in October 1974, when Turner did tour with Basie.

JOE TURNER/COUNT BASIE (Turner, vo; Harry Edison, tp; J.J. Johnson, tb; Eddie Davis, Zoot Sims, ts; Count Basie, p, p&org-1; Irving Ashby, g; Ray Brown, b; Louis Bellson, d).

Los Angeles – December 11, 1973

(a)	The Honeydripper	(LP)	Pablo	2310	709
(b)	Honey Hush	(LP)	Pablo	2310	709
(c)	Cherry Red -1	(LP)	Pablo	2310	709
(d)	Night Time Is The Right Time				
	(To Be With The One You Love)	(LP)	Pablo	2310	709
(e)	Blues Around The Clock	(LP)	Pablo	2310	709
(f)	Since I Fell For You	(LP)	Pablo	2310	709
(g)	Flip, Flop and Fly	(LP)	Pablo	2310	709
(h)	Wee Baby Blues	(LP)	Pablo	2310	709
(i)	Good Mornin' Blues	(LP)	Pablo	2310	709
(j)	Roll 'Em Pete	(LP)	Pablo	2310	709

(a)(d)(h) have accompaniment by Basie and the rhythm section only. (c) omit Johnson. (f) omit Edison & Johnson.. album title: The Bosses

Other issues: all titles on (CD) Original Jazz Classics OJCD-821; b on CD) Rhino R2-71550

DELLA REESE (no details)

Los Angeles – 1973

Trojan   unissued?

This recording is mentioned in *Blues Who's Who*. One possibility is that JoeTurner made a guest appearance on a Della Reese television show which was considered for an LP issue.

THE LAST OF THE BLUE DEVILS (Big Joe Turner, vo; Jay McShann, p; James Whitcomb, b; Paul Gunther, d).

Musicians Foundation Hall, Kansas City - March 20, 1974

(a)	Piney Brown Blues	(DVD)	Eforfilms	2869012
(b)	Shake, Rattle and Roll	(DVD)	Eforfilms	2869012
(c)	Piney Brown Blues	(DVD)	Eforfilms	2869012

Note: (a) also has unknown, g. (b) add tp & as; (c) is *New Kansas City Blues*.

(vo; with Jay McShann Big Band: Arthur Mitchell, Dave Christie, Bill Drybread, Orestus Tucker, tp; Godfrey Powell, R. Powers, Richard Smith, tb, Arthur Jackson, Donald Parsons, John Jackson, Al Zanders, Ben Kynard, reeds; Jay McShann, p; James Whitcomb, b; Paul Gunther, d).

(d)   Roll 'Em, Pete   (DVD)   Eforfilms   2869012

(Turner, vo; Jay McShann, p; James Whitcomb, b; Paul Gunther, d)

(e)   Honey Hush   (DVD)   Eforfilms   2869012
(f)   Rose Garden   (DVD)   Eforfilms   2869012
(g)   Chains of Love   (DVD)   Eforfilms   2869012
(h)   Shake, Rattle and Roll (incomplete) (DVD)   Eforfilms   2869012
Other tracks without Turner feature Count Basie, Jay McShann, etc.
Other issue: all on (DVD) Kino K168

OSCAR PETERSON PRESENTS (Joe Turner, guest, vo; Oscar Peterson, p; Niels Pedersen, b; Louis Bellson, d).

BCTv telecast, Vancouver, Canada - early 1974
(a)   Flip, Flop and Fly   private   tapes   exist
(b)   Wee Baby Blues   private   tapes   exist
(c)   Honey Hush   private   tapes   exist
This series of eight shows premiered on Canadian TV on June 23, 1974.

BIG JOE TURNER (vo; unknown ts; p; g; b; d).

live - early 1974
(a)   I'm On My Way To Denver Blues   (CD) Fuel 302 062 008 8
(b)   Shoo-Shoo Boogie Boo   (CD) Fuel 302 062 008 8

JOE TURNER (vo; Mack Johnson, tp; Gene 'Mighty Flea' Connors, tb; Clifford Solomon, ts, bar; Big Jim Wynn, bar; Johnny Otis, p (except -1), d; Shuggie Otis, p-2, g; Theresa and Alesia Butler, duo vo -2; band vo-3).

Hawk Studios, Los Angeles - c. 1974
(a)   Honey Hush -3   (LP) Blues Spectrum BS-104
(b)   Chains of Love   (LP) Blues Spectrum BS-104
(c)   Shake, Rattle and Roll -3   (LP) Blues Spectrum BS-104
(d)   Corrine Corrina -1, -2   (LP) Blues Spectrum BS-104
(e)   Wee Baby Blues   (LP) Blues Spectrum BS-104

(vo; Johnny Otis, p-5, d; Shuggie Otis, p, g, b-g).

Hawk Studio, Los Angeles - c. 1974
(f)   Roll 'Em Hawk -3   (LP) Blues Spectrum BS-104
(g)   Piney Brown Blues   (LP) Blues Spectrum BS-104
(h)   Cherry Red   (LP) Blues Spectrum BS-104
(i)   Nothin' From Nothin' Blues   (LP) Blues Spectrum BS-104
(j)   T.V. Mama -5   (LP) Blues Spectrum BS-104
(k)   Squeeze Me, Baby   (LP) Blues Spectrum BS-104
Sleeve quotes 1974 as year of recording; record is copyright 1973.

Album title: Big Joe Turner: Great Rhythm & Blues Oldies, Volume 4.
Other issues include: all on (LP) Bulldog BDL1003, Frog BRP2024; and
probably (AC) Jewel JC-5059. all on (LP) Magnum Music MFLP064, (CD)
Magnum Music CDMF098. (f) to (k) on (CD) Tomato R2 71666.

JOE TURNER (vo; Roy Eldridge, tp; Al Grey, tb; Lee Allen, ts; Jimmy
Robins, org, p-1; Thomas Gadson, g; Ray Brown, b; Earl Palmer, d).

MGM Studio, Los Angeles - June 3, 1974

(a)	Plant Your Garden	(LP) Pablo 2310-883
(b)	Kick The Front Door In	(LP) Pablo 2310-883
(c)	So Long	(LP) Pablo 2 310-883
(d)	Morning Glory -1	(LP) Pablo 2310-883
(e)	For Growin' Up	(LP) Pablo 2310-883
(f)	Life Ain't Easy	(LP) Pablo 2310-883

Album title: Life Ain't Easy. *So Long* is credited to Woody Guthrie, should be
to James Brown.
Other issues: all on (CD) Original Jazz Classics OJCCD 809-2.

JOE TURNER (vo; Dizzy Gillespie, Roy Eldridge, Harry Edison, Clark
Terry, tp; Jimmy Robins, p-1, p&org-2; Pee Wee Crayton, g; Charles Norris, b;
Washington Rucker, d).

MGM Studios, Hollywood - September 19, 1974

(a)	Mornin', Noon and Night -1	(LP) Pablo 2310 717
(b)	I Know You Love Me Baby -1 ,-2	(LP) Pablo 2310 717
(c)	T'Aint Nobody's Bizness If I Do -1	(LP) Pablo 2310 717
(d)	T.V. Mama -,1-2	(LP) Pablo 2310 717
(e)	Stormy Monday -1,-2	(LP) Pablo 2310-943

(d) listed as *T.V. Momma* on sleeve.
Album title (2310-717) The Trumpet Kings Meet Joe Turner; (2310-943)
Stormy Monday.
Other issues: all on (CD) Pablo PACD-2310-943-2, Original Jazz Classics
OJCCD497-2

JOE TURNER with COUNT BASIE and his Orchestra (Turner, vo;
Oliver Beener, Franklin 'Lyn' Biviano, Sonny Cohn, Pete Minger, tp; Al Grey,
Lincoln Ross, Mel Wanzo, tb; Bill Hughes, b-tb; Bobby Plater, fl, as; Curtis
Peagler, as; Eddie 'Lockjaw' Davis, Jimmy Forrest, ts; John C. Williams, bar;
Count Basie, p; Freddie Green, g; Bill Davis, b; Skeets Marsh, d).

(a)	Hide and Seek	(LP) Pablo 2310-937
(b)	TV Momma	(LP) Pablo 2310-937
(c)	Corrine, Corinna	(LP) Pablo 2310-937
(d)	Cherry Red	(LP) Pablo 2310-937
(e)	Shake, Rattle and Roll	(LP) Pablo 2310-937
(f)	Since I Fell For You	(LP) Pablo 2310-937
(g)	Flip, Flop and Fly	(LP) Pablo 2310-937
(h)	Everyday I Have The Blues	(LP) Pablo 2310-937
(i)	Good Morning Blues	(LP) Pablo 2310-937

The album sleeve states recorded in Paris and Frankfurt on April 17 and 24, 1972, but Joe Turner, although booked, did not make the tour. The above are assumed details for these titles.

Chris Sheridan's *Count Basie: A Bio-Discography* gives above personnel for the 1974 tour, which lasted from September 28 to October 14. If the above titles came from Paris and Frankfurt, then the dates would be October 4, Salle Pleyel, and October 13, Jahrhunderthalle.

Album title: Flip, Flop and Fly

Other issues: (h) on (LP) Pablo 2310-848; all on (CD) Original Jazz Classics OJC-1053

JOE TURNER (vo; Sonny Stitt, as-1, ts-2; J.D. Nicholson, p; Pee Wee Crayton, g; Charles Norris, b; Washington Rucker, d).

(a)	Stormy Monday	(LP) Pablo 2310 818
(b)	Piney Brown (K.C.)	(LP) Pablo 2310 818
(c)	Martin Luther King Southside -2	(LP) Pablo 2310 818
(d)	Everyday I Have The Blues	(LP) Pablo 2310 818
(e)	Shake, Rattle and Roll -1	(LP) Pablo 2310 818
(f)	Lucille -2	(LP) Pablo 2310 818

Album title: Everyday I Have The Blues. (c) is a reworking of *Miss Brown Blues.*

Other issue: all titles on (LP) Original Jazz Classics OJC-634-2

JOE TURNER (vo; Roy Eldridge, tp; Milt Jackson, vb; J.D. Nicholson, p; Pee Wee Crayton, g; William Walker, b; Charles Randall, d).

(a)	I Want A Little Girl	(LP) Pablo 2310 760
(b)	Nobody In Mind	(LP) Pablo 2310 760
(c)	The Chicken and the Hawk	(LP) Pablo 2310 760
(d)	I Just Didn't Have The Price	(LP) Pablo 2310 760
(e)	How Long, How Long Blues	(LP) Pablo 2310 760
(f)	Crawdad Hole	(LP) Pablo 2310 760

| (g) | Juke Joint Blues | (LP) | Pablo | 2310 | 760 |
| (h) | Red Sails In The Sunset | (LP) | Pablo | 2310 | 760 |

(d)(h) omit Eldridge and Jackson. album title: *Nobody In Mind*
Other issues include: (e) (g) on (LP) Pablo 2310 848 and (CD) Pablo 2405-404. all on (CD) Original Jazz Classics OJC-729-2

JOE TURNER (vo; Bob Smith, as; J.D. Nicholson, p; Pee Wee Crayton, Herman Bennett, g; Winston McGregor, b; Charles Randall, d).

Los Angeles - March 10, 1976

(a)	In The Evening (When the sun goes down)	(LP)	Pablo	2310	776
(b)	Summertime	(LP)	Pablo	2310	776
(c)	Sweet Lorraine	(LP)	Pablo	2310	776
(d)	Too Late, Too Late	(LP)	Pablo	2310	776
(e)	I've Got The World On A String	(LP)	Pablo	2310	776
(f)	Chains of Love	(LP)	Pablo	2310	776
(g)	Corrine, Corrina	(LP)	Pablo	2310	776
(h)	J. T. Blues	(LP)	Pablo	2310	776
(i)	Pennies From Heaven	(LP)	Pablo	2310	776
(j)	Two Loves Have I	(LP)	Pablo	2310	776

Album title: In The Evening. Other issues include: (d)(g)(h) on (LP) Pablo 310 848. All on (CD) Original Jazz Classics OJC-852-2.

JOE TURNER (vo; Jake Porter, tp; Curtis Kirk, hca-1; Curtis Peagler, as, ts-2; Roy Brewster, bar. horn; Sylvester Scott, p; Cal Green, g; Bobby Haynes, b; Washington Rucker, d).

RCA Studios, Los Angeles - May 27, 1976

(a)	I Left My Heart In San Francisco -1,-2	(LP)	Pablo	2310-844
(b)	I Left My Heart In San Francisco (take -3) -1,-2			
		(CD)	OJC	OJCCD-1077-2
(c)	I'm Gonna Sit Right Down and Write Myself A Letter			
		(LP)	Pablo	2310-844
(d)	I'm Gonna Sit Right Down and Write Myself A Letter (take -10)			
		(CD)	OJC	OJCCD-1077-2
(e)	I Can't Give You Anything But Love -1	(LP)	Pablo	2310-844
(f)	I Can't Give You Anything But Love (take -2) -1			
		(CD)	OJC	OJCCD-1077-2
(g)	You're Driving Me Crazy	(LP)	Pablo	2310-844
(h)	You're Driving Me Crazy (take -2)	(CD)	OJC	OJCCD-1077-2
(i)	So Long -1	(LP)	Pablo	2310-844
(j)	After My Laughter Came Tears	(LP)	Pablo	2310-844
(k)	The Midnight Special -1	(LP)	Pablo	2310-844
(l)	Stoop Down Baby -1	(LP)	Pablo	2310-844
(m)	The Things That I Used To Do	(LP)	Pablo	2310-943

Album title: (2310-844) The Midnight Special: (2310-943) Stormy Monday.

Other issues include: all takes on (CD) Original Jazz Classics OJC-1077-2. *So Long* is credited to Woody Guthrie (and even titled *So Long It's Been Good To Know Yuh* on the CD); it is actually *So Long*, by James Brown.

BIG JOE TURNER (vo; Phil Smith, ts; Mark Naftalin, p; Mike Bloomfield, g; Pat Campbell, b; Tom Dolinger, d).

The Palms Cafe, San Francisco - January 20-22, 1977
This three-day engagement was taped and it is believed that these tapes may be the source of some of the myriad titles featuring Mike Bloomfield on LP and CD. Refer to notes after the March 5, 1977 recordings.

JOE TURNER (vo; Blue Mitchell, tp; Eddie Vinson, as; Rashid Ali, Wild Bill Moore, ts; Lloyd Glenn, p; Gildo Mahones, org; Greg Beck, Gary Bell, g; Lawrence Gales, b; Bruno Carr, d).

Sunwest Studios, Hollywood - February 8, 1977

(a)	Things That I Used To Do	(LP)	Pablo	2310	800
(b)	S.K. Blues	(LP)	Pablo	2310	800
(c)	Jelly Jelly Blues	(LP)	Pablo	2310	800
(d)	Hey Little Girl	(LP)	Pablo	2310	800
(e)	Shake It and Break It	(LP)	Pablo	2310	800
(f)	St. Louis Blues	(LP)	Pablo	2310	800
(g)	Oke-She-Moke-She-Pop	(LP)	Pablo	2310	800
(h)	My Train Rolled Up In Texas	(LP)	Pablo	2310	800
(i)	Time After Time	(LP)	Pablo	2310	943

Album titles: (2310 800) Things That I Used To Do; (2310 943) Stormy Monday
Other issues include: (a) (d) on (LP) Pablo 2310 848; (i) on (CD) Pablo 2310-943, Original Jazz Classics OJC-862-2

BIG JOE TURNER (vo: John Stafford, as; Phil Smith, ts; Mark Naftalin, p; Mike Bloomfield, g; Pat Campbell, b; Bob Scott, d; unidentified (perhaps Stafford) cl-1)..

live, The Palms Cafe, San Francisco - March 5, 1977

(a)	The Night Time Is The Right Time (7:19)	(CD)	Rock Beat ROC-3388
(b)	Flip, Flop and Fly (6:15)	(CD)	Rock Beat ROC-3388
(c)	Honey Hush (Hi Ho Silver) (5:54)	(CD)	Rock Beat ROC-3388
(d)	TV Mama (5:14)	(CD)	Rock Beat ROC-3388
(e)	Chains of Love (7:23)	(CD)	Rock Beat ROC-3388
(f)	Corrine, Corrina (5:42)	(CD)	Rock Beat ROC-3388
(g)	I Hear You Knocking -1 (8:03)	(CD)	Rock Beat ROC-3388
(h)	How Long Blues (6:49)	(CD)	Rock Beat ROC-3388
(i)	Give Me An Hour In Your Garden (11:27)	(CD)	Rock Beat ROC-3388
(j)	Shoo Shoo Boogie Boo (7:21)	(CD)	Rock Beat ROC-3388
(k)	Early One Morning (6:22)	(CD)	Rock Beat ROC-3388

(l)   Everyday I Have The Blues (10:00)   (CD) Rock Beat ROC-3388
(m)   medley: I've Got A Pocketful of Pencils /
        I Want My Baby To Write Me (13:14) (CD) Rock Beat ROC-3388
(n)   Ain't Gonna Be Your Low Down Dog (3:31) (CD) Rock Beat ROC-3388
(o)   Stormy Monday Blues (6:29)   (CD) Rock Beat ROC-3388
(p)   When The Sun Goes Down (3:26)   (CD) Rock Beat ROC-3388
(q)   Morning, Noon and Night (3:22)   (CD) Rock Beat ROC-3388
(r)   Hide and Go Seek (4:42)   (CD) Rock Beat ROC-3388
(s)   Shake, Rattle and Roll (3:22)   (CD) Rock Beat ROC-3388
(t)   The Things I Used To Do -1 (9:38) (CD) Rock Beat ROC-3388
(u)   Chicken and the Hawk (4:49)   (CD) Rock Beat ROC-3388
(v)   On My Way To Denver Blues (11:07) (CD) Rock Beat ROC-3388
(w)   Write Me A Letter (5:47)   (CD) Rock Beat ROC-3388

Notes: Tracks (a) to (k) shown as "Set 1" on the first CD; tracks (l) to (w) as "Set 2" on the second.
The Rock Beat 2-CD set is the most comprehensive issue of this material and is used here as the base on which the research is built. For this purpose, it is assumed that the notes are accurate in reference to date of recording and separation into two sets.
On (h), (q), (r) the reed players seem to be absent.
On (c), (i), (j), (k), (l), (m), (p), (v), (w) Stafford may not be present. This might suggest that some of these titles are from the January 1997 engagement.
Album title: Big Joe Turner: San Francisco 1977.

The following titles, not on the Rock Beat CDs, are from either the January or March 1977 engagements:
(x)   Roll 'Em Pete
(y)   Jump For Joy (Roll 'Em Pete)   (rhythm section only)
(z)   Roll Me Baby   (two reed players)
(aa)   Piney Brown Blues   (tenor only?)
(ab)   Cherry Red   (rhythm section only)
Also to be found on Google are audio recordings by Turner and Bloomfield of *Wee Baby Blues* and *I Know You Love Me*.

Refer to Appendix 1 to the Discography which endeavours to identify the other known issues of the material, including the original LPs. It also tries to indicate which titles have been edited.

Turner and Bloomfield played a three-day engagement at The Palms, January 20-22, in addition to two days, March 4-5, in 1977. Apparently all the sessions were recorded, making it difficult to allocate dates, other than that of March 5th. In January the personnel was Phil Smith, ts; Mark Naftalin, p; Mike Bloomfield, g; Pat Campbell, b; Tom Dolinger, d.

(A website names Ben "King" Perkoff as the tenor saxophonist, though this seems unlikely. The Perkoff band was advertised to accompany Turner at The Palms for an engagement on July 15/16, 1977) [www.thediscography.dk/vinyl/bloomfield]

BIG JOE TURNER and the Bill Dicey-Robert Ross Band (vo; Bill Dicey, hca; Lloyd Glenn, p; Robert Ross, g; Danny Counts, b-g; Kenny Covell, d; Washboard Doc, wbd; Brenda Bell, vo-1)

City Studio, New York City - March 18, 1977

(a)	I'm Gonna Sit Right Down and Write Myself A Letter	(LP) Spivey LP-1020
(b)	Let Me Be Your Dog	(LP) Spivey LP-1020
(c)	T'Ain't Nobody's Biz-ness If I Do -1	(LP) Spivey LP-1020
(d)	Red Sails In The Sunset -1	(LP) Spivey LP-1020
(e)	Boss of the House	(LP) Spivey LP-1020
(f)	Little Birdie Tweet-Tweet-Tweet	(LP) Spivey LP-1020

All titles are first takes, except (d) which is one of four. Unissued titles include one other duet with Brenda Bell.
Album title: I'm Gonna Sit Right Down and Write Myself A Letter.

BIG JOE TURNER (vo; unknown p; org-1; 2 g; b-g; d).

Los Angeles - February 1978

(a)	Jelly On My Mind	(LP) Big Town BT-1007
(b)	Bring It On Home (parts 1 & 2)	(LP) Big Town BT-1007
(c)	S.K. Blues -1	(LP) Big Town BT-1007
(d)	Get Me A Rockin' Chair	(LP) Big Town BT-1007
(e)	Yack Yack This and That	(LP) Big Town BT-1007
(f)	Flying All Day -1	(LP) Big Town BT-1007
(g)	Hanging On The Wall	(LP) Big Town BT-1007
(h)	Rolling In To Your Big Town	(LP) Big Town BT-1007

Album title: Big Joe Turner: Really The Blues
Other issues: (a) as *Jelly, Jelly* and (g) on (45) Kickback 101; (b) on (45) Big Town BT722 parts 1 & 2, as *Bring It On Home, Corina*. (a)(b) on (EP) Ripete REP-1025. (e)(h) on (45) Topflight T-107

BIG JOE TURNER: AXEL ZWINGENBERGER (vo; Axel Zwingenberger, p; Torsten Zwingenberger, d).

Hawk Sound Studios, Los Angeles - May 22, 1978

(a)	Roll 'Em Boy	(LP) Telefunken 6.23624
(b)	New Goin' Away Blues	(LP) Telefunken 6.23624
(c)	In The Evening	(LP) Telefunken 6.23624
(d)	Corrine Corrina Boogie	(LP) Telefunken 6.23624
(e)	Rock The Joint Boogie	(LP) Telefunken 6.23624
(f)	John's and Louis' Blues	(LP) Telefunken 6.23624
(g)	Jelly Jelly Blues	(LP) Telefunken 6.23624

(h)	(Sit Down) On Your Daddy's Knee	(LP) Telefunken 6.23624
(i)	The Chicken and the Hawk Boogie	(LP) Telefunken 6.23624
(j)	Low Down Dog	(LP) Telefunken 6.23624
(k)	Crawdad Hole	(LP/CD) Vanguard 8.885005

Album title: Let's Boogie Woogie All Night Long. There are two piano solo tracks on the album. other issues: all on (LP/CD) Vanguard 8.85005

JOE TURNER (vo; Joe Banks, tp; Bobby Smith, as; Bill Clark, Hollis Gilmore, ts; Lloyd Glenn, p; Evans Walker, Pee Wee Crayton, g; Bill Walker, b; Charles Randall, d; Frederick Woods, cga).

Group IV Studios, Hollywood – June 22, 1978

(a)	Rocks In My Bed	(LP) Pablo 2310-863
(b)	So Long	(LP) Pablo 2310-863
(c)	Howlin' Wind	(LP) Pablo 2310-863
(d)	Woman You Must Be Crazy	(LP) Pablo 2310-863
(e)	How Come My Dog Don't Bark	(LP) Pablo 2310-863
(f)	Long Way From Home	(LP) Pablo 2310-943
(g)	Somebody Loves Me	(LP) Pablo 2310-943
(h)	Love Is Like A Faucet	(LP) Pablo 2310-943

Album title: Have No Fear, Big Joe Is Here.
(b) *So Long* is incorrectly credited to Woody Guthrie, it is the James Brown composition.
Other issues: all on (CD) Pablo PACD-2310-943-2. Pablo 2310-863 also on (CD) Original Jazz Classics OJC-905-2

COUNT BASIE, JOE TURNER, EDDIE "CLEANHEAD" VINSON
(Joe Turner, vo; Eddie Vinson, as, vo; Count Basie and his Orchestra: Pete Minger, Sonny Cohn, Dale Carley, David Stahl, tp; Mitchell 'Bootie' Wood, Bill Hughes, Dennis Wilson, Grover Mitchell, Dennis Rowland, tb; Eric Dixon, Bobby Plater, Danny Turner, Kenny Hing, John Williams, reeds; Count Basie, p; Freddie Green, g; Cleveland Eaton, b; Duffy Jackson, d; Ernie Wilkins, arr).

Group IV Studios, Hollywood – April 7/8, 1980

(a)	Blues For Joe Turner vJT	(LP) Pablo D2310.859
(b)	Everyday I Have The Blues vJT, aEW	(LP) Pablo D2310.859
(c)	Stormy Monday vJT	(LP) Pablo D2310.859

(b)(c) Eddie Vinson added on alto. other tracks have Eddie Vinson vocals or are instrumentals.
Album title: Kansas City Shout.
Other issues: all on (CD) Pablo 2310 943, 3112-52

JOE TURNER (vo; Axel Zwingenberger, p).

6121 Cimarron Street, Los Angeles - May 23, 1981

(a)	Chains of Love	(LP) Telefunken 6.28572
(b)	Flip Flop and Fly	(LP) Telefunken 6.28572
(c)	Piney Brown Blues	(LP) Telefunken 6.28572
(d)	Wee Baby Blues	(LP) Telefunken 6.28572
(e)	Backyard Boogie	(LP) Telefunken 6.28572

(add Roy Milton, d)

same session

(f)	Hide and Seek Boogie	(LP) Telefunken 6.28572
(g)	Cherry Red	(LP) Telefunken 6.28572
(h)	St. Louis Blues	(LP) Telefunken 6.28572
(i)	Boogie Woogie 'Round The Clock	(LP) Telefunken 6.28572
(j)	Back Door Getaway (version 1)	(LP) Telefunken 6.28572
(k)	Back Door Getaway (version 2)	(LP) Telefunken 6.28572
(l)	Cimarron St. Breakdown	(LP) Telefunken 6.28572

(add Eddie 'Cleanhead' Vinson, vo; Margie Evans, vo, Roy Milton, vo)

same session

(m)	Boogie Woogie Jubilee	(LP) Telefunken 6.28572

Album title: Boogie Woogie Jubilee.
Other issue: all titles, except (d), on (LP/CD) Vagabond VRCD-8.81010.

ROOMFUL OF BLUES (Bob Enos, tp; Porky Cohen, tb; Rich Lataille, as; Greg Piccolo, ts, leader; Doug James, bar; Al Copley, p; Ronnie Earl Horvath, g; Jimmy Wimpfheimer, b; John Rossi, d; Joe Turner vo).

live, Lupo's Heartbreak Hotel, Providence, R.I. - July 22, 1982

	Shake, Rattle and Roll	vJT (CD) Rounder 1166-11589-2

Turner is not present on the other titles on this CD.
CD title: The Blues'll Make You Happy, Too.

BIG JOE TURNER & ROOMFUL OF BLUES (personnel as for July 22, 1982, except Preston Hubbard, b; replaces Wimpfheimer; Dr. John, p; replaces Copley on (e))

JAC Studio, New York City - January 26, 1983

(a)	Crawdad Hole	(LP) Muse MR-5293
(b)	Red Sails In The Sunset	(LP) Muse MR-5293
(c)	Cocka-Doodle Doo	(LP) Muse MR-5293
(d)	Jumpin' For Joe (non-vocal)	(LP) Muse MR-5293
(e)	I Want A Little Girl	(LP) Muse MR-5293
(f)	Blues Train	(LP) Muse MR-5293
(g)	I Know You Love Me	(LP) Muse MR-5293
(h)	Last Night (non-vocal)	(LP) Muse MR-5293

(i)   I Love The Way My Baby Sings The Blues   (LP) Muse MR-5293
There are no unissued titles from this session.
Album title: Blues Train
Other issues: all on (CD) Muse MCD-5293, 32 Blues 32015; (a) on (CD)
Rhino R2-71550

BIG JOE TURNER (vo; with Knocky Parker and the Houserockers: Eddie
Chamblee, as-1, ts; Knocky Parker, p; Jim Lawyer, g; David Ostwald, tu, bsax-2;
Fred Stoll, d).

Dreamland Studios, New York City - May 18, 1983

(a)	You Mighty Beautiful	(LP) Southland SLP-13
(b)	Be With The One You Love	(LP) Southland SLP-13
(c)	Doggin' The Dog	(LP) Southland SLP-13
(d)	Seventy-Two -1	(LP) Southland SLP-13
(e)	Careless Love	(LP) Southland SLP-13
(f)	Corrine Corrina	(LP) Southland SLP-13
(g)	One Hour In Your Garden -1	(LP) Southland SLP-13
(h)	Woke Up This Morning	(LP) Southland SLP-13
(i)	Everyday -1, -2	(LP) Southland SLP-13
(j)	St. Louis Blues	(LP) Southand SLP-13

There are no unissued titles from this session. Changes to titles include; (a)
is *Roll 'Em*, Pete; (b) *The Night Time Is The Right Time*; (c) *Low Down Dog*.
album title: Big Joe Turner with Knocky Parker and the Houserockers.

BIG JOE TURNER and THE BLASTERS (Lee Allen, ts; Steve Berlin,
sax, kbd; Gene Taylor, p; Dave Alvin, g; Phil Alvin, g, vo; John Bazz, b; Bill
Bateman, d).

Club Lingerie, Los Angeles - October 15, 1983

(a)	Hide and Seek	
(b)	Jump For Joy	
(c)	Crawdad Hole	
(d)	Honey Hush	This is a CD issue, but probably
(e)	Chains of Love	a private one, not commercial.
(f)	Flip, Flop and Fly	Quoted as an example of Turner's
(g)	Morning, Noon and Night	appearances with The Blasters.
(h)	Rock Me, Baby	These titles may still be
(i)	Roll 'Em Pete	heard on YouTube.
(j)	Chicken and the Hawk	
(k)	Do That One More Time	

BIG JOE TURNER (vo; Lee Allen, ts ; Steve Berlin, bar; Gene Taylor, p; Johnny Taylor, g; Dennis Riggs, d).

live, The Music Machine, Santa Monica, CA – October 27, 1983

(a)	Hide and Seek	(CD)	Rock Beat Roc-CD-3198
(b)	Corrine, Corrina	(CD)	Rock Beat Roc-CD-3198
(c)	Chains of Love	(CD)	Rock Beat Roc-CD-3198
(d)	Honey Hush	(CD)	Rock Beat Roc-CD-3198
(e)	Shake, Rattle and Roll	(CD)	Rock Beat Roc-CD-3198
(f)	Early One Morning	(CD)	Rock Beat Roc-CD-3198
(g)	Roll 'Em Pete	(CD)	Rock Beat Roc-CD-3198
(h)	Around The Clock Blues	(CD)	Rock Beat Roc-CD-3198

The CD also contains two titles by Eddie 'Cleanhead' Vinson and two by the Lee Allen band. The last track is *Walkin' With Mr. Lee* by the Allen band, which is followed by an unlisted *Well Oh Well* by Joe Turner, from Mexico, January 1966, qv.
Other issues: all titles, including *Well Oh Well*, on (CD) Retroworld FLOATM6212. CD title: Big Joe Turner: Live 1983.

JOE TURNER (vo; Ike Williams, tp; Jerry Jumonville, as, bar; Lee Allen, ts; Bobby Blevins, p; Alvin Robinson, Terry Evans, g; Rudy Brown, bg; Al Dunkin, d).

Ocean Way Studios, Hollywood - February 14, 1984

(a)	Down Home Blues	(LP) Pablo 2310 904
(b)	Call The Plumber	(LP) Pablo 2310 904
(c)	Since I Fell For You	(LP) Pablo 2310 904
(d)	Kansas City Here I Come	(LP) Pablo 2310 904
(e)	Big-Legged Woman	(LP) Pablo 2310 904
(f)	Sweet Sixteen	(LP) Pablo 2310 904
(g)	Time After Time	(LP) Pablo 2310 904

Album title: Kansas City Here I Come. (e) as *Big Leg Woman* on sleeve.
Other issues: all on (CD) Original Jazz Classics OJC-743-2

PEE WEE CRAYTON featuring Big Joe Turner (Pee Wee Crayton Blues Orchestra: Rod Piazza, hca; Pee Wee Crayton, g; unknown ts p, b-g, d; Joe Turner, vo).

Long Beach Blues Festival, CA, September 15, 1984

(a)	Good Thing
(b)	CC Rider
(c)	Are You Ready
(d)	Call the Plumber

A 2022 CD issue, compiled by The Bootlegger. Label perhaps Good Thing. Titles can be heard on YouTube.

JOE TURNER meets JIMMY WITHERSPOON (Turner, vo; Witherspoon, vo-1; Ike Williams, tp; Red Holloway, as; Lee Allen, ts; Jerry Jumonville, bar; Bobby Blevins, kbd; Gary Bell, g; Rudy Brown, b; Al Dunkin, d).

Group IV Studios, Hollywood, April 11, 1985

(a)	Patcha, Patcha	-1	(LP) Pablo 2310-913
(b)	Blues Lament	-1	(LP) Pablo 2310-913
(c)	Kansas City On My Mind		(LP) Pablo 2310-913
(d)	J.T.'s Blues		(LP) Pablo 2310-913

Other titles are by Jimmy Witherspoon. Drummer is named as Al Duncan on the sleeve.
Album title: Patcha, Patcha, All Night Long.
Other issues: all on (CD) Original Jazz Classics OJCCD-887-2

BIG JOE TURNER with Barney McClure Quartet (Turner, vo; McClure, p; Dave Peterson, g; Chuck Deardorf, b; Dean Hodges, d, plus Joe Houston, ts-1, vo).

concert, Mount Baker Theater, Bellingham, Washington May 8, 1985

(a)	Hide and Seek	-1	(CD) BMP Records (no number)
(b)	Call The Plumber	-1	(CD) BMP Records (no number)
(c)	Sweet Little Angel	vJH,BJT	(CD) BMP Records (no number)
(d)	Kansas City	-1	(CD) BMP Records (no number)
(e)	Corrine, Corrina		(CD) BMP Records (no number)

Oh Boy, credited to Joe Turner, is by Joe Houston. *Hide and Seek* is not in the track listing and, as a result, the remaining Turner titles are wrongly named. The above has the correct titles.
Corrine, Corrina appears as an unlisted track 14.
The BMP CD was privately issued by Barney McClure. It also has tracks by Joe Houston and by Eddie 'Cleanhead' Vinson.
Other issues: (b)(d) on (CD) Sunset Boulevard SBR-7009.

****

Record release for which information is missing:

Joe Turner:
Can't Read, Can't Write/No, You Can't Come Back   (45) 4 Sale 150

****

Discography Appendix 1 – Recordings with Mike Bloomfield

from The Palms Cafe, San Francisco. Long-play and CD issues of the January and March 1977 recordings

1.	Rock Beat ROC-3388 (CD)	("San Francisco 1977")
2.	Fuel 302 062 008 8 (CD)	("Night Time Is The Right Time")
3.	Blues Cafe 382 5222 (CD)	("Stormy Monday")
4.	Pilz 449319-2 (CD)	("Live: Shake, Rattle and Roll")
5.	Elap 16234 (CD	("Every Day I Have The Blues")
6.	Super Doubles SD886362 (CD)	("Blues Anthology")
7.	Pilz 449300-2 (CD)	("Blues Summit: Percy Mayfield")
8.	Cleo 0018983 (LP & AC)	("Every Day I Have The Blues")
9.	Cleo 0019983 (LP & AC)	("Rock This Joint")
10.	Intermedia QS-5030 (LP)	("Boss Blues")
11.	Intermedia QS-5026 (LP)	("The Very Best of Joe Turner")
12.	Intermedia QS-5036 (LP)	("Every Day I Have The Blues")
13.	Success 16234 (CD)	("Every Day I Have The Blues")
14.	Rajon RJSUC 16234 (CD)	("Every Day I Have The Blues")
15.	Time Music TM1026 (CD)	("Blues" anthology)
16.	Tomato R2 71666 (CD)	("Shake, Rattle and Roll")
17.	Blue Dog KRB5104-1 (CD)	("Live in Concert")
18.	P-Vine PCD-908 (CD)	("Live!") (not audited)
19.	Aim 0013 (CD)	(Shake, Rattle and Roll) (not audited)
20.	Magnum Music MFM 22 (LP)	("Rock This Joint") (not audited)
21.	Intermedia QS-5043 (LP)	("Roll Me Baby") (not audited)
22.	Intermedia QS-5008 (LP)	("Rock This Joint") (not audited)
23.	SRI Jazz 312142 (CD)	(not audited)

The Night Time Is The Right Time (7:19)	1, 2, 5, 10, 13, 14, 16, 17, 18
Flip, Flop and Fly (6:15)	1, 8, 18, 19, 21
Honey Hush (Hi Ho Silver) (5:54)	1, 8, 18, 19, 21
TV Mama (5:14)	1, 2, 7. 8, 18, 19, 21
Chains of Love (7:23)	1, 2, 3, 4, 6, 11, 17, 18
Corrine, Corrina (5:42)	1, 2, 3, 4, 11, 17, 18
I Hear You Knocking (8:03)	1, 3, 4, 11, 16
How Long Blues (6:49)	1, 3, 5, 9, 13, 14, 16, 19, 20, 22
Give Me An Hour In Your Garden (11:27)	1, 3, 4, 11, 18
Shoo Shoo Boogie Boo (7:21)	1, 5, 10, 13, 14, 16, 18
Early One Morning (6:22)	1, 2, 5, 8, 12, 13, 14, 17
Everyday I Have The Blues (10:00)	1, 5, 8, 12, 13, 14
medley: I've Got A Pocketful of Pencils	

/I Want My Baby To Write Me (13:14)	1, 3, 5, 8, 12, 13, 14
Ain't Gonna Be Your Low Down Dog (3:31)	1, 2, 9, 19, 20, 21, 22
Stormy Monday Blues (6:29)	1, 3, 5, 9, 13, 14, 19, 20, 22
When The Sun Goes Down (4:20)	1, 3, 5, 9, 13, 14, 19, 20, 22
Morning, Noon and Night (3:23)	1, 2, 9, 15, 17, 19, 20, 22
Hide and Go Seek (4:42)	1,2,5,9,13,14,17,19,20,22
Shake, Rattle and Roll (7:20)	1,2,4,5,9,11,13,14,17,19,20,22
The Things I Used To Do (9:38)	1, 6, 10, 16
Chicken and the Hawk (4:49)	1, 2, 8, 19, 21
On My Way To Denver Blues (11:07)	1, 10
Write Me A Letter (5:47)	1, 8, 12
Roll 'Em Pete (3:58)	2, 3, 5, 9, 13, 14, 19, 20, 22
Jump For Joy (Roll 'Em Pete) (3:21)	17
Roll Me Baby (8:04)	7, 9, 20, 21, 22
Piney Brown Blues (3:45)	16
Cherry Red (3:03)	16

Notes:

The timings shown in brackets after each title above are, with one exception*, for the unedited versions. The edited tracks are:
The Night Time Is The Right Time (2:35) on Fuel   (track faded out)
Chains of Love (2:58) on Fuel (intro is deleted and track is cut short by four minutes)
How Long Blues (3:26) on Elap, Blues Cafe (faded out during guitar solo, losing over 3 minutes)
The Things I Used To Do (8:04) on Tomato (clarinet solo cut by 37 seconds; guitar solo by 42)
Morning, Noon and Night (3:02) on Rock Beat, Fuel, Cleo. (track faded out, short 3 minutes)
Roll 'Em, Pete (3:31) on Elap, Rajon, Success, Blues Cafe and (3:21) Blue Dog, as *Jump For Joy*.
(guitar solo shortened by 40 seconds, eliminating microphone feedback. The track is not faded out as it is on Cleo and Fuel)

When The Sun Goes Down is the exception, as both versions heard have been edited. The one (3:26) on Rock Beat and Cleo has the tenor solo deleted, but the (4:26) version on Blues Cafe is missing the guitar solo.

Shake, Rattle and Roll:
Three versions have been released. One is timed at 7:22 (Intermedia QS-5026, Pilz) and a second has been edited (with the tenor solo heavily redacted) to 5:26 (Elap, Blue Dog, Success, Rajon). The third (Rock Beat, Fuel and Cleo), timed at 3:33, with no tenor sax, is a different version, suggesting it may be from the January sessions.

On Magnum Music MMF22, *Stormy Monday Blues* is printed as *Storing Monday Blues*.

On Cleo CL0018983, *T.V. Mama* is given on sleeve; *T.V. Mamma* on the label. Reference the Intermedia QS releases, *Intermedia* is printed on the labels and front of the sleeves; *Quicksilver* is printed on the back of the sleeves. Much of the material from The Palms first appeared on *Intermedia*.

www.the discographer.dk/bloomfield has a Mike Bloomfield discography by Réne Aagaard. It suggests Ben 'King' Perkoff as tenor player for these titles. This seems unlikely, though Perkoff's band was scheduled to accompany Joe Turner for a two-day engagement at The Palms in July 1977.

With the exception of the unidentified clarinet soloist on *The Things I Used To Do*, Phil Smith on tenor saxophone is the primary front-line soloist. John Stafford's role is, apparently, limited to harmonising with Smith in the ensembles, though he is hard to discern on some tracks. As noted, several numbers have accompaniment by the rhythm section only, though it is difficult to be certain with all the musicians playing fortissimo. It has been stated that a clarinet can be heard also on *Shake, Rattle and Roll, Morning Noon and Night* and *I Hear You Knocking,*

The Elap, Success and Rajon CDs contain the same tracks, have the same catalogue number and the same CD title, "Every Day I Have The Blues". Elap and Success use same insert design and colour, and minimal notes. Elap has no notes, with a different cover photograph on a brighter colour insert.

A Blues Boulevard CD advertised on the Amazon website contains tracks (b) (d)(e)(g)(h)(i)(n)(o)(p)(q)(r)(s)(u)(x). (x) *Roll 'Em Pete* is timed at 4:00. Notes state recorded at The Palms on March 5, 1977. Release number is unknown.

Discography Appendix 2 - Record Labels with Country of Origin (other than U.S.A,)

Ace (UK)

Acrobat (UK)
Affinity (UK)
Amiga (German)
Avid (UK)

Bear Family (German)
Bellaphon (German)
Black and Blue (France)
Black Lion (UK)
Blue Jazz (France)
Blue Moon (Spain)
Bulldog (UK)

Charly (UK)
Classics (France)
Cleo (Holland)
Curcio (Italy)

Denon (Japan)

Europa Jazz (Italy)

Fabulous (UK)
Fontana (UK & Germany))
Fresh Sounds (Spain)
Frog (Italy)

Giganti del Jazz (Italy)

Hip Shakin' (UK)

Jackson (France)
Jasmine (UK)
Jazz Connoisseur Cassettes (UK)
JSP (UK)
Juke Box Lil (Sweden)

Intermedia (USA)

KC (France)

London (UK)

Magnum Music (UK)
Magpie (UK)
Masters of Jazz (France)

Neatwork (France)

Official (Denmark)
Orfeon (Mexico)

Philips (UK)
Phontastic (Sweden)

Rajon (Australia)
RCA (UK)
RCA Bluebird (Germany)
Retro-World (UK)

Scout (Germany)
Sequel (UK)
Stateside (UK)
Storyville (Denmark)
Success (UK)
Swing House (UK)
Swingtime (Italy)

Telefunken (German)

Vagabond (German)
Vanguard (German)
Vogue (France)

Wolf (Germany)

Discography Appendix 3 – Atlantic Reissues

A selective listing of long-play and compact disc releases of Atlantic 78 rpm and 45 rpm recordings.

A600 (LP) Atlantic 8033, London HA-E2231, Charly CRB1070; (CD) Rhino R2-71550, JSP 7709E, Jasmine JASMCD3032, Sequel RSACD809, Proper P1456, Acrobat ADDCD375

A601 (LP) Atlantic 8033, London HA-E2231; (CD) Atlantic 781752-2, JSP 7709E, Jasmine JASMCD3032, Sequel RSACD809, Proper P1456, Acrobat ADDCD3275

A602 (LP) Atlantic 8033, London HA-E2231, Charly CRB1070; (CD) Atlantic 781752-2, Rhino R2-71550, JSP 7709E, Jasmine JASMCD3032, Sequel RSACD809, Proper P1456, Acrobat ADDCD3275

A603 (EP) Atlantic 536; (LP) Atlantic 8005; (CD) Atlantic 781752-2, Rhino R2 71550, Charly CBMCD011, JSP 7709E, Jasmine JASMCD3032, Sequel RSCACD809, Proper P1456, Acrobat ADDCD3275

A786 (Alt) (LP) Atlantic 8023, London HA-E2231; (CD) Atlantic 781752-2, JSP 7709E, Jasmine JASMCD3032, Sequel RSACD809, Proper P1456, Acrobat ADDCD3275

A787 LP) Atlantic 8005; (CD) Atlantix 781752-2, Rhino R2-71550, Charly CBMCD011, JSP 7709E, Jasmine JASMCD3032, Sequel RSACD809, Proper P1456, Acrobat ADDCD3275

A789 (LP) Atlantic 8033, London HA-E2231; (CD) Rhino R2-71550, JSP 7709E, Jasmine JASMCD3032, Proper P1456, Acrobat ADDCD3275

A790 (LP) Atlantic 8033, London HA-E2231; (CD) JSP 7709E, Jasmine JASMCD3032, Proper P1456, Acrobat ADDCD3275

A906 (LP) Atlantic 8023, London HA-E2173; (CD) Rhino R2-71550, Charly CBMCD011, JSP 7709E, Jasmine JASMCD3032, Proper P1456, Acrobat ADDCD3275

A907 (LP) Atlantic 8033, London HA-E2231; (CD) Atlantic 781752, JSP 7709E, Jasmine JASMCD3032, Sequel RSACD809, Proper P1456, Acrobat ADDCD3275

A1072 (LP) Charly CRB1070; (CD) Real Gone Music RGMCD200 , Prism PLATCD1349

A1073 (EP) Atlantic 606; (LP) Atlantic 8005, Charly CRB1070; (CD) Atlantic 781752-2, Rhino R2-71550, Charly CBMCD011, Jasmine JASMCD3032, Sequel RSACD809, Proper P1456, Acrobat ADDCD3275

A1074 (EP) Atlantic 536; (LP) Atlantic 8005; (CD) Atlantic 781752-2, Rhino R2-71550, Charly CBMCD011, Jasmine JASMCD3032,

Sequel RSACD809, Proper P1456, Acrobat ADDCD3275

A1126   (LP) Atlantic 8033, 81663-1, London HA-E2231, Charly CRB1070; (CD) Rhino R2-1550, Jasmine JASMCD3032, Acrobat ADDCD3275, Real Gone Music RGMCD200

A1127   (LP) Atlantic 8005; (CD) Atlantic 781752-2, Rhino R2-71550, Charly CBMCD011, Jasmine JASMCD3032, Proper P1456, Sequel RASCD809, Big Three 3136, Sequel SACD809, Proper P1456, Acrobat ADDCD3275

A1128   (EP) Atlantic 536; (LP) Atlantic 8023, 81663-1, London HA-E2173, Charly CRB1070; (CD) Rhino R2-71550, Charly CBMCD011, Jasmine JASMCD3032, Proper P1456, Acrobat ADDCD3275

A1209   (EP) Atlantic 565; (LP) Atlantic 8005, Charly CRB1070; (CD) Atlantic 781752-2, Rhino R2-71550, Charly CDMCD011, Jasmine JASMCD011, Sequel RSACD809, Proper P1456, Acrobat ADDCD3275

A1211   (EP) Atlantic 565; (LP) Atlantic 81663-1, Charly CRB1070; (CD) Rhino R2-71550, Proper P1456

A1212   (LP) Atlantic 8005, Charly CRB1070; (CD) Atlantic 781752-2, Rhino R2-71550, Charly CBMCD011, Sequel RSACD809, Proper P1456, Acrobat ADDCD3275

A1220   (LP) Atlantic 8023, 81663-1, London HA-E 2173; (CD) Rhino R2-71550, Charly CBMCD011, Jasmine JASMCD3032, Proper P1456, Acrobat ADDCD3275

A1225   (LP) Atlantic 8033, 81663-1, London HA-E2231; (CD) Rhino R2-71550, Jasmine JASMCD3032, Proper P1456, Acrobat ADDCD3275

A1226   (LP) Atlantic 8033, 81663-1, London HA-E2231; (CD) Rhino R2-71550, Jasmine JASMCD3032, Proper P1456, Acrobat ADDCD3275

A1424   (LP) Atlantic 8023, 81663-1, London HA-E2173, Charly CRB1070; (CD) Rhino R2-71550, Charly CD CD011, Jasmine JASMCD3032, Acrobat ADDCD3275

A1425   (EP) Atlantic 586; (LP) Atlantic 8005, Charly CRB1070; (CD) Charly CBMCD011, Jasmine JASMCD3032, Proper P1456, Acrobat ADDCD3275

A1427   (EP) Atlantic 565; (LP) Atlantic 8005, Charly CRB1070; (CD) Atlantic 781752-2, Rhino R2-71550, Charly CBMCD011, Jasmine JASMCD3032, Proper P1456, Acrobat ADDCD3275

A1687   (EP) Atlantic 586; (LP) Charly CRB1070; (CD) Atlantic 781752-2, Rhino R2-71550, Charly CBMCD011, Jasmine JASMCD3032, Sequel RSACD809, Acrobat ADDCD3275

A1688*   (EP) Atlantic 606; (LP) Charly CRB1070; (CD) Atlantic 781752-2, Rhino R2-71550, Charly CBMCD011, Jasmine JASMCD3032, Real Gone Music RGMCD200 Sequel RSACD809,

Acrobat ADDCD3275

A1884   (EP) Atlantic 586; (LP) Atlantic 8005; (CD) Atlantic 781752-2, Rhino R2-71550, Charly CBMCD011, Jasmine JASMCD3032, Sequel RSACD809, Acrobat ADDCD3275

A1885   (LP) Atlantic 8023, 81663-1, London HA-E2173, Charly CRB1070; (CD) Rhino R2-71550, Charly CBMCD011, Jasmine JASMCD3032, Acrobat ADDCD3275

A1886   (LP) Atlantic 8033, 81663-1, London HA-E2231; (CD) Rhino R2-71550, Jasmine JASMCD3032, Acrobat ADDCD3275

A2219   (LP) Atlantic 8023, 81663-1, London HA-E2173; (CD) Charly CBMCD011, Jasmine JASMCD3032, Acrobat ADDCD3275

A2220   (EP) Atlantic 606; (LP) Atlantic 8005; (CD) Atlantic 781752-2, Charly CBMCD011, Jasmine JASMCD3032, Sequel RSACD809, Acrobat ADDCD3275

A2221   (LP) Atlantic 8023, London HA-E2173; (CD) Atlantic 781752-2, Charly CBMCD011, Jasmine JASMCD3032, Sequel RSACD809, Acrobat ADDCD3275

A2223   (EP) Atlantic 586; (LP) Atlantic 8005; (CD) Charly CBMCD011, Jasmine JASMCD3032, Sequel RSACD809, Acrobat ADDCD3275

A2533   (LP) Atlantic 8023, 81663-1, London HA-E2173; (CD) Charly CBMCD011, Jasmine JASMCD3032, Acrobat ADDCD3275

A2535   (LP) Atlantic 8023, 81663-1, London HA-E2173; (CD) Charly CBMCD011, Jasmine JASMCD3032, Acrobat ADDCD3275

A2536   (LP) Atlantic 8023, 81663-1, London HA-E2173; (CD) Rhino R2-71550, Charly CBMCD011, Jasmine JASMCD3032, Acrobat ADDCD3275

A2537   (LP) Atlantic 8023, 81663-1, London HA-E2173; (CD) Charly CBMCD011, Jasmine JASMCD3032, Acrobat ADDCD3275

A2802   (LP) Atlantic 8023, 81663-1, London HA-E2173; (CD) Rhino R2-71550, Charly CBMCD011, Jasmine JASMCD3032 Acrobat ADDCD3275

A2803   (LP) Atlantic 8033, 81663-1, London HA-E2231; CD) Jasmine JASMCD3032, Acrobat ADDCD3275

A2927   (CD) Atlantic 81663-1, Jasmine JASMCD3032, Real Gone Music RGMCD200, Acrobat ADDCD3275

A2930   (LP) Atlantic 8023, 81663-1, London HA-E2173, Charly CRB1070; (CD) Rhino R2-71550, Charly CBMCD011, Jasmine JASMCD3032, Acrobat ADDCD3275

A2931   (LP) Atlantic 8023, London HA-E2173; (CD) Charly CBMCD011, Jasmine JASMCD3032, Sequel RSACD809, Acrobat ADDCD3275

A3554   (LP) Atlantic 81663-1; (CD) Jasmine JASMCD3032, Acrobat ADDCD3276

A3555   (LP) Atlantic 81663-1; (CD) Jasmine JASMCD3032, Acrobat ADDCD3275

A3556   (LP) Atlantic 81663-1; (CD) Jasmine JASMCD3032, Acrobat
        ADDCD3275
A3809   (LP) Atlantic 81663-1; (CD) Jasmine JASMCD3032, Acrobat
        ADDCD3275
A3810   (LP) Atlantic 81663-1; (CD) Rhino R2-71550, Jasmine
        JASMCD3032, Acrobat ADDCD3275
A3811   (LP) Atlantic 81663-1; (CD) Jasmine JASMCD3032, Acrobat
        ADDCD3275
A3812   (LP) Atlantic 81663-1; (CD) Jasmine JASMCD3032, Acrobat
        ADDCD3275

Bibliography

Articles

Mary Katherine Aldin, "Hey cousin, how you doin'?", *Blues & Rhythm* 18, April 1986, originally published in the *Los Angeles Reader*.

James Austin, "Conversations with a Legend, Big Joe Turner," *Goldmine*, No. 78, November 1982.

George M. Avakian, "Backdrop to Jazz, No. 6, The Cafe", *Jazz Notes* (Australian), No.54, July 1945

Bruce Baker, article/interview with Joe Turner, "Been to Kansas City - -," *Jazz Quarterly*, Summer 1945

Whitney Balliett, *"Majesty"*, *The New Yorker, November 29, 1976* (reprinted in *American Singers)*

Bart Becker, *interview with Jay McShann, Cadence, August 1979*

Ernest Borneman, *"A picture of those 'bootleg' years," Melody Maker, October 6, 1951* (quoting extensively from "Joe Turner, as told to Inez Cavanaugh," qv.)

Fred Broekman, "Big Joe Turner, Boss of the Blues", *Revival (Dutch)*, No. 7, July, No. 8, August 1983

Frank London Brown, "Boss of the Blues, from Kansas City to Copenhagen," *Down Beat*, December 11, 1958

Tony Burke & Dave Penny, "Big Joe Turner: Have No Fear, Big Joe Is Here," (part 1), Blues & Rhythm, No. 11 (July 1985), (part 2), *Blues & Rhythm* No. 12 (September 1985)

Tony Burke & Dave Penny, "In Search of Gene Norman," Blues & Rhythm No. 15 (December 1985)

Ulf Carlsson, "Big Joe Turner," *Jefferson (Swedish)* 60, 1983

Benjamin Cauthra, "Duke Ellington's *Jump For Joy* And The Fight For Equality in Wartime Los Angeles," *Southern California Quarterly*, Vol. 98, No. 1, Spring 2016

Paul Clinco, "Joe Turner", *Living Blues*, No.10, Autumn 1972

Mike Corbett, interview with Jay McShann, *Cadence*, October 1979

Terry Currier, *BluesNotes*: see website, Cascades Blues Association.

Stanley Dance, column, "Jump For Joy", *Jazz Journal*, November 1967

Jim Delehant, "Tempo" (article on Pete Johnson) *Hit Parader*, Vol. xv, No. 28, October 1966 (quoting from Carroll Hardy, qv)

Wilma Dobie, "Joe Turner The Originator," *Jazz Forum* 46, 1977

David Driver, "Rock A While with Big Joe Turner: a memoir," *Now Dig This*, No. 338, May 2011.

Leonard Feather, "Why Big Joe Had To Stay Home", *Melody Maker*, May 13, 1972

Gary Giddins, "Big Joe Turner Cooks Up A Shrine", *Village Voice*, November 29, 1976

Ralph J. Gleason, "Blues Sweetened: Joe Turner," *Down Beat*, July 14, 1954

Peter Guralnick, "Big Joe Rolls On", *Melody Maker*, December 30, 1978

Gene Gray (Bob Porter), "Joe Turner/Charles Kynard/Leo Blevins," *Down Beat*, November 13, 1969

Peter Haining, "Boss of the Blues," *Jazz News*, June 14, 1961

Carrol Hardy & Pete Johnson, "Pete Johnson's Music". *Rhythm & Blues*, April 1964

Jack Hutton, "Boss of the Blues Joe Turner says – I'm Dying To Visit Britain", *Melody Maker*, March 7, 1964

David Illingworth, "Second Opinion: Big Joe Turner", *Melody Maker*, May 24, 1969

Jorgen G. Jepsen, "Boss of the Blues", *Orkester Journalen (Swedish)*, December 1957

Lee Jeske. "Big Joe Turner/Jay McShann," *Down Beat*, July 1983

Tony Kisch, "A Date with Joe Turner," *Broadside*, December 2000

Edward Komara, "From The Archive," *Living Blues*, March/April 1994

Andre Miller and Jorg"George" Koran, "From the singing waiter to world fame: Big Joe Turner", *Dig It (Bulletin of the New Jazz Club, Zurich) (Swiss)*, Vol. 7, No.1, November 1965. (script for Turner presentation on January 13, 1965)

George A. Moonoogian, "Big Joe Was Here: Blues Classics Revisited," *Whiskey, Woman and …* No. 6, March 1974

Dan Morgenstern, "Caught In The Act: Joe Turner," *Jazz Journal*, January 1977. (reprinted in *Living With Jazz: A Reader*)

Pete O'Gorman, "Well All Reet Then!!: The Joe Turner Story," *Now Dig This*, No. 338, May 2011.

Dara O'Lochlainn, "Never Fear, Big Joe Turner Was Here", *Jazz News*, No. 2, March/April 1987, No. 4, July/August 1987

Paul Oliver, "Boss of the Blues", *Jazz Music Mirror*, Vol.5, no. 5, 1958

Robert Palmer, "An Old Blues Singer Still Belts It Out", *The New York Times*, November 12, 1976

Doc Pomus, "Joe Turner", *Whiskey, Women And …*, No. 11, June 1983

Bob Porter, see Gene Gray.

Mike Price, "Big Joe Turner: The Atlantic Years", *Now Dig This*, No. 39, June 1986

Steve Propes, "Joe Turner interview", October 23, 1983, KLON radio, *Blues & Rhythm*, No. 362, September 2021

Gary Richards, "The Big Boss From K.C.", *Alley Music*, Vol. 1, No.1, 1968.

Tony Russell, "Big Joe Turner: All-round Entertainer," *The Blues Collection*, No. 50, 1995

Brian Smith, "Big Joe in the UK 1966," Brian Smith, *Now Dig This*, No. 338, May 2011

Serge Tonneau, "Joe Turner", *R 'n' B Panorama (Belgian)*, No. 2, March 1960, No. 42, 1966 (Belgian)

Topanga Dick, "Big Joe Turner, 50 Years in Show Business," *Whiskey, Woman and …* No. 7, May 1975

Joe Turner, as told to Inez Cavanagh, "Kansas City Moods," *Metronome*, March 1945

Joe Turner, "It's Joe Turner, 'Boss of the Blues', with Kansas City Memories," *Crescendo*, September 1965

uncredited, "Boss of the Blues". *Ebony*, Vol. 9, No. 5, March 1954

uncredited (Max Jones?), "That Town Was Really On Fire, Says Big Joe", *Melody Maker*, May 15, 1965

uncredited, "B.B. King With a Little Help From His Friends," *Hit Parader*, November 1970

uncredited, "The South's Blues Singer", *The Negro South*, June 1946

uncredited, Joe Turner interview, *Beano Magazine* No. 12, December?, 1984

Gary Von Tersch, "Live Blues: Big Joe Turner," *Living Blues* 8, Spring 1972

John White, "Putting His Trust in Jazz" (John Hammond), *Jazz Journal*, December 2018

Patricia Willard, "Jump For Joy", essay for Duke Ellington LP, Smithsonian label.

Valerie Wilmer, "Blues for Mr. Turner", *JazzBeat*, Vol. 2, No. 7, July 1965

Valerie Wilmer, "Big Joe's Still Boss", *Melody Maker*, July 10, 1976

Valerie Wilmer, "The Boss of the Blues: Joe Turner", *Down Beat*, November 18, 1965

Theo Zwicky, "Pete Johnson", *VJM* (*Vintage Jazz Mart*), January 1964

plus many and various news items in *Capitol News, Down Beat, Jazz Journal, The Melody Maker, Wavelength*.

Books

Whitney Balliett, "Majesty: Joe Turner", chapter in *American Singers*, Oxford University Press, 1979 (reprint from *The New Yorker*, November 29, 1976)

Count Basie, with Albert Murray, *Good Morning Blues, The Autobiography of Count Basie*, Heinemann, 1986

Tony Biggs, *Shout It Out, The Recordings of Big Joe Turner*, privately published, 2011, (second edition)

Red Callendar with Elaine Cohen, *Unfinished Dream, The Autobiography of Red Callendar*, Quartet Books, 1985

Ray Charles with David Ritz, *Brother Ray: Ray Charles' Own Story*, McDonald and Jane's, 1974

John Chilton, *Who's Who of Jazz*, MacMillan London Ltd., 1985 (first edition Bloomsbury Book Shop, 1972)

Donald Clarke, editor, *The Penguin Encyclopedia of Popular Music*, Penguin Books, 1998

Buck Clayton, with Nancy Miller Elliott, *Buck Clayton's Jazz World*, The MacMillan Press Ltd., 1986

Lawrence Cohn (editor), "Bright Lights, Big City: Urban Blues," by Mark A Humphrey, *Nothing But The Blues*, Abbeville Press, 1999

Rick Coleman, *Blue Monday: Fats Domino and the Lost Dawn of Rock 'n' Roll*, Da Capo Press, 2006

Stanley Dance, *The World of Count Basie*, Sidgwick & Jackson, 1980

Dave Dexter, "Jazz in the West," *Jazz Cavalcade*, Criterion Music Corp., 1946

David Dicaire, "Big Joe Turner: Shoutin' The Blues," *Blues Singers*, Jefferson, McFarland, 1999

Frank Driggs, Chuck Haddix, *Kansas City Jazz: From Ragtime to Bebop - A History*, Oxford University Press, 2005

Art Farmer in *Central Avenue Sounds: Jazz in Los Angeles*, University of California, Press, 1998

Ted Fox, *Show Time at the Apollo*, Quartet Books, 1985

Galen Gart, First Pressings, *The History of Rhythm & Blues*, Volumes 1-9, 1951-1959, Big Nickel Publications, 1990s.

Gary Giddins, "Joe Turner: Unmoved Mover". *Rhythm-a-ning: Jazz Tradition and Innovation in the 80's, Oxford University Press, 1985*

Charlie Gillett, *The Sound of the City: The Rise of Rock and Roll*, Outerbridge & Dienstfrey, 1970

Charlie Gillett, *Making Tracks: Atlantic Records and the Growth of a Multi-Billion-Dollar Industry*, W. H. Allen, 1975

Leslie Gourse, *The Story of Joe Williams*, Quartet Books, 1985

Leslie Gourse, "A Loving Proposition", *Louis' Children: American Jazz Singers*, Cooper Square Press, 2001

Peter Guralnick, "Big Joe Turner: Big Joe Rides On", *Lost Highway: Journals & Arrivals of American Musicians*, David R. Godine, Publisher, Inc., 1979

Sheldon Harris, *Blues Who's Who, A Biographical Dictionary of Blues Singers*, Arlington House, 1979, Da Capo reprint

Nat Hentoff and Albert J. McCarthy, (editors): "Kansas City and the Southwest", chapter by Franklin S. Driggs, *Jazz*, Rinehart & Co. 1959

Tad Hershorn, *Norman Granz: The Man Who Used Jazz for Justice* , University of California Press, 2011

Mary Lou Hester, "Boss Man", *Going To Kansas City"*, Sherman, Early Bird, 1980

Franz Hoffmann, New England Negro Press 1950-1967. (7 volumes)

Barney Josephson with Terry Trilling-Josephson, *Cafe Society: The wrong place for the Right people*, University of Illinois Press, 2009

Barry Kernfeld (editor), *The New Grove Dictionary of Jazz*, MacMillan Press, 1988 (includes entry on Joe Turner by Paul Oliver)

Lawrence H. Larsen and Nancy L. Hulston, *Pendergast*, University of Missouri Press, 1997

Sanda Lieb, *Mother of the Blues: A Study of Ma Rainey*, The University of Massachusetts Press, 1981

Jimmy Lyons, with Ira Kamin, *Dizzy, Duke, The Count and Me: The Story of the Monterey Jazz Festival*, A California Living Book, 1978

Humphrey Lyttelton, "Big Joe," *Take It From The Top*, Robson Books Ltd.,1975

Hans J. Mauerer (editor), *The Pete Johnson Story (German)*, Fund Raising Project, 1965

Albert McCarthy, Alun Morgan, Paul Oliver, Max Harrison, "Joe Turner," *Jazz On Record: A Critical Guide to the First 50 Years*, Hanover Books Ltd., 1968

Dan Morgenstern, "Joe Turner", *Living With Jazz: A Reader*, Pantheon Books, 2004 (originally in *Jazz Journal*, 1977)

Paul Oliver, *Screeening The Blues*, Cassell & Co. Ltd, 1968.

Paul Oliver, *The Story of the Blues*, Barrie and Rockliff, 1969

Nathan W. Pearson, Jr., *Goin' To Kansas City*, MacMillan Press, 1988

Tom Reed, *The Black Music History of Los Angeles*, Black Accent Press, 1994

Paul Roland (editor), "Joe Turner", *Jazz Singers: The great song stylists in their own words*, Octopus Publishing Group, 1999

Bobby Rush, with Herb Powell, *I Ain't Studdin' Ya: My American Blues Story*, Hachette Books, 2021

Ross Russell, *Jazz Style in Kansas City and the South-west*, University of California Press, 1971

Eric Sackheim, *The Blues Line, A Collection of Blues Lyrics*, Schirmer Book, 1975

Gunther Schuller, *The Swing Era: The Development of Jazz 1930-1945*, Oxford University Press, 1991

Nat Shapiro and Nat Hentoff (editors), *Hear Me Talkin' To Ya*, Rinehart & Co., 1955

Chris Sheridan, *Count Basie: A Bio-Discography*, Greenwood Press, 1986

Peter Silvester, *A Left Hand Like God: A Study of Boogie-Woogie*, Quartet Books Ltd, 1988

Michael P. Smith, New Orleans Jazz Fest: A Pictorial History, Pelican Publishing Company, 1991

Rowena Stewart (editor), *Kansas City ... and All That's Jazz*, Andrews McMeel Publishing/The Kansas City Jazz Museum, 1999

John Swenson, *Bill Haley, The Extraordinary Life and Career of the World's First Rock and Roll Idol*, Arrow Book, W. H. Allen & Co. Ltd, 1983

Terry Teachout, "A Message For The World, Jump for Joy 1941-1942," *Duke: The Life of Duke Ellington*, The Robson Press, 2013

Nick Tosches, *Unsung Heroes of Rock 'N' Roll*, Secker & Warburg 1984

Dorothy Wade & Justin Picardie, *Music Man: Atlantic Records and the Triumph of Rock 'n' Roll*, W. W. Norton & Company, 1990.

Todd Bryant Weeks, *Luck's In My Corner: The Life and Music of Hot Lips Page*, Routledge, 2008

Pete Welding and Toby Byron (editors), "Big Joe Turner: The Holler of a Mountain Jack", by Murray & Arthur Kempton, *Bluesland, Portraits of Twelve Major American Blues Masters*. Penguin Books/Dutton, 1991

Jerry Wexler, with David Ritz, *Rhythm and the Blues: A Life in American Music*, Jonathan Cape, 1994

Valerie Wilmer, "The Boss of the Blues", *Jazz People*, Allison & Busby, Ltd. 1971

Obituaries

A few of the more important tributes:

Todd Everett, *Los Angeles Herald-Examiner*, November 25, 1985
Leonard Feather, *Jazz Express*, No. 68, January 1986
Jon Pareles, *The New York Times*, November 25, 1985
Steve Voce, *Jazz Journal*, February 1986
uncredited, *Afro-American*, December 14, 1985
uncredited, *Cash Box*, December 7, 1985
uncredited, The Daily Telegraph, November 26, 1985
uncredited, Joslin's Jazz Journal, Vol. 5, No. 1, February 1986
uncredited, The Times, November 26, 1985
uncredited, *The Times Picayune*, November 25, 1985

Sleeve & Insert Notes

There are many, many such notes on Joe Turner LP sleeves and CD inserts, but the majority consist of a basic biography and/or comments on the recordings on the disc. For that reason, only a selection of these writings is listed here:

Ron Bartolucci, "Johnny Otis Show: Live 1970," Wolf 120.612 (CD)
Bob Blumenthal, "Joe Turner: Every Day In The Week," MCA GRP16212 (CD)
Jean Buzelin, "Big Joe Turner, Volume 1, 1938-1940," Masters of Jazz MJCD 134 (CD)
Ulf Carlsson, "Big Joe Turner: I Don't Dig It," Jukebox Lil JB-618 (LP)
Colin Escott, "The Boss of the Blues, Joe Turner Sings Kansas City Jazz," Bear Family B17505 (CD)
Rolph Fairchild, "Joe Turner: Tell Me Pretty Baby," Arhoolie CD-333 (CD)
Benny Green, "Nobody In Mind: Joe Turner," Pablo 2310 760 (LP)
Peter Grendysa, "The Big Joe Turner Anthology: Big Bad & Blue," Atlantic R2 71550 (CD)
Jeff Hannusch, "Joe Turner: Jumpin' Tonight," Imperial 1561431(LP)
Nat Hentoff, "Patcha, Patcha, All Night Long: Joe Turner Meets Jimmy Witherspoon," Pablo 2310-913 (LP)
Lee Hildebrand, "Joe Turner: Stormy Monday," Pablo PRCD2310-943-2
Dan Morgenstern, "Boogie Woogie and Blues Piano," Mosaic Select MS-030 (CD)
Neil Slaven, "Big Joe Turner: All The Classic Hits, 1938-1952", JSP7709 (5-CD set)
Paul Watts, "Big Joe Turner, The Singles Collection 1950-60," Acrobat ADDCD3275
Pete Welding, "Big Joe Turner," Tomato R271 (CD)

Cliff White, Jumpin' With Joe," Charly CRB1070 (LP)
Axel Zwingenberger, "Rare Live Cuts," Document DOCD-1003 (CD)

Websites

Terry Currier, Cascades Blues Association (reprints of article from *BluesNotes*,
October 2002, originally in January and February 1997 issues)
Jerry Fuentes, A Rock 'n' Roll Historian blog
Dave Stephens: a detailed essay on Big Joe Turner, with numerous references to
his recordings and data connected with them.
setlistfm: a random list of engagement dates.
Wikipedia.org (numerous biographies and other sites)
Daily Breeze blog: dailybreeze.com/history2014/04/05

Newspapers

Franz Hoffman, *Jazz Advertised (mainly) in the Negro Press* series.
Baltimore Afro-American / Chicago Defender / New York Amsterdam News /
New York Times / Pittsburgh Courier
Galen Gart, *First Pressings* (1951-1959) Big Nickel Publications, 1990s,
Billboard reprints..
Ray Astbury's research used the following websites:
https://newspaperarchive.com
https://www.genealogybank.com

A random selection of lesser-known newspapers from the approximately
300 which Ray Astbury quoted included the Arizona Republic, Austin
American Statesman, Brunswick News, Charleston Gazette, Dallas
Morning News, Durham Morning Herald, Fresno Bee, Gulf Informer,
Morning Call (Allentown, PA), Morning Call (Paterson, NJ), Omaha Star,
Pulaski Southwest Times, San Antonio Register, Seattle Post-Intelligence,
Tallahassee Democrat, and The Tennesseean.

Notes

Chapter 1   Kansas City and Boss Pendergast

1. *Dave Dexter, Jr., The Jazz Story, Prentice-Hall Inc., 1964*
2. *Frank Driggs & Chuck Haddix: Kansas City Jazz, Oxford University Press, 2005*
3. *James C. Fitzpatrick, Kansas City Times, January 2, 1985*
4. *Dave Dexter, Jr. Jazz Cavalcade, Criterion Music Corp., 1946*
5. *Dave Dexter, Jr. The Jazz Story, Prentice-Hall, Inc., 1964*
6. *ibid*
7. *The Gangsters, by Timothy Jacobs, Magna Books, 1990*
8. *Lawrence H. Larsen & Nancy J. Hulston, Pendergast, University of Missouri Press, 2013*
9. *The Encyclopedia Britannica*

Chapter 2   "I had singing on my mind" (1911-1930)

1   United States Population Census for 1910. Details courtesy of Howard Rye.
2   Whitney Balliett, *American Singers* (Oxford University Press, 1988). (The "Majesty" chapter is a modified version of an article originally in *The New Yorker*.)
3   Joe & Geraldine Turner letter to author, May 1964. (At least four publications, including John Chilton's *Who's Who of Jazz*, aver that Joe was 15 when his father died, with one stating it was a car accident.)
4   Whitney Balliett, *American Singers* (Oxford University Press, 1988).
5   ibid
6   Frank London Brown, "Boss of the Blues", *Down Beat*, December 11, 1958
7   Joe & Geraldine Turner, letter to author, May 1964.
8   Paul Clinco, "Joe Turner", *Living Blues* 10, Autumn 1972
9   Whitney Balliett, *American Singers* (Oxford University Press, 1988)
10 Frank London Brown, "Boss of the Blues", *Down Beat*, December 11, 1958
11 Whitney Ballett, *American Singers* (Oxford University Press, 1988)
12 Joe & Geraldine Turner letter to author, May 1964
13 Whitney Balliett, *American Singers* (Oxford University Press, 1988)
14 Valerie Wilmer, *Jazz People* (Allison & Busby, Ltd., 1971)
15 Peter Guralnick "Big Joe Rolls On", *Melody Maker*, December 30, 1978
16 Frank London Brown, "Boss of the Blues", *Down Beat*, December 11, 1958
17 Whitney Balliett, *American Singers* (Oxford University Press, 1988)
18 Frank London Brown, "Boss of the Blues", *Down Beat*, December 11, 1958
19 Leslie Gourse, *Louis' Children* (Cooper Square Press, 2001)
20 Whitney Ballett, *American Singers* (Oxford University Press, 1988)
21 Max Jones, *Melody Maker*, May 16, 1965
22 Whitney Ballett, *American Singers*, (Oxford University Press, 1988)

23 Paul Clinco, "Joe Turner", *Living Blues*, No. 10, Autumn, 1972
24 Frank London Brown, "Boss of the Blues", *Down Beat*, December 11, 1958
25 Whitney Balliett, *American Singers* (Oxford University Press, 1988)
26 Valerie Wilmer, *Jazz People* (Allison & Busby, Ltd., 1971)
27 ibid
28 Whitney Balliett, *American Singers* (Oxford University Press, 1988)
29 ibid
30 Joe Turner, "Kansas City Memories", *Crescendo*, September 1965
31 Stanley Dance, *Jazz Journal*, May 1964
32 Joe Turner, "Kansas City Memories", *Crescendo*, September 1965
33 Peter Guralnick, "Big Joe Rolls On", *Melody Maker*, December 30, 1978
34 Leslie Gourse, *Louis' Children* (Cooper Square Press, 2001))
35 Joe Turner, "Kansas City Memories", *Crescendo*, September 1965
36 Whitney Balliett, *American Singers* (Oxford University Press, 1988)
37 Valerie Wilmer, "Joe's Still Boss", *Melody Maker*, July 10, 1976
38 Peter Guralnick, "Big Joe Rolls On", *Melody Maker*, December 30, 1978
39 Whitney Balliett, *American Singers* (Oxford University Press, 1988)
40 Valerie Wilmer, *Jazz People* (Allison & Busby, Ltd., 1971)
41 Joe Turner, "Kansas City Memories", *Crescendo*, September 1965
42 Valerie Wilmer, *Jazz People* (Allison &Busby Ltd., 1971)
43 Joe Turner, "Kansas City Memories",*Crescendo*, September 1965
44 Paul Clinco, "Joe Turner", *Living Blues* 10, Autumn 1972
45 Leslie Gourse, *Louis' Children (Cooper Square Press, 2001)*
46 Whitney Balliett, *American Singers* (Oxford University Press, 1988)
47 Leslie Gourse, *Louis' Children* (Cooper Square Press,2001)
48 U.S. Population Census for 1930. Details courtesy of Howard Rye.

Chapter 3 "Let me sing with your band" (1930-1934)

1 Count Basie with Albert Murray, *Good Morning Blues* (William Heinemann Ltd. 1986)
2 Joe & Geraldine Turner letter to author, October 3, 1965
3 anonymous (Max Jones?), "That Town Was Really on Fire", *Melody Maker*, May 15, 1965
4 Bruce Baker, "Been To Kansas City", *Jazz Quarterly*, Summer 1945
5 Valerie Wilmer, *Jazz People*, (Allison & Busby, Ltd., 1971)
6 Robert Palmer, *New York Times*, November 2, 1976
7 Marshall Stearns, *The Story of Jazz (Oxford University Press, 1957)*
8 Count Basie with Albert Murray, *Good Morning Blues* (William Heinemann Ltd. 1986)
9 Jay McShann to Mike Corbett, *Cadence*, October 1979
10 John Williams to Andy Klein, *IAJRC Journal*, Winter, 1996
11 Frank London Brown, "Boss of the Blues ...", *Down Beat*, December 11, 1958
12 Whitney Balliett, *American Singers* (Oxford University Press, 1988)
13 Inez Cavanaugh, "Kansas City Moods", *Metronome*, March 1945

14 ibid

15 Max Jones, *Melody Maker*, May 15, 1965

16 Inez Cavanaugh, "Kansas City Moods", *Metronome*, March 1945

17 Jack Hutton, *Melody Maker*, March 7, 1964

18 Joe & Geraldine Turner, letter to author, May 1964

19 Ulf Carlsson, sleeve notes, "I Don't Dig It", Juke Box Lil JB-618

20 Joe Turner, "Kansas City Memories", *Crescendo*, September 1965

21 George Melly, *The Observer*, May 16, 1965

22 quoted in Ulf Carlsson sleeve notes, "I Don't Dig It", Juke Box Lil JB-618

23 Pete Johnson to Johnny Simmen, *The Pete Johnson Story*, (Fund Raising Proiject, 1965)

24 Joe Turner, "Kansas City Memories", *Crescendo*, September 1965

25 Valerie Wilmer, "Joe's Still The Boss", *Melody Maker*, July 10, 1976

26 Whitney Balliett, *American Singers* (Oxford University Press, 1988)

27 Joe Turner, "Kansas City Memories", *Crescendo*, September 1965

28 Valerie Wilmer, "Blues for Mr. Turner", *Jazz Beat*, July 1965

29 Pete Welding, insert notes, "Shake, Rattle & Roll", Tomato R2 71666

30 Count Basie with Albert Murray, *Good Morning Blues (William Heinemann Ltd., 1986)*

31 Whitney Balliett, American Singers (Oxford University Press 1988)

32 Joe Turner to James Austin, *Goldmine* 78, November 1982

33 *Kansas City ... and all that's Jazz* (Andrew McMeel Publishing, 1999)

34 Frank Driggs & Chuck Haddix, *Kansas City Jazz* (Oxford University Press, 2005)

35 Joe & Geraldine Turner, letter to author, October 3, 1965

36 Inez Cavanaugh, "Kansas City Moods", *Metronome*, March 1945

37 Whitney Balliett, *American Singers* (Oxford University Press, 1988)

38 Frank Driggs & Chuck Haddix, *Kansas City Jazz* (Oxford University Press, 2005)

39 Whitney Balliett, *American Singers* (Oxford University Press, 1988)

40 Todd Bryant Weeks, *Luck's In My Corner*, (Routledge, 2008)

41 Valerie Wilmer, "The Boss of the Blues", *Jazz People*, (Allison & Busby Ltd., 1971)

42 Whitney Balliett, *American Singers* (Oxford University Press, 1988)

43 Joe & Geraldine Turner, letter to author, September 1965

44 Inez Cavanaugh, "Kansas City Moods", *Metronome*, March 1945

45 Joe & Geraldine Turner, letter to author, September 1965

46 Hans J. Maurer (editor), *The Pete Johnson Story* (Fund Raising Project, 1965)

47 *Kansas City ... and all that's Jazz* (Andrews McMeel Publishing, 1999)

48 Ross Russell, *Jazz Style in Kansas City and the Southwest* (University of California Press, 1971)

Chapter 4 "That town was really on fire" (1934-1936)

1   Nathan W. Pearson, Jr., *Goin' To Kansas City* (MacMillan Press 1988)
2   Frank Driggs & Chuck Haddix, *Kansas City Jazz* (Oxford University Press, 2005)
3   Count Basie with Albert Murray, *Good Morning Blues* (William Heinemann Ltd, 1986)
4   Buck Clayton, with Nancy Miller Elliott, *Buck Clayton's Jazz World* (The MacMillan Press 1986)
5   *Kansas City … and All That's Jazz*, (Andrews McMeel Publishing 1999)
6   *Kansas City Star*, August 11, 1989
7   Chuck Haddix e-mail to author, June 4, 2019
8   Inez Cavanaugh, "Kansas City Moods", *Metronome*, March 1945
9   Frank Driggs & Chuck Haddix, *Kansas City Jazz* (Oxford University Press 2005)
10 Count Basie with Albert Murray, Good Morning Blues (William Heinemann Ltd. 1986)
11 Hans J. Maurer (editor), *The Pete Johnson Story* (Fund Raising Project, 1965)
12 Joe & Geraldine Turner, letter to author
13 Jesse Price letter to George Koran, *Dig It* (1964)
14 Nat Shapiro & Nat Hentoff, *Hear Me Talkin' To Ya* (Penguin Books, 1962)
15 ibid
16 John Williams to Andy Klein, *IAJRC Journal*, Winter 1996
17 Dave Dexter, Jr., *The Jazz Story* (Prentice-Hall Inc., 1964)
18 Ben Webster to Max Jones, *Melody Maker*, May 8, 1971
19 Pete Guralnick, *Lost Highway* (David R. Godine, Publisher, Inc. 1979)
20 Earl Hines, *Jazz Journal*, March 1966
21 Frank Driggs & Chuck Haddix, *Kansas City Jazz* (Oxford University Press 2005)
22 Count Basie with Albert Murray, *Good Morning Blues* (William Heinemann Ltd., 2005)
23 Buck Clayton with Nancy Miller Elliott, *Buck Clayton's Jazz World* (The MacMillan Press 1986)
24 Jay McShann to Bart Becker, *Cadence*, September 1979
25 Nathan Pearson, *Goin' To Kansas City* (MacMillan Press, 1988)
26 Jay McShann to Mike Corbett, *Cadence*, October 1979
27 Dave Dexter, *Down Beat*, January 15, 1941
28 Andy Kirk with Amy Lee, *Twenty Years on Wheels* (Bayou Press, 1989)

Chapter 5 "We're just waiting for John Hammond" (1936-1938)

1   Nathan Pearson, *Goin' To Kansas City* (MacMillan Press 1988)
2   Frank Driggs & Chuck Haddix, *Kansas City Jazz* (Oxford University Press 2005)
3   Nathan Pearson, *Goin' To Kansas City* (MacMillan Press 1988)

4 Count Basie with Albert Murray, *Good Morning Blues*, (William Heinemann Ltd. 2005)

5 Neal Slavin, insert notes to "Big Joe Turner 1938-1952", JSP 7709

6 Ulf Carlsson, sleeve notes, "I Don't Dig It", Juke Box Lil JB-618

7 Pete Johnson to Johnny Simmen, The Pete Johnson Story (Fund Raising Project, 1965)

8 Ulf Carlsson, sleeve notes, "I Don't Dig It", Juke Box Lil JB-618

9 John Williams to Andy Klein, *IAJRC Journal*, Winter 1996

10 Whitney Balliett, *American Singers* (Oxford University Press 1988)

11 Valerie Wilmer, *Jazz People* (Allison & Busby Ltd. 1971)

12 Frank Driggs & Chuck Haddix, *Kansas City Jazz* (Oxford University Press 2005)

13 Mary Lou Hester, *Going To Kansas City* (Early Bird Press, 1980)

14 Stanley Dance, *The World of Count Basie*, (Sidgwick & Jackson 1980)

15 ibid

16 Nathan Pearson, *Goin' To Kansas City* (MacMillan Press 1988)

17 *Kansas City ... and All That's Jazz (*Andrews McMeel Publishing 1999)

18 Pete Johnson letter to George Koran *Dig It*, November 1965

19 Myra Taylor in *Kansas City ... and All That's Jazz* (Andrew McMeel Publishing, 1999)

20 Frank Driggs & Chuck Haddix, *Kansas City Jazz* (Oxford University Press 1988)

21 ibid

22 George Hoefer, sleeve notes to "Joe Turner singing the blues", BluesWay BL-6006

23 Jerry Wexler and David Ritz, *Rhythm and The Blues* (Random House, 1993)

24 Jay McShann in *Kansas City ... and All That's Jazz* (Andrew McMeel Publishing, 1999)

25 ibid

26 Nathan Pearson, *Goin' To Kansas City* (MacMillan Press 1988)

27 *Kansas City Call*, April 23, 1937

28 *Kansas City Call*, December 17, 1937

29 *Kansas City Call*, May 27, 1938

30 Chris Sheridan, *Count Basie: A Bio-Discography* (Greenwood Press 1986)

31 Ken Vail, compiler, quoting Bob Inman diary, *Swing Era Scrapbook*, The Scarecrow Press 2005)

32 Marge Johnson, *The Pete Johnson Story* (Fund Raising Project, 1965)

33 Guy Remark, sleeve notes to "rock & roll Joe Turner", Atlantic 8005

34 Whitney Balliett, *American Singers* (Oxford University Press 1988)

35 Frank Driggs & Chuck Haddix, *Kansas City Jazz* (Oxford University Press 2005)

Chapter 6 "The boogie got moving" (1938)

1 John Hammond with Irving Townsend, *John Hammond on Record,* (Penguin Books Ltd, 1981)
2 Bruce Baker, "Been To Kansas City", *Jazz Quarterly*, Summer 1945
3 John Hammond with Irving Townsend, *John Hammond on Record* (Penguin Books Ltd., 1981)
4 *Kansas City Times*, December 24, 1938
5 *The Milwaukee Journal*, December 24, 1938
6 *Daily News*, December 24, 1938

Chapter 7 Cafe Society – Jump for Joy (1938-1941)

1 Ken Vail, *Lady Day's Diary, The Life of Billie Holiday* (Castle Communications plc, 1996)
2 Barney Josephson with Terry Trilling-Josephson, *Cafe Society* (University of Illinois Press, 2009)
3 George Avakian, *Jazz Notes*, July 1945
4 Billie Holiday with William Duffy, *Lady Sings The Blues* (Barrie Books, 1958)
5 Ulf Carlsson, sleeve notes, "I Don't Dig It", Juke Box Lil JB-618
6 Jim Turner e-mail to author, October 21, 2019
7 Mark A. Humphrey, *Nothing But The Blues*, editor Lawrence Cohn (Abbeville Press Publishers, 1993)
8 Barney Josephson with Terry Trilling-Josephson, *Cafe Society* (University of Illinois Press, 2009)
9 George Avakian, *Jazz Notes*, July 1945
10 Joe Turner to James Austin, "Conversation with a Legend," *Goldmine*, No. 78, November 1982.
11 Barney Josephson with Terry Trilling-Josephson, *Cafe Society* (University of Illinois Press 2009)
12 George Hoefer, sleeve notes to "Joe Turner Singing The Blues" BluesWay BL-6006
13 Drew Page, *Drew's Blues* (L.S.U. Press 1999)
14 Joe & Geraldine Turner, letter to author, September 1965
15 *Indianapolis Recorder*, May 25, 1940 / *Pittsburgh Courier*, May 25, 1940
16 *New York Times*, October 7, 1940
17 sleeve notes to "The Joe Turner Anthology: Big, Bad and Blue", Atlantic R2-71550
18 Dave Dexter, *Playback* (*Billboard* Publications 1976)
19 Gunther Schuller, *The Swing Era* (Oxford University Press, 1989)
20 Pat Willard, sleeve notes to "Jump For Joy", Smithsonian LPR037
21 ibid
22 Ulf Carlsson, sleeve notes to "I Don't Gig It", Juke Box Lil JB-618
23 Pat Willard to author, May 1985
24 Jack Hutton, "Boss of the Blues", *Melody Maker*, March 7, 1964

25 Bill Oliver, *Herald-Express*, August 8, 1941 (quoted by Pat Willard, note 18)
26 Dave Green e-mail to author, May 3, 2019
27 John Franceschina, *Duke Ellington's Music for the Theatre* (McFarland & Co. 2001)
28 Duke Ellington interview with John Pittman, quoted in Mark Tucker, editor, *The Duke Ellington Reader* (Oxford University Press, 1993)
29 Stuart Nicholson, *A Portrait of Duke Ellington* (Sidgwick & Jackson, 1999)
30 Mark Cantor e-mails to author, May 30 and June 2, 2019
31 Ken Vail, *Duke's Diary (Part One)* (Vail Publishing, 1999)

Chapter 8 "Joe Turner has gone Hollywood" (1941-1946)

1   *Metronome*, April 1944
2   Red Callender with Elaine Cohen, *Unfinished Dream* (Quartet Books, 1985)
3   ibid
4   Ken Vail, *Lady Day's Diary, The Life of Billie Holiday* (Castle Communications plc, 1996)
5   Bryant et al, *Central Avenue Sounds* (University of California Press, 1998)
6   Ken Vail, *Lady Day's Diary, The Life of Billie Holiday* (Castle Communications plc, 1996)
7   Jacqueline Cogdell DjeDje & Eddie S. Meadows (editors), *California Soul: Music of African Americans in the West* (University of California Press, 1998)
8   *Los Angeles Tribune*, September 13, 1943
9   *Los Angeles Tribune*, September 30, 1943
10 *Philadelphia Enquirer*, October 27, 19431
11 Billy Rowe, *Pittsburgh Courier*, December 4, 1943
12 Mark Cantor, e-mail to author, August 23, 2018
13 *Capitol News*, May 1944
14 Neil Slaven, insert notes to JSP 7709
15 *Detroit Tribune, April 29, 1944*
16 *Chicago Defender, August 5, 1944*
17 *Detroit Times*, September 9/16, 1944
18 *Detroit Free Press*, September 24, 1944
19 *Hollywood Note*, June 1946
20 Charlie Gillett, *Making Tracks* (W.H. Allen & Co. Ltd., 1975)
21 John Chilton, *Who's Who of Jazz* (Macmillan London Limited, 1985)
22 *Dallas Morning News*, March 28, 1945
23 *Jazz Record* No. 36, September 1945
24 *Capitol News,* September 1945
25 *Louisiana Weekly*, December 21, 1945
26 Bryant et al, *Central Avenue Sounds* (University of California Press, 1998)
27 Peter Vacher, *Swingin' on Central Avenue* (Rowman & Littlefield Publishers, 2015)
28 Walter C. Allen, *Hendersonia* (self-published, 1973)

Chapter 9 "Don't play no be-bop in here" (1947-1950)

1   *Hattiesburg American*, January 10, 1947
2   *Richmond Afro-American*, April 5, 1947
3   Neil Slaven, insert notes to JSP 7709
4   Jacqueline Cogdell DjeDje & Eddie S. Meadows (editors), *California Soul, Music of African Americans in the West (University of California Press, 1998)*
5   *Down Beat*, November 5, 1947, December 5, 1947
6   Jack McVea, letter to Jorg Korna, *Dig It*, November 1965
7   Rick Coleman, *Blue Monday, Fats Domino and the Lost Dawn of Rock 'n' Roll* (Da Capo Press 2006)
8   *Jazz Journal*, March 1984
9   Pete Johnson letter to Hans J. Maurer, *The Pete Johnson Story (Fund Raising Project, 1965)*
10 Ulf Carlsson sleeve notes to "I Don't Dig It", Juke Box Lil JB-618
11 Ian Carr, Digby Fairweather and Brian Priestley *Jazz, The Essential Companion* (Grafton Books, 1987)
12 Mack McCormick, letter to author, December 21, 1964
13 Joe Turner to Dick Shurman, 1983, *Blues & Rhythm* 343, October 2019
14 Jeff Hannusch sleeve notes to *"Jumpin' Tonight"*, Imperial 1561431
15 Big Joe Laredo sleeve notes to "Jumpin' with Joe", EMI 7 99293
16 Almost Slim, *Wavelength*, March 1987
17 Brian Wood, *The Song For Me, A Glossary of New Orleans Musicians* (self published 2002)

Chapter 10 "Best R&B Artist of 1954" (1951-1954)

1   Ray Charles and David Ritz, *Brother Ray* (Macdonald & James, 1979)
2   *Detroit Free Press*, January 18, 1951, February 2, 1951, *Detroit Times*, January 18 & 24, 1951
3   Charlie Gillett, *Making Tracks*, (W.H. Allen, 1975)
4   Tom Fox, *Show Time at the Apollo* (Quartet Books, 1985), *Billboard*, April 1951
5   Charlie Gillett, *Making Tracks*, (W.H. Allen, 1975)
6   Tom Fox, *Show Time at the Apollo* (Quartet Books, 1985)
7   Doc Pomus, sleeve notes to "Rhythm & Blues Years", Atlantic 81663
8   *New Orleans Music*, December 2006
9   Jeff Hannush, *The Soul of New Orleans* (Swallow Publications, 2001)
10 Valerie Wilmer, *Jazz Beat*, July 1965
11 *Wavelength*, October 1985
12 Jerry Wexler and David Ritz, *Rhythm and the Blues* (Random House, 1993)
13 Joe Turner to Steve Propes, KLON, October 23, 1983, *Blues & Rhythm* no. 362
14 Charlie Gillett, *Making Tracks* (W.H. Allen, 1975)
15 Jerry Wexler and David Ritz, *Rhythm and the Blues* (Random House, 1993)
16 Mark Cantor, e-mails to author, August 23/27, 2018, January 21, 2019

Chapter 11 "I made all those things before Haley" (1955-1950)

1   Nesuhi Ertegun to Richard Williams, *Melody Maker*, August 12, 1972
2   Neil Slaven insert notes to "Big Joe Turner: All The   Classic Hits, 1938-1952," JSP 7709
3   Dorothy Wade & Justine Picardie, *Music Man: Ahmet Ertegun, Atlantic Records, and the Triumph of Rock 'n' Roll* (W.W. Norton & Company Ltd, 1990) (Published in the U.K. as *Atlantic and the Godfathers of Rock and Roll.*)
4   Bob Porter e-mail to author, January 10, 2020
5   Charlie Gillett, *Making Tracks* (W.H. Allen, 1975)
6. Ahmet Ertegun, *What'd I Say: The Atlantic Story* (Welcome Rain Press, 2001)
7   Paul Watts insert notes to "Big Joe Turner: The Singles Collection, 1950-1960," Acrobat ADDCD3275
8   John Swanson, *Bill Haley* (W.H. Allen, 1982)
9   Jim Dawson, *Rock Around The Clock* (Backbeat Books, 2005)
10 George Buck sleeve notes to "Big Joe Turner with Knocky Parker...," Southland SLP-13
11 Valerie Wilmer, *Jazz People* (Allison & Busby, Ltd, 1971)
12 Ulf Larsson, sleeve notes to "I Don't Dig It," Juke Box Lil B-618
13 John Swanson, *Bill Haley* (W.H. Allen, 1982)
14 Ray Connelly, *Being Elvis* (W&N, 2017)
15 Jesse Stone to Alyn Shipton, BBC Radio 3, 1997
16 *Down Beat*, May 30, 1956
17 Charlie Gillett, *The Sound of the City: The Rise of Rock and Roll* (Outerbridge & Diensfrey, 1970)
18 Rick Colman, *Blue Monday: Fats Domino and the Lost Dawn of Rock n' Roll* (Da Capo Press, 2006)
19 Galen Gart (compiler), *First Pressings: The History of Rhythm & Blues, volume 5, 1955*
(Big Nickel Publications, 1990)
20 *Rocky Mountain Telegram*, May 29, 1955
21 Valerie Wilmer, *Jazz People* (Allison & Busby, Ltd. 1971)
22 *News and Observer* (Raleigh), November 2, 1955
23 Charlie Gillett, *Making Tracks* (W.H. Allen, 1975)
24 Joe Turner to Steve Propes, station KLON, October 23, 1983, *Blues & Rhythm* no. 362
25 Michael Lydon, *Ray Charles, Man and Music* (Payback Publications, 1998)
26 Jerry Fuentes website, A Rock n' Roll Historian
27 Jerry Wexler and David Ritz, *Rhythm and the Blues* (Random House, 1993)

Chapter 12 "Long as it sounds good" (1957-1961)

1   Jacques Demetre, letter to author, May 1, 1964
2   Yannick Bruynoghe, letter to author, May 12, 1964
3   Kurt Mohr, letter to author, July 7, 1964

4   Yannick Bruynoghe, letter to author, May 12, 1964
5   Tad Hershorn, *Norman Granz: The Man Who Used Jazz for Justice* (University of California Press, 2011)
6   ibid
7   Valerie Wilmer, "Joe's Still The Boss", *Melody Maker*, July 10, 1976
8   Nat Hentoff, *Jazz Monthly*, September 1958
9   Ralph Gleason, *San Francisco Chronicle*, July 8, 1958
10   Frank London Brown, "Boss of the Blues ...", *Down Beat*, December 11, 1958
11   Peter Guralnick, *Lost Highway* (David R. Godine, Publisher Inc.,1979)
12   Paul Garon, letter to author, March 31, 1964
13   Paul Clinco, Living Blues, no. 10, Autumn 1972
14   Gary Kramer, notes to "Rockin' The Blues", Atlantic 8203
15   Joseph F. 'Big Joe' Laredo, sleeve notes to "Jumpin' with Joe", EMI 0777 7 99293
16   Kansas City.... and all that's jazz (Andrew McMeel Publishing, 1999)
17   Peter Guralnick, Lost Highway (David R. Godine, Publisher Inc.,1979)
18   Joe Turner to James Austin, "Conversation with a Legend", *Goldmine* no. 10, November 1982)
19   George Moonoogian, *Whiskey, Women and ....*, no. 6, March 1974
20   Nesuhi Ertegun, letter to author, July 25, 1963

Chapter 13 "That's what it takes today, daddy" (1962-1968)

1   Joe & Geraldine Turner, letter to author, May 1964
2   Joe & Geraldine Turner, letter to author, March 13, 1964
3   Nesuhi Ertegun, letter to author, July 25, 1963
4   Hans J. Maurer (editor), *The Pete Johnson Story* (Fund Raising Project, 1965)
5   Lars Edegran, e-mail to author, July 30, 2019
6   Joe & Geraldine Turner, letter to author, March 13, 1964
7   Willie The Lion Smith & George Hoefer, *Music On My Mind: The Memoirs of an American Pianist (MacGibbon & Kee, Ltd., 1964)*
8   *Jazz Journal*, January 1965
9   *Melody Maker*, March 7, 1964
10   Joe & Geraldine Turner, letter to author, March 13, 1964
11   Richard Hadlock, sleeve notes to "Joe Sullivan", Time-*Life* STL-J27
12   *Melody Maker*, March 7, 1964
13   *Melody Maker*, May 16, 1965
14   Alan Bates, tel-con with author, October 26, 2020
15   *Melody Maker*, May 22, 1965
16   Buck Clayton, *Buck Clayton's Jazz World* (Macmillan Press, 1986)
17   Dave Green to author
18   BBC 2 "Jazz Score" radio broadcast, December 27, 1993
19   Humphrey Lyttelton, *Take It From The Top* (Robson Books, 1975)
20   Valerie Wilmer, letter to author, November 3, 2018

21 *Melody Maker*, April 2, 1966

22 *The Observer*, October 2, 1966

23 *Whiskey, Women and ....* no. 11, June 1983

24 Joe Turner to Steve Propes, KLON, October 23, 1983, *Blues & Rhythm* no. 362

25 Roni Failows, *Coda*, Feb./Mar. 1967

26 *Jazz Journal*, March 1967

27 *Blues Unlimited*, no. 58, December 1968

28 *Los Angeles Times*, October 7, 1968

Chapter 14 "My sister got on my case" (1969-1976)

1 Frank Bostwick, *Coda*, February, 1970

2 *Down Beat*, July 23, 1970, August 6, 1970

3 Mary Katherine Alden, e-mails to author, January 21, 2020, March 3, 2020

4 *Blues Unlimited*, July 1970

5 John Breckow, e-mail to author, October 2, 2019

6 Ross Russell, *Jazz Style in Kansas City and the Southwest* (University of California Press, 1971) : *San Diego Union*, November 11, 1970

7 *Melody Maker*, October 2, 1971

8 Dave Alvin to Jim Allison, *INDY Week*, October 2015

9 *Melody Maker*, January 8 & 15, 1972

10 Mary Katherine Alden, e-mail to author, January 21, 2020

11 *Melody Maker*, May 13, 1972

12 Johnny Otis to Richard Williams, *Melody Maker*, August 5, 1972

13 Mary Katherine Alden, e-mail to author, March 8, 2020

14 *Whiskey, Women and ....* No. 7, May 1975

15 Mary Katherine Alden, e-mail to author, January 21, 2020

16 George Hulme, *Names & Numbers*, number 29, April 2004

17 *Coda*, May 1974 : *Victorian*, March 20, 1974

18 Topanga Dick, *Whiskey, Women and ...* , no. 7, May 1975

19 John Chilton, *Roy Eldridge, Little Giant of Jazz* (Continuum, 2002)

20 Max Jones, *Melody Maker*, October 5, 1974

21 Peter Guralnick, *Lost Highway* (David R. Godine, Publisher, Inc. 1979)

22 *Melody Maker*, July 10, 1976

23 Val Wilmer, letter to author, November 3, 2018

24 Lynn Abbott (Tulane University), e-mail to author, February 15, 2019

25 Dan Morgenstern, *Jazz Journal*, December 1976

26 Wayne Wright to Bill Crow, *Jersey Jazz*, July 2008

Chapter 15 "A voice to stop an army in its tracks" (1977-1985)

1 Mark Naftalin, thediscography website

2 Peter Guralnick, *Melody Maker*, December 30, 1978

3 Nathan Pearson, *Goin' To Kansas City* (MacMillan Press, 1988)

4   *Now Dig This*, No. 338, May 2011
5   Bernie Pearl, e-mail to author, March 19, 2021
6   Bernie Pearl, e-mail to author, October 2, 2020
7   Doug MacLeod, tel-con with author, November 16, 2020 and e-mail November 18, 2020.
8   *Jazz Journal*, May 1981
9   Axel Zwingenberger, *Blues & Rhythm*, number 317, March 2017
10 Paul Roland (editor), *Jazz Singers* (*Billboard* Books 2000)
11 *Melody Maker*, July 18, 1981
12 Gary Giddins, *Rhythm-A-Ning* (Oxford University Press, 1985)
13 *Jazz Journal*, February 1982
14 *Now Dig This*, No. 338, May 2017
15 *Jazz Journal*, February 1982
16 Leslie Gourse, *Louis' Children* (First Cooper Square, 2001)
17 *Daily Breeze* website, April 5, 2014
18 Mark A. Humphrey, *Nothin' But The Blues, Lawrence Cohn, editor,* (Abbeville Press Publishers, 1993)
19 Bob Porter, e-mail to author, December 31, 2019
20 Guy Stock to author (uncertain date)
21 *Freemont Tribune*, August 1, 1983
22 *Cadence*, October & November, 1983: *New York Newsday*, November 29 1985
23 John Breckow, e-mail to author, October 2, 2019
24 obituary, *Jazz Express* No. 68, January 1986
25 obituary, Todd Everett, *Los Angeles Herald Examiner*, November 25, 1985

Chapter 16 "Thank you, Joe Turner" (1985)

1   obituary, *The Times-Picayune*, November 25, 1985
2   Mary Katherine Alden, e-mail to author, January 21, 2020
3   ibid
4   Sharyn Felder, tel-con with author, March 18, 2020
5   Mark A. Humphrey, *Nothin' But The Blues, Lawrence Cohn, editor* (Abbeville Press Publishers, 1993)
6   Charlie Gracie, BBC Radio interview, March 17, 1980
7   reprinted by permission of Dave Alvin, through the good offices of Nancy Sefton, GS Management.

Appendix 1 - The Man

1   Doc Pomus, *Whiskey, Women and ....*, No. 11, June 1983
2   Joe Turner to James Austin, *Goldmine* No. 78, November 1982
3   *Austin-American-Statesman*, September 21, 1984
4   *Cash Box*, December 7, 1985
5   Humphrey Lyttelton, *Take It From The Top* (Robson Books, 1975)
6   Jacques Demetre, letter to author, July 4, 1964

7   Whitney Balliett, American Singers (Oxford University Press, 1988)
8   Barney Josephson with Terry Trilling-Josephson, *Cafe Society* (University of Illinois Press, 2009)
9   Valerie Wilmer, *Jazz People* (Allison & Busby, Ltd. 1971)
10 Nevil Skrimshire to author, January 7, 1993
11 Roy Pellett (editor): Humphrey Lyttelton in *The Best of Jazz Score*, BBC Books, 1992
12 letter to author, June 29, 1966
13 letter to author, January 5, 1967
14 letter to author, October 5, 1963
15 Bob Porter, e-mail to author, December 31, 2019

Appendix 2 - The Appetites

1   Johnny Otis, *Upside Your Head* (University Press of New England, 1993)
2   Humphrey Lyttelton, *Take It From The Top* (Robson Books, 1975)
3   Freddie King to Max Jones, *Melody Maker*, December 18, 1971

Appendix 3 – The Money

1   Whitney Balliett, American Singers (Oxford University Press, 1988)
2   Nick Tosches, *Unsung Heroes of Rock 'n' Roll* (Secker & Warburg, 1991)
3   Joe Turner to Steve Propes, KLON, October 23, 1983, *Blues & Rhythm* no 362
4   ibid
5   ibid
6   Doc Pomus, *Whiskey, Women and ....*, No. 11, June 1983
7   Joe Turner to Steve Propes, KLON, October 23, 1983, *Blues & Rhythm* no. 362
8   Peter Guralnick, *Lost Highway* (David R. Godine, Publisher Inc. 1979)

Appendix 4 - The Voice

1   Bob Hite to Max Jones, *Melody Maker*, June 5, 1976
2   Eddie Lambert, *Jazz Monthly*, July 1965
3   Humphrey Lyttelton, *The Best of Jazz* (Robson Books, 1978)
4   Stanley Dance, sleeve notes to "Super Black Blues," BluesTime BTS-9003
5   George Melly, *The Observer*, May 16, 1965
6   Mimi Clar, *The Jazz Review*, February 1959
7   Sandy Ingham, *Central New Jersey Home News*, September 2, 1982
8   Paul Oliver letter to author, January 5, 1967
9   Paul Oliver, *Jazz Music Mirror, Vol. 5, No. 5, 1958*
10 Stanley Dance, insert notes to "Bosses of the Blues" Volume 1, Bluebird ND88311
11 Paul Roland (editor), *Jazz Singers* (Octopus Publishing, 1999))
12 Gunther Schuller, *The Swing Era* (Oxford University Press, 1989)

Appendix 5 - The Songs

1 Paul Oliver letter to author, January 5, 1967
2 Michael Steinman, "Jazz Lives" blog, October 12, 2020
3 George Melly, *The Observer*, May 16, 1965
4 Ulf Carlsson, sleeve notes to "I Don't Dig It", Juke Box Lil JB-618
5 Joseph F. 'Big Joe' Laredo, insert notes to "Jumpin' With Joe," EMI 0777 7 99293
6 Valerie Wilmer, *Jazz People* (Allison & Busby Ltd. 1971)
7 Peter Guralnick, *Lost Highway* (David R. Godine, Publisher, Inc. 1979)
8 Whitney Balliett, *American Singers* (Oxford University Press 1988)
9 Joseph F. 'Big Joe' Laredo, insert notes to "Jumpin' with Joe", EMI 0777 7 99293
10 *Melody Maker*, May 15, 1965
11 Valerie Wilmer, *Melody Maker*, July 10, 1976
12 ibid

Appendix 8 - The Recordings

1 Alun Morgan in *Jazz On Record* (Hanover Books, Ltd., 1968)
2 Dan Morgenstern, insert notes to "Boogie woogie and blues piano", Mosaic Select MS-030
3 ibid
4 Mimi Clar, *The Jazz Review*, February 1959
5 Paul Oliver (editor): Dave Penny in *The Blackwell Guide to Blues Records* (Blackwell Ltd. 1989)
6 anonymous, *Bulletin du Hot Club de France*, no. 257, November/December 1976
7 Lee Hildebrand, insert notes to "Stormy Monday," Pablo PACD-2310-943-2
8 John Chilton, *Roy Eldridge, Little Giant of Jazz* (Continuum, 2002)

Appendix 9 - The Lyrics

1 Paul Oliver, *Screening The Blues: Aspects of the Blues Tradition* (Cassell, 1968)

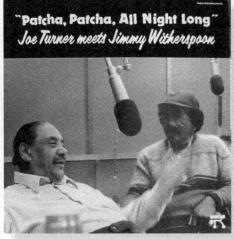

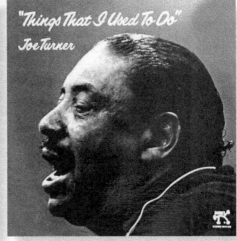

Biography - Index of Song Titles

Biography Index of Names

Let 'em Roll

Over three decades of Blues, R&B, Gospel and Soul.
Published 6 times a year. Subscriptions and back issues can be
purchased on-line via PayPal at www.bluesandrhythm.co.uk
email mikestephenson@mac.com call +44 (0) 130 482 5102
or write to 80, Lewishaam Road, Dover, Kent CT OQQ, UK

BLUES&RHYTHM

Discography Index of Song Titles

Discography Index of Names

428

Printed in the USA
CPSIA information can be obtained
at www.ICGtesting.com
LVHW011027190424
777812LV00002B/145